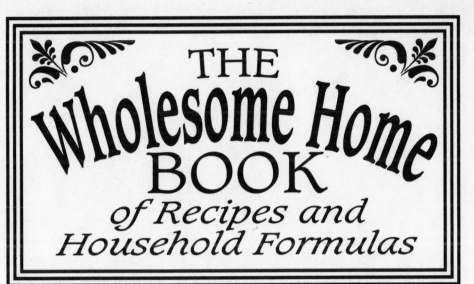

# THE Wholesome Home BOOK
## of Recipes and Household Formulas

*1996*

*Happy Birthday Amy*
*Love forever,*
*Linda*

# THE
# Wholesome Home
# BOOK
## of Recipes and Household Formulas

## YVONNE YOUNG TARR

**WINGS BOOKS**
New York • Avenel, New Jersey

ORIGINALLY TITLED *THE UP-WITH-WHOLESOME,*
*DOWN-WITH-STORE-BOUGHT BOOK OF HOUSEHOLD RECIPES AND FORMULAS*

THIS 1995 EDITION IS PUBLISHED BY WINGS BOOKS,
DISTRIBUTED BY RANDOM HOUSE VALUE PUBLISHING, INC
40 ENGELHARD AVENUE, AVENEL, NEW JERSEY 07001,
BY ARRANGEMENT WITH YVONNE YOUNG TARR.


RANDOM HOUSE
NEW YORK • TORONTO • LONDON • SYDNEY • AUCKLAND


PRINTED AND BOUND IN THE UNITED STATES OF AMERICA


LIBRARY OF CONGRESS CATALOGING-IN-PUBLICATION DATA


TARR, YVONNE YOUNG.
THE WHOLESOME HOME BOOK OF RECIPES & HOUSEHOLD FORMULAS /
YVONNE YOUNG TARR.
P. CM.
REV. ED. OF : THE UP-WITH-WHOLESOME, DOWN-WITH-STORE-BOUGHT
BOOK OF RECIPES & HOUSEHOLD FORMULAS. 1ST ED. C1975.
INCLUDES INDEX.
ISBN 0-517-12342-8
1. COOKERY. 2. RECIPES. I. UP-WITH-WHOLESOME, DOWN-WITH-STORE-BOUGHT
BOOK OF RECIPES & HOUSEHOLD FORMULAS. II. TITLE.
TX652.T37 1995          95-7609
641.5—DC20          CIP


8 7 6 5 4 3 2

ART FROM THE YVONNE YOUNG TARR
TURN OF THE CENTURY ARCHIVES
DESIGN BY MARGARET McCUTCHEON WAGNER

*I dedicate this book*
*to Ruth Grossman, my editorial assistant,*
*for help and devotion*
*above and beyond the call*
*of duty**

=====

*\* with a special thank you to Jill*
*Loewen, Jill Costigan, Jacqueline*
*Little and Susan Trulli*

# Contents

===

FIVE

*Household Helps* 215

# FOREWORD

═══

When I was very young I lived in the farm community of Powys in central Pennsylvania. Powys wasn't a town or even a hamlet; it was no more than a few houses dotted out here and there along the highway. It had no streets, no movies, no drugstores and no dry cleaner. What it did have was "The Store."

"The Store" was run by an ample lady named Mrs. Shepherd, who always wore an apron, a housedress and a smile. There were no big glass front windows in "The Store." It was dark inside, and homey, with a few shelves of merchandise, a woodburning stove, a rocking chair and a glass case near the door with penny candy for sale.

"The Store" carried only absolute necessities— some canned goods, a few boxes of this and that, a barrel of pickles, a barrel of crackers, some smaller measures of flour and cornmeal and sugar, dried fruits for winter pies and a glass soft-drink case that contained large blocks of ice and a sign that said "Please keep top closed." "The Store" didn't sell produce—a few apples in season or a basket of choice peaches from a nearby farm, perhaps—but then produce was not much in demand. Everybody thereabout had his or her own garden. It would have been unthink-

able, in that time and place, to buy things you could grow and preserve for yourself. "The Store" didn't have a meat counter either, but that was no inconvenience. My aunt had a poultry house, so we had as many eggs and chickens as we needed, and a farmer nearby sold the best smoked bacon and ham in the world.

Not many of the farmhouses had telephones in those days, and when the doctor had to be called or an emergency reported, "The Store" was the place to go . . . or, if need be, "The Store" came to you. It was Mrs. Shepherd who warned us that a flood was due and helped my mother carry to safety my baby brother, while I saved my paperdolls and my cat.

I loved Mrs. Shepherd's store, and felt it belonged to me as much as to anyone. It stocked the staples important to children as well as the ones for adults—a box of crackerjacks, a few greenleaves, a soft drink sweating with cold on a summer afternoon. What more could any reasonable person ask?

Once every two or three weeks almost everybody in Powys went to town. Our town had everything that a town needed, including a grocery store with a big brass and glass meat counter. We went to "The Grocery" to buy the items "The Store" didn't carry—rice perhaps, and bananas, and occasionally a steak. "The Grocery" was run by a friend of my father's, and when times were bad, and they were bad in the early thirties, the store manager, our friend, would tuck a few extra oranges, a baker's dozen rolls, or even a chocolate bar in the shopping bag to show that he appreciated our business, was pleased to see us and cared enough to want us to have some treat my parents would have thought it frivolous to buy, since times were difficult and people were going hungry.

There was a link between "The Store" and "The Grocery" and our lives. We knew the people who ran those stores. We knew they cared about us. We could count on them to tell us when the cider wasn't up to par or the meat was tough. We were important to them and they were important to us.

Our town has supermarkets now, like every other town. Not one supermarket, but eight or ten, filled with thousands of senseless items as well as necessities. Nowadays supermarket managers are rarely trusted neighborhood friends (as is evidenced by price tickets pasted over fat in the meat and can tops with multiple price marks, each higher than the last), and while the size and the glitter of the markets have grown, the quality of the foods sold has not kept pace. In these difficult times we don't need ever-bigger supermarkets with seeing-eye doors, fancy packages and junk foods. We don't need hi-fis piping sprightly Christmas carols, wall to wall, when our food dollar allows little left over for holiday presents. We don't need plastic decorations or clever promotional mobiles. What we do need is a dollar's worth of value for a dollar spent, and if the supermarket owners won't or can't protect us, what we need is the will power and the know-how to protect ourselves. We need the determination to buy only those products that are necessary and healthful and the resolve to buy little or nothing at all until prices come down.

We must not allow manufacturers to determine whether the vitamins should be removed from our breads, dangerous preservatives and chemicals should be pumped into our foods or insecticides grown into our produce. In this time of accelerating prices everyone who has a back yard, a flower bed, a window box or even a sunny window sill should be home-growing as much food as possible. We must freeze or can or preserve foods in the summer season to tide us over the months when produce is most expensive.

This book is meant to help you to help yourself and to save money in the bargain. It will show you how to make your own mixes if mixes you must have, how to manage without expensive cuts of meats, how to freeze summer bounties for winter pleasures, how to make cheese and yogurt and sausages without preservatives, how to make your own soft drinks and inexpensive wines, your own household products and polishes and cleaners. How to clean your own clothes, how to make your own soaps and natural cosmetics. How to raise chickens, goats, sheep, ducks and geese, how to keep a cow—and much other useful information that will help you to find your way back to independence and the security of knowing that your life truly is in your own hands.

# ONE

## Supermarket Staples You Can Make Yourself

*WHEN I was young, the shelves of our country store*
*were frequently only partially filled and "The Store's" solitary*
*light bulb provided so little light that brand names, if there*
*were any, were impossible to read. There were no shoulder-*
*to-shoulder packages, boxes or bags on Mrs. Shepherd's*
*shelves. She stocked only one brand of most staples and*
*you bought what she carried (always a respectable product),*
*and planned your meals around the items you*
*and she had on hand.*
*When Mother baked bread or cake, she baked it "from*
*scratch." She measured and sifted and mixed from the items*
*stored on her pantry shelf, and the entire process took her*
*much less time than it usually takes us to drive to and*
*from our supermarkets to pick up a "mix."*
*One of the most seductive myths of supermarket shopping*
*is that on these shelves, and only there, is it possible to*
*obtain the time-saving foods so vital to our frenetic lives.*
*Convenience foods are convenient, I will admit. But the*
*truth is that most of these can be made by you in your own*
*kitchen in just a few minutes, and usually for much,*
*much less money. The recipes that follow are designed to*
*save you money—not only because they actually cost you less*
*but also because they save you time and keep you far*
*from the temptation of buying those unnecessary necessities*
*that line your supermarket shelves. Set aside one morning*
*per month to package your own dry mixes (breads, cakes,*
*puddings, etc.), then spend the time and money saved on*
*something worthwhile—pleasure.*

# YOUR
# OWN DRY MIXES

## Your Own Batter and Bake Mix

*This rather biscuity topping helps keep baked chicken unusually moist.*

(YIELD: ENOUGH FOR 5 2½-POUND CHICKENS)

INGREDIENTS AND DIRECTIONS FOR
BASIC MIX

    *5 Cups all-purpose flour*
    *5 Teaspoons baking powder*
    *1 Tablespoon onion powder*
    *1 Teaspoon thyme*
    *1 Teaspoon paprika*
    *1 Tablespoon granulated sugar*

Shake all the ingredients in a double-thick plastic bag. Fasten and store on a kitchen shelf until needed.

ADDITIONAL INGREDIENTS AND
DIRECTIONS FOR 1 2½-POUND CHICKEN

    *½ Cup milk*
    *1 Large egg*

Preheat the oven to 400 degrees F.

Shake the bag of Basic Mix to incorporate all the ingredients. Measure 1 cup into a small, shallow bowl. Stir in the milk and egg with a fork. (Do not overmix; the batter should be slightly lumpy.)

Rinse the chicken and pat dry with paper towels. Dip only the top or skin side of each piece in the batter; coat fairly thickly. Place the chicken pieces, batter side up, on a well-greased cookie sheet. Bake for 50 minutes, or until golden brown.

## Barbecue Batter Bake for Chicken

*If you prefer a sweet/piquant Deep South dip for your baked chicken, try this.*

(YIELD: ENOUGH FOR 4 2½-POUND CHICKENS)

INGREDIENTS AND DIRECTIONS FOR
BASIC MIX

    *1 Cup light brown sugar*
    *2 ⅔ Cups all-purpose flour*

¾ Cup fine bread crumbs
1 Teaspoon onion powder
½ Teaspoon ground ginger

Mix all the ingredients together. Place in a jar or double-thick plastic bag, seal and store in closet or refrigerator.

### ADDITIONAL INGREDIENTS AND DIRECTIONS FOR 1 2½-POUND CHICKEN

2 Tablespoons vegetable oil (not olive oil)
1 Tablespoon yellow prepared mustard
2 Tablespoons water

Preheat the oven to 400 degrees F.

Shake the bag of Basic Mix to incorporate all the ingredients. Measure 1 cup into a small, shallow bowl. Stir in the oil and mustard. Add the water and mix well.

Rinse chicken pieces and pat them dry with paper towels. Use a knife to spread one side of each piece with the batter (as you would ice a cake). Place the chicken pieces, batter side up, on a well-greased baking sheet and bake for 55 minutes.

Serve with baked peaches, using any leftover batter in the peach hollows.

## Herb-Flour Bake Mix for Pork Chops or Chicken

(YIELD: ENOUGH FOR 40 CHOPS OR CHICKEN PIECES)

### INGREDIENTS AND DIRECTIONS FOR BASIC MIX

2¼ Cups all-purpose flour
2½ Teaspoons each marjoram and thyme
5 Teaspoons each onion powder and paprika
1 Teaspoon white pepper
3 Teaspoons salt

Mix all the ingredients together. Place in a jar or double-thick plastic bag, seal and store in closet or refrigerator.

### DIRECTIONS FOR BAKING 8 CHOPS OR 8 CHICKEN PIECES

Preheat the oven to 425 degrees F.

Shake the bag to remix the ingredients. Measure ½ cup of the Basic Mix into a fairly small paper (or plastic) bag.

Rinse each chop or chicken piece and dry with paper towels. Pour ¼ cup cooking oil onto a cookie sheet or other shallow baking pan. Dip the meat or fowl, one piece at a time, in the oil. Drop into the bag of mix and shake until well covered on all sides. Set the meat aside and grease the baking pan with the remaining oil. Arrange the meat on the pan and bake for 40 to 50 minutes, or until cooked through and well browned.

## Curry Crumb Bake Mix for Pork Chops

This crumb mix is ever so slightly sweet and flavored with curry powder. Pork chops stay moist and shrink very little when they are baked in this easy-to-use mix.

(YIELD: ENOUGH FOR 40 CHOPS)

### INGREDIENTS AND DIRECTIONS FOR BASIC MIX

1¼ Cups all-purpose flour
1¾ Cups Homemade Bread Crumbs (see page 6)
¾ Cup free-pouring brown sugar
4 Teaspoons curry powder
3 Teaspoons salt

Mix all the ingredients together. Place the mix in a double-thick plastic bag, seal and store in closet or refrigerator.

### DIRECTIONS FOR BAKING 8 CHOPS

Preheat the oven to 450 degrees F.

Shake the bag of Basic Mix to remix the ingredients. Measure ¾ cup into a fairly small paper (or plastic) bag.

Rinse the chops and shake off the excess moisture. Drop the moist chops, 2 at a time, into the bag with the mix and shake well until the meat is covered on all sides. Place on a well-greased cookie sheet or other shallow baking pan and bake for 40 to 50 minutes, or until the pork is well cooked but not dried out. (Baking times will differ with the thickness of the chops.)

## Curry-Crumb Mix for Broiled or Fried Lamb Chops

*Curry powder enhances the flavor of lamb. Dip chops in this mix prior to cooking, set aside and let dry for half an hour, then fry or broil. These crumbs may also be used to dress up roast lamb. Press the mix into the top of a roast and bake as you normally would. Delicious!*

(YIELD: ENOUGH FOR 40 TO 50 CHOPS)

### INGREDIENTS AND DIRECTIONS FOR BASIC MIX

> 1 Cup all-purpose flour
> 2 Cups Homemade Bread Crumbs (see page 6)
> 4 Teaspoons curry powder
> 2 Teaspoons salt
> 1 Teaspoon thyme

Mix all the ingredients together. Store in a jar or double-thick plastic bag until needed.

### DIRECTIONS FOR BROILING OR FRYING 8 CHOPS

Shake the container of Basic Mix to incorporate all the ingredients. Measure ¾ cup into a fairly small paper (or plastic) bag.

Rinse the chops and shake off excess moisture. Place the moist chops, 2 at a time, in the bag with the mix and shake well until the meat is covered on all sides. Arrange the chops on a rack or plate and allow to dry for half an hour. Fry or broil as you like them.

## Herb Stuffing Mix

(YIELD: 12 CUPS)

### INGREDIENTS AND DIRECTIONS FOR BASIC MIX

> 12 Cups bread cubes
> 4 Envelopes powdered beef or chicken broth
> 3 Teaspoons onion salt
> 2 Teaspoons leaf thyme or 1 teaspoon ground thyme
> 1½ Teaspoons each sage and marjoram

Spread the bread cubes thinly over the surface of a large cookie sheet. Bake, stirring occasionally, in an oven preheated to 250 degrees F. long enough to dry, but not brown, the bread. Remove the bread cubes from the oven and allow to cool. Place the powdered broth, seasonings and bread cubes in a double-thick plastic bag, shake well to mix and seal tightly. Store on a pantry shelf until needed.

### ADDITIONAL INGREDIENTS AND DIRECTIONS FOR PREPARING STUFFING

> 1 Large onion, peeled
> 3 Large stalks celery
> 2 Tablespoons butter or margarine
> ½ Cup hot water
> 1 Egg

Shake the bag of Basic Mix several times to distribute the seasonings evenly. Measure 3 cups into a large bowl.

Chop the onion. Wash, trim and coarsely chop the celery. Heat the butter or margarine in a skillet and sauté the onions and celery until they are not quite tender. Remove from the heat and stir the vegetables into the bread cubes. Add the hot water and stir thoroughly. Beat the egg lightly and stir into the mixture.

### Your Own Quickie Stuffing

Prepare Herb Stuffing as directed above. Mix in 2 tablespoons finely chopped leftover meat and/ or gravy if any is available. Place the stuffing in a colander and set in a large kettle with ¾ inch of water in the bottom (the water should not touch the stuffing). Cover the top of the pan with a tight lid or aluminum foil and bring the water to a boil. Lower the heat and simmer for 25 to 30 minutes. Serve hot.

## Cornbread Stuffing Mix

(YIELD: 12 CUPS)

INGREDIENTS AND DIRECTIONS FOR
BASIC MIX

    8  Cups cornbread cubes
    6  Cups other bread cubes
    4  Envelopes powdered onion or
       chicken broth
    3  Teaspoons onion salt
    2  Teaspoons leaf thyme or 1 teaspoon
       ground thyme
 1½  Teaspoons sage

Preheat the oven to 250 degrees F.

Spread the bread cubes thinly over the surface of a large cookie sheet and bake, stirring occasionally, until the bread is dry but not brown. Remove from the oven and cool. Combine the bread cubes, powdered broth and seasonings in a double-thick plastic bag. Shake the bag to mix the ingredients thoroughly and seal tightly. Store on a pantry shelf until needed.

ADDITIONAL INGREDIENTS AND
DIRECTIONS FOR PREPARING STUFFING

    1  Large onion, peeled and chopped
    3  Large stalks celery, trimmed and
       chopped
    2  Tablespoons butter or margarine
  ½  Cup hot water
    1  Egg

Shake the bag of Basic Mix long enough to distribute its contents evenly. Measure 3 cups into a large bowl.

Sauté the onion and celery in the butter until they are not quite tender; remove from the heat and stir into the seasoned bread cubes. Add the hot water, blend well, then beat the egg lightly and stir into the mixture.

## Homemade Bread Crumbs

Prepare your own money-saving bread crumbs from leftover or slightly stale bread. Arrange quartered bread slices, or crusts cut from bread prepared for other recipes, on a cookie sheet. Bake in an oven preheated to 150–200 degrees F. until the bread is bone-dry but not brown. Whirl the bread in your blender, grind in your food chopper, or grate coarsely. Spoon into an airtight container and store on your pantry shelf or in your freezer.

If desired, mix the bread crumbs with fresh or dried herbs just before using to produce your own seasoned version. Thyme, basil, oregano, chives and parsley are all superb.

## Griddle Cake Mix

(YIELD: ENOUGH FOR 56 TO 64 GRIDDLE
CAKES 4 INCHES IN DIAMETER)

INGREDIENTS AND DIRECTIONS FOR
BASIC MIX

    5  Cups all-purpose flour, sifted before
       measuring
    2  Tablespoons plus 2 teaspoons
       baking powder
  ¼  Cup granulated sugar
    2  Teaspoons salt

Sift all the ingredients together and place in a double-thick plastic bag or other airtight container. Store on a shelf until ready to use.

ADDITIONAL INGREDIENTS AND
DIRECTIONS FOR MAKING 14 TO 16
4-INCH GRIDDLE CAKES

    1  Cup milk
    1  Egg, beaten
    2  Tablespoons melted margarine

Shake the container of Basic Mix long enough to distribute its contents evenly. Measure 1⅓ cups into a mixing bowl. Combine the milk and the egg. Add to the dry ingredients and mix until the batter is fairly smooth. Fold in the melted margarine.

To bake, spoon 3 tablespoons batter for each cake onto a hot, lightly greased griddle. Turn when the top of the cakes develop tiny bubbles and the bottoms are lightly browned. Brown the other side and serve immediately with butter and syrup.

## Make-Ahead Waffle Mix

*Waffles are versatile and economical family pleasers. They always seem to be welcome at breakfast, lunch or dinner—especially when they are dressed and delivered forth in any one of the following variety of combinations.*

(YIELD: 6 LARGE WAFFLES)

INGREDIENTS AND DIRECTIONS FOR
BASIC MIX

*5 Cups sifted all-purpose flour*
*2 Tablespoons plus 2 teaspoons baking powder*
*4 Tablespoons granulated sugar*
*2 Teaspoons salt*

Combine the sifted flour with the other ingredients and sift again. Place the mixture in a double-thick plastic bag and fasten securely. Store on a cool, dry pantry shelf.

ADDITIONAL INGREDIENTS AND
DIRECTIONS FOR PREPARING 3
LARGE WAFFLES

*2 Eggs, at room temperature, separated*
*1 Cup milk, at room temperature*
*2 Tablespoons shortening, melted*

Beat the egg yolks in a small bowl, then beat in the milk and the cooled shortening.

Shake the bag of Basic Mix vigorously to mix the ingredients. Measure 1 cup plus 2 tablespoons into a large bowl and add the egg yolk mixture. Stir only long enough to blend. Beat the egg whites until stiff but not dry and fold them into the batter. Pour the batter, about ⅓ cup at a time, onto a hot waffle iron and bake about 4 to 5 minutes. Serve hot.

### Blueberry Waffles

Add 1 tablespoon sugar to the additional ingredients (see above). Fold ½ cup blueberries into the waffle batter along with the beaten egg whites. Bake as directed above.

### Nut Waffles

Fold ⅔ cup of your favorite chopped nuts into the waffle batter, along with the beaten egg whites. Bake as directed above.

### Bacon Waffles

Fold ½ cup crisp bits of crumbled bacon along with the beaten egg whites. Substitute bacon fat for the shortening if desired. Bake as directed above.

### Cheese Waffles

Fold ½ cup of your favorite cheese, grated, into the batter along with the egg whites. Bake as directed above.

### Apricot Waffles

Fold ½ cup of finely chopped dried apricots into the batter along with the egg whites. Bake as directed above.

### Currant or Raisin Waffles

Fold ½ cup currants or chopped raisins into the batter along with the egg whites. Bake as directed above.

### Coconut Waffles

Fold ½ cup flaked coconut into the batter along with the egg whites. Bake as directed above.

### Butterscotch or Chocolate Chip Waffles

Fold ½ cup butterscotch or semisweet chocolate chips into the batter along with the egg whites. Bake as directed above.

### Cherry Waffles

Fold ½ cup finely chopped maraschino cherries into the batter along with the egg whites. Bake as directed above.

### Pineapple Waffles

Fold ½ cup well-drained, canned crushed pineapple into the batter along with the egg whites. Bake as directed above.

### Lemon Waffles

Fold 4 drops lemon extract and 1 tablespoon grated lemon zest (the thin outer layer of skin with none of the bitter white underskin included) into the batter along with the egg whites. Bake as directed above.

### Orange Waffles

Follow the directions for Lemon Waffles (see above), but substitute orange extract for the lemon extract and orange zest for the lemon zest.

### Corn Waffles

Fold ¾ cup well-drained canned corn into the batter along with the egg whites. Bake as directed above.

### Spice Waffles

Add 1 tablespoon granulated sugar to the additional ingredients (see above). Fold ½ teaspoon ground cinnamon and ¼ teaspoon each ground nutmeg and allspice into the batter along with the egg whites. Bake as directed above.

### Date Waffles

Add ⅓ cup chopped dates to the batter along with the egg whites. Bake as directed above.

### Waffles With Chipped Beef and Hard-Cooked Egg Sauce with Peas

Top plain waffles with bits of chipped beef and cover with hot Hard-Cooked Egg Sauce with Peas (see page 172).

### Cheese Waffles with Turkey and Mixed Vegetable Sauce

Top Cheese Waffles (see page 7) with warm leftover turkey slices. Cover with Mixed Vegetable Sauce (see page 172).

### Corn Waffles with Chicken Slices and Herb Sauce

Top Corn Waffles (see above) with warm leftover chicken slices and Herb Sauce (see page 172).

### Bacon Waffles with Hard-Cooked Egg Sauce with Peas and Grilled Tomato

Spoon Hard-Cooked Egg Sauce with Peas (see page 172) over crispy Bacon Waffles (see page 7) and top with a grilled tomato.

### Bacon Waffles with Fried Eggs and Mornay Sauce

Top a Bacon Waffle (see page 7) with two fried eggs and spoon over a bit of Mornay Sauce (see page 172).

### Corn Waffles with À la King Sauce and Hard-Cooked Eggs

Top a Corn Waffle (see above) with À la King Sauce (see page 172). Set two hard-cooked egg halves on top.

### Corn Waffles with Crisp Bacon Slices and Mornay Sauce

Top a Corn Waffle (see above) with hot bacon slices and Mornay Sauce (see page 172).

### Nut Waffles with Chicken Slices and Curry Sauce

Top Nut Waffles (see page 7) with warm leftover chicken slices and Curry Sauce (see page 172).

### Waffles with Veal, Green Peppers and Mushroom Sauce

Top plain waffles with leftover sautéed veal and green pepper slices. Cover with Mushroom Sauce (see page 172).

### Waffles with Ground Beef, Onions and Leftover Chili Sauce

Top plain waffles with ground beef fried with onions. Cover with hot chili sauce.

### Cheese Waffles with Ham and Hard-Cooked Egg Sauce

Top Cheese Waffles (see page 7) with thin slices of ham and top with Hard-Cooked Egg Sauce (see page 172).

### Enchilada Waffle

Fry ground beef with garlic, chili and chopped onions. Heap this chili-beef combination on a Corn Waffle (see page 8), top with grated mild Cheddar or jack cheese, and broil until the cheese melts.

### Pizza Waffle

Cook Italian sausages as directed on page 74, then cut into slices. Sprinkle a plain waffle generously with grated mozzarella cheese and place under the broiler until the cheese melts. Top with a little spaghetti sauce, the sausage slices and sautéed mushroom slices and broil again until the sausage is hot.

---

## Tortillas

(YIELD: ABOUT 48 TORTILLAS)

---

INGREDIENTS AND DIRECTIONS FOR
BASIC MIX

    9 Cups all-purpose flour
    4½ Teaspoons salt
    4½ Teaspoons baking powder
       (optional)

Mix the flour, salt and baking powder together in a large, double-thick plastic bag. Store on your pantry shelf until needed.

ADDITIONAL INGREDIENTS AND
DIRECTIONS FOR MAKING 16 TORTILLAS

    4½ Tablespoons shortening
    1 Cup water

To make the tortillas, shake the bag well to mix ingredients thoroughly. Measure 3 cups plus 2 tablespoons mix into a large bowl. Cut the shortening into the Basic Mix until the mixture resembles very coarse meal, then add the water a little at a time, mixing well after each addition. The dough should be fairly stiff.

Pinch off a piece of the dough and shape it, in your hands, into a small ball about 1 inch in diameter. Continue until all the dough has been used. Set each ball of dough on a lightly floured pastry board and flatten as thin as possible, using your floured hand or a second lightly floured pastry board.

Fry the tortillas on a lightly greased griddle for 2 minutes on one side. As soon as the edges start to lift, flip over and brown on the other side. Arrange in stacks and keep warm. Serve dripping with butter.

### Tacos

Tacos—literally "snack"—are tortillas that have been folded and crisply fried so that they resemble a half-circle-shaped pocket. Into this pocket can go any one of a number of delicious meat or cheese fillings. Topped off with a garnish and/or a spicy sauce, tacos are an excellent way to use up your leftovers and delight your family at one and the same time.

To prepare tacos, make tortillas according to the directions above. Arrange the tortillas in stacks and keep them warm. Spoon your choice of fillings (see below) slightly off center on each warm tortilla, then fold or roll up. Secure with a toothpick. Fry the tacos in ½ inch of hot, deep fat until crisp and golden brown. Drain briefly on paper towels. Serve piping hot.

### Tostadas

Tostadas are simply tortillas that have been crisp-fried in hot fat without bending. Top whole tostadas with your choice of fillings to produce a kind of crunchy open-faced sandwich.

### Tostada Chips

Cut the warm tortillas into triangular-shaped chips and crisp-fry in hot fat. Drain on paper towels and serve with dips.

### Fillings for Tacos and Tostadas

Use the following meats, vegetables and cheeses in any combination you prefer:

MEATS: Leftover beef, veal, ham, turkey or chicken, finely chopped
Ground cooked beef or lamb
Leftover chili con carne

VEGETABLES: Coarsely chopped avocados, tomatoes, onions, scallions
Shredded lettuce
Sweet peppers, green or red, chopped
Hot chili peppers, minced
Leftover refried beans

CHEESES: (in order of preference):
Jack or mild Cheddar, cubed or grated; American, cut in strips
By all means, try other cheeses, if you have bits you would like to use up

OTHERS: Don't hesitate to experiment with your leftovers. One unusual and highly tasty example is ground lamb topped with grated raw apple, chopped scallion and shredded lettuce. Delicious!

### Making Your Own Baking Powder

*To make baking powder at home simply combine the following ingredients:*

4 Ounces cream of tartar
2 Ounces baking soda
2 Ounces cornstarch

Sift together several times, then store in an air-tight container.

### Make-it-Yourself Quick Biscuit Mix

*One hundred percent better than any mix you can buy in the store, and it takes all of 5 minutes to put together.*

(YIELD: ENOUGH FOR ABOUT 2 DOZEN BISCUITS OR 2 SHORTBREADS)

INGREDIENTS AND DIRECTIONS FOR BASIC MIX

4 Cups all-purpose flour
½ Cup granulated sugar
1 Teaspoon salt
2½ Tablespoons baking powder

Sift all the ingredients into a large, double-thick plastic bag. Fasten securely and store on a kitchen shelf.

ADDITIONAL INGREDIENTS FOR BAKING 1 DOZEN BISCUITS OR 1 9-INCH SHORTBREAD

6 Tablespoons butter or margarine
2 Eggs
¼ Cup milk

DIRECTIONS FOR BAKING THE BISCUITS

Preheat the oven to 400 degrees F.

Shake the bag of Basic Mix thoroughly to incorporate the ingredients. Measure out half the mixture (2 cups) into a large bowl. Use 2 knives or a pastry cutter to cut the butter into the dry ingredients until the mixture resembles coarse meal.

Beat the eggs and milk together and stir into the butter-flour mixture to form a soft dough. On a floured surface pat out a circle of dough about 12 inches in diameter. Cut out 12 biscuits and bake for 15 minutes on a greased baking sheet. Serve hot with butter and jam.

DIRECTIONS FOR BAKING THE SHORTCAKE

Preheat the oven to 375 degrees F.

Shake the bag of Basic Mix thoroughly to incorporate all ingredients. Measure out half the mix (2 cups) and place in a large bowl. Use 2 knives or a pastry cutter to cut the butter into the dry ingredients until the mixture resembles coarse meal.

Beat the eggs and milk together and stir into the butter-flour mixture to form a soft dough. On a floured surface pat out a thick circle of dough about 8½ inches in diameter. Grease a 9-inch skillet (with an ovenproof handle) and press the dough in to fit. Bake for 20 minutes, or until golden brown.

## Scone Mix

(YIELD: ENOUGH FOR 32 SCONES)

INGREDIENTS AND DIRECTIONS FOR BASIC MIX

8 Cups all-purpose flour
5½ Teaspoons baking powder
1 Tablespoon baking soda
6 Tablespoons granulated sugar
½ Teaspoon salt

Sift all the ingredients together into a double-thick plastic bag. Fasten and store on your pantry shelf until needed.

ADDITIONAL INGREDIENTS AND DIRECTIONS FOR BAKING 16 SCONES

1 Egg
1 Cup sour milk or buttermilk
½ Cup melted butter

Preheat the oven to 375 degrees F.

Shake the bag of Basic Mix for several minutes to incorporate all the ingredients. Measure 4 cups into a mixing bowl.

Beat the egg and sour milk together and stir into the mix. Add the melted butter to the dough, a little at a time, mixing well after each addition. Roll the dough out to ¼-inch thickness on a lightly floured board and cut into 3-inch rounds, using the top edge of a drinking glass. Cut the rounds into quarters and bake for 10 minutes on a greased baking sheet.

## Cornmeal Fritters

(YIELD: ENOUGH FOR 60 FRITTERS)

INGREDIENTS AND DIRECTIONS FOR BASIC MIX

2 Cups yellow cornmeal
⅔ Cup all-purpose flour
1 Tablespoon granulated sugar
½ Cup instant nonfat dry milk
½ Teaspoon salt

Measure the ingredients and sift them into a double-thick plastic bag. Fasten the bag and store on a pantry shelf until needed.

ADDITIONAL INGREDIENTS AND DIRECTIONS FOR MAKING 30 FRITTERS

2 Eggs, separated
1 Tablespoon melted butter
1½ Cups water
Vegetable oil for deep frying
Confectioners' sugar
1 Apple, peeled and grated (optional)

Shake the bag of Basic Mix well to incorporate all the ingredients. Measure 1½ cups into a bowl. Beat in the egg yolks, butter and water. Beat the egg whites until stiff and fold them in. Add the grated apple if desired.

Drop by large spoonfuls into hot oil (365 degrees F.) and fry until golden (about 3 minutes). Remove with a slotted spoon and sprinkle with confectioners' sugar. Serve with maple syrup.

## French Bread Mix

*I find it psychologically helpful to have the dry ingredients for even the most simple breads premeasured and waiting on the shelf or in the refrigerator. This mix must be refrigerated once the yeast is added and baked within 4 days.*

(YIELD: 2 LOAVES OR 1 GIANT ONE)

INGREDIENTS AND DIRECTIONS FOR
BASIC BREAD MIX

> 8 Cups all-purpose flour
> 1 Tablespoon salt
> 2 Packages dry active yeast

Shake all the ingredients together in a large, double-thick plastic bag until well mixed. Store in the refrigerator.

ADDITIONAL INGREDIENTS AND
DIRECTIONS FOR BAKING

> 3 Cups warm (not hot!) water
> 1 Tablespoon melted butter
> About 1½ Cups all-purpose flour
> 2 Tablespoons white cornmeal (yellow will do)
> 1 Egg white mixed with 1 tablespoon cold water

Shake the bag of Basic Mix to incorporate the ingredients, then transfer to a large bowl. Stir in the water and melted butter. Cover and let rise until doubled in bulk in a warm, draft-free place (about 1½ hours).

Punch down the dough. Spread 1 cup of the additional flour on a flat surface, scoop the dough onto it and sprinkle the top with flour. Knead in the flour (adding extra flour if necessary) to form a fairly stiff dough. Cover and set aside to double in bulk in a warm, draft-free place (about 1¼ hours).

Punch the dough down once more and knead for 2 minutes. Roll the dough into 2 long loaves and place on a cookie sheet sprinkled with cornmeal. (I, personally, prefer to bake this bread as one giant loaf the size of a cookie sheet. It is not only quite impressive and very delicious, but it eliminates the need for an especially large pan and oven. To form this giant bread simply arrange the unbaked loaves in 2 facing semicircles, the end of one inside the center of the other.) Slash the tops of the loaves in 5 or 6 places with a sharp knife. Brush with the egg white–water mixture.

Cover and place in a warm, draft-free place for about 25 minutes. Place a shallow pan of hot water in the bottom of the oven. Bake the bread on the middle shelf of the oven for 50 to 60 minutes. Serve hot, if possible.

## Irish Yeastbread Mix

(YIELD: ENOUGH FOR 2 VERY LARGE LOAVES)

INGREDIENTS AND DIRECTIONS FOR
BASIC MIX

> 8 Cups all-purpose flour
> 1½ Cups granulated sugar
> 4 Teaspoons salt
> 2 Teaspoons ground allspice
> ⅔ Cup instant nonfat dry milk
> Zest from 1 lemon, with none of the bitter white underskin

Sift all the ingredients except the lemon zest into a plastic bag. Add the zest and shake the bag to mix. Fasten the top and set aside until needed.

ADDITIONAL INGREDIENTS AND
DIRECTIONS FOR BAKING 1 LOAF

> 2 Packages dry active yeast
> 1 Cup warm water
> ½ Cup milk
> ⅓ Cup soft butter
> ½ Cup each currants and raisins
> All-purpose flour, if necessary

Sprinkle the yeast over the warm water and let stand for 5 minutes.

Meanwhile, shake the bag of Basic Mix until the ingredients are well incorporated. Measure 2 cups into a large mixing bowl. Stir in the milk, butter, and yeast mixture and beat for several minutes, or until well blended. (An electric mixer set on medium speed makes this job much easier.) Place the dough in a bowl, cover it, and allow to rise for 30 minutes in a warm, draft-free place.

Shake the bag of mix again and measure 2 cups of it onto the surface of the dough. Beat for several minutes, or until well blended. Sprinkle a pastry board with a little flour, the currants and the raisins, and incorporate these into the dough as you knead it for 8 to 10 minutes. (If necessary, knead in additional plain all-purpose flour to make a fairly stiff dough.) Place the dough in a large, greased bowl and turn once to grease the top. Cover and set aside in a warm, draft-free place for 1½ to 2 hours, or until doubled in bulk.

Punch the dough down, knead into a rounded loaf and place on a greased baking sheet. Once again cover the dough and set it aside in a warm, draft-free place to double in bulk (about 1½ to 2 hours).

Bake in an oven preheated to 350 degrees F. and bake for 50 minutes, then remove the bread from the baking sheet and cool on a wire rack.

## Pull-Apart White Bread

*One of the most intriguing breads you can bring to your table is this fine-textured white bread that pulls apart like a dinner roll. Brush the unbaked bread with garlic or chive butter for additional flavor.*

(YIELD: ENOUGH FOR 4 LOAVES)

INGREDIENTS AND DIRECTIONS FOR
BASIC MIX

14 Cups all-purpose flour
½ Cup granulated sugar
4 Teaspoons salt

Shake all the ingredients in a large, double-thick plastic bag. Store on a pantry shelf.

ADDITIONAL INGREDIENTS AND
DIRECTIONS FOR BAKING 2 LOAVES

1 Package dry active yeast
6 Tablespoons butter
½ Cup milk
1½ Cups water
⅓ Cup melted butter
All-purpose flour, if necessary
Garlic or minced chives (optional)

Shake the bag of Basic Mix until the ingredients are well incorporated. Measure 2 cups of the mix into the large bowl of your mixer. Add the yeast and use your fingers to blend it in.

Place the butter, milk and water in a small saucepan and heat to lukewarm (not hot!); the butter will not be melted. Add the liquid ingredients to the dry ingredients and beat at medium speed for 2 minutes.

Measure out 1 cup additional mix from the bag, add it to the bowl, and beat at high speed for 3 minutes more, scraping the bowl occasionally. Stir in 4 cups more mix from the bag, adding

additional plain all-purpose flour if necessary to form a stiff dough; knead 8 to 10 minutes. Place the dough in a greased bowl, turning once to grease the top. Cover and let rise in a warm, draft-free place until doubled in bulk (1 to 1½ hours).

Punch the dough down and divide into 2 equal parts. Set aside for 15 minutes, then roll out into 2 rectangles, each about 14 by 9 inches. Brush each rectangle with melted butter (take your choice of plain, garlic or chive) and cut one into 4 9-inch-long strips. Place these strips one on top of the other, and slice the stack into 4 2¼-inch pieces. Stand the pieces of dough in a line down the center of a standard-sized loaf pan. Repeat this procedure with the second 14- by 9-inch rectangle of dough. Cover the 2 pans and set them aside in a draft-free place for 1 hour, or until they are doubled in bulk.

Meanwhile, preheat the oven to 400 degrees F.

Bake the loaves for 30 minutes, or until they are golden brown. Remove the loaves from the pans immediately and cool on a wire rack.

## Anadama Bread

*It is a good idea to have in your files at least one rich, dark Early American bread recipe. This particular bread is so tasty that I usually triple the Basic Mix recipe and store the "three bags full" on my pantry shelf to be ready and waiting for bread-baking day.*

(YIELD: ENOUGH FOR 2 LOAVES)

INGREDIENTS AND DIRECTIONS FOR
BASIC MIX

9 Cups all-purpose flour
1½ Cups yellow cornmeal
2¾ Teaspoons salt

Place the dry ingredients in a double-thick plastic bag and shake vigorously to mix.

ADDITIONAL INGREDIENTS AND
DIRECTIONS FOR BAKING 2 LOAVES

2 Packages dry active yeast
2½ Cups warm water
¾ Cup molasses

1 Stick softened margarine
All-purpose flour, if necessary

Add the yeast to the bag of Basic Mix and shake well. Stir together the water and molasses in a large bowl. Add the margarine and let stand for 5 minutes. Sprinkle the yeast and mix over the liquid and work it in, a little at a time, until a stiff dough is formed, adding extra flour if the dough is sticky. Knead 8 to 10 minutes, then place the dough in a large, greased bowl, turning once to grease the top. Cover and set aside in a draft-free place until the dough doubles in bulk (about 1½ hours).

Punch the dough down and divide in two. Roll each piece into a rectangle about 14 by 9 inches, then, starting at the short end, roll each piece up tightly to form a loaf. Tuck the ends under and place the loaves in greased standard-sized loaf pans. Cover and set aside again in a draft-free place for 50 to 60 minutes, or until the dough doubles in bulk.

Meanwhile, preheat the oven to 375 degrees F.

Bake the loaves for 50 minutes, or until they are a rich brown. Remove from the pans and cool on a wire rack.

## 100 Percent Whole-Wheat Bread Mix

(YIELD: ENOUGH FOR 6 LOAVES)

INGREDIENTS AND DIRECTIONS FOR
BASIC MIX

15 Cups 100 percent whole-wheat flour
8¼ Cups all-purpose flour
3 Tablespoons baking soda
1½ Cups granulated sugar

Combine all the ingredients in a large, double-thick plastic bag, fasten securely and shake well to mix. Store on a kitchen shelf until needed.

ADDITIONAL INGREDIENTS AND
DIRECTIONS FOR BAKING 1 LOAF

¼ Pound (1 stick) butter
1 Cup milk
2 Tablespoons lemon juice
1 Egg

Shake the Basic Mix in its plastic bag until it is well incorporated. Measure 3¾ cups of the mix into a bowl. Using 2 knives, cut in the butter until the mixture resembles coarse meal. Clabber the milk with the lemon juice, then beat the egg into the soured milk. Make a well in the dry ingredients and stir in the milk, a little at a time. Mix well; the dough should be fairly stiff.

Knead for 10 minutes on a lightly floured board and form into a rounded loaf. Place on a baking sheet and bake in an oven preheated to 400 degrees F. for 50 minutes, or until crusty and brown. Remove from the oven and cool on a wire rack.

## Fruited Wheat Bread Mix

If you are looking for a bread that tastes as good as it is good for you, try this.

(YIELD: ENOUGH FOR 6 LOAVES)

INGREDIENTS AND DIRECTIONS FOR
BASIC MIX

14½ Cups 100 percent whole-wheat flour
8 Cups all-purpose flour
3 Tablespoons baking soda
1½ Cups granulated sugar
1 Cup raisins
1 Cup chopped candied fruits

Combine all the ingredients in a large, double-thick plastic bag, fasten securely and shake well to mix. Store on a kitchen shelf or in your refrigerator.

ADDITIONAL INGREDIENTS FOR BAKING
2 LOAVES

½ Pound (2 sticks) margarine
2 Cups milk
¼ Cup lemon juice
2 Eggs
All-purpose flour, if necessary

Shake the Basic Mix in its plastic bag until it is well mixed. Measure 8 cups of the mix into a large mixing bowl. Using 2 knives, cut the margarine into the Basic Mix until the mixture resembles coarse meal.

Clabber the milk with the lemon juice, then beat the eggs into the clabbered milk. Make a well in the dry ingredients, pour in the egg-milk mixture and blend with your fingers until well mixed. Add extra all-purpose flour, if necessary, to form a stiff dough. Knead the dough for 8 to 10 minutes, then divide it in half and form each piece into a rounded loaf. Slash an X ½-inch deep in the top of each loaf.

Place the loaves on a well-greased cookie sheet and bake in an oven preheated to 400 degrees F. for 1 hour. Cool on a wire rack.

## Oatmeal-Raisin Quick Bread Mix

(YIELD: ENOUGH FOR 4 LOAVES)

INGREDIENTS AND DIRECTIONS FOR
BASIC MIX

- 4 Cups all-purpose flour
- 4 Teaspoons each salt and baking soda
- 4 Cups rolled oats
- 4 Cups currants or raisins
- 2 Cups coarsely chopped almonds, pecans or walnuts

Sift together the flour, salt and soda and divide into 4 sturdy plastic bags. Add 1 cup of the oats, 1 cup of the raisins and ½ cup of the nuts to each plastic bag and shake them well to mix. Store in the refrigerator or freezer until needed.

ADDITIONAL INGREDIENTS AND
DIRECTIONS FOR BAKING 1 LOAF

- ½ Cup light brown sugar
- 1 Egg
- 1 Cup milk
- 2 Tablespoons lemon juice
- 2 Tablespoons vegetable oil

Beat the sugar and egg until fluffy. Measure the milk, stir in the lemon juice and set in a warm place to sour. Add the soured milk to the sugar and egg and beat until smooth. Add the contents of 1 bag of Basic Mix to the milk-sugar mixture and stir just enough to combine. Fold in the oil. Pour the batter into a greased loaf pan and bake

in an oven preheated to 350 degrees F. for 40 to 50 minutes, or until the loaf is nicely browned and has pulled away from the sides of the pan. Cool on a rack.

## Crispy Cornbread Mix

(YIELD: ENOUGH FOR ABOUT 35 2-INCH
SQUARES)

INGREDIENTS AND DIRECTIONS FOR
BASIC MIX

- 1½ Cups yellow cornmeal
- 1½ Cups all-purpose flour
- ¾ Cup granulated sugar
- 1 Teaspoon salt
- 1 Tablespoon baking powder

Sift all the ingredients together and store in a plastic bag.

ADDITIONAL INGREDIENTS AND
DIRECTIONS FOR BAKING

- 1½ Tablespoons melted butter
- 1¾ to 2 Cups milk

Put the Basic Mix into a large bowl.

Stir the butter into 1¾ cups of milk and beat into the mix, adding a little more milk if necessary to bring to spreading consistency. Spread the batter evenly on a buttered cookie sheet and bake in an oven preheated to 400 degrees F. for about 20 minutes, or until crisp. Cut into 2-inch squares and butter while hot.

## Mixed Grain Muffin Mix

*There are no mixing bowls to wash when you make this super-nutritious muffin mix. Just measure the ingredients into a plastic bag, shake well and set aside. When you're ready to bake up a batch, simply measure part of the mix in a smaller plastic bag, add the Additional Ingredients and knead the bag with your fingers to mix. Bake and serve for the best cornmeal muffins you've ever tasted. And you've eliminated most of the preservatives.*

(YIELD: ENOUGH FOR 4 DOZEN MUFFINS)

INGREDIENTS AND DIRECTIONS FOR
BASIC MIX

    2¼  Cups yellow cornmeal
    2¼  Cups whole-wheat flour
    ⅓  Cup granulated sugar
    1¾  Teaspoons salt
    2  Teaspoons each baking powder and
        baking soda

Shake all the ingredients together in a large, sturdy plastic bag. Seal and store in closet or refrigerator.

ADDITIONAL INGREDIENTS AND
DIRECTIONS FOR BAKING 1 DOZEN
MUFFINS

    1  Large egg
    ½  Cup sour cream
    3  Tablespoons milk
    2  Teaspoons vegetable oil

Shake the bag of Basic Mix until the ingredients are well incorporated. Measure 1¼ cups of the mix into a sturdy plastic bag. Add all the Additional Ingredients and fasten the top of the bag securely. Using your fingers, knead the ingredients together through the plastic bag. Fill greased muffin cups ⅔ full and bake in an oven preheated to 425 degrees F. for 18 minutes, or until muffins are nicely browned.

### Healthful Mixed Grain Bread

*Because this bread is made from Mixed Grain
Muffin Mix, it is a bit more dense
than most cornbreads. It is crunchy and
delicious and particularly nutritious.*

(YIELD: 1 LOAF)

    2½  Cups Mixed Grain Muffin Mix
        (see page 15)
    ½  Cup sour cream
    ⅓  Cup milk
    2  Large eggs
    1½  Tablespoons vegetable oil

Place all the ingredients in a large, sturdy plastic bag and knead (through the bag) with your fingers until well mixed. Squeeze all of the mix out of the bag and into a well-greased loaf pan. Bake in an oven preheated to 425 degrees F. for 20 minutes, or until golden brown. Cool the bread for 5 minutes in the pan, then loosen the sides with a knife and turn out onto a plate. Serve warm with soft butter on the side.

### Graham Muffin Mix

(YIELD: 2 DOZEN MUFFINS)

INGREDIENTS AND DIRECTIONS FOR
BASIC MIX

    4¼  Cups graham flour
    ¾  Teaspoons salt
    1  Teaspoon baking soda

Mix all the ingredients well and store in a plastic bag.

ADDITIONAL INGREDIENTS AND
DIRECTIONS FOR BAKING 1 DOZEN
MUFFINS

    1  Tablespoon lemon juice
    1  Cup milk
    5  Tablespoons molasses
    1  Large egg

Shake the bag of Basic Mix to incorporate all the ingredients. Measure 2 cups plus 2 tablespoons of the mix into a large bowl.

Add the lemon juice to the milk and set in a warm place to sour. Beat the molasses and egg into the soured milk. Stir the milk-egg mixture into the dry ingredients only until the mix is thoroughly moistened. Divide equally into well-oiled muffin tins and bake in an oven preheated to 425 degrees F. for 25 minutes.

### Shoofly Pie Mix

*There is no dessert that can surpass a really well-baked
shoofly pie. If you think "shoofly" is not your dish,
you probably never tasted one like this.*

(YIELD: ENOUGH FOR 2 PIES)

INGREDIENTS AND DIRECTIONS FOR
BASIC MIX

> *4 Cups all-purpose flour*
> *2 Cups light brown sugar*
> *2 Teaspoons baking soda*

Sift together all the ingredients, place in a double-thick plastic bag, fasten and store on a pantry shelf.

ADDITIONAL INGREDIENTS AND
DIRECTIONS FOR BAKING 1 PIE

> *1 Cup molasses*
> *1 Cup hot water*
> *6 Tablespoons each butter and margarine*
> *Instant Pie Crust for 1 pie shell (see page 48)*

Simmer the molasses and water together for 1 minute and remove from the heat.

Shake the bag of Basic Mix until the ingredients are well incorporated. Measure 3 cups of the mix into a bowl, then cut 6 tablespoons of margarine and 4 tablespoons of the butter into the mix until the mixture resembles coarse meal.

Line a pie plate with the pie dough and sprinkle about one-third of the Basic Mix buttercrumbs over the bottom. Pour ½ cup of the molasses mixture over the crumbs. Repeat the procedure (using about 1 cup crumbs and ½ cup liquid) until all of the mix and liquid are used, ending with the crumbs. Dot with the remainder of the butter and bake in an oven preheated to 375 degrees F. for 50 minutes. Serve warm or at room temperature.

## Graham Cracker Crust Mix

(YIELD: ENOUGH FOR 2 SINGLE CRUSTS)

INGREDIENTS AND DIRECTIONS FOR
BASIC MIX

> *About 38 single graham crackers (enough to make 3 cups crumbs)*
> *½ Cup granulated sugar*
> *1 Tablespoon ground walnuts, pecans or blanched almonds (optional)*

Place the crackers, in batches, between 2 sheets of waxed paper or into a plastic bag and use your rolling pin to crush them as fine as possible. Spoon the 3 cups of crumbs into a double-thick plastic bag as you crush each batch. Add the sugar, seal the bag tightly, and shake well to mix. Store on your pantry shelf. (If you have some nuts on hand, grind them and add along with the sugar for extra delicious flavor.)

ADDITIONAL INGREDIENTS AND
DIRECTIONS FOR PREPARING
1 SINGLE CRUST

> *4 Tablespoons softened butter or margarine*

Shake the bag of Basic Mix several times to redistribute the contents. Measure out 1½ cups of the mix and place in a bowl, then work in the softened butter.

Arrange the buttered crumbs in a 9-inch pie plate. Set an 8-inch pie plate over the crumbs and press down firmly with both hands; this assures an even layer on the sides and bottom. Remove the smaller pie plate and bake the crust for 7 or 8 minutes in an oven preheated to 375 degrees F. Cool and fill as desired.

Graham cracker pie crusts may also be frozen, with or without prior baking. Thaw at room temperature before filling.

## Party Fudge Cake Mix

*This cake mix has one of those small secret bags of special ingredients occasionally included in grocery store cake mixes. This assures that the chocolate will mix smoothly with the other cake ingredients. As the name indicates, this is a 3-layer party cake that stands about 10 inches high and will serve 12 to 16 persons. If you prefer, however, you may bake the 3 layers, frost one, serve it, and freeze the other two for future use.*

(YIELD: 1 3-LAYER CAKE OR 3 SINGLE LAYERS)

INGREDIENTS AND DIRECTIONS FOR
BASIC MIX

> *1½ Teaspoons baking soda*
> *½ Teaspoon salt*
> *3 Cups all-purpose flour*

*1½  Cups granulated sugar*
*1  Cup instant nonfat dry milk*

Sift the soda, salt and flour into a large, double-thick plastic bag. Add the sugar and nonfat dry milk and shake the bag to mix.

SPECIAL INGREDIENTS

*4½  1-ounce squares unsweetened chocolate, chilled*
*1  Cup granulated sugar*

Grate the chilled chocolate, removing each square from the refrigerator as you grate it and refrigerating each mound of grated chocolate as soon as possible afterwards (it is important that the chocolate bits do not melt and stick together). Place the grated chocolate and the sugar in a small, double-thick plastic bag and shake well to mix. Seal the bag and add it, bag and all, to the large plastic bag of Basic Mix. Refrigerate or freeze until baking day.

ADDITIONAL INGREDIENTS AND
DIRECTIONS FOR BAKING

*1¾  Cups water*
*1  Cup granulated sugar*
*¾  Cup vegetable shortening*
*2  Teaspoons vanilla extract*
*5  Eggs*

Mix the small bag of Special Ingredients with ¾ cup of the water and simmer over low heat, stirring occasionally, until the chocolate melts. Cool to room temperature. Meanwhile, cream the sugar, shortening and vanilla together and add the eggs, one at a time, beating well after each addition.

Shake the bag of Basic Mix and add it to the creamed ingredients alternately with the remaining 1 cup of water, beating well after each addition. Spoon the chocolate mixture into the batter and stir until well incorporated. Divide the batter into 3 greased 9-inch layer cake pans and bake for 40 to 45 minutes, or until the middle of the cake springs back when pressed lightly with the finger. Cool the layers for 20 minutes in the pans, then remove them and frost or freeze.

## Gingerbread Mix

(YIELD: ENOUGH FOR 2 CAKES)

INGREDIENTS AND DIRECTIONS FOR
BASIC MIX

*4  Cups all-purpose flour*
*3  Teaspoons each ground ginger and cinnamon*
*½  Teaspoon ground cloves*
*4  Teaspoons baking powder*
*1  Teaspoon each baking soda and salt*
*¾  Cup instant nonfat dry milk*

Sift all the ingredients together into a large, double-thick plastic bag. Fasten the bag and store on a pantry shelf.

ADDITIONAL INGREDIENTS AND
DIRECTIONS FOR BAKING
1 CAKE

*⅓  Cup granulated sugar*
*5  Tablespoons margarine*
*1  Egg*
*¾  Cup each molasses and warm water*

Cream the sugar and margarine. Beat in the egg. Mix the molasses and water and stir it into the creamed shortening alternately with 2 cups of the Basic Mix; do not overmix. Grease a 9-inch-square baking pan, pour in the batter and bake in an oven preheated to 350 degrees F. for 45 minutes, or until a wooden toothpick comes out clean. Serve warm or at room temperature topped with whipped cream or ice cream.

## Oatmeal Coconut Cookie Mix

*These are perhaps the most delicious cookies ever.*

(YIELD: ENOUGH FOR 6 DOZEN COOKIES)

INGREDIENTS AND DIRECTIONS FOR
BASIC MIX

*1½  Cups all-purpose flour, sifted*
*¼  Teaspoon baking powder*

½ Teaspoon each baking soda, salt
  and ground cinnamon
1 Cup grated coconut
2½ Cups rolled oats
½ Cup each walnut halves, broken
  into quarters, and raisins
1½ Cups semisweet chocolate chips

Into a large, double-thick plastic bag, sift the flour, baking powder, baking soda, salt and cinnamon. Add the coconut, oats, walnuts, raisins and chocolate chips and shake the bag until all ingredients are incorporated. Fasten the bag and store the mix on a pantry shelf or in your refrigerator until ready to use.

ADDITIONAL INGREDIENTS AND
DIRECTIONS FOR BAKING
3 DOZEN COOKIES

½ Cup vegetable shortening
1 Cup brown sugar, tightly packed
1 Egg

Shake the Basic Mix to incorporate ingredients. Measure out half the mix into a large bowl.

Beat the shortening and sugar in a large mixing bowl until fluffy. Add the eggs and beat well. Stir in the Basic Mix from the plastic bag and mix well. Drop in heaping teaspoonfuls onto ungreased cookie sheets and bake in an oven preheated to 350 degrees F. for 12 to 15 minutes, or until lightly browned.

## Ginger Snap Mix

(YIELD: ENOUGH FOR 20 DOZEN WAFERS)

INGREDIENTS AND DIRECTIONS FOR
BASIC MIX

3½ Cups all-purpose flour
2 Cups dark brown sugar
½ Teaspoon baking soda
1 Tablespoon ground ginger
1½ Teaspoons salt
¼ Teaspoon allspice

Sift together all the ingredients and place in a double-thick plastic bag. Fasten the bag and store on a pantry shelf.

ADDITIONAL INGREDIENTS AND
DIRECTIONS FOR BAKING
10 DOZEN WAFERS

½ Cup molasses
4 Tablespoons margarine

Shake the bag of Basic Mix until the ingredients are well blended. Measure 2¼ cups of the mix into a large mixing bowl. Heat the molasses, pour it over the margarine and beat it into the dry ingredients. Chill the dough for 45 minutes.

Divide the dough into 4 portions. Return 3 portions to the refrigerator and roll out the remaining portion as thinly as possible. Cut into 1½-inch rounds with a small cookie cutter (the top of a large kitchen salt shaker is what I use) dipped in flour. Arrange the ginger snaps on a greased cookie sheet and bake in an oven preheated to 350 degrees F. for 6 to 8 minutes. Repeat the process with the remaining 3 portions of dough.

## Vanilla Wafers

(YIELD: ENOUGH FOR 10 TO 12 DOZEN WAFERS)

INGREDIENTS AND DIRECTIONS FOR
BASIC MIX

3 Tablespoons instant nonfat dry milk
2½ Cups all-purpose flour
2 Teaspoons baking powder
½ Teaspoon salt

Sift all the ingredients into a double-thick plastic bag. Fasten the bag and store on a pantry shelf.

ADDITIONAL INGREDIENTS AND
DIRECTIONS FOR BAKING ABOUT
3 DOZEN WAFERS

⅓ Cup butter
⅓ Cup margarine or other vegetable
  shortening
1 Cup granulated sugar
1 Egg
¼ Cup water
2 Teaspoons vanilla extract

Cream together the butter, margarine and sugar. Beat the egg and the water together in a small bowl.

Shake the bag of Basic Mix until the ingredients are well incorporated. Measure out 2 cups of the mix. Add the egg mixture and the Basic Mix alternately to the creamed ingredients, beginning with the Basic Mix. Stir in the vanilla extract. Chill the dough.

Cut the dough into 4 portions; return 3 portions to the refrigerator. Roll out the remaining portion as thinly as possible. Cut into small rounds with a small cookie cutter or the end of a can or glass dipped in flour. Arrange the wafers on a greased cookie sheet and bake in an oven preheated to 350 degrees F. for 6 minutes. Repeat the process with the remaining 3 portions of dough.

## Crunchy Oat Crust Mix for Tortes

(YIELD: ENOUGH FOR 8 CRUSTS)

INGREDIENTS AND DIRECTIONS FOR BASIC MIX

    4 Cups quick-cooking oats
    2 Cups all-purpose flour
    4 Cups light brown sugar

Measure 1 cup of the oats, ½ cup of the flour and 1 cup of the brown sugar into each of 4 small, double-thick plastic bags; press any lumps of sugar away with your fingers. Shake each bag to mix, fasten and store on a pantry shelf until needed.

ADDITIONAL INGREDIENTS AND DIRECTIONS FOR BAKING 2 CRUSTS

    ½ Cup melted butter

Empty 1 bag of Basic Mix into a small mixing bowl. Stir in the melted butter and press the mixture into the bottoms of 2 well-greased cake pans. Bake in an oven preheated to 400 degrees F. for 20 minutes. Cool the crusts for a few minutes, then, while they are still warm, loosen with a long, narrow spatula.

Transfer the crusts to a serving plate and top with sliced fresh fruit and whipped cream.

## Chocolate Pudding Mix

(YIELD: ENOUGH FOR 12 ½-CUP SERVINGS)

INGREDIENTS AND DIRECTIONS FOR BASIC MIX

    6 1-ounce squares unsweetened
        chocolate
    ¾ Cup cornstarch
    2 Cups granulated sugar
    1 Cup instant nonfat dry milk
    ⅓ Teaspoon salt

Finely grate the chocolate squares, removing one square at a time from the refrigerator and returning the grated chocolate to the refrigerator while the remainder of the chocolate is being prepared (the chocolate must not melt or become too sticky). Measure the cornstarch, sugar, dry milk and salt into a sturdy plastic bag. Add the grated chocolate, fasten the top of the bag, and shake well to mix. Refrigerate until needed.

ADDITIONAL INGREDIENTS AND DIRECTIONS FOR COOKING 4 ½-CUP SERVINGS

    1½ Cups cold water
    2 Tablespoons butter
    1 Teaspoon vanilla extract

Measure the water into a small, heavy saucepan. Add 1½ cups of the Basic Mix and stir well. Cook over a very low flame, stirring constantly, until pudding is thick and creamy. (Do not worry if the chocolate remains separated from the other ingredients during cooking. It will be incorporated by the time the pudding has thickened if your burner is on very low heat and if you stir without interruption.)

When the pudding is thick, remove the pan from the heat and stir in the butter and vanilla. Divide into 4 small bowls, chill and serve.

## Lemon-Cinnamon Pudding Mix

(YIELD: ENOUGH FOR 12 ½-CUP SERVINGS)

INGREDIENTS AND DIRECTIONS FOR
BASIC MIX

    1 Cup instant nonfat dry milk
    2 Cups granulated sugar
    6 Tablespoons all-purpose flour
1½ Teaspoons ground cinnamon
    1 Tablespoon grated lemon zest, with
       none of the bitter white underskin
   ½ Teaspoon salt

Place all the ingredients into a plastic bag, fasten and shake to mix. Store on a pantry shelf until needed.

ADDITIONAL INGREDIENTS AND
DIRECTIONS FOR COOKING
4 ½-CUP SERVINGS

  ¾ Cup cold water
  2 Tablespoons lemon juice
  2 Egg yolks
  2 Tablespoons sherry

Shake the bag of Basic Mix until the ingredients are well incorporated. Place the cold water in a heavy saucepan. Measure 1 cup plus 3 tablespoons of the mix, add to the water and mix thoroughly. Add the lemon juice. Place over very low heat and cook, stirring constantly, for about 10 minutes, or until thick.

Remove the mixture from the heat and beat a few tablespoons of it into the egg yolks. Quickly beat the egg yolk mixture into the hot pudding mixture until thoroughly incorporated. Beat in the sherry. Divide evenly into 4 small bowls, chill and serve.

## Hot Cocoa Mix

*If your family loves hot cocoa, it may be handy to have it premixed on your kitchen shelf. The milk is already in it, so just mix with water and serve.*

(YIELD: ENOUGH FOR ABOUT 14 TO 20
SERVINGS)

INGREDIENTS AND DIRECTIONS FOR
BASIC MIX

1½ Cups cocoa
  2 Cups granulated sugar
4½ Cups instant nonfat dry milk

Measure all the ingredients into a double-thick plastic bag and shake well to mix. Fasten securely and store on a kitchen shelf.

ADDITIONAL INGREDIENTS FOR MAKING
1 GENEROUS MUG OF HOT COCOA

  1 Cup boiling water
 ¼ Cup milk (optional)

Shake the bag of mix to incorporate the ingredients. Measure out ½ cup of mix into a heatproof pot. Add ½ cup of boiling water and stir until the mixture is smooth. Stir in the remaining ½ cup of boiling water and ¼ cup of hot milk if desired.

### Mexican Chocolate

Add 2 teaspoons ground cinnamon to the Basic Mix for a delectable variation in flavor.

# SUPERMARKET STAPLES

Time was when the air was perfumed every autumn with pungent aromas, arising like incense from pots of catsup, India relish and chutney simmering on every stove. The abundant harvest reaped from country gardens was most often turned to excellent eating with a handful of spices, a bit of patience and a good recipe.

There are, of course, many supermarket items we would find it very hard to do without—sugar, flour, salt, paper products—but many of the things we think of as supermarket staples can be made much cheaper and better at home. A good many of these following recipes do have as prerequisites a profusion of inexpensive or garden-grown produce and the time and interest to make-it-yourself. Given these, however, you will find you can turn out products so far superior to their store-bought counterparts that you are bound to be stunned. Brown sugar syrup is every bit as tasty as maple. Homemade catsup resembles a deep red, thick steak sauce with indescribably exquisite flavor. Kitchen-made chutney, with its plump pieces of fruit, whole raisins and nuts, and extra thick sauce is guaranteed to turn you away from the store-bought variety for life.

Buy only the staples you need and take a vacation from those artificially flavored, unnatural, manufactured foods.

---

### Your Own Meat Extender

*Here is a good way to make meat go twice as far. Serve the mushroom caps sautéed as a vegetable or sliced in a sauce and grind the stems to add flavor to the meat.*
*This recipe is extremely tasty served on its own as a meat substitute. Just form into patties and fry as you would hamburger.*

(YIELD: ABOUT 1 POUND)

---

1 Cup partially cooked soybeans
   (see below)
¼ Pound fresh mushroom stems
   (optional)
1 Large carrot, scraped
1 Small onion, peeled
1 Teaspoon meat extract
¼ Teaspoon sage
¼ Teaspoon thyme
   Dash of nutmeg
1 Slice stale whole-wheat bread

Put all the ingredients through the fine blade of your food grinder or mince them.

Mix well with 2 pounds ground beef. Form the mixture into patties and place on paper towels to blot out excess moisture. Brown over medium-low heat in ⅛-inch hot oil, turning once. Serve hot.

### How to Cook Soybeans

Place 1 cup dried soybeans in 3 cups cold water. Bring to a boil over medium heat. If your recipe calls for partially cooked soybeans, drain the beans at this point and continue as the recipe directs.

Beans that are to be fully cooked prior to their inclusion in other recipes should be further cooked over low heat until they are tender but still have a bit of "crunch" when you bite into them (about 40 minutes). Remove the soybeans from their cooking water, rinse them in fresh cold water and drain them well.

### Your Own Meat Extender II

*Add this to ground beef or form the extender alone into patties, fry and serve in place of meat.*

(YIELD: ABOUT 1 POUND)

1 Cup cooked soybeans (see above)
6 Ounces mushrooms
1 Small clove garlic, peeled
1 Slice whole-wheat bread
1 Tablespoon catsup
1 Tablespoon meat extract

Put all the ingredients through the fine blade of your food grinder or chop finely. Add to 2 pounds chopped beef and mix well. Form the mixture into patties and place on paper towels to blot out excess moisture. Brown over medium-low heat in ⅛-inch hot oil, turning once. Serve hot.

### Brown Sugar Syrup

*Old-fashioned brown sugar syrup is far superior in taste to the supermarket kind.*

(YIELD: ABOUT 4⅓ CUPS)

3 Cups boiling water
4 Cups light brown sugar
6 Tablespoons butter

Bring the water to a boil in a saucepan. Add the sugar and butter and boil over medium heat, stirring constantly, until the syrup thickens "as you like it."

### Natural Cereal I

(YIELD: ABOUT 6 CUPS)

1 Cup wheat germ
3 Cups old-fashioned hull-less rolled oats
1 Cup flaked coconut
1 Cup sunflower seeds
1 Cup chopped natural nuts
12 Dates, pitted
12 Dried apricots, chopped
1 Cup currants or ⅔ cup raisins

Mix the wheat germ, rolled oats, coconut, sunflower seeds and nuts and sprinkle on a cookie sheet. Bake for 5 minutes in an oven preheated to 350 degrees F. Lower the heat to 300 degrees and continue to bake for 20 minutes, stirring every few minutes. As the cereal begins to dry out it will smell toasty and be light brown in color.

Cool the toasted ingredients and mix them with the dates, apricots and raisins. Store in an airtight container in the refrigerator.

### Natural Cereal II

(YIELD: ABOUT 10 CUPS)

1½ Cups flaked coconut
4 Cups old-fashioned rolled oats

2 Cups wheat germ
1 Cup chopped nuts
¼ Cup sesame seeds
1½ Cups raisins
1 Cup chopped dates
½ Teaspoon ground cinnamon
¼ Teaspoon ground ginger
1½ Cups molasses
⅔ Cup salad oil (not olive)
1 Teaspoon vanilla extract

Mix the dry ingredients, then stir in the remaining ingredients. Spread on a greased baking sheet and bake in an oven preheated to 300 degrees F. for 30 minutes, stirring frequently. Cool and store in airtight containers; refrigerate if desired.

## Peanut Butter

(YIELD: ¾ CUP)

*Peanut butter is best when it is very fresh. Make only a small amount at a time.*
1½ Cups salted peanuts
Vegetable oil

Put the peanuts, a handful at a time, into your blender jar. Whirl at high speed until the peanuts reach the consistency of flour. If necessary, stop the blender now and then to push the nuts down with a rubber spatula. Mix in only enough oil to thicken the peanut butter to your liking. Store, covered, in the refrigerator.

## Tomato Catsup

*Plant your garden with no fear of waste. Any excess or slightly imperfect tomatoes will provide you with catsup so piquant it tastes like steak sauce.*

INGREDIENTS FOR MAKING
4 8-OUNCE BOTTLES

10 Pounds (about 15 large) ripe tomatoes (you may include imperfect specimens, but cut away all bad spots, please)
2 Sweet red peppers, seeded

2 Large onions, peeled
2 Cups granulated sugar, more if desired
1 Teaspoon each paprika, salt and allspice
2 Teaspoons ground cinnamon
¼ Teaspoon ground cloves
½ Teaspoon each celery salt and dry mustard
Juice of 1 lemon

INGREDIENTS FOR MAKING
20 8-OUNCE BOTTLES

50 Pounds (about 80 large) tomatoes (same admonition as above)
10 Sweet red peppers
10 Large onions, peeled
10 Cups granulated sugar (slightly under 5 pounds), more if desired
5 Teaspoons each paprika, salt and allspice
2½ Teaspoons each celery salt and dry mustard
Juice of 5 lemons

Plunge the tomatoes, a few at a time, in boiling water for a minute or two. Remove the tomatoes one at a time and pull off the skins and remove the stem ends. Cut the peeled tomatoes, the seeded peppers and the onions into quarters and run through the fine blade of your grinder. Simmer this mixture in a large, heavy kettle for 40 to 50 minutes, or until the bits of vegetable are quite soft.

Rub the cooked vegetables through a fine strainer. (If this is difficult and you have a blender, blend the pulp for a few seconds, return it to the strainer and continue to rub it through.) Do not give up too quickly on this process; every bit of strained pulp means more flavor and substance for your catsup. Ideally, only the tomato seeds should be discarded.

Add all the remaining ingredients except the lemon juice. Mix well and cook over a medium flame, stirring every 5 or 10 minutes, for 1½ hours. Stir in the lemon juice and taste the catsup; add more sugar if you prefer a sweeter sauce.

Cook over a medium-low flame, stirring every 5 minutes, until the catsup is quite thick (about one hour longer if you are making the smaller quantity; about 2 hours longer for the larger amount). When the catsup begins to reach the consistency of the commercial variety, stir it more frequently. The catsup is ready to bottle when no liquid fills in the empty space if a spoon is drawn across the bottom of the pot.

Spoon the hot catsup into sterilized bottles or jars and top with commercial caps or paraffin. Use a funnel to avoid spilling. This ownmade catsup is darker in color (a deep, rich reddish-brown) and more piquant than the bland store-bought variety.

## Super-Spicy Peach Chutney

*If you have a "hot tooth" as well as a sweet one, this is the chutney to spice your table. I have also included an ingredient list to prepare 30 jars in case you have your own peach tree and would like to give a few jars for gifts.*

### INGREDIENTS FOR MAKING 6 6-OUNCE JARS

    1 Large onion, peeled
3½ Cups dark raisins
    2 Cloves garlic, peeled
    4 Pounds fresh peaches, peeled
    2 Sweet red or green peppers, seeded
    ½ Cup fresh ginger root, peeled and cut into ¼-inch strips
1½ Teaspoons allspice
    ¾ Teaspoon dry mustard
    1 Teaspoon each dried, crushed red pepper and ground cinnamon
    2 Teaspoons salt
    3 Cups cider vinegar
    5 Cups light brown sugar
      Zest from 1 lemon, with none of the bitter white underskin

### INGREDIENTS FOR MAKING 30 6-OUNCE JARS

    5 Large onions, peeled
16 Cups dark raisins
10 Cloves garlic, peeled
20 Pounds fresh peaches, peeled
10 Sweet red or green peppers, seeded
2½ Cups fresh ginger root, peeled and cut into ¼-inch strips
2½ Tablespoons allspice

3¾ Teaspoons dry mustard
    5 Teaspoons each dried, crushed red pepper and ground cinnamon
    3 Tablespoons salt
15 Cups cider vinegar
25 Cups light brown sugar (about 6 1-pound boxes)
      Zest from 5 lemons, with none of the bitter white underskin

Cut the onion (or onions) into quarters and put it, along with 2 cups (or 10 cups) of the raisins and the garlic cloves, through the coarse disk of your grinder (or finely chop with a sharp knife). Cut the peaches into ¾-inch slices and the peppers into ½-inch dice. Slice the lemon zest into strips. Mix all the ingredients (including the remaining whole raisins) in a large, heavy pot and cook at a low boil for about 1½ hours, or until the chutney is quite thick and dark brown in color. Store in sterilized jars.

## Grape Chutney

### (YIELD: ABOUT 6 8-OUNCE JARS)

    4 Cups full-sized, unripe grapes, seeded
    4 Cups peeled, cored and sliced tart apples
    4 Large cloves garlic, peeled and finely chopped
    3 Tablespoons chopped preserved ginger
    1 Tablespoon each dry mustard and salt
    ⅓ Teaspoon cayenne pepper
1½ Cups cider vinegar
1½ Cups light brown sugar, firmly packed
    2 Cups seedless raisins
    ¾ Cup finely chopped blanched almonds

Combine the grapes, apples, garlic, ginger, mustard, salt and cayenne in an unchipped enamel kettle. Stir thoroughly, then add the vinegar and cook over low heat until the grapes are soft. Mix in the sugar, raisins and almonds and simmer the mixture for about 1 hour, or until it is thick.

Divide the hot mixture into sterile jars. Seal, cool and store in a cool, dark place.

### India Relish

(YIELD: 6 8-OUNCE JARS)

3 Quarts green tomatoes
2½ Tablespoons salt
6 Cups finely chopped cabbage
4½ Cups cider vinegar
1 Cup finely chopped onion
1 Cup finely chopped sweet green pepper
½ Cup finely chopped sweet red pepper
3 Cups granulated sugar
2¼ Teaspoons each celery seed and mustard seed
1 Teaspoon cardamom seed
½ Teaspoon each dry mustard and coarsely crushed whole peppercorns
1½ Teaspoons whole cloves
1 2-inch stick cinnamon

Rinse the tomatoes, then chop them coarsely and place in a large bowl. Sprinkle with the salt and toss well. Allow the mixture to stand overnight, covered loosely with cheesecloth.

Drain the tomatoes and place in a preserving kettle. Add the cabbage and vinegar and boil the mixture for 25 to 30 minutes. Remove from the heat and stir in the onion, peppers, sugar, celery seed, mustard seed, cardamom seed, dry mustard and peppercorns. Cut a piece of cheesecloth large enough to hold the cloves and cinnamon stick and tie up the corners to make a small bag. Add to the kettle. Stir the relish mixture thoroughly to blend all ingredients.

Simmer over low heat until it is fairly thick (about 1½ hours). Discard the spice bag and divide the relish into sterile jars. Seal tightly. Turn the jars upside down to cool before storing.

DRIED APPLES

### Carrot–Green Tomato Relish

(YIELD: 6 8-OUNCE JARS)

3 Quarts chopped green tomatoes
5 Tablespoons salt
4½ Cups cider vinegar
18 Large carrots, scraped and chopped
¾ Cup chopped onion
¾ Cup chopped sweet green pepper
½ Cup chopped sweet red pepper
4 Cups granulated sugar
2¼ Teaspoons each celery seed and mustard seed
1 Teaspoon each cardamom seed and coarsely crushed whole peppercorns
¼ Teaspoon dry mustard
1½ Teaspoons whole cloves
1 ¾-inch stick cinnamon

Place the chopped tomatoes in a large bowl and sprinkle with the salt. Stir gently to mix, then cover with cheesecloth and allow the tomatoes to stand overnight.

Drain the tomatoes, place them in a large kettle and add the vinegar and carrots. Boil over medium heat for 25 to 30 minutes, then add the onion, peppers, sugar, celery seed, mustard seed, cardamom seed, dry peppercorns and mustard. Tie the whole cloves and cinnamon stick in a small cheesecloth bag and add to the kettle. Stir the mixture to blend all ingredients, return to low heat and simmer until the relish is fairly thick, usually a little over an hour.

Discard the spice bag and immediately pour the relish into hot, sterile jars. Seal tightly before turning the jars upside down to cool. Store in a cool, dry place.

### Applesauce

(YIELD: ENOUGH TO SERVE 8)

12 Medium McIntosh apples
2½ Cups water
½ Cup honey
½ Teaspoon ground cinnamon

⅛ Teaspoon ground cardamom
¼ Teaspoon nutmeg (optional)

Peel the apples, core them, then cut into ½-inch slices. Place in a saucepan with the water and cook over medium heat until soft. Remove from the heat and press through a strainer into another saucepan.

Stir the honey and spices into the puréed apple and simmer over low heat until fairly thick. Serve hot or cold, topped with a sprinkling of cinnamon or brown sugar.

## Homemade Noodles

6 Eggs plus 3 egg yolks
6 Tablespoons water
⅛ Teaspoon salt
4½ Cups hard-wheat flour
1 Tablespoon vegetable oil

Combine the eggs, egg yolks, water and salt in your blender container. Beat at high speed for 2 minutes, then turn the mixture out into a large bowl. Beat in 3 cups of the flour to form a smooth paste. Allow to stand, uncovered, for 10 to 15 minutes, then work in the rest of the flour, kneading with your fingers until the dough becomes smooth and elastic. Sprinkle the oil over the dough, a little at a time, incorporating it thoroughly as you knead.

Shape the dough with your hands into a long thin roll. Break off a 3-inch section and roll out on a lightly floured board to form a thin, narrow rectangle, about 2 by 14 inches. Set the rolled-out dough aside to dry, then proceed to cut and roll out the remaining dough, setting each piece aside to dry as you finish it.

Allow about 35 minutes for the pieces of dough to dry slightly, then cut into noodles about ¼-inch wide. Set the noodles on towels after cutting them, and let them stand in a warm, dry place until they become brittle (about 2 to 3 hours). Store in airtight containers.

To cook half the noodles, bring 3 quarts of water to a boil in a large kettle, add the noodles and boil gently for 10 minutes. Serve the noodles with any kind of clear soup, or use them as a substitute for potatoes.

## Golden Noodles

To add a unique flavor and a lovely bit of color to your homemade noodles, try this variation: place 2 teaspoons whole saffron (or, if saffron is not available, substitute ½ teaspoon ground turmeric) in ⅔ cup of water and bring to a boil. Cover the mixture, reduce the heat and simmer for 15 minutes. The result should be about 3 to 4 tablespoons of liquid. Pour into the blender jar, add the other ingredients and proceed as directed above.

## Pot-Pie Noodles

*Pot-pie noodles are traditionally more chewy than the ribbon-cut kind. This recipe duplicates my grandfather's Pennsylvania Dutch one. Add these to any stew that is a little short of meat and the meat will never be missed.*

(YIELD: ABOUT 2 POUNDS OF NOODLES)

Half of this recipe should be enough to serve 8. To freeze the remaining noodles, arrange them on plastic wrap so they do not touch and place in a freezer container.

4½ Cups all-purpose flour
2 Teaspoons baking powder
⅛ Teaspoon salt
2 Tablespoons vegetable shortening
2 Eggs
1 to 1½ Cups milk

Combine 4 cups of the flour, the baking powder and salt and sift together into a large bowl. Using 2 knives, cut the shortening into the dry ingredients. When the mixture resembles coarse meal, add the lightly beaten eggs. Stir in enough of the milk, a bit at a time, to produce a firm dough.

Spread ½ cup flour on a pastry board. Cut the dough into 4 pieces and roll out, 1 piece at a time, working excess flour well into each piece. Cut the rolled-out dough into 1-inch squares.

Make pot pies out of your beef stew or chicken fricassee by adding a bit of extra broth and water and arranging these pastry squares over the surface, taking care that the edges do not overlap.

Spoon the broth over the noodles frequently while they cook for 1 hour. Serve hot.

## Croutons

*These savory cubes of sautéed bread make delicious go-withs or garnishes for soups or salads. They also put your slices of slightly stale bread to good use.*

(YIELD: ABOUT 3 CUPS)

12 Slices leftover bread
3 Tablespoons each vegetable oil and butter

Trim the crusts from the bread and cut into small cubes. Heat the oil and butter together in a large skillet and sauté the bread cubes, stirring frequently, until golden brown on all sides. Cool and store in an airtight container.

Reheat before serving.

## Seasoned Croutons

(YIELD: ABOUT 3 CUPS)

12 Slices white bread
3 Tablespoons each vegetable oil and butter
1½ Teaspoons garlic salt, onion salt, marjoram or thyme (or any other herbs you may prefer)

Trim the crusts from the bread, then cut the slices into cubes. Sauté gently in the oil and butter, stirring constantly and sprinkling to taste with any one, or any combination, of the above seasonings. As soon as the croutons reach a golden brown on all sides, remove and drain briefly on paper towels. Cool and store in an airtight container.

Reheat before serving.

## Fried Bread Croutons

*Nothing dresses up a soup or salad more than crunchy fried croutons. These cost practically nothing when they are made from stale bread normally thrown away, or from bread from a day-old-bread outlet.*

(YIELD: 64 LARGE CROUTONS)

16 Slices slightly stale bread
⅓ Cup butter and margarine, combined to your liking
½ Teaspoon sage, thyme or marjoram (or any combination of these)

Trim the crusts from the bread if you prefer. Make a criss-cross cut diagonally across each slice to form 4 triangles.

Heat the butter and margarine in a heavy skillet, stir in the herbs and fry the bread triangles to a golden brown on each side, turning once. Serve at once or cool and freeze in a plastic container until needed. Reheat under the broiler and serve in soups.

## Banana Chips

*When really green bananas are available, they fry up as crispy as potato chips. If only partially green bananas are available, the chips will be softer but equally tasty.*

(YIELD: 6 CUPS)

8 Large green bananas, peeled
Vegetable oil for deep frying
Salt (optional)

If the bananas are hard enough you may use a vegetable peeler to cut them into paper-thin slices, but since it is difficult to find really green bananas in supermarkets, you will, most likely, have to use a knife to cut slices as thin as possible.

Heat oil, 1½ inches deep, in a large, heavy skillet. When the temperature of the oil is 375 degrees F. (See How to Deep-Fry, page 46), drop the banana slices in, one at a time, until the surface of the oil is covered. Fry approximately

3 to 4 minutes, turning any slices that are light brown. When the banana chips are golden brown, scoop them from the oil with a slotted spoon and arrange them on paper towels to blot out excess oil. Salt lightly if desired.

### Potato Chips

(YIELD: ABOUT 28 CUPS)

*4 All-purpose potatoes, 7 ounces each*
*Vegetable oil for deep-frying*
*Salt to taste*

Peel, wash and dry the potatoes. Using a vegetable peeler, cut the potatoes in broad, paper-thin slices. As they are cut, arrange the slices several deep on paper towels. Cover the slices with additional paper towels and press with the palms of your hands to blot up excess moisture.

Heat oil to boiling in a fairly deep, broad pan. Add the potato slices, one at a time, until the surface of the oil is covered and stir with a slotted spoon for approximately 30 seconds, or until golden brown; do not overbrown. Remove the potato chips with a slotted spoon and turn onto several thicknesses of paper towel.

When the chips are cool, store them in an airtight container or securely fastened plastic bag. Salt prior to serving.

### Mustard with Beer

*This is not your usual store-bought mustard, but it is inexpensive and unusually zesty.*

*Powdered mustard*
*Beer*

Combine mustard with as much beer as needed to reach spreading consistency.

# SAVING MONEY
# WITH YOUR FREEZER

Although the wholesome, fresh-tasting foods of yesteryear are much noted and longingly remembered in this book, there are, of course, some priceless modern-day conveniences. Among these is your friendly home freezer. Grandmother would have been delirious with joy, could she have traded her dripping icebox for today's modern refrigerator-freezer (even though, to my mind, there is nothing so marvelous for drinks as hand-chipped block ice). The home freezer is a modern miracle!

Do you actually save money by owning a freezer? Can the convenience of having foods at your fingertips, or the advantage of buying in quantity when prices are low, compensate for the high cost of electricity? Is your time and the work you save with a freezer worth money to you?

I believe it is, for while relatively few people take the time or go to the trouble of canning foods, many freezer owners take advantage of seasonal savings, since freezing is so easy to do. But savings are realized best by (1) those who plant and harvest their own gardens; and (2) those who save hours by cooking two meals and freezing one to help them manage an outside job and a family at the same time.

The question of whether or not your freezer saves you money depends on a great many factors, but the primary factor is you. Do you freeze the right foods? Carrots, for example, freeze well but they cold-store conveniently too, so why give them relatively expensive freezer space when they will do nicely in the vegetable bin of your refrigerator, or cheaper yet, in a root cellar? Do you freeze foods that would otherwise go to waste? If there is a fisherman or hunter in the house, you can save—and use—the fish and wild game that you were once forced to give away.

Perhaps most important, if you use your freezer properly you will save a fortune in time, and time is money because it gives you more of an opportunity to participate in the enjoyable and productive endeavors that make your life more rewarding.

## HOW YOUR FREEZER HELPS YOU SAVE MONEY

Here are a few ways your freezer works for you.

· Leftovers that might ordinarily be thrown away may be saved and served at a later date.

· Foods that are less expensive due to seasonal surpluses may be stored and used weeks and even months later.

· Extra portions of food may be cooked and the surplus stored for future use. You save cooking time and fuel because it is quicker to reheat foods than to cook them from scratch.

· Foods may be bought in larger quantities and on special sale days to save you dollars.

· Fish and game, caught, shot or given by household members or family friends, may be stored and served where normally they might go to waste.

· Having food in the freezer can save you fuel-consuming trips to the supermarket.

## FREEZER WRAPS AND CONTAINERS

There are three requisites for the containers and/or materials you will use to store foods in your freezer.

It is essential that these be airtight. Air contains oxygen, and oxygen not only alters the flavor of freezer foods but it also imparts that seared, burned look, called "freezer burn," when the surface of the meat comes into prolonged contact with oxygen.

Wraps must also be moisture-proof. Freezer air is damp, and excessive dampness can, over a period of time, drain flavor from frozen foods.

Effective freezer wraps are nonporous and therefore odorproof. Fresh spices, strong cheeses or for that matter all pungent foods, can pass on their characteristic odor when stored in the refrigerator or freezer.

Fortunately, effective freezer wraps are easy to obtain. Supermarkets, department stores and many hardware stores and groceries carry meat wraps, freezer sealing tapes, plastic containers with tight-fitting lids, waxed cardboard freezer cartons with plastic liners, reusable polyethylene food bags and other convenient containers and wraps.

Of course, not all freezer wrappings have to be store-bought. A wide variety of the foodstuffs you normally purchase come packaged in containers suitable for freezing. Milk cartons make fine containers. When they are empty, open them up carefully and wash them out well, but don't use water hot enough to melt the wax. The 1-quart and 2-quart sizes both do well. Fill, leaving expansion room at the top, then refold and staple securely shut. If you don't have a stapler, a couple of stitches with a heavy needle and coarse thread will do the trick.

Ice cream and other foodstuffs frequently come in plastic containers with tight lids. These make ideal freezer containers. Be sure to save them for future use.

Glass jars and jelly glasses should not be used as freezer containers. Glass, when frozen, becomes brittle and shatters easily, and a freezer full of broken glass can be troublesome and dangerous as well.

Polyethylene bags are easy to use and relatively inexpensive, but these must be well sealed to exclude as much air as possible. After filling the bag, squeeze out as much air as you can. Then, holding the bag by the neck, spin it to twist it shut and tightly wrap a few inches of freezer tape around the neck to form an airtight seal. Covered wire closures, like those used to seal garbage bags, are even more effective, as well as easier to use. After filling the bag and squeezing out the air, twist the top, fold it back once and apply the wire closure, twisting it well.

Heavy-duty aluminum foil makes an effective and easy-to-use wrap for meats, fish and other foodstuffs. It is particularly handy for wrapping oddly shaped packages.

## TRAY-FREEZING—THE NEWEST TECHNIQUE

A great many foods—basically those which take the form of individual pieces, like chops, steaks, asparagus spears, mushrooms and so on—may be tray-frozen.

Simply prepare the food for freezing, either cooked or uncooked, just as you would ordinarily do, then lay the pieces out on a baking tray, unwrapped and not touching one another. Slide them into your freezer, tray and all. When they are solidly frozen, remove the tray from the freezer and pop the individually frozen pieces into polyethylene bags, seal, label and store in the freezer.

There are several obvious advantages to tray-freezing. You don't have to wrap as carefully as you ordinarily would, pieces don't stick together because they have been placed into bags after they have been frozen, and they may be removed from the bags individually, or in any amount you desire.

## GENERAL TIPS ON FREEZING

· Do not refreeze foods unless you cook them between the first freezing and the second. For example, raw meat or vegetables may be frozen only once. They may be frozen a second time after they have been cooked, but never a third time.

· Do not fill your freezer to capacity. It is always a good idea to leave your freezer from one-quarter to one-third empty. Then, if an opportunity arises to pick up a special buy, you have the room to take advantage of it.

· Process promptly and keep all foods refrigerated until you are ready to freeze them.

· Space packages at least one inch apart. They will freeze more rapidly that way.

· Leave room at the top! Never fill freezer containers all the way. Like water, foods that are on the liquid side expand when they are frozen. If you don't leave room at the top they will quite literally flip their lids.

· Freeze a comparatively small amount of warm foods at a time. This keeps freezer temperature low so that foods freeze more quickly.

· Keep your freezer at zero degrees or below. When you put in a substantial amount of food to be frozen, set the dial to the lowest setting and then return it to the appropriate setting to maintain zero degrees after the new additions have frozen. A freezer thermometer is very helpful in maintaining proper temperatures.

· Date all packages, and always use the oldest packages first! There is a limit to how long a

given food may be kept frozen and still maintain its flavor.

## DO-NOT-FREEZE LIST

Following are a number of items that simply do not freeze well. For full particulars, consult the item under its heading in the pages that follow.

| | |
|---|---|
| Buttermilk | Mayonnaise |
| Celery | Meat, seasoned |
| Cottage cheese, creamed | Meringues |
| Cream, sour | Pasta, fully cooked |
| Cream, sweet (un-whipped) | Potatoes, raw |
| Custard | Potato salad (or any salad that contains mayonnaise) |
| Eggs, hard cooked | |
| Eggs in the shell | Radishes |
| Egg white frostings | Tomatoes, fresh |
| Fried foods, fully cooked | Vegetables, unblanched |
| Lettuce | |

If you are in doubt about whether or not a particular item will freeze well, try a small quantity and see. In general, firm, crispy items—raw celery, radishes and such—go limp during thawing.

While it is not generally recommended, in an emergency you may freeze cream or milk. All the nutritional values stay intact, but it does not look too appetizing when it thaws out. If you do freeze milk or cream, thaw it in your refrigerator.

## MEAT

Although freezing preserves the fresh, natural quality of meat better than any other method, remember that it cannot make tough meat tender, so purchase meats wisely. The most you can expect is that your meat will emerge from the freezer as appetizing as the day you put it in, and that will only happen if you prepare it properly.

If you expect to maintain quality, you cannot casually toss a package of meat into your freezer in its supermarket wrappings. There are a few simple rules that you should observe even if you are in a hurry. The extra time and trouble it takes to wrap correctly will save you money in the long run by eliminating spoilage and assuring that the quality you paid for in the first place is the quality your family enjoys when the meat is served.

Following are a few helpful tips on freezing meat:

· Trim excess fat away and pad the sharp bone points with folded freezer wrap to prevent punctures in the outer wrapping.

· Whenever you can, remove the bones; they only take up valuable freezer space.

· Stack meat patties, thin chops and other small cuts with two pieces of freezer wrap in between. This makes them easier to separate and consequently helps them to thaw faster.

· Preshape ground meat in the form in which it will be used.

· Generally, larger cuts of meat maintain their quality for longer periods of time than smaller cuts of the same meat do, so plan your shopping accordingly.

· Salted meats, for example, smoked ham, have a shorter freezer life. The salt tends to turn them rancid sooner.

· Freshly butchered beef and lamb—whether you do it yourself or have it done for you—should be aged at about 34 degrees F. for five to seven days before freezing. Pork and veal, however, should be frozen as soon as the various cuts are chilled.

· Wrap all meats with tender, loving care. Remember that air causes freezer burn, so use freezer paper that is air and moisture resistant, and seal well with freezer tape.

### Freezer Timetable for Fresh Meat

| Beef | 8 to 12 months |
|------|----------------|
| Veal | 8 to 12 months |
| Lamb Roasts | 8 to 12 months |
| Pork Roasts | 4 to 8 months |
| Chops (all kinds) | up to 4 months |
| Cutlets (all kinds) | up to 4 months |
| Ground Meats | 2 to 3 months |
| Stewing Meat | 2 to 3 months |
| Variety Meats | 2 to 3 months |

### Cooking Frozen Meats

Whether you cook meats frozen or thawed does not make a great deal of difference in the end results. However, meats brown more evenly if they are thawed first, and of course you do save a good deal of fuel (and dollars) by doing so. Thaw your meats in their freezer wraps, preferably in the refrigerator to prevent drying.

## WILD GAME

### Birds

Game birds should be prepared and frozen in the same manner as domestic poultry. Try to clean and dress the birds as soon after they have been killed as possible. Keep your birds iced or refrigerated for between twenty-four and thirty-six hours before freezing. Remove as much fat from ducks and geese as possible, since this becomes rancid quickly.

### Small Animals

The above also holds true for rabbit and other small game. There should be as little delay between the time the game was shot and the time you clean them as you can manage. Cool the carcass, skin it, remove and discard the internal organs, and cut the meat into convenient sections. Then wash all the parts thoroughly, refrigerate for twenty-four to thirty-six hours, wrap well and freeze.

### Deer and Other Large Game

Venison, bear, moose, elk and other big game are generally too large and therefore too unwieldly to be handled conveniently at home. Ideally they should be butchered by a professional in the same manner as a side of beef. Commercial freezer lockers are generally the best source for this service, so unless you or someone close to you is an old hand at butchering, you would do best to have your animal cut, freezer-wrapped and frozen at a convenient freezer-locker plant. Incidentally, request that as many large bones as possible be removed. A great many people experienced in these matters believe the bone marrow is responsible for the excessively gamy flavor.

### Getting Your Kill Home

If the hunting grounds are a substantial distance from your home—and freezer—you may find it makes more sense to ship your game home as soon after the kill as possible. If the hunting lodge is equipped with a freezer—and many of them are—your game should be cleaned, wrapped and frozen in the usual fashion and then shipped home in the frozen state.

Pack the various parts, cleaned and well wrapped, in a clean carton, using between twenty-five and thirty pounds of dry ice per seventy to eighty pounds of frozen game. That quantity of ice is sufficient to keep your game frozen for around five days or so. After the carton has been well taped and sealed, place it in a somewhat larger carton and fill in the empty spaces around the sides, bottom and top with sawdust, bits of polyurethane foam or crumpled newspapers. Seal the outer carton and your game should be well protected.

When your carton arrives home, check to be sure that all packages are still well frozen and, if they are, put them into your freezer immediately. Any defrosted meat that is not spoiled should be cooked immediately.

### Freezer Timetable for Game

| Animals | 9 months |
| Birds | 9 months |

## POULTRY

Poultry, like meat, freezes well. Just remember to wrap well in the usual airtight, moisture-resistant, well-sealed packages, and to date each package so that you can use them in the proper order. Incidentally, don't be alarmed if you spot dark areas around the bones of roasters, fryers and broilers. This slight discoloration is caused by the oxidation of bone marrow. It is perfectly normal, perfectly harmless and doesn't affect the quality or the flavor of the bird. Following are a few helpful tips:

· Separate small parts with freezer paper and then wrap enough for one meal together in a large package.

· Be sure whole birds are clean and well drained before packaging. Tie wings and legs close to the body to make a more compact package, and mold your freezer paper around the bird to eliminate as many air pockets as possible.

· Do not freeze freshly killed birds; they tend to be tough when cooked. Dress and chill them in your refrigerator for twenty-four to thirty-six hours, or until they have lost their stiffness. When you can rotate their legs and wings easily, you know they are ready to be frozen.

· Wrap and freeze giblets separately. They have a shorter freezer life, and tend to impart an unpleasant flavor to the rest of the poultry.

· Never stuff your poultry before freezing. Stuffed birds take longer to freeze, and that gives undesirable bacteria a chance to breed, multiply and perhaps cause dangerous spoilage.

### Freezer Timetable for Uncooked Poultry

| Chicken | 6 to 9 months |
| Turkey | 6 to 9 months |
| Goose | 6 to 7 months |
| Duck | 6 to 7 months |
| Giblets | 2 to 3 months |

### Cooking Frozen Poultry

Cooking frozen poultry presents no particular problems. Simply thaw it first in its freezer wrapper in your refrigerator or place it in a plastic bag and immerse it in cold water until it defrosts. Then cook as usual.

## VEGETABLES

Most vegetables are completely accommodating when it comes to taking up residence in your freezer. As a general rule, anything that may be canned may be frozen. There are, however, a few exceptions. Crispy vegetables—those high in water content like radishes, cabbages, lettuce, white potatoes, whole tomatoes and a few others —do not do well in the polar temperatures of your freezer. The formation of ice crystals during freezing breaks down their delicate cellular structure, and when they are thawed out they become limp and lifeless. Commercial food-processing companies are often able to bypass this problem by freezing at extremely low temperatures, but your home equipment will not be able to reach the temperature needed for this.

## Preparing Your Vegetables for Freezing

The first rule is to select young, tender, garden-fresh specimens. If you possibly can, freeze your vegetables the same day they are picked. If you cannot do this, at least be sure to keep them refrigerated until you get around to processing them. All vegetables should be well washed in cold water, and those like broccoli and cauliflower, which tend to harbor insects, should be soaked for half an hour in cold salt water to draw out any reluctant tenants.

BLANCHING—WHY AND HOW: Nature, in her grand plan, builds into her fruits and vegetables certain enzymes whose function it is to assure that the produce has a chance to ripen and mature. When vegetables are stored—whether in bin, refrigerator or freezer—this enzyme action continues in varying degrees and consequently, so does the ripening process. In order to stop that action cold (which is what freezing is all about), vegetables should be blanched to prepare them for their stay in your freezer.

Basically, blanching is a partial cooking process that consists of bringing a particular vegetable to a particular temperature for a specified amount of time. Here is how it is done.

Use a large aluminum or unchipped enamel-ware pot (iron or copper will not do, since these metals react badly to certain vegetables). If you do not own one, perhaps you can borrow one. A large 8 to 10-quart kettle is ideal. In addition you will require a wire basket, colander or, if neither is available, a large piece of cheesecloth.

Add a minimum of 4 quarts of water to your kettle and bring to a vigorous boil. Place no more than 1 pound at a time of the vegetables you are working with into your colander, basket or cheesecloth bag. Lower the vegetable into the still boiling water, cover the kettle tightly and continue to boil for the length of time specified for that particular vegetable. (Start to time from the exact moment your vegetables are completely submerged in boiling water. A minute extra can make or break a vegetable's crispness and/or fresh taste at this point.) If you happen to live in an area that is 5,000 feet or more above sea level, add one minute to the boiling time.

As soon as the boiling time is up, remove your vegetables and plunge them into a cold water bath. A well-scoured, rinsed and stoppered sink filled with cold water and ice is best, but any large container will do as long as it is not copper or iron. If you do not have an endless supply of ice, use cold running tap water. Keep the vegetables in their cold water bath for twice as long as they were blanched. Then remove them, place in appropriate containers, label and freeze.

Prepare the following vegetables for freezing according to the directions for each:

ASPARAGUS: Wash well, cut off tough ends, leave in spears or cut into 2-inch lengths. Blanch small stalks 2 minutes, thick stalks 4 minutes. Chill, drain and freeze.

BEANS: Shell tender, fresh beans and sort for size. Blanch small beans 2 minutes, medium beans 3 minutes and larger beans 4 minutes. Chill, drain and freeze.

BEANS (SHELL): Shell and blanch for one minute. Chill, drain and freeze.

BEANS (SNAP, STRING, GREEN): Wash young, tender beans, cut off both ends, slice crosswise and blanch for 3 minutes. Chill, drain and freeze.

BEETS: Select tender young beets less than 3 inches across. Wash, trim tops to within ½ inch, leave on tails and blanch until tender (about 25 minutes). Cool quickly, drain and slip off skins. Slice or dice and freeze.

BROCCOLI: Soak in salt solution for 30 minutes (1 tablespoon of salt per quart of cold water). Trim off leaves and stalks, cut lengthwise into uniform pieces, and blanch for approximately 3 minutes. Chill, drain and freeze.

BRUSSELS SPROUTS: Wash, cut from stems and soak in a salt-water solution for half an hour if you think insects may be present. Remove coarse outer leaves and blanch 3 minutes for small heads, 4 minutes for medium heads, 5 minutes for large heads. Chill, drain and freeze.

CABBAGE: Do not freeze unless you plan to use in soup or other cooked dishes. Trim off outer leaves, shred or separate into individual leaves and blanch between 1 and 2 minutes. Chill, drain and freeze.

CARROTS: Since carrots store well elsewhere, it normally does not pay to freeze ordinary specimens. However, if you have an abundance of very small, tender, fancy young carrots that might go to waste, do freeze them by all means. Trim tops, wash and peel. Leave small carrots whole; blanch for 4 minutes. Chill, drain and freeze.

CAULIFLOWER: Break into 1-inch pieces. Soak in salt water if you think insects are present. Wash well and blanch in salted water (1 teaspoon of salt water per quart of water) for 3 minutes. Chill, drain and freeze.

CORN (WHOLE KERNEL): Select very fresh young corn with thin, sweet milk. Husk, remove silk and trim. Blanch for 5 to 7 minutes, depending on size. Chill, drain and cut the tops of the kernels from the cob with a sharp knife. For cream-style corn, scrape the milk from the cobs with a knife. Freeze.

CORN (ON THE COB): Select very fresh ears with thin, sweet milk. Husk, remove silk and trim. Blanch small ears for 7 minutes, medium ears for 9 minutes, large ears for 11 minutes. Chill, drain and freeze.

MUSHROOMS: Select small to medium mushrooms. If larger than 1 inch across, cut or slice. Wash in salt solution (4 teaspoons per quart of cold water), then blanch 3 to 5 minutes. Chill, drain and freeze.

OKRA: Wash and carefully remove stems but leave pods uncut. Blanch small pods 3 minutes, large pods 4 minutes. Chill, drain, slice if preferred and freeze.

PARSNIPS: Select young, small specimens. Remove tops, wash well and slice or dice. Blanch for 2 minutes. Chill, drain and freeze.

PEAS: Select tender young peas. Shell and blanch for 1 to 2 minutes. Chill, drain and freeze.

PEPPERS (SWEET, RED AND GREEN): These require no blanching unless you plan to use them for cooking. In this case, wash, remove stems and seeds and cut into desired shape. Blanch for 2 minutes.

POTATOES: Potatoes store best in your root cellar and do not take well to freezing unless specially prepared. Raw potatoes become soft and mushy after freezing. Boiled potatoes also freeze badly. If you have a large surplus and wish to experiment, freeze baked potatoes. These freeze fairly well and may be used for frying (unthawed), or in potato salad (thawed), or in any manner you prefer.

Mashed potatoes (made without milk) may be prepared as usual, placed in a pie plate, freezer wrapped and frozen.

Fried potatoes should be done to a light, golden brown, packaged and frozen. To reheat, place on a cookie sheet in a 450 degree F. oven for approximately 20 minutes.

PUMPKIN: Wash, cut into pieces and remove seeds. Blanch, unpeeled, until soft. Scrape pulp from rind and purée. Cool and freeze.

RUTABAGA: Wash tender, young, medium-sized specimens. Cut into small (½-inch) cubes and blanch for 2 minutes. Chill, drain and freeze.

SOYBEANS: Select young, green beans. Wash well, blanch for 5 minutes and remove hulls. Chill, drain and freeze.

SPINACH: Select tender young leaves. Wash well, cut away thick stems and blanch for 2 minutes. Chill, drain and freeze.

SQUASH (SUMMER, YELLOW OR ZUCCHINI): Select only young, tender squash with small seeds. Wash and cut into ½-inch slices. Blanch for 3 minutes. Chill, drain and freeze.

SQUASH (WINTER): Select well-ripened specimens with hard rinds. Wash well, remove seeds, cut into 1-inch cubes and blanch for 3 minutes. Chill, drain and freeze.

SWEET POTATOES: Select medium- to large-sized sweet potatoes. Wash and cook without peeling until almost done, then cool to room temperature. Slice, and to keep from discoloring, dip the slices into ½ cup lemon juice mixed with 1 quart of water. For mashed sweet potatoes, mix 2 table-spoons of lemon juice into each quart of mashed potatoes. Package and freeze.

TOMATOES (FRESH): Whole fresh tomatoes cannot be frozen successfully. During thawing they become soft, mushy, shapeless and singularly unappetizing. These do, however, can well, and that is the process recommended. If you find canning irksome and you have tomatoes that will go to waste, they may be frozen stewed or as tomato juice or sauce.

TOMATOES (STEWED): Trim, quarter and peel. Cook gently in a covered enamel or stainless steel vessel until tender (about 15 minutes). To cool, place the pot in cold water. Package and freeze.

TOMATO JUICE: Cut ripe tomatoes into eighths and simmer in their own juices for approximately 10 to 12 minutes. Put through a sieve, and freeze in an appropriate container. Salt before using.

TOMATO SAUCE INGREDIENTS (UNCOOKED): Follow the recipe for Tomato Catsup (see page 24), up to (but *not* including) the point of the first cooking, but omit the onions, allspice and dry mustard. Be sure to use an enamel pan. Freeze in appropriate containers.

TOMATO SAUCE (PARTIALLY COOKED): Follow the recipe for Tomato Catsup (see page 24), up to (*and* including) the first cooking, but omit the onions, allspice and dry mustard. Be sure to use an enamel pan. Cool by plunging the pan into cold water. Freeze in appropriate containers.

TURNIPS: Pick young, tender specimens. Wash, peel and cut in cubes. Blanch the cubes 2 minutes, or cook the cubes fully and mash them. Cool and store in appropriate containers. Freeze.

### Cooking Frozen Vegetables

Frozen vegetables taste better, look better and actually are better (because most of the nutrients remain intact) if they are cooked in a small amount of water for a brief period of time. The moment they become tender, stop cooking and serve immediately.

## FRUITS

### Preparing Fruits for the Freezer

The rules here are simple and logical—work with only that amount of fruit you can handle conveniently . . . generally two or three quarts at a time. Begin the preparation process in much the same way you would if you were serving the fruit immediately. Trim, peel, cut or pit in the usual fashion.

There is, however, one extra precaution you must take to prevent spoilage. Some fruits—specifically peaches, nectarines, pears, apples and apricots—if left untreated darken almost immediately when their flesh is exposed to air. Other fruits will suffer a similar fate a bit later on while they are already in the frozen state. Fortunately, there are steps you can take to prevent this from happening.

HOW TO KEEP FRUIT FROM DARKENING: The easiest procedure, and probably the most effective, is the use of ascorbic acid. You can buy ascorbic acid (vitamin C) in convenient tablet form from your local druggist or health food store. Ascorbic acid comes in aspirin-sized tablets in various potencies ranging from 100 milligrams per tablet on up to 500 milligrams. To use, simply crush the required number of tablets into cold water, mix and apply to the cut fruit as directed. Because this is used in small quantities, it will not affect the flavor of the foods you are freezing as will the relatively larger amounts of lemon juice required to do the same job.

Steam blanching is a more economical procedure, because you have nothing extra to buy. It does take more time, however, and of course creating steam means using fuel. To steam you will require a fairly large pot, with an inside rack (one that will hold your fruit three or four inches above the bottom) and a tight-fitting lid. There are special steam-blanching pots, or you can improvise nicely by using a colander or metal basket with legs set inside your large boiling pot.

Bring about an inch and a half of water to a boil in the bottom of your pot. Place a single layer of fruit on the bottom of the rack and lower it into the pot. Cover the pot tightly and continue to boil for the recommended length of time, starting from the moment the lid is fastened in place. If you happen to live in an area that is 5,000 feet or more above sea level, add one minute to the boiling time. Cool your fruit just as quickly as possible after steaming.

As an alternative, you may use lemon juice to prevent darkening, but this gives the fruit a very tart taste, which must be compensated for by using additional sugar.

Crystalline ascorbic acid is a safe and effective antioxidant. It is sold by the ounce in some drugstores and freezer-locker plants. Directions for freezing given in this section call for the use of ascorbic acid tablets. If, however, you would like to try it and you can buy it in your area, ¼ teaspoon of crystalline ascorbic acid is equal to about 750 milligrams of ascorbic acid in tablet form. Dissolve it in cold water or fruit juice.

FREEZING WITH SUGAR SYRUPS: Adding sugar syrup to your fruits prepared for freezing is easy if you mix, cook and chill the mixture ahead of time.

Use granulated sugar and add it to water in the following proportions:

| | |
|---|---|
| 30 percent syrup: | 2 cups sugar to 1 quart water |
| 35 percent syrup: | 2½ cups sugar to 1 quart water |
| 40 percent syrup: | 3 cups sugar to 1 quart water |
| 50 percent syrup: | 4¾ cups sugar to 1 quart water |
| 60 percent syrup: | 7 cups sugar to 1 quart water |

To prepare any syrup, combine the sugar and water in a saucepan, stir to dissolve the sugar and heat to the boiling point. Remove from the heat, cool and chill. Always be sure your syrup is cold before adding to the fruit.

When adding ascorbic acid to syrups, crush the tablets into a small amount of cold water and mix into the syrup *just before using.*

### Fruits You Can Freeze

Prepare the following fruits for freezing according to the directions for each:

APPLESAUCE: Select juicy apples. Wash and core. Peel or not as you prefer and cook over a low flame until soft enough to strain. Mix in sugar to taste. Pack in rigid plastic containers, cap well and freeze.

APPLE SLICES FOR PIE: Wash firm, mature apples. Core, peel and slice. Soak in salt water (2 tablespoons per gallon) for 15 minutes. Rinse and drain. Cover all surfaces thoroughly with sugar, pack in appropriate containers and freeze.

Alternate method:

Wash, peel, core and slice, and treat with 1,500 milligrams of ascorbic acid per 3 tablespoons of water. Rinse and drain. Cover all surfaces with sugar. Pack and freeze.

APRICOTS: Select firm, well-ripened fruit. Peel, halve and remove pits. Pack and cover with 40 percent syrup to which has been added 2,000 milligrams of ascorbic acid per quart of syrup. Cap well and freeze.

Alternate method:

Dissolve 750 milligrams ascorbic acid tablets in ¼ cup cold water. Toss the apricot halves in this mixture. Sprinkle with sugar, pack and freeze.

BLACKBERRIES (DESSERT): Select firm, ripe berries and discard any that are bruised or soft. Wash gently and pack in 40 percent syrup in rigid plastic containers. Freeze.

BLACKBERRIES (JAMS, PIES OR TARTS): Pack in plastic bags or rigid, well-capped containers in ¾ cup of sugar per quart of berries. Freeze.

BLUEBERRIES: Use large, well-ripened berries. Steaming for 1 minute is optional but recommended for wild berries. Cool quickly and dry well. Pack with no sugar if berries are to be used for cooked dishes; pack in 40 percent syrup if they are to be used for desserts. Freeze.

CHERRIES (SOUR): Wash firm, red cherries. Pit and pack in containers with ¼ cup of sugar per cup of cherries. Freeze.

CHERRIES (SWEET): Select large, firm cherries. Stem, wash and pit if desired. Pack in well-capped rigid containers in 40 percent syrup into which has been stirred 1,500 milligrams of ascorbic acid per quart of syrup. Freeze.

CRANBERRIES (WHOLE): Wash, drain well and pack in firm containers without sugar or syrup. Freeze.

CRANBERRIES (PURÉED): Wash and drain berries. Boil in 2 cups of water per quart of berries until the skins burst. Force through a sieve. Mix in 2 cups of sugar per quart of purée. Pack in well-capped rigid containers, with a minimum of 1-inch head room. Freeze.

CURRANTS (WHOLE) : Wash, drain and pack without sugar or syrup. Freeze.

GRAPEFRUIT: Freezing is not particularly economical unless you have an abundance of cheap fruit. Select ripe, firm fruit. Wash, cut into sections and remove skins, seeds and membranes. Cover with 40 percent syrup to which has been added 1,500 milligrams of ascorbic acid per quart. Pack in rigid containers, cap well and freeze.

GRAPES: Select ripe, mature grapes, eliminating any bruised specimens. Remove stems. Leave seedless grapes whole. For other varieties, cut in half, remove seeds and pack in 40 percent syrup. Freeze.

JUICE (ORANGE, GRAPEFRUIT) : Squeeze the fruit, removing seeds and pulp. Add 600 milligrams of ascorbic acid and 2 tablespoons of sugar per quart. Freeze in well-capped rigid containers.

MELONS (BALLS, CUBES OR SLICES) : Wash firm, ripe melons and halve. Remove seeds and rind. Cut pulp into desired shape, or keep skin intact and scoop out melon balls. Pack in well-capped rigid containers. Pour over 30 percent syrup to which has been added 1,500 milligrams of ascorbic acid. Freeze.

NECTARINES: Nectarines do not freeze as well as most fruits, but if you have an abundance, try this method. Wash well and peel. Remove pits and halve or slice and pack in 40 percent syrup to which has been added 1,500 milligrams of ascorbic acid tablets per quart of syrup. Cap tightly and freeze.

ORANGES: Refer to GRAPEFRUIT.

PEACHES: Select firm, mature, unblemished fruit. Wash and peel. Remove pits and halve or slice the fruit. Pack, in rigid containers, in 50 percent syrup to which has been added 1,500 milligrams of ascorbic acid per quart of syrup. Cap tightly and freeze.

PINEAPPLE: Select firm, ripe pineapples. Pare, remove eyes and core. Cut into desired shape (sticks, slices or cubes), or crush. Pack in rigid containers. Cover with 30 percent syrup made with pineapple juice or water, cap tightly and freeze.

Pineapple pieces may also be frozen dry, without sugar, tightly packed in rigid containers.

PLUMS AND PRUNES: Select firm, mature specimens. Wash and halve or quarter. Remove pits or leave whole. Pack in rigid containers and cover with 40 or 50 percent syrup to which has been added 1,500 milligrams of ascorbic acid per quart. Cover tightly and freeze.

RASPBERRIES: Select firm, ripe berries. Wash gently, pack in rigid containers, cover with 40 percent syrup and freeze.

RHUBARB: Wash, trim well and cut into 1- or 2-inch pieces. Blanch for 1 minute, cool well and pack without sugar or in 40 percent syrup, as desired. Freeze.

STRAWBERRIES: Select firm, ripe berries. Wash in cold water, drain and hull. Slice or leave whole as desired. Cover with 40 percent syrup or sprinkle well with sugar (¼ cup sugar per cup of berries) . Freeze.

---

## *Freezer Timetable for Fresh Fruits*

| | |
|---|---|
| Citrus fruits | 4 to 6 months |
| Citrus juices | 4 to 6 months |
| Other fruits | 8 to 12 months |

## BAKED GOODS

As a general rule, baked goods freeze well. Cake, cookies and breads of various types are all perfect candidates for your freezer. There are a few exceptions, of course. The custard in pies and pastries, meringue, egg white frosting and soft, cream-type fillings in layer cakes do not hold up well when frozen. Almost everything else does. Here is more detailed information to help guide you when freezing baked goods.

BREAD (STORE-BOUGHT) : Overwrap in heavy-grade freezer paper and seal well. Thaw at room temperature in unopened freezer bag. Storage time: 2 to 4 months.

BREAD (QUICK) : Cool after baking, place in freezer, unwrapped, until frozen. Place in plastic bag and return to freezer. Thaw at room temperature in unopened freezer bag. Storage time: 2 to 4 months.

BREAD (YEAST, BAKED) : Cool after baking. Place, unwrapped, into freezer until frozen. When frozen, place in freezer bag. Thaw at room temperature in unopened freezer bag. Storage time: 2 to 4 months.

BREAD (YEAST, UNBAKED): After mixing, allow dough to rise the first time. Punch down, wrap in airtight package and freeze. To thaw, remove from wrapping and cover with damp cloth. Allow to rise. Punch down, knead, shape and allow to rise again. Bake. Storage time for the unbaked dough: 1 week.

CAKE (ICED): Bake, cool and frost. Omit cream or custard fillings until after the cake has thawed. Place in freezer, unwrapped, until frozen. Then remove, place in freezer bag and return to freezer. To thaw, remove from bag and let stand at room temperature. To avoid condensation on icing, thaw under a deep plastic cake cover or pan. Storage time: 3 to 4 months.

CAKE (WITHOUT ICING): Cool, place in freezer, unwrapped, until frozen. Place in freezer bag and return to freezer. Thaw at room temperature, unwrapped, or unwrap and warm in oven at 300 degrees F. for 10 minutes. Storage time: 3 to 4 months.

COOKIES (BAKED): Freeze in freezer bags or cartons. Thaw, wrapped, at room temperature. Storage time: 4 to 6 months.

COOKIES (UNBAKED): Roll dough into tight cylinder, wrap and freeze. To thaw, cut into thin (usually ¼-inch) slices, position on cookie sheet and bake. Storage time: 2 months.

PIES (FRUIT, BAKED): Cool and freeze in pie pan. Remove from pan and place in plastic freezer bag on a sturdy paper plate. Thaw at room temperature in unopened wrappings. When thawed, remove wrappings and bake in oven at 325 degrees F. for approximately 20 minutes. Storage time: 2 to 4 months.

PIES (FRUIT, UNBAKED): Fruit pies freeze better when they are unbaked. Tapioca is preferred as a thickening agent in preference to cornstarch. Freeze in pie plate before wrapping. Then remove from freezer, place in plastic bag and replace in freezer on a sturdy paper plate. To thaw, unwrap, brush top of pie with egg white, slit top crust and bake in an oven at 450 degrees F. for about 25 minutes. Then turn oven down to 350 degrees F. and bake until done. Storage time: 2 to 4 months.

PIE CRUSTS (UNBAKED): Make crust in your usual fashion, roll it out and stack on a cookie sheet. Place 2 layers of freezer wrap or waxed paper between each crust and freeze. Place the stack of frozen crusts in a flat box, wrap and seal well, and place in the freezer. You may freeze pie dough in bars (each bar enough dough for one pie; see page 48). Wrap in aluminum foil.

To thaw, remove crusts, reseal the box and replace the balance in the freezer. Allow crusts to stand at room temperature 7 to 12 minutes. Then shape into your pie plate as usual.

Bars of dough may be unwrapped and crumbled into a bowl and allowed to defrost for 10 minutes. Sprinkle in water, stir with a fork, roll out and bake as usual.

Storage time for both crusts and bars: 2 to 4 months.

## TIPS ON FREEZING COMBINATION DISHES

Preparing, cooking and freezing main dishes ahead of the time you plan to serve them saves time and energy. Choose only the highest-quality ingredients for these dishes, and plan to keep them in the freezer at 0 degrees F. no longer than 3 months (although if properly packaged and stored, no serious loss of quality will result if they are held in storage a few weeks longer).

· Experiment with small amounts of your favorite recipes to see which of them store well. Those that remain fresh-tasting when reheated are the ones to depend on for future freezer storage.

· Prepare the dish as you would if you were serving it right away, but *undercook* slightly, especially if it contains ingredients such as vegetables, cooked dried beans and macaroni products. These can finish cooking as the dish reheats.

· Fresh vegetables lose crispness and can become soggy when precooked and frozen. Cook these separately and add them to frozen stews and soups just before serving to minimize texture changes.

· Cook fried foods just to the barely brown stage before freezing. Crispness will be restored through further cooking at serving time.

· Although soups, gravies and sauces thickened with ordinary wheat flour tend to separate or curdle when thawed, they can be satisfactorily quick-frozen at o degrees F. (and stored for no longer than 3 months) when tapioca or waxy rice flour is used as a thickening agent. Commercial frozen food processors use these to make their soups, gravies and sauces smoother and less prone to curdling. Concentrated canned cream soups may also be used as the basis for creamed dishes. Stir sauces or stews frequently while reheating.

· If possible, add seasonings to combination main dishes when reheating, since freezing frequently affects these in mysterious ways. Salt loses flavor and helps turn fatty meats and sauces rancid. Large quantities of pepper, onion, garlic, cloves and vanilla extract may become strong or bitter or both when used in frozen dishes.

· Keep combination main dishes containing foods of high fat content in your freezer for only short periods of time to prevent them from turning rancid.

· Sprinkle crumb or cheese toppings over your foods when reheating them for serving. Results will be crispier and have more fresh-cooked flavor.

· When preparing cooked foods for the freezer, follow safe and sane freezing rules. Use only clean equipment and food. Do not let foods linger too long at room temperature after cooking; bacteria grow most rapidly at temperatures between 40 degrees F. and 120 degrees F. Cool your foods quickly by setting the pans in cold or iced water and change the water frequently. Quick cooling prevents further cooking, helps maintain natural flavor, texture and color, and prevents bacteria growth.

· Use freezer containers or wrappings that are moisture- and vapor-proof. Pack foods tightly to eliminate air. Leave ample headspace when packing liquid and semiliquid foods to allow for expansion when frozen. Choose appropriate containers of aluminum or plastic, seal all packages tightly and freeze promptly at o degrees F.

· Choosing containers that hold a planned number of servings is an added convenience. You can estimate that quart containers hold four to six servings, while pints will provide enough for two or three.

· When preparing casseroles for the freezer, choose an aluminum pot slightly smaller than your casserole dish. Line the pot with aluminum foil, spoon the partially cooked food in, then cool quickly, cover and freeze. To store, lift both the foil and the frozen food from the pot, fold the foil over and place in a plastic freezer bag. Keep well frozen. Remove from plastic bag and set the foil-wrapped food into the casserole to reheat.

· Some ingredients that generally go into combination main dishes do not freeze well. Check the Do-Not-Freeze List (page 32) and plan your combination dishes to avoid these foods.

· Freeze your prepared main dishes at o degrees F. or below as soon as they are packaged. You may count on good results from cooked and frozen main dishes if used within 2 to 4 months. Soups, gravies and sauces may be held at o degrees F. storage for 2 to 3 months.

· Reheat your precooked combination main dishes in the oven or on top of the stove without thawing them first (although some foods may require partial thawing if transfer to another container is necessary). Always thaw foods in the refrigerator if they must be partially defrosted.

· Oven reheating generally keeps food texture better and requires less attention, but reheating on top of the stove in a double boiler is faster.

Keep foods covered when reheating in the oven. The cover holds the heat inside and foods cook more uniformly. Take the cover off near the end of the heating time if you want to brown the food surface.

Reheating over direct heat calls for considerable attention and frequent stirring. Keep the heat low and the food covered for best results. When using a double boiler, start with warm, not hot or cold, water in the bottom pan. Blocks of frozen foods should be laid side by side in a wide pan if possible; stacking slows the reheating and causes uneven cooking.

· Once food is thawed, use it immediately. Never refreeze! Organisms which grow as the food thaws will cause spoilage and/or loss of quality.

## FREEZER RECIPES

### *Chili con Carne*

(YIELD: ENOUGH TO SERVE 10)

BASIC INGREDIENTS AND DIRECTIONS

>   3 Pounds lean beef, cut in small cubes
>   2 Tablespoons vegetable oil
>   2 28-ounce cans tomatoes
>   4 20-ounce containers of partially
>     cooked red kidney beans from your
>     freezer or 4 20-ounce cans of same

Brown the beef in the oil in a heavy kettle, turning to brown on all sides. Drain the tomatoes, reserving the juice, then chop the tomatoes coarsely. Stir the chopped tomatoes and reserved juice into the kettle. Stir in the partially cooked kidney beans with their juice (if canned beans are to be used, add later) . Bring to just under a boil, then reduce the heat and cover the kettle.

ADDITIONAL INGREDIENTS AND
DIRECTIONS FOR SERVING

>   2 Large onions, peeled and chopped
>   4 Cloves garlic, peeled and minced
>   ¼ Cup chili powder
>   2 Teaspoons each salt, ground cumin
>     and oregano

If you should change your mind and decide to serve the chili instead of freezing it, add the onions, garlic, chili powder, cumin and oregano. Simmer for 2 hours, stirring occasionally. Add a little water if the chili becomes too thick. Stir in canned beans at this point and heat well. To stretch the chili a bit further, place 1 or 2 spoonfuls of cooked macaroni or rice in each bowl before ladling in the chili.

DIRECTIONS FOR FREEZING
IMMEDIATELY

To freeze, prepare the chili to the point of bringing to just under a boil and covering, without the Additional Ingredients. Simmer for 1½ hours, stirring occasionally.

Remove from the heat, chill quickly, then pour into suitably sized freezer containers, leaving 1 inch headspace. Freeze at 0 degrees F. or below.

DIRECTIONS FOR COOKING
AFTER FREEZING

To prepare for serving, thaw slightly in the refrigerator. Place in a large kettle, add a small amount of water, stir in the Additional Ingredients (see above) and cook over low heat, covered, for about ½ hour. Stir frequently to prevent sticking.

### *Meat Loaf*

(YIELD: ENOUGH TO SERVE 8)

>   3½ Pounds lean ground beef
>     1 Tablespoon vegetable oil
>     2 Cups finely chopped onion
>    ¼ Cup finely chopped green pepper
>     3 Tablespoons finely chopped celery
>     5 Slices bread
>     3 Tablespoons rolled oats
>     1 Cup beef broth
>    ½ Cup catsup
>    ¼ Cup mild mustard
>     1 Teaspoon salt
>    ½ Teaspoon each sage and thyme
>    ¼ Teaspoon pepper

Place the meat in a large mixing bowl. Heat the oil in a skillet over low heat and sauté the onion, green pepper and celery until tender. Meanwhile, cut the bread into ½-inch cubes and add them, along with the oats, to the beef broth. Squeeze out the excess broth and mix the moistened bread and oats into the meat. Add the sautéed vegetables, catsup, mustard and spices. Pack the mixture into an aluminum foil-lined loaf pan.

TO PREPARE FOR FREEZER

Meat loaf may be frozen unbaked or baked.

Freeze unbaked meat loaf in foil-lined pan. Rewrap in moisture-resistant wrapping material and seal tightly. Freeze at 0 degrees F. or below.

To bake meat loaf before freezing, place in an oven preheated to 350 degrees F. and bake for 1 hour. Pour off any grease. Cool quickly, then cover and wrap as above. Seal and freeze.

### TO PREPARE FOR SERVING

Set frozen uncooked meat loaf in an appropriately sized loaf pan. Place in a cold oven; do not cover. Bake at 350 degrees F. for 1½ hours, or until done.

Frozen baked meat loaf may be thawed in the refrigerator, then sliced and served cold. If you prefer your meat loaf warm, arrange the slices in a cake pan, cover with tomato sauce or gravy and heat until warmed through.

## White Beans with Sausage Slices

(YIELD: ENOUGH TO SERVE 6)

### BASIC INGREDIENTS AND DIRECTIONS

*1 Pound dried white beans*
*4 Cups water*
*3 Tablespoons vegetable oil*
*2 Tomatoes, seeded and chopped*
*⅛ Teaspoon sage*

Soak the beans in water to cover overnight. Drain well. Place the beans, 4 cups water, tomatoes and sage in a large, heavy skillet. Cover and simmer for 1 hour, then cool quickly by setting the pan in ice water. Place in an airtight container and freeze at 0 degrees F.

### ADDITIONAL INGREDIENTS AND DIRECTIONS FOR COOKING

*Salt and pepper to taste*
*½ Pound homemade Italian-style sausage (see page 75) or other spicy precooked sausage*
*2 Tablespoons olive oil*
*1 Clove garlic, peeled*
*1 Large onion, peeled and chopped*

Place the frozen bean mixture in an ovenproof dish and bake at 350 degrees F. until thawed, stirring occasionally. Stir in salt and pepper to taste.

Cut the sausage in ⅓-inch slices and fry in the olive oil until nicely browned. Remove the meat with a slotted spoon. Sauté the garlic and onion in the oil remaining in the pan and stir these vegetables and the oil into the beans. Arrange the sausage slices on top of the casserole and bake 10 minutes more.

## Refried Beans

*Beans freeze well, and these refried pinto beans are especially delicious. Serve them with chili, heap them on tostadas or use as a change of pace from potatoes.*

(YIELD: ENOUGH TO SERVE 16)

### BASIC INGREDIENTS AND DIRECTIONS

*3 Pounds dried pinto beans*
*2 Quarts cold water*
*4 Serrani chili peppers, chopped, or 1 teaspoon dried, crumbled chilies (optional)*

Place the beans in a large kettle, cover with water and allow to soak overnight.

Bring the beans to a boil. Add the fresh or dried chilies, then lower the heat and simmer, partially covered, for 2½ to 3 hours. Check occasionally to see that the beans do not boil dry; add a little water if necessary.

### ADDITIONAL INGREDIENTS AND DIRECTIONS FOR SERVING IMMEDIATELY

*4 Onions, chopped*
*1½ Cups bacon fat*
*Salt*

To serve immediately, drain the beans thoroughly and mash with a potato masher. Sauté the onions in the bacon fat until quite soft and transparent, then stir the onions and fat into the mashed beans. Cook over medium heat, stirring occasionally, until the fat has been absorbed and the beans are piping hot. Salt to taste and serve.

### DIRECTIONS FOR FREEZING IMMEDIATELY

To freeze, cook the beans until tender, then chill quickly. Pack into freezer containers and freeze at 0 degrees F. or below.

DIRECTIONS FOR COOKING
AFTER FREEZING

To cook, thaw the beans in the refrigerator until fairly soft. Place in a saucepan over very low heat, covered, until well heated through. Sauté the onions in the bacon fat and stir into the beans, stirring until the fat is absorbed. Salt to taste and serve hot.

## Baked Beans

(YIELD: ENOUGH TO SERVE 8)

BASIC INGREDIENTS AND DIRECTIONS

>    4 Cups dried pea beans
>    2 Quarts water, more if necessary

Pick over the beans and place them in a large kettle. Cover with the 2 quarts water and allow to soak overnight. The beans will probably absorb most of this liquid; add as much additional water as is necessary to cover the beans, then simmer over low heat in a tightly covered pot for 1 hour.

ADDITIONAL INGREDIENTS AND
DIRECTIONS FOR SERVING

>    ¾ Pound salt pork
>    1 Cup molasses
>    1½ Teaspoons grated onion
>    1 Teaspoon dry mustard
>    ½ Teaspoon paprika

Should you decide to serve beans immediately, cut about one-third of the salt pork into thick strips and place the pieces in the bottom of an earthenware or other heavy deep casserole. Drain the beans (reserving their liquid) and pour over the salt pork. Score the remaining piece of salt pork in several places, then bury it about halfway down in the beans.

Combine the molasses with 1 cup reserved bean liquid. Add the onion, mustard and paprika, blend the mixture well and pour over the beans in their pot. Stir gently to allow the seasonings to seep down (take care not to crush the beans too much). Set the bean pot, covered, in an oven preheated to 300 degrees F. to cook for 6 hours,

or until tender. (Lift the cover once in a while to check the liquid level in the pot; it should not be higher or lower than the level of the beans. If the level of the liquid falls too low, add a bit of the reserved bean liquid.) Uncover the beans during the last hour of cooking to brown the top.

DIRECTIONS FOR FREEZING
IMMEDIATELY

To freeze, cool the beans quickly after simmering for 1 hour. Drain the beans, reserving the liquid, then spoon carefully into freezer containers and seal tightly. Pour the reserved bean liquid into suitable freezer containers, leaving 1-inch headspace, and seal. Label and store beans and liquid at 0 degrees F. or lower.

DIRECTIONS FOR COOKING
AFTER FREEZING

To prepare the baked beans from the frozen beans and their liquid, allow both to thaw completely in the refrigerator, then combine with the Additional Ingredients (see above) and proceed as directed.

## Osso Buco

*This classic Italian recipe for veal makes one of the most delectable economy meat meals. If possible, ask your butcher to saw the shanks into 3-inch pieces for you, but do not shun the 2-inch packaged pieces if the larger cuts are not available.*

(YIELD: ENOUGH TO SERVE 6)

BASIC INGREDIENTS AND DIRECTIONS

>    6 3-inch pieces veal shank, with surrounding meat
>    1 Tablespoon butter
>    3 Tablespoons vegetable oil
>    3 Carrots, scraped and grated
>    1 Cup chopped celery
>    ⅛ Teaspoon each rosemary and sage
>    ¼ Cup tomato paste
>    1 Cup chicken stock or broth, more if necessary
>    1 Cup white wine (you may substitute chicken stock for the wine if your budget does not permit wine)

In a large, heavy pot, brown the veal pieces on all sides in the butter and oil. (Set them upright so the marrow will not cook out.) Add the carrots, celery, rosemary and sage, then cover and simmer for 10 minutes.

Mix the tomato paste, broth and wine and pour over the meat and vegetables. Cover and simmer over very low heat for 2 hours, adding more broth or water occasionally so the vegetables are just covered.

Set the pan in cold water and chill quickly. Freeze at 0 degrees F. in snap-top freezer containers.

### ADDITIONAL INGREDIENTS AND DIRECTIONS FOR COOKING

> 2 Teaspoons cornstarch
> ½ Cup water
> 1 Teaspoon lemon zest, with none of the bitter white underskin
> ¼ Cup minced fresh parsley
> 2 Cloves garlic, peeled and minced
> Salt and pepper to taste
> Hot cooked rice

Defrost overnight in the refrigerator. Simmer until thoroughly heated through (about 30 to 40 minutes). Just prior to serving, mix the cornstarch and the water, add to the vegetables in the pan and stir continuously until the sauce is thick and clear. Stir in the lemon zest, parsley and garlic and serve immediately over hot rice.

## Oven Stew with Macaroni

### (YIELD: ENOUGH TO SERVE 6)

#### BASIC INGREDIENTS AND DIRECTIONS

> 1 2-Pound slice chuck beef or bottom round
> 2 Tablespoons vegetable oil
> 2 Teaspoons butter
> ½ Teaspoon rosemary
> 2 Cups tomato sauce
> 1½ Cups beef stock (see page 145) or 1 10¾-ounce can beef broth
> 2 Cups uncooked elbow macaroni

Brown the meat on both sides in the oil and butter. Add the rosemary, tomato sauce and beef stock, then cover and bake for 1 hour in an oven preheated to 350 degrees F.

Meanwhile, cook the macaroni according to package directions, but allow only half the cooking time specified. Drain well.

Remove the meat from the pan and cut into 1-inch cubes. Stir the partially cooked macaroni into the sauce in the pan. Chill the stew quickly and freeze at 0 degrees F.

### ADDITIONAL INGREDIENTS AND DIRECTIONS FOR COOKING

> Salt to taste
> Buttered bread crumbs (optional)

To cook, thaw overnight in the refrigerator or place directly in a heavy cooking pot and bake at 350 degrees F. for 40 minutes, or until the stew is piping hot. Salt to taste. If desired, you may sprinkle stew with buttered bread crumbs 20 minutes prior to removing from the oven.

## Eggplant Parmesan

### (YIELD: ENOUGH TO SERVE 6)

> 1 Large eggplant
> ½ Cup vegetable oil
> 2½ Cups tomato sauce
> 2 Cups fine Homemade Bread Crumbs (see page 6)
> 2 Tablespoons minced fresh parsley
> ½ Cup grated Parmesan cheese
> ⅓ Pound mozzarella cheese, cut in thin slices

Cut the eggplant into ⅓-inch-thick slices and place in a glass dish. Cover with boiling water and let stand for 5 minutes. Drain well on paper towels.

Heat 2 tablespoons of the oil in a large skillet. Brush the eggplant slices with the remaining oil and sauté them, a few at a time, until all are lightly browned on each side.

Line an ovenproof bowl with 2 layers of aluminum foil. Arrange half the eggplant slices in the bottom, sprinkle these with half each of the bread crumbs, parsley and cheese. Top with half the tomato sauce and mozzarella slices.

Repeat the procedure, using the remaining ingredients in the order mentioned above. Freeze at 0 degrees F. and wrap in additional foil.

### DIRECTIONS FOR BAKING

To cook, place the foil-wrapped eggplant Parmesan in a baking dish and bake at 350 degrees F. for 45 minutes, or until sizzling hot.

## Freezer Rice

*Real cooked rice with flavor and texture intact is a handy freezer staple. It takes only a few minutes from freezer to serving dish, and lends itself admirably to a multitude of jiffy economy meals.*

Long-grain rice
Water

Cook rice according to package directions, only cut the cooking time in half. Rinse the rice in cold water, drain well and freeze in containers large enough to serve your family.

### DIRECTIONS FOR COOKING

To serve, bring salted water to a boil, add the frozen rice and return to a boil. Cook on low heat for 1 minute. Drain well and serve hot. (Keep warm in a baking dish placed in a warm oven.)

## Frozen Shoestring French-Fried Potatoes

### (YIELD: ABOUT 16 CUPS)

*16 8-ounce all-purpose potatoes, peeled
Vegetable oil for deep frying*

Rinse the potatoes and dry them well. Cut each potato into ¼-inch sticks, to form shoestring potatoes. Place these potato sticks onto several thicknesses of paper towel to blot dry.

Pour the oil into a deep fryer with a metal mesh basket and bring to 375 degrees F. (See How to Deep-Fry, below).

Add the potato sticks to the hot oil, a handful at a time. (Do not fry too many at once.) When the potatoes are *very* light brown, remove them from the oil and spread them on paper towels to cool and to drain off excess oil. Arrange the cooled potato sticks carefully in snap-top plastic freezer containers or freezer bags, allowing enough in each package to feed 4 or 8 persons, to suit your family needs. Freeze as quickly as possible.

To serve, spread the frozen French-fried potatoes on a well-greased cookie sheet, sprinkle liberally with salt and bake in an oven preheated to 400 degrees F. for 7 to 10 minutes, or until golden brown.

## How to Deep-Fry

The secret of successful deep-frying lies in cooking foods at correct temperatures. Fats for uncooked foods need a temperature of 370 degrees F., while precooked foods require a temperature of 390 degrees F. An electric frying pan or deep-fat fryer will indicate the correct temperature without any fuss on your part, but cooks who lack these conveniences can test temperatures this easy way. Simply drop a small cube of bread into the fat when you suspect it may be hot enough. If the temperature is 370 degrees F., the bread will brown in 60 seconds. At 390 degrees F., the bread cube should brown nicely in 40 seconds.

## Frozen Home Fries

### (YIELD: ABOUT 16 CUPS)

*16 all-purpose potatoes, 8 ounces each
Vegetable oil for frying*

Peel, wash and dry the potatoes. Cut into ¼-inch-thick slices, placing the slices in cold water as they are cut. Drain well, then turn onto several thicknesses of paper towel to blot dry.

Cover the bottom of a large skillet ¼ inch deep with oil. Heat the oil and drop the potato and onion slices evenly over the bottom of the pan. Brown lightly, then turn and brown on the other side; the potatoes should be lightly browned and fairly well cooked. Cool the home fries and place them in a snap-top freezer container or plastic bag. Freeze until needed.

To serve, arrange the frozen home fries on greased cookie sheet. Sprinkle with salt and brown in an oven preheated to 450 degrees F., turning after 4 minutes. Continue to bake for several minutes, or until nicely browned.

### Frozen German Hot Potato Salad Base

*Mix this incredibly delicious hot potato salad base at your leisure and freeze it until company comes.*

(YIELD: ENOUGH TO SERVE 8)

INGREDIENTS AND DIRECTIONS FOR POTATO SALAD BASE

   6 *Strips of bacon, minced*
   3 *Small onions, peeled and sliced*
  ½ *Cup each vinegar and hot water*
   2 *Bouillon (chicken or beef) cubes*
   2 *Tablespoons light brown sugar*
  ½ *Teaspoon salt*
   1 *Teaspoon cornstarch*
   2 *Tablespoons cold water*

Fry the bacon bits until they begin to take on color, separating them with a spoon as they cook. Separate the onion slices into rings and sauté them with the bacon for 4 to 5 minutes; do not overcook! Add the vinegar, hot water, bouillon cubes, sugar and salt and bring to a boil.

Combine the cornstarch and the cold water and stir rapidly into the hot mixture. Continue cooking, stirring constantly, until the mixture bubbles and thickens. Cool to room temperature, place in a plastic freezer container and freeze until needed.

ADDITIONAL INGREDIENTS AND DIRECTIONS FOR MAKING POTATO SALAD

  10 *Large potatoes*
   3 *Egg yolks*

Cook potatoes in their jackets in enough water to cover, making sure the water stays at a low boil until the potatoes are cooked through. Drain, peel and cut the potatoes into ½-inch dice while they are still hot.

Meanwhile, bring the frozen potato salad base to a boil, remove from the heat and rapidly beat in the egg yolks, one at a time. Pour the hot base over the warm potatoes and mix well. Serve immediately.

### Breakfast Fried Toasts

*Here is another good use for leftover bread. Serve hot, with a sprinkling of cinnamon and sugar. These taste better than cinnamon toast.*

(YIELD: 64 TRIANGULAR PIECES)

  16 *Slices slightly stale bread*
 5⅓ *Tablespoons butter and margarine, combined to your liking*
     *Sugar*
     *Cinnamon*

Trim the crusts from the bread if you prefer. Make a criss-cross cut diagonally across each slice to form 4 triangles. Heat the butter and margarine in a heavy skillet and fry the bread triangles to a golden brown on each side, turning once. Serve at once, sprinkled with sugar and cinnamon, or cool and freeze in a plastic container until needed.

To reheat, place under broiler a few seconds.

### How to Make a Perfect Pie Crust

Tender, flaky, melt-in-the-mouth pie crusts can be yours every time if you follow these few simple rules.

· Mix your ingredients together lightly with a fork and only long enough to bind them. Don't overmix.

· Use ice water in your recipe.

· Keep your pastry board *lightly* floured, and try to roll your crust to the correct size the first time. Rolling and re-rolling tends to toughen the dough.

· Roll your dough to a size slightly larger than the pie plate. Avoid stretching when fitting it in the plate.

## Instant Pie Crust

(YIELD: ENOUGH FOR 6 SINGLE CRUSTS)

INGREDIENTS AND DIRECTIONS FOR
BASIC MIX

    8  Cups all-purpose flour
3¾  Teaspoons salt
    3  Cups vegetable shortening

Sift the flour and salt, then sift again into a large bowl. Using 2 knives, cut in the shortening until the mixture resembles coarse meal. Divide the dough into 6 equal parts, place each piece on a separate sheet of aluminum foil and shape into a bar. Fold the aluminum foil up and over each bar, sealing the ends. Freeze until needed.

GENERAL DIRECTIONS FOR BAKING
1 2-CRUST PIE

Defrost 2 bars of pie dough.

Crumble the pie dough gently between your fingers into a mixing bowl. Sprinkle 3 tablespoons of water over the mixture and stir with a fork. Add 3 tablespoons more water and stir again. Add more water, a tablespoon at a time, until the dough holds together and forms a ball. (If you should miscalculate and add too much water, and the mixture becomes sticky, sprinkle 2 tablespoons flour on a pastry board and knead the dough a few seconds.) Chill the dough for 15 minutes before rolling out into 2 circles.

Line a 9-inch glass pie plate with dough, spoon in the filling and cover with the second circle of dough. Slash the top in 4 or 5 places to allow steam to escape. Bake for 15 minutes in an oven preheated to 450 degrees F., then reduce the heat to 375 degrees F. and continue baking for 30 to 40 minutes, or until the crust is nicely browned.

## Frozen Fudge Brownie Mix

(YIELD: 2 DOZEN)

   3  1-ounce squares unsweetened
     chocolate
12  Tablespoons (1½ sticks) butter

1½  Cups granulated sugar
   3  Eggs
1½  Teaspoons vanilla extract
   ¾  Cup all-purpose flour
1½  Cups coarsely chopped walnuts,
     pecans or peanuts

Place the chocolate squares in the top of a double boiler and melt over hot water. Beat the butter until fluffy and cream in the sugar. Beat the eggs slightly and add them to the butter and sugar mixture. Stir in the vanilla, flour, melted chocolate and nuts. Incorporate all ingredients thoroughly, then chill the mixture for 2 hours.

Turn the thickened mix onto aluminum foil and form into a roll. Wrap tightly with foil and freeze.

DIRECTIONS FOR BAKING

Cut the frozen dough into ½-inch slices and arrange in a buttered 8- by 8-inch pan. Bake for 30 minutes in an oven preheated to 350 degrees F.

## Chocolate-Chip Oatmeal Freezer Cookies

(YIELD: 9 DOZEN)

INGREDIENTS AND DIRECTIONS FOR
BASIC MIX

1½  Cups vegetable shortening
   8  Tablespoons margarine
   ½  Pound (2 sticks) butter
   3  Cups each light brown sugar and
     granulated sugar
   6  Eggs
4½  Cups sifted all-purpose flour
   1  Tablespoon each salt and baking
     soda
9¾  Cups rolled oats
   1  Tablespoon vanilla extract
1½  Cups chopped walnuts
   2  Cups chocolate chips

Beat the vegetable shortening, margarine and butter together until fluffy. Cream in the two sugars; beat in the eggs. Sift the flour, salt and baking soda into the mixture and mix well. Stir in the oats, vanilla, nuts and chocolate chips.

Knead the dough for 1 minute, then divide it equally onto 3 sheets of aluminum foil. Shape each piece of dough into a bar 2 inches in diameter. Fold the aluminum foil up and around each bar, double-wrapping if necessary. Freeze until needed.

### DIRECTIONS FOR BAKING
### 3 DOZEN COOKIES

Cut ¼-inch slices from one bar and place on a well-greased baking sheet. Bake in an oven preheated to 375 degrees F. for 10 to 12 minutes, or until golden brown. Use a spatula to transfer the hot cookies to a cooling rack.

## Molasses Freezer Cookies

### (YIELD: 9 DOZEN)

### INGREDIENTS AND DIRECTIONS FOR
### BASIC MIX

6 Cups sifted all-purpose flour
¾ Teaspoon salt
1½ Teaspoons baking soda
¾ Teaspoon each ground cinnamon and cloves
½ Teaspoon ground ginger
1½ Cups granulated sugar
1½ Cups molasses
1½ Cups vegetable shortening
3 Eggs

Sift together all the dry ingredients except the sugar. Heat the molasses and the shortening and beat in the sugar by hand. Cool slightly. Place the eggs in a large mixing bowl and beat them lightly. Pour the molasses-shortening-sugar mixture over the beaten eggs, add the dry ingredients and mix thoroughly. Divide the dough equally on 3 sheets of aluminum foil and shape each piece into a bar about 2 inches in diameter. Wrap the foil up and over each bar and fold in the ends. Freeze until needed.

### DIRECTIONS FOR BAKING
### 3 DOZEN COOKIES

Cut 1 bar of dough into ¼-inch slices and roll them out to a thickness of ⅛ inch on a lightly floured board, shaping with a cookie cutter if the pieces become ragged-looking. Arrange on ungreased baking sheets and bake for 8 minutes in an oven preheated to 350 degrees F. Use a spatula to transfer cookies from baking sheets to cooling rack.

## Oatmeal-Currant Freezer Cookies

### (YIELD: 3 DOZEN)

1 Cup margarine
½ Cup each granulated sugar and light brown sugar
1 Cup all-purpose flour
½ Teaspoon each ground cinnamon, baking powder and baking soda
1 Egg
1 Tablespoon milk
1 Teaspoon vanilla extract
¾ Cup rolled oats
½ Cup currants

Beat the margarine until fluffy. Add the sugars and beat until light and airy. Sift the dry ingredients together and add half to the margarine and sugars; beat until well mixed. Add the egg and beat once again. Add the other half of the dry ingredients and beat until fully moistened. Finally add the milk and vanilla and beat once more. Stir in the rolled oats and currants.

Spoon the cookie dough onto aluminum foil and shape into a roll about 2 inches in diameter. Freeze until ready to use.

### DIRECTIONS FOR BAKING

Cut the cookie dough into ¼-inch slices and place on a greased cookie sheet. Bake for 5 to 7 minutes, or until the cookies are nicely browned. Cool the cookies several minutes on the cookie sheet, then remove them carefully with a spatula.

## Lace Nut Freezer Cookies

*These cookies are fancier and more delicate than most freezer cookies—real special occasion cookies to take the place of a bakery cake.*

(YIELD: 2½ DOZEN)

1 Cup margarine
1 Cup light brown sugar
1 Cup all-purpose flour
½ Teaspoon each ground cinnamon, baking powder and baking soda
1 Egg
1 Tablespoon milk
1 Teaspoon almond flavoring
1 Cup chopped almonds

Beat the margarine until puffy. Add sugars and beat until light. Sift the dry ingredients together and add half to the margarine and sugar; beat until mixed. Add the egg and beat once again until the egg is fully incorporated. Add the other half of the dry ingredients and beat until all of the mixture is moist. Finally add the milk and almond flavoring and beat once more. Stir in the almonds.

Spoon the cookie dough onto aluminum foil and shape into a roll about 2 inches in diameter. Freeze until ready to use.

### DIRECTIONS FOR BAKING

Cut the cookie dough into ¼-inch slices and place on a greased cookie sheet. Bake in an oven preheated to 400 degrees F. for 5 to 7 minutes, or until the cookies are lightly browned. Remove from the oven and cool for several minutes on the cookie sheet, then remove the cookies carefully with a spatula and set them on a rack to dry a bit and become crisp.

## Peanut Butter Freezer Cookies

(YIELD: 9 DOZEN COOKIES)

5 Cups sifted all-purpose flour
2 Tablespoons baking powder
1½ Teaspoons salt

1½ Cups vegetable shortening
2 Cups peanut butter
1½ Cups each light brown sugar and granulated sugar
3 Eggs
1 Tablespoon vanilla extract

Sift together the flour, baking powder and salt and set aside. Beat the shortening, peanut butter and the two sugars until well blended. Add the eggs and vanilla, then beat again. Stir in the dry ingredients a little at a time and mix thoroughly.

Divide the cookie dough equally on 3 sheets of aluminum foil. Shape each piece of dough into a bar about 2 inches in diameter. Fold the aluminum foil up and over the dough and freeze until ready to bake.

### DIRECTIONS FOR BAKING
### 3 DOZEN COOKIES

Take one bar of the frozen dough and cut into ½-inch slices with a sharp knife. Roll each slice into a small ball and place, 1½ inches apart, on a lightly greased baking sheet. Use a fork to flatten each ball into a fat little cookie slightly less than ½ inch thick. Bake for 10 to 12 minutes, or until very lightly browned. Use a metal spatula to transfer the hot cookies immediately from the baking sheet to a cooling rack.

## Special Frozen Apple Pie Filling

(YIELD: ENOUGH FILLING FOR 3 9-INCH PIES)

### INGREDIENTS AND DIRECTIONS FOR
### PIE FILLING

18 Large McIntosh apples, peeled and cored
6 Tablespoons butter
3 Cups granulated sugar
3¾ Teaspoons nutmeg
⅛ Teaspoon each ground allspice and ginger

Cut the apples into ½-inch-thick slices. Melt the butter in a large, heavy pot, then add the apple slices and all the remaining ingredients. Partially cook the fruit over very low heat for 15 minutes, stirring now and then with a wooden spoon.

Cool the filling, stirring occasionally, and divide evenly into 3 snap-top plastic freezer containers. Freeze until needed.

### ADDITIONAL INGREDIENTS AND DIRECTIONS FOR BAKING 1 PIE

Instant Pie Crust for a 2-crust pie
(see page 48)
2 Tablespoons all-purpose flour
2 Tablespoons butter

Turn 1 container of pie filling out into a bowl to defrost.

Roll out and line a 9-inch ovenproof pie plate with half the pie dough. Spoon the pie filling into the crust, sprinkle with the flour and dot with butter. Cover with the remaining pie dough. Crimp the edges of the dough together and slash the top in several places to allow the steam to escape. Bake in an oven preheated to 450 degrees F. for 15 minutes, then turn the oven to 375 degrees F. and bake for 30 to 40 minutes longer, or until the crust is nicely browned.

### Pumpkin Pie Filling

*Not too spicy, not too bland, not too custardy, not too firm—in fact, this pie recipe may be the "just-right" one you have been looking for.*

(YIELD: ENOUGH FILLING FOR 4 10-INCH PIES)

### INGREDIENTS AND DIRECTIONS FOR PIE FILLING

6 Cups cooked, strained pumpkin
4 Cups dark brown sugar
2 Cups light brown sugar
3¼ Teaspoons each ground cinnamon, ginger and salt

Stir all ingredients together until well mixed. Divide equally into 4 snap-top freezer containers and freeze until needed.

### ADDITIONAL INGREDIENTS AND DIRECTIONS FOR BAKING 1 PIE

Instant Pie Crust for a 1-crust pie
(see page 48)

4 Eggs
3 Cups milk

Defrost 1 container of the pie filling. Roll out the pie dough and line a 10-inch pie plate.

Beat together the defrosted pie filling, the eggs and the milk. Pour into the pie shell and bake in an oven preheated to 400 degrees F. for 1½ hours, or until a knife blade inserted in the center comes out clean.

### Blueberry Pie Filling

(YIELD: ENOUGH FILLING FOR 4 PIES)

### INGREDIENTS AND DIRECTIONS FOR PIE FILLING

4 Cups granulated sugar
¾ Teaspoon each ground cinnamon and salt
10 Cups blueberries

Toss all the ingredients together and divide equally into 4 snap-top plastic freezer containers. Freeze until needed.

### ADDITIONAL INGREDIENTS AND DIRECTIONS FOR BAKING 1 PIE

Instant Pie Crust for a 1-crust pie
(see page 48)
3 Tablespoons all-purpose flour
1¼ Cups sour cream
1 Egg
¾ Teaspoon vanilla extract

Defrost 1 container of the pie filling. Roll out and line a 9-inch pie plate with the pie dough.

Beat together the flour, sour cream, egg and vanilla. Combine the defrosted pie filling with the cream-egg mixture, taking care not to crush the berries. Spoon the blueberry filling into the crust and bake in an oven preheated to 450 degrees F. for 35 to 40 minutes. Serve hot or cool.

### Frozen Waffles

Waffles freeze beautifully. Make some ahead of time (see recipes on pages 7–9), cool thoroughly, then wrap in foil or laminated paper and freeze at 0 degrees F. To serve, heat briefly under your broiler, turning once, or divide into quarters and pop into your toaster.

### Frozen Lemonade Cubes

*These make-ahead cubes save time and effort on party day.*

(YIELD: 12 LEMONADE CUBES; ENOUGH FOR 6 12-OUNCE GLASSES)

6 Lemons (about 15 tablespoons juice)
Enough water to fill ice-cube tray

Squeeze the lemons and strain the juice if you prefer (in any case, remove the seeds). Add water. Pour the juice-water mixture into the ice-cube tray and freeze.

#### TO MAKE LEMONADE BY THE GLASS

Place 1 or 2 frozen lemon juice cubes in a glass. (The number of cubes will depend on what size glass you use and how strong you prefer your lemonade.) Fill the glass ¼ full with warm water, add sugar to taste, and stir. When the cubes have melted, add several plain ice cubes and water to the top of the glass.

#### TO MAKE A PITCHER OF LEMONADE

Place 12 lemon juice cubes in a 10-cup pitcher. Stir in 1½ cups warm water and sugar to taste. When the cubes are melted and the sugar is dissolved, add 2 trays of plain ice cubes. Fill the pitcher with water and adjust the sweetening if necessary.

### Frozen Iced Tea Cubes

*The frozen tea cube is a nice hot weather convenience.*

(YIELD: 12 TEA CUBES; ENOUGH FOR 6 12-OUNCE GLASSES)

5 Tea bags
2 Cups water
Enough additional water to fill ice-cube tray

Steep the tea for 5 minutes in 2 cups boiling water. Remove the tea bags and pour the tea into an ice-cube tray. Add water to fill and freeze the iced tea. Make as many trays as you need, then remove the cubes and store them loose in a plastic bag in your freezer.

#### TO MAKE ICED TEA BY THE GLASS

Place 1 tea cube and several plain ice cubes in a tall glass. Add plain water to the top of the glass and sweeten if desired. Stir well several times as the tea cube melts.

#### TO MAKE ICED TEA BY THE PITCHER

To make a larger quantity of tea, place 12 tea cubes in a pitcher, pour in 10 cups water and stir occasionally as the tea cubes melt. Add additional plain ice cubes to chill.

### Frozen Lemon Iced Tea Cubes

Add the juice of 2 lemons to the tea before freezing.

### Frozen Mint Tea Cubes

Add 1 cup fresh mint leaves while the tea is steeping. Proceed as directed for plain tea cubes.

### Bloody Mary Mix

*Party day is more relaxed when the drinks are made beforehand.*

(YIELD: ENOUGH FOR 8 4-OUNCE DRINKS)

#### INGREDIENTS AND DIRECTIONS FOR BASIC MIX

3 Cups tomato juice
2 Tablespoons lemon juice
2 Teaspoons Worcestershire sauce
1 Tablespoon granulated sugar
¼ Teaspoon salt
¼ Teaspoon freshly ground black pepper (this may be added later if desired)

Stir all the ingredients in a 1-quart pitcher. Immediately divide the mix equally into 2 plastic 1-pint containers. Refrigerate or freeze.

ADDITIONAL INGREDIENTS AND
DIRECTIONS FOR MAKING 4 DRINKS

> ½ Teaspoon Tabasco sauce
> 6 Ounces vodka (more or less if you desire)
> 8 Ice cubes

Remove one container Basic Mix from the freezer and allow to thaw. Stir the Tabasco sauce and vodka into the mix. Place 2 ice cubes in each glass and pour the mix over. Serve immediately.

### Bloody Mary Ice Cubes for Individual Drinks

If you prefer, you may pour the Bloody Mary Mix (see above) into an ice-cube tray and freeze. Remove the cubes from the tray and store in a plastic bag.

To make 1 drink, place 4 cubes in a glass and allow to thaw. Add Tabasco sauce, 1½ ounces vodka and 2 ice cubes to the glass and serve immediately.

### Fruit Juice Pops

Freeze fresh fruit juice in your refrigerator trays. When the cubes are partially frozen, insert sticks and continue to freeze. These are better-tasting, more nutritious and less expensive than commercial pops. Make several flavors, remove the frozen pops from the trays and store in plastic bags in your freezer.

# TWO

## How to Make Your Own Cheese, Butter, Yogurt, Sausage, Wine, Cordials, Cider, Mock Beers, Teas & Punches

*THE country store carried few staples, but quite often there would be, set in quiet prominence on the counter, the prize product of some local resident. A round of mellow, golden farm-pressed cheese found its way to that store fairly frequently, and any child who was about when that treasure was cut had the right and the privilege of eating the "crumbles" that fell onto the board as the cheese was cut to order.*

*Homemade cider made its appearance at "The Store" in the autumn, just about the same time that we were planning our Halloween costumes. The cloudy, sweet cider came from a local farm and the clear, bitey, slightly fermented variety came from the orchards over near Pleasant Valley. There was nothing casual about buying this nectar, no "Pick up a gallon of cider if you happen to be passing" attitude. We waited. We counted the days until the Day of the Cider came. And the wait enhanced the flavor. To my memory, no drink has ever surpassed it.*

*The butter in "The Store" was freshly churned and came in a chunk the size of a block of ice. Any person lucky enough to have tasted a piece of homemade bread spread with that sweet butter topped with salt and pepper would never forget the experience. From that day to this day of impoverished supermarket buying, I remember those homemade products of "The Store."*

*This section is really a group of small books within a book. Instructions are included here to give you a chance, if you desire, to taste "real" cheese, butter, yogurt, sausage, wine, cider, root beer and all the rest. You may not have time to make these special foods on a regular basis, but please do yourself a favor and try each at least once.*

# CHESEMAKING

## THE CHEESEMAKING PROCESS SIMPLIFIED

· First, cure or ripen the milk by adding buttermilk and heating the mixture to 86 degrees F.

· Next, curdle the milk by adding rennet and/or allowing it to stand at 86 degrees F. until a curd forms.

· Cut the curd into uniform pieces.

· Slowly raise the heat and cook the curds until they reach a firm consistency.

· Drain the curds, separating them from the whey.

· Salt the curds to taste.

· When making hard or semihard cheese, continue by hooping and pressing the curds.

· Allow the cheese to dry, then prepare it for storage.

· Finish by curing (aging) the cheese.

## CHEESEMAKING EQUIPMENT

Improvise equipment from objects you have around the house—cooking pots, canning kettles, tin cans, some boards, a broomstick handle, a few bricks.
You will need:

8-QUART COOKING POT: Stainless steel is best, but any good, unchipped enamelware or heavily tinned pot will do. Use an enamel water-bath canner if you have one. Avoid aluminum or galvanized iron, since the acid in the curd will react on these.

SECOND CONTAINER: This should be about 2 inches larger in diameter than your 8-quart cooking pot. Use whatever you have on hand: a large galvanized milk pail, a restaurant-sized tin can or a water-bath canner.

FLOATING DAIRY THERMOMETER: Drugstores sometimes carry them, or you can obtain one from a dairy supply company. A candy or jelly thermometer which plainly measures each degree between 75 and 175 degrees F. will do nicely.

SPOON OR STIRRER: One long enough to reach to the bottom of the 8-quart cooking pot.

KNIFE WITH A STAINLESS STEEL BLADE: One long enough to do the same.

GLASS MEASURING CUP: One with a handle for dipping off whey.

SET OF MEASURING SPOONS.

CHEESECLOTH.

COLANDER: A good-sized one.

DEEP PAN OR BOWL: One large enough to hold the colander.

CHEESE HOOP: You can make your own from 1- or 2-pound empty coffee cans or any other can 4 to 5 inches in diameter. File or sandpaper any jagged edges. Punch about a dozen small holes in the bottom of the can from the inside out so the whey can drain during the pressing process.

FOLLOWER: This is a circular piece of wood or weight which is set inside the cheese hoop directly over the curds when making hard cheese. When pressure is applied, the follower squeezes out the whey and forces the cheese into a solid mass. A follower is usually made of hardwood from 2 to 4 inches thick, cut ¼ inch smaller than the circumference of the hoop.

Actually I usually find that it's easier to improvise a follower by using a can slightly narrower than the can you use for your hoop. A 46-ounce tomato juice can makes a perfect hoop, and a large-sized (13-ounce) tuna fish can with contents still inside is exactly the right size to use as a follower. Use the can unopened. Just be sure that the improvised follower can move up and down with ease.

CHEESE PRESS: Devise your own from two boards, 1 inch thick and 1-foot square, and a broomstick handle. Drill holes, if you like, in the center of the bottom board to allow the whey to drip freely.

In a pinch you can improvise a press of sorts to use with the can-within-a-can method described above. Simply balance a board on the inside can (follower) and pile bricks on the board to press the cheese.

BANDAGE: For wrapping the cheese when it is pressed. Use several layers of cheesecloth or other light cotton cloth.

ORDINARY CONSTRUCTION BRICKS: At least eight or ten, or enough rocks or other 4-pound weights to total 30 to 40 pounds. Wrap the bricks, rocks or weights in aluminum foil.

PARAFFIN: This is used in the final process of cheesemaking to cover hard cheeses. Paraffin prevents mold growth and keeps cheese from drying out.

## INGREDIENTS FOR CHEESEMAKING

MILK (the basic ingredient): When you make cheese, what you do is ripen or curdle milk so that the solid part of it (curd) separates from the liquid part (whey). From this point on, cheeses differ only in the way the curd is cut, cooked, pressed and cured.

Good cheeses start with good milk. Use only the freshest high-grade pasteurized whole milk, skim milk or instant nonfat dry milk reconstituted with water. This should be pasteurized first to kill off any harmful bacteria that may be in the water.

One gallon of milk will make approximately ¾ pound of hard cheese, 1 pound of soft cheese and slightly more than 1 pound of cottage cheese. (The butterfat in milk varies, so yields cannot be estimated exactly.)

If you have your own livestock, making cheese may solve the problem of what to do with surplus milk, but be sure to pasteurize first (see Sanitation and Pasteurization, page 204). Goat's milk is also suitable for making cheese, but be prepared for a subtle difference in flavor.

STARTER: Buttermilk, the natural starter, increases the lactic acid level in milk, helps it to curdle and develop good cheese flavor.

Use only the *freshest* cultured buttermilk, with no salt or preservatives added. Local dairies in farm communities or health food stores are a good source. Commercial starters are also available. Follow manufacturer's directions.

RENNET: A solidifying enzyme added to milk when preparing some cheeses. It hastens separation of curds and whey and gives the cheesemaker more control over the curdling process. Rennet is produced commercially in tablet form and is available at your drugstore or grocery. Ask for junket tablets, which *are* rennet, but don't settle for junket powder, which is not. Rennet is also available by mail (see Sources of Supply, pages 273–74).

CHEESE COLOR: An optional ingredient in cheesemaking. It adds nothing to the taste or nutritional value, but does give a professional look to your cheese.

Cheese color is available from dairy supply houses (see Sources of Supply, pages 273–74).

SALT: Essential for bringing out the flavor of cheese. Coarse, kosher or flake salt works best, but ordinary table salt will do. Coarse salt dissolves slowly and is therefore more easily absorbed, making a tastier finished cheese.

## CLEANLINESS IN CHEESEMAKING

Because milk and milk products present an almost irresistible attraction to bacteria, take special precautions to keep your equipment spotless. Scrub all utensils with soap and hot water immediately after using and rinse thoroughly with boiling water.

Wash cheesecloth (or other cloths) with soap and water immediately after using, boil them and, if possible, hang in the sun to dry.

When aging hard or semihard cheeses, scrub the curing cupboard or shelf (see page 65) with soap and water at least once a week while the cheese is aging. If conditions permit, dry the curing shelf in the sun.

To guard against mold, make sure there are no cracks or holes in your cheese before setting to dry. (See page 64). Dip the cheese into hot paraffin only when it is perfectly dry.

When mold does appear, as it sometimes will, scrape it off immediately! As long as the mold is confined to the surface the cheese will still be edible. If the mold extends clear through the cheese, throw the cheese away.

### Small-Curd Cottage Cheese

Cottage cheese is the everything food that is just about everybody's diet favorite. With its low-key taste and interesting texture, it is delicious dressed with fruit, raw vegetables and/or seasonings and can be pressed into service at a moment's notice as a main course, side dish, salad or snack. What's even better, cottage cheese fills you up with a minimum of calories while retaining most of the nutrients found in fresh milk.

There are basically two types of cottage cheese, small-curd and large. Small-curd cottage cheese is a bit more acid than the large-curd variety, has a tangier flavor and a bit more bite. Difference in taste and curd size depends upon whether the cheese is prepared with or without rennet. Rennet, a substance commercially produced from the stomach linings of young animals, has a most important function in cheesemaking. It is used to hurry curdling of the milk and to keep the curd from breaking up too easily after it forms. Whenever rennet is used in preparing cottage cheese, the end product is the large-curd, low-acid variety.

Homemade cottage cheese, whether small-curd or large, has a fresh, creamy, delightful flavor very different from its commercial counterpart. You haven't really tasted cottage cheese until you have sampled the homemade kind. Try your hand at making some—small-curd, a recipe for which is below, or large-curd, a recipe for which follows on page 60.

(YIELD: 1 TO 1½ POUNDS)

1 Gallon skim milk
½ Cup instant nonfat dry milk
1 Cup buttermilk (or ½ cup commercial starter)
Salt
4 to 6 Tablespoons heavy sweet or sour cream (optional)

Use the equipment as listed on pages 57–58, up to and including the deep bowl or the dishpan.

Pour the milk into the 8-quart cooking pot, add the dry milk powder and buttermilk or commercial starter, heat to 86 degrees F. and hold at that temperature from 12 to 18 hours, while the milk mixture incubates and forms a curd. Test for "clean break" (see page 63). (In cheeses made without rennet the curd may never become tough enough to break smoothly; proceed with the cheesemaking even if curd is a bit custardlike.) Cut the curd into ¼-inch pieces (see page 63).

Allow the cut curds to stand at 86 degrees F. for 30 minutes while the whey separates from the curd, then slowly cook to 100 to 104 degrees F. (see page 64). Allow the curds to remain at this temperature for 30 minutes. If the curds fail to firm, increase the curd temperature gradually to 110 to 115 degrees F. Stir frequently. (Take care not to overheat or scald curds; overheating means death to a good cheese, while slightly undercooked curds can usually be salvaged.)

Remove the curds from the heat as soon as they firm. Dip or strain off the whey and retain it for breadmaking. Pour the curds and remaining whey into a cheesecloth-lined colander set over a deep bowl. Drain for a minute or two, then rinse by dipping the curds (in their cheesecloth sling) into lukewarm water. Return to the colander and drain thoroughly.

Turn the curds into a bowl and season to taste with salt. Chill the cheese and add 4 to 6 tablespoons of heavy sweet or sour cream if desired.

## Large-Curd Cottage Cheese

(YIELD: 1 TO 1½ POUNDS)

Large-curd cottage cheese is prepared in basically the same way as the small-curd variety. The difference is the addition of rennet, which curdles the milk mixture in less time and produces a less acid cottage cheese.

Bring milk, dry milk and buttermilk or commercial starter to 86 degrees F. as directed in making Small-Curd Cottage Cheese (see page 59). Dissolve ⅛ tablet rennet thoroughly in 2 tablespoons cool water, add to the warm milk, and stir in thoroughly. Let stand, undisturbed, overnight until the milk curdles and whey forms on the surface.

Cut into ½-inch pieces (see page 63). Allow the cut curds to stand at 86 degrees F. for 30 minutes, then gradually increase the curd temperature (see page 64). When the curds reach 100 to 104 degrees F., hold at this temperature

for 30 to 60 minutes. If the curds are still soft, gradually raise the heat to 110 to 115 degrees F. as described in preparing the small-curd cottage cheese. Do not overcook!

When the curds are firm, remove them from the heat, skim off the whey and proceed as directed for small-curd cottage cheese. Salt, chill and add cream if desired.

## Cream Cheese

*A soft, unripened cheese that is always used fresh, delicately smooth cream cheese is easy to make and can easily be combined with herbs or spices for interesting flavor variations.*

(YIELD: ABOUT ¼ POUND)

INGREDIENTS

 2 Cups sour cream
 ¼ Rennet tablet
 2 Tablespoons water
 ¼ Teaspoon salt

EQUIPMENT

 1-Quart stainless steel or glass saucepan
 2-Quart saucepan or double-boiler bottom
 Dairy thermometer
 Cheesecloth or similar cotton cloth

Spoon the sour cream into the 1-quart saucepan. Crush the piece of rennet tablet, mix it with the 2 tablespoons water and stir until completely dissolved before adding to the sour cream. Mix thoroughly.

Fill the larger saucepan one-third full with warm water and set over a low flame. Place the saucepan with the sour cream mixture over the heating water, and bring the temperature of the mixture gradually to 100 degrees F. Keep the temperature of the sour cream mixture steady at 100 degrees F. for 20 minutes by turning the heat off and on as necessary.

Lift the saucepan with its sour cream mixture out of the warm water and set it aside to cool. As soon as it reaches room temperature, spoon it into a cheesecloth square. Tie the corners of the cheesecloth together to form a bag. Suspend the bag in a cool place free from drafts, with a bowl set underneath to catch the drips, or hang it on your kitchen faucet spout.

Unloosen the bag every few hours to check the progress of the cheese. When it is quite stiff and completely drained, remove it from the cheesecloth and turn into a bowl. Mix in the salt, form into a bar and wrap in waxed paper or aluminum foil. Refrigerate.

### *Cheddar Cheese*

*The best Cheddar I have ever tasted is a cheese I made last year using this recipe. I aged the cheese 4 months in the refrigerator.*

(YIELD: ABOUT 1 TO 1¼ POUNDS)

1 *Gallon whole milk*
1 *Cup buttermilk*
  *Cheese color (optional)*
1 *Rennet tablet*
¼ *Cup tepid or cool water (never hot)*
1 *Tablespoon salt*

Use the equipment as listed on pages 57–58, plus a flat, rectangular baking pan and a wire roasting rack. Pour the milk into the 8-quart cooking pot. Stir in the buttermilk starter, cover the pot and allow the mixture to stand for 4 hours (or even overnight) at room temperature (72 degrees F. is just right).

Pour several inches of warm water into the larger container and set over a low flame. As soon as the water temperature registers 100 degrees F. on your dairy thermometer, turn the heat off. Set the pot with the milk in the larger container of water. Allow the milk mixture to reach 86 degrees F.

If you choose to color your cheese, prepare the color according to the manufacturer's directions (mixing thoroughly) and stir into the warm milk for at least 2 minutes to ensure even color distribution. Slowly raise the milk temperature to 88 to 90 degrees F. by turning the heat on and off under the container of water. Crush the rennet tablet in the ¼ cup of tepid or cool water and mix it into the milk mixture. Stir continuously for 1 minute. Never add color and rennet together.

Remove the milk mixture from the heat. Cover and allow to stand undisturbed for 30 to 40 minutes while the curd forms to a custard-like firmness. Check to see whether coagulation is complete by making the clean break test (see page 63). If the curd splits evenly as you bring thumb and forefinger together, it is ready to be cut.

Use your long-bladed knife to slice the curd into ½-inch pieces as directed on page 63.

Stir the cut curd gently with your hand for 15 minutes, using a long, slow, sweeping movement; too rapid or rough stirring will cause the curds to distintegrate. Cut to ½-inch any large pieces of curd you may have missed during the cutting process.

Add enough warm water to the larger container to bring the water to a level slightly higher than the curds in their cooking pot. Slowly increase curd temperature to 100 degrees F. by turning the heat on and off every few seconds (this should take at least 20 to 30 minutes).

Stir the curds gently every 3 to 5 minutes. Move those in the center to the outside of the pan to make sure that all get the benefit of the heat (see page 64). Don't worry if the thermometer slides 1 or 2 degrees above 100 degrees F. (but no higher, please); the important thing to remember is to increase the heat slowly enough to warm the curds uniformly and steadily until they firm.

Cook the curds at 100 to 102 degrees F. for about 1 hour, stirring every few seconds. To test for firmness, remove a few curds from the cooking pot and let them cool in your hand. If the curds hold their shape when very lightly squeezed, they are ready to be drained. If they crumble in your hand, cook the curds in the pot for 10 minutes and test again.

Line your colander with cheesecloth and set over the deep bowl or dishpan. Remove some of the whey from the cooking pot by scooping it out with your measuring cup, then pour the curds and remaining whey into the cloth-lined colander. Holding the ends of the cheesecloth in each hand, tilt the curds back and forth in a rolling motion to drain off any excess whey.

Carefully drape a double layer of cheesecloth over the wire roasting rack, then set the rack in the baking pan. Gently heap the curds onto the cheesecloth, building them into a layer 1 inch thick.

Turn your oven temperature to warm. The

correct temperature is very important at this point; the curd must cook at *exactly* 98 degrees F., so check with your thermometer before setting the pan inside the oven and keep the thermometer right in the oven alongside the pan. Switch the oven on and off as necessary to maintain the designated heat throughout the cooking time.

Cook the curds until they mat together in a large mass (this should take about 20 minutes). Slice the lumped curds into 1-inch strips, then continue to cook for 1 hour, turning the strips every 15 minutes to make sure each side is cooked. Take care to maintain a temperature of 98 degrees F. throughout the cooking process.

Remove the curd strips from the oven and cut them into approximately 1-inch squares. Place the squares back in the colander and sprinkle with salt, working the salt in with your hands to distribute it evenly. Let the salted curds absorb the salt for about 20 minutes.

Line your hoop with cheesecloth and spoon in the curds. Cover the curds with cheesecloth, insert the follower and put into the press.

Begin with a weight of 12 to 16 pounds for 5 to 10 minutes, then remove the weights and follower and pour off any collected whey. Return the hoop to the press, insert the follower and gradually increase the number of weights until the poundage totals 25 to 30 pounds. Maintain this pressure for 30 to 60 minutes, or until the cheese is very firm.

Remove the weights and follower and take the hoop from the press. Turn the cheese out of its hoop and unwrap the cheesecloth liner carefully. Dip the cheese into a bowl filled with warm water (100 degrees F.), rinse off any fat and smooth out any cracks. Trim clean cheesecloth 2 inches wider than the cheese and long enough to wrap completely around the cheese with a 1-inch overlap. Place the cheese on its side at one end of the bandage and roll up tightly. Cover the top and bottom with 2 cheesecloth circles cut to fit. Return the bandaged cheese to the hoop. Replace the follower and add weights one at a time until a total of 24 to 30 pounds is achieved. Press for 16 to 20 hours.

When pressing time has elapsed, unwrap and wipe the cheese surface. Check the cheese for any holes, openings or cracks. The cheese should be smooth before it begins to dry. Dip the cheese

in warm water and smooth any imperfections with your fingers.

Dry, paraffin and cure the cheese as directed on pages 64–65. Cheddar cheese cured for 6 to 8 weeks at 50 to 60 degrees F. will develop a smooth, firm texture and mild flavor. If you prefer a sharper flavor and mellower texture, cure for 3 to 5 months, or even longer if exceptionally sharp flavor is desired.

## American-Type Cheese

(YIELD: 2 TO 3 POUNDS)

2½  Gallons whole milk
  1  Cup buttermilk or ½ cup
     commercial starter
     Cheese color (optional)
  1  Rennet tablet
  ¼  Cup cool water
1¾ to 2  Tablespoons coarse or kosher salt

Use the equipment as listed on pages 57–58, but use a 10- to 12-quart pot and a gallon-sized cheese hoop. Pour the milk into the 10- to 12-quart pot, set this in 3 inches of hot water in larger pan and let stand until the milk temperature is 86 degrees F. Stir in the buttermilk or commercial starter and mix thoroughly for 1 minute. Maintain the heat for 60 minutes.

Meanwhile, prepare the cheese color according to manufacturer's directions. Pour this into the milk mixture and stir for 2 minutes to ensure even color distribution. Crush the rennet tablet completely in the ¼ cup cool water and stir into the milk mixture for 1 minute. Never add the color and the rennet at the same time. Cover the milk to prevent chilling and let stand, undisturbed, for 40 minutes, or until the curd firms (see Testing for "Clean Break," page 63).

Use your long-bladed knife to slice the curd into ⅜-inch pieces as directed on page 63. Allow the cut curds to stand for 15 minutes, using your hand to stir the curds very gently every 5 minutes.

Slowly increase the cooking temperature by turning the heat on and off, a few seconds at a time, under the pot of water until the dairy thermometer reads 100 degrees F. (see page 64). Maintain this temperature until the curds are firm (about 50 minutes).

When the curds test firm, line the colander with cheesecloth and set over the deep bowl or dishpan. Pour the curds into the colander to drain, tilting the colander from side to side so the whey runs off. Stir the curds occasionally with your fingers to keep them from lumping together.

When the curd temperature cools to 90 degrees F., enough acidity should have developed for the curds to be ready for salting. Chew a curd or two. When a sample feels rubbery and squeaks between your teeth, sprinkle salt over the curds. Stir in until the salt dissolves.

Cool the curds to 85 degrees and spoon into the hoop, lined with a large piece of cheesecloth. Cover the top surface of the curds with a circle of cheesecloth and insert the follower.

Begin with a weight of 12 to 15 pounds for 5 to 10 minutes, then remove the weights and follower (but not the cheese) and pour off any collected whey. Return the hoop to the press, insert the follower and gradually increase the number of weights until poundage totals 25 to 30. Maintain this pressure for 30 to 60 minutes, or until the cheese is very firm.

Remove weights, follower and hoop and pull the cheese out with a tug or two at the cheesecloth liner. Carefully unwrap the cheese and dip it into a bowl of warm (100 degrees F.) water to rinse away any surface fat. Trim clean cheesecloth 2 inches wider than the cheese and long enough to wrap completely around the cheese with a 1-inch overlap. Place the cheese on its side at one end of the bandage and roll up tightly. Cut 2 cheesecloth circles to fit over the top and bottom of the cheese, and return to the hoop. Reposition the follower and press the cheese for 16 to 20 hours, increasing the pressure gradually to 30 or 40 pounds by adding weights one at a time.

Dry the cheese after the final pressing and inspect for cracks or holes where mold could form. If any imperfections exist, dip the cheese in lukewarm water and smooth the softened surface with your fingers. Rebandage the cheese and put it back in the press for 1 hour.

Dry, paraffin and cure the cheese as directed on pages 64–65. It will take about 6 weeks at 50 to 60 degrees F. for the cheese to develop smooth, firm texture and mild flavor. If more mellow texture and sharper flavor are desired, cure the cheese for 3 to 6 months.

## CHEESEMAKING PROCESSES EXPLAINED

### Curing or Ripening the Milk

Fill the larger container one-third full of warm (92 degrees F.) water. Set on the stove, but do not turn on the heat. Place the cooking pot of milk in the larger container in a double-boiler arrangement. Let stand for 1 hour.

### Taking the Temperature of the Milk

Take the temperature of the milk with a dairy thermometer. If it registers less than 86 degrees F., turn the heat on under the larger container for 2 to 3 minutes. Wait 15 minutes, then repeat the process until the milk warms to 86 degrees F. Occasionally the milk will accidentally be heated too high. In this case, cool to 86 degrees before adding the starter.

### Testing for "Clean Break"

To determine whether the curd is firm enough to cut, test for "clean break":

Insert your finger at an angle into the center of the curd and bring your thumb down to meet it. The curd is ready to cut when it breaks cleanly over your finger as you lift it and clear whey fills the opening.

Cheeses made without rennet may sometimes fail to firm sufficiently to pass the "clean break" test. In this case, proceed with cheesemaking when the milk appears fairly firm and custard-like.

### Cutting the Curd

To cut the curd, make deep perpendicular strokes at designated intervals with a long-bladed knife. The general rule is to cut vertically in two directions, then diagonally in two directions.

Insert your knife down to the bottom of the curd on the side of the pot opposite you. Pull through the curd cleanly. Continue cutting in parallel lines until the curd is completely cut in one direction. Turn the cooking pot and make parallel cuts perpendicular to the previous cuts.

Return the cooking pot to its original position. Hold your knife at a slant and slice through the curd in deep diagonal strokes, following your original cuts as closely as possible. Turn the cooking pot a final time and cut diagonally in the opposite direction.

If curd cubes are not uniform, they may be cut to size later on during the cooking process.

### Cooking the Curds

Whenever you have to bring milk to a recommended temperature, set the pot of milk inside a larger container partially filled with water, and heat. This prevents the milk from scorching.

After the cut curds have been allowed to stand for the specified time, bring the level of the warm water in the outer container to a point just above the level of the curds in their inner pot. Gradually heat the water until curd temperature reaches 100 to 104 degrees F. Allow at least 30 to 40 minutes for this process; take care not to hurry the cooking. Quick or uneven heating results in hard curds with mushy centers. Stir the curds frequently while they are heating or move them around with your hand to maintain even heat distribution. If you should turn up any oversized curds, cut them to size.

Once the curds reach the required temperature range, hold them at this heat for one hour by turning the heat on and off for a few seconds at a time, every 15 minutes or so. Stir occasionally to keep the curds from matting together. As they cook they will grow firmer. Cooking is finished as soon as the curds take on the texture and appearance of scrambled eggs, or retain their shape even when a few are lightly pressed in your fist.

### Drying the Cheese

Unwrap the cheese, wipe it dry with a clean cloth, and inspect it for cracks or holes. To correct any imperfections, soften the cheese surface in warm water and smooth it with your fingers. Pare off any uneven surfaces with a sharp knife. Cheeses with cracks or holes that do not respond to this treatment should be re-bandaged and pressed for about 1 hour.

Set the cheese in a cool, clean, moisture-proof storage place where it can dry and form a rind (usually within 3 to 5 days). Bandage (wrap loosely in cheesecloth) your cheese or leave it as is to dry. In either case, turn and wipe the cheese daily. Bandaged cheeses do not form a hard rind and therefore must be paraffined.

Cheese is ready for paraffining as soon as it develops a dry, unbroken surface, generally within 3 days. Unparaffined cheeses require a few days longer to dry. Should a hard rind fail to form on any cheese within 6 days, your storage place may not be dry enough. Remedy this by transferring the cheese to a drier spot to cure.

### Paraffining the Cheese

Before preparing paraffin, make sure that your cheese has a perfectly dry surface.

Use an old double boiler to melt enough paraffin to immerse half the cheese at once. Use low to medium heat to raise the paraffin temperature to between 210 and 220 degrees F. Be particularly careful when heating the paraffin—it is extremely flammable! Color the paraffin if you want a professional touch.

Dip one end of the cheese into the hot paraffin, hold for 10 seconds, then remove and cool for 1 or 2 minutes. Repeat with the other half. Be sure to completely cover all surface areas.

If you prefer not to paraffin, you may seal the cheese inside a plastic bag. Flatten the bag to expel all air. Although this type of covering cannot be made perfectly airtight, there is the advantage that the cheese can be checked easily for mold. Wipe or cut away any mold that forms.

### Curing the Cheese

The curing (aging) process gives cheese its characteristic texture and flavor. The ideal storage place for curing should have a temperature range between 50 and 60 degrees F., but it is also possible to age cheese in your refrigerator if you are in no hurry for the finished product.

Pick a clean, dry cupboard shelf in a cool cellar or shed. Turn the cheese over daily during the first few weeks of curing; thereafter, turn once a week. Scrub the storage shelf weekly with soap and water. If the shelf is removable, dry it in air and sunshine.

With proper storage conditions, cheese should develop a firm body and mild flavor within 6 weeks. Cheesemakers whose taste runs to sharp, distinctive cheese, however, should plan on longer periods of storage. The longer the cheese is cured, generally speaking, the sharper the flavor and more mellow the texture.

# BUTTERMAKING

Whether prepared with conventional kitchen equipment or with dasher and churn, almost anyone who bakes bread should, at least occasionally, turn their hand to churning butter. Those who live near an inexpensive source for whole milk, or who keep their own livestock, should consider the pleasure of making their own butter on a regular basis.

Butter is produced from milk by separating out and then churning the cream. Once upon a time the sole method was to place the milk in a skin bag (hair side out, naturally) then agitate until a butter of sorts was formed. Visions arise of Tartars riding across The Steppes, their yak's milk frenetically turning to butter underneath their saddlebags (or wherever). The advent of the hand-operated dasher and churn turned buttermaking into a more predictable, less romantic but only slightly less arduous process. The wooden dasher and churn that were standard household fixtures for generations of rural families have been replaced by more efficient materials—glass, lined wood or stainless steel—and muscle power has been replaced in most instances by electricity. Now it is possible for cooks to

whip up a bar of butter in their kitchen mixer or blender in minutes.

## Homemade Butter

If your farm or country home includes a cow or a pair of goats, or if the farmer down the road will quote a low price for his surplus milk or cream, allow yourself the luxury of fresh-baked bread and fresh-churned butter. You can figure roughly that 2½ to 3 gallons of whole, nonhomogenized milk will provide enough cream for 1 pound of butter. If you are buying just the cream, 1 quart will do.

An electric or hand-powered churn is perfect for making butter. A 1-gallon glass churn with wooden paddles will probably suit most families who raise only a few milkers, but if you prefer not to invest in a specialized piece of equipment, an excellent product can also be turned out with an electric mixer or a combination of eggbeater and muscle power.

If you have no cream separator, raise the cream from whole milk by using one of Great-grandmother's techniques. Allow the freshly drawn milk to cool a bit, then strain it into the widest bowl you own. Set the bowl, uncovered, in the refrigerator for 12 to 24 hours. During this time enough cream will rise for you to skim off the surface of the milk. Keep the skimmed and cooled cream from each day's milk in a screw-top jar in the refrigerator until you have collected enough to make butter. Skimming this way does leave some of the cream behind, but the partly skimmed milk is richer and more drinkable as a consequence.

Let the cream stand at room temperature (65 to 75 degrees F.) for a day or two until it just begins to sour (ripen). Cool the cream for a couple of hours once it is mildly ripe and has a thick, glossy look, then pour it into a chilled mixing bowl. Chill the beaters, too, to help the butter "come" faster. (When using a churn, rinse it first with scalding water, then chill it with cold water and pour in the cream. Do not fill the churn more than half full; too much cream prolongs the churning process.)

Bring the electric mixer gradually to high speed, or turn the churn handle slowly for 15 to 20 minutes. As the cream changes to butter and buttermilk, slow down the electric beaters. Pour off the buttermilk from bowl or churn as soon as the butter "comes." Save the buttermilk for cooking or drinking.

Leave the butter in the mixing bowl or churn. Rinse a wooden spoon, or butter paddle if you have one, with cold water and use it to press and fold the butter over and over again until all the milk has been worked out. Fill the bowl or churn with ice water and continue to work the butter until the last drop of milk has been washed away and poured off. Refill the bowl or churn with water as many times as necessary for the water to come clear.

If you like your butter salted, work in about ¾ ounce of salt with your spoon or paddle after the washing process is finished. Pack the finished butter into crocks or shape it into bars, and cover it tightly with moisture-resistant wrap before refrigerating. Do not forget that butter, like milk, will develop off-flavors if left uncovered or loosely wrapped. Any butter you are not using immediately can safely be stored in the freezer until needed. Cover the original wrappings with aluminum foil before freezing.

Great-grandmother usually kept her own cow, so if she needed a small amount of butter in a hurry she had only to put new milk in a jar with a tight-fitting lid and let it stand a few hours. A vigorous shaking of the jar would produce clots of butter, which were then strained, washed and pressed together.

Should you need a small amount of instant homemade butter for a special recipe or occasion, you can do the same thing. Pour any amount of heavy whipping cream into a jar, seal tightly and shake. Sooner or later (depending on your stamina), lumps of butter will form. Strain out and drink the buttermilk with freshly ground black pepper as a reward for your labors, then mash the lumps of butter together until all the buttermilk has been pressed out. Sweet butter at the ready!

### Nut Butter

*Fresh butter can also be blended with nuts or spices to give special zip to meats and vegetables.*

(YIELD: 1 CUP)

⅓ Cup finely chopped pecans or walnuts
¾ Cup butter
1¼ Teaspoons chopped fresh chives
¼ Teaspoon Tabasco sauce

Gently sauté the nuts in 3 tablespoons of the butter until crisp and light brown, then remove from the heat and allow to cool. Soften the remaining butter, blend in the nuts, chives and Tabasco and beat the mixture until light and creamy. Spread over hamburgers or steak before grilling.

### Corn Butter

(YIELD: ½ CUP)

½ Cup butter, softened
½ to 1 Teaspoon any of the following herbs (fresh are best) or spices: celery salt, chili powder, nutmeg, oregano, savory or tarragon

Blend the butter thoroughly with the herb or spice of your choice and use with freshly cooked corn or any hot vegetable.

### Rose Butter

*Here's another old-fashioned recipe, this time for a delicate butter with the flavor of roses.*

Freshly opened rose petals
Salt
1 Pound very fresh butter

Place alternate layers of rose petals and salt in a stone crock and weight down with a saucer or small plate. Set the butter in on the plate, then cover and store in the refrigerator. Use the fragrant butter to spread on plain bread or toast, or in the following way:

#### Rose Butter Tea Sandwiches

*The custom of "taking tea" in the afternoon is out of fashion in most places. More's the pity. There is absolutely nothing more relaxing in the middle of a harried day than sipping tea and eating delicate sandwiches of homebaked white bread spread with butter and topped with a flavorful bit of "something or other." Take some tea yourself one day and treat yourself to these elegant reminders of yesteryear.*

Spread slices of untrimmed white bread (homebaked is best) with Rose Butter (see above). Cut the slices into triangles. Top each triangle with a rose petal. Refrigerate for several hours, then sprinkle with a few grains of sugar.

### Devonshire Cream

*This unique and tasty clotted cream is especially delicious served with fresh berries. Traditional in Great Britain, where it is used for a spread on toast, as well as a topping for fresh fruits, this is a treat that harks back to more peaceful days.*

A recipe from an early nineteenth-century American cookbook shows that Devonshire cream or "clot" was also popular in the colonies. Directions for this delicacy were given as follows:

Allow the milk to ripen in the milk closet for 12 hours, then set it on a stove or on top of a furnace still aglow with embers. Heat for 5 hours, but take care not to scald. Return it to the milk closet to cool. When cold, take off the clotted cream and use for coffee or for making butter.

You can still make Devonshire cream in essentially the same way should you find yourself with whole, nonhomogenized milk. Simply pour the milk into a wide and fairly shallow heatproof baking dish and allow to stand at room temperature for 12 hours. Heat the milk *very* slowly over a very low flame (an asbestos pad is helpful here), taking care not to let it boil. As soon as bubbles show on the rim surface, remove from the heat and place in a cool place for 24 hours. Skim off the clotted cream and refrigerate. Serve very cold.

Not everyone has access to whole nonhomogenized milk, unfortunately, so if you really have an insatiable desire to try this, you will have to settle for using light cream mixed with milk for clotting. Mix one cup light cream with 2 cups milk and clabber with 3 tablespoons fresh cultured buttermilk. Follow the directions given for clotting nonhomogenized milk above.

Two cups of light cream will yield about ¼ pound of clot. If your family is not diet-conscious, try making Devonshire cream this way using heavy cream.

# MAKING YOGURT

Smooth, silky-white yogurt is one of nature's most perfect foods. It is easy and inexpensive to prepare, has a marvelous flavor and is marvelous for you as well. Versatile yogurt can serve as a delicious snack, a tempting dessert, a piquant basis for mayonnaise, salad dressing or soup, a cooling side dish for lamb or a suitable substitute for sour cream.

Although it is often thought of as an exotic food, yogurt is simply milk that has been fermented in a special manner. Ever since the time in unrecorded history when man first recognized that milk from his domesticated livestock might be safely preserved through fermenting, yogurt has been an important and exceptionally healthful food staple in the diets of many of the world's peoples.

Whether yogurt has a lasting or an especially beneficial effect upon human health has long been debated by nutritionists and health food enthusiasts. Folklore has it that yogurt promotes health and increases life expectancy by controlling harmful bacteria in the digestive tract, but this has never been authenticated with any scientific certainty. What counts is that yogurt is a nutritious and tasty food rich in vitamin B

complex. My own opinion is that while yogurt may not be a miracle food, it almost certainly can improve the standard American diet. Even those who do not get along well with plain milk can often tolerate yogurt, since the presence of helpful lactic bacteria makes yogurt particularly easy to digest. Milk, for instance, requires an average of 3 hours before it is digested. Yogurt possesses all the food value of milk while taking only about 1 hour to be digested.

You can prepare your own yogurt at home from pasteurized whole or skim milk, or from any combination of the two. Instant nonfat dry milk that has been reconstituted with water will also do very nicely, but it should be pasteurized first to kill off any harmful bacteria that may be lurking in the water.

Your homemade yogurt will taste sweet or tart depending upon the milk you use. The higher the fat content of the milk, the sweeter your yogurt will be. Milk with a high butterfat content understandably also tends to produce a creamier yogurt, but be careful—if you add too much cream the result will be too similar to sour cream. The best idea is to experiment with varying percentages of skim and whole milk until you discover the combination best suited to your taste. To make a firmer yogurt without cream, try adding 2 or 3 level tablespoons of instant nonfat dry milk to each quart of milk you use.

You will also need some kind of a starter to get the fermentation process under way. Any food product cultured with lactic bacteria is suitable (buttermilk or yogurt for example), or you may prepare a lactic-acid culture at home using a commercially packaged starter culture. I generally use 2 or 3 tablespoons of plain, unflavored commercial yogurt (the freshest I can find) to each quart of milk. The kind prepared without preservatives works best. If you decide to use a commercially packaged culture, simply follow the manufacturer's directions.

A reliable thermometer is essential in yogurt-making. You will need it to tell exactly when to add the starter and whether each particular batch of yogurt is at the proper incubation temperature. Milk that ferments at too cool a temperature produces a weak-textured yogurt; too warm a temperature will separate your yogurt into curds and whey. The floating dairy-type thermometer is best. Drugstores sometimes carry them, or you can obtain one from a dairy supply company.

(YIELD: ABOUT 4 CUPS)

1 Quart pasteurized whole or skim milk in any combination
2 to 3 Tablespoons instant nonfat dry milk
2 to 3 Tablespoons plain, unflavored yogurt, at room temperature

Place the milk and nonfat dry milk in the top of a double boiler and bring it just to the boiling point. Allow the milk to barely boil for 30 seconds, stirring constantly (Boiling the milk this half-minute will produce a firmer curd.) Remove the milk from the heat and let it stand until the temperature of the mixture drops to 112 to 115 degrees F. on your thermometer. Measure the room-temperature commercial yogurt and stir it into the lukewarm milk until the ingredients are thoroughly blended. Pour the mixture into warm sterilized cups or glasses and cover tightly with sterile lids or screw tops.

The next step is the most crucial in making yogurt. The warm milk must stay at the proper incubating temperature (98 to 108 degrees F.) for several hours until fermentation produces the firmness you prefer. You can incubate your yogurt in a number of ways, but the important thing to remember is to have the milk at 100 degrees F. (not below) prior to and during incubation.

An electric yogurt maker will brew yogurt for you with little effort on your part. Preferably it should be large enough to hold 1 quart of milk and have an automatic temperature control. Follow the directions that come with your machine, but take care to clean it thoroughly with sterile water after each use and before using again to prevent contamination of future batches.

If you have no electric yogurt maker, you will need to be a bit more resourceful. Follow one of these methods:

· Set the covered cups or glasses of yogurt in a pan of warm water placed over the pilot light on a gas stove. Fit an aluminum foil cover over the cups to contain the heat.

· A gas or electric oven turned to 100 degrees F., and with the door left open, will supply enough heat for a properly firmed yogurt. If your oven is well insulated, preheat it to 100 degrees F., shut off the heat, and set the yogurt into the oven in a pan of warm water. Keep the oven door shut while the yogurt brews.

· An electric frying pan makes an excellent yogurt maker. Set the thermostat to warm, add 1 inch of water and heat. Arrange the cups of milk in the water and fit a cover loosely on top to keep the heat evenly distributed.

· Pour the milk mixture into a wide-mouthed thermos bottle, cover tightly, and wrap with a heavy towel.

· If you are making yogurt during the winter months, try incubating the cups of milk in a pan of warm water set on top of a radiator.

The yogurt may vary a bit in taste and texture depending upon the incubation method used. Experiment with several different methods to find the one that produces yogurt suited to your taste.

Refrigerate the yogurt as soon as it is as firm as you like it. Milk that ferments at the proper temperature will generally be ready for chilling within 3 to 6 hours. If you prefer yogurt with a tangier flavor, incubate for up to 10 hours.

Homemade yogurt has a unique taste and texture, quite unlike the store-bought variety and even more delectable. It is less sour, for one thing, and when stirred a bit, has a creamlike consistency. For unusual flavor combinations, try adding honey, fresh or cooked fruit or preserves to your homemade product.

Reserve a small quantity (about 2 or 3 tablespoons) from one jar to use as a starter for the next batch. Keep this starter sealed tightly in a sterilized container in the refrigerator. Yogurt kept for this purpose may be stored for up to a week without losing its strength. Reserve a starter from successive batches each week for about a month; after that time the bacterial strain will have lost its vitality, so you will have to start again with commercially prepared yogurt.

# SAUSAGEMAKING

*Higher Protein, Lower Fat, No Preservatives*

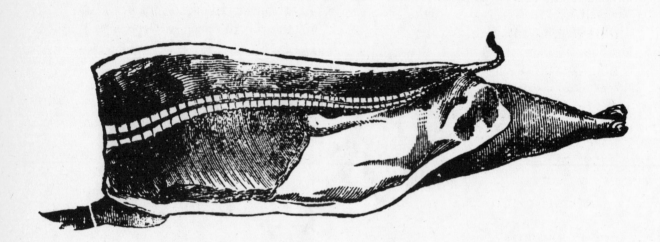

There are sausages . . . and sausages . . . and almost all of them are delicious. The advantages of making your own sausages are many. First, the homemade variety tastes better than the store-bought kind. Second, you flavor the meat to suit your taste and use the kinds of meat and amounts of fat you prefer (increasing the meat and decreasing the fat content if you wish to make the sausages higher in nutrition). Third, the sausages you make yourself may be made without dangerous preservatives, and fourth, homemade sausages are naturally good because they are made from high-quality ingredients and are as fresh and sanitary as you make them.

## MONEYSAVING SAUSAGE EXTENDERS

An equally important factor in home sausage-making is that the homemade ones are money savers. Sausages take naturally to being extended with wholesome fillers like oatmeal, soybeans and kasha—even bread crumbs may be added with great success. The sausages that come to your table full of protein can cost dollars less than comparable sausages from your butcher, or from your supermarket. One of the most delicious sausages I ever sampled was in an English pub. The contents were mostly grain with meat added for flavoring, but I still remember the scrumptious taste.

I have tested recipes with additions of oatmeal and soybeans (see page 75) to help stretch your meat dollars. These sausages are as good if not better than any I've tasted. Anyone who is on a diet—or a budget—should definitely not pass them by. Experiment with them, then hold a family sausage-tasting session. Whichever are family favorites, *those* are the sausages you should use to stock your freezer.

Since sausages and sausage meat freeze so well, it is a good idea to make enough extra to freeze at least a few. Properly prepared sausages may be frozen for up to 3 months, and I know cooks who freeze them for much longer.

## THE SAUSAGEMAKING PROCESS SIMPLIFIED

· Prepare the meat by chopping or grinding it.

· Mix all ingredients together.

· Shape the sausage mixture into patties or rolls, or stuff it into casings, tying off at appropriate intervals.

· If the recipe so indicates, precook the sausages in water.

· Store the sausages properly in refrigerator or freezer until cooking time.

## GENERAL DIRECTIONS FOR MAKING SAUSAGES

### Chopping or Grinding the Meat

There are two ways to make sausage—one is by hand-chopping the meat, the other is by putting the meats through a grinder. Really superior sausages are usually the result of chopping by hand. These have the chunky, slightly chewy texture that enhances the flavor of the meat.

If working over a chopping board does not appeal to you, and you have a meat grinder or a grinding attachment for your electric mixer, a really decent sausage can be made if you use a large-holed disk. Professional sausagemakers frequently use a hand grinder fitted with a disk with holes as large as the tip of your little finger. This equipment makes sausages as good as the chopped variety, so if you can manage to obtain a machine like this, by all means do so. If your grinder has only a fine disk (or you have mislaid your larger one), make sausage patties instead of stuffed sausages.

Cut pork and fat into ¼-inch dice with a very sharp knife. If you do not intend to freeze your sausages or patties, chopping is made much easier if the meat is first partially frozen.

### Mixing

Mix all ingredients, working spices in well with your fingers. If the meat is to be formed into a roll instead of individual sausages, work in ice water to keep the meat from crumbling when it is cut. Cover tightly and refrigerate overnight if the sausage is to be used within 2 or 3 days. Sausage that is to be frozen may be shaped into patties or stuffed into casings immediately and then refrigerated overnight before freezing.

### Preparing the Casings

I recommend the use of natural casings, and these require a bit of preparation before you stuff them. Most natural casings come in the dry, salted form. When you are ready to stuff your sausage, rinse the casing under running water, then soak it for a while in warm water. Insert 2 fingers in one end of casing to separate it. Hold this open end under the faucet and let water run through the entire length. Some casings have an inner membrane that should be removed. If casing is too long to handle comfortably, cut into lengths of about 24 inches. After rinsing, place the casing on paper towels until ready to stuff.

Rinse only enough casing for the amount of sausage to be stuffed. If casings are left over, rinse them thoroughly, dry, then repack in salt in their original container and return to the refrigerator for storage. If you buy casings in quantity, sprinkle additional table salt over them from time to time while they are stored in your refrigerator. Most casings packed in salt can be kept for up to 2 years if they are well refrigerated and salted.

### Filling Casings Using Funnel and Spoon

This process looks and sounds more difficult than it actually is. With a little practice you will have no trouble at all.

First wash casings thoroughly, inside and out as directed (see above). While the casing is still wet, open one end and slip it over the funnel spout. Next, slide the entire length of casing (whatever size is convenient) *onto* the funnel spout. Force some sausage meat through the funnel with the handle of a wooden spoon that has been soaked in ice water to prevent meat from sticking to it. When the meat is flush with the end of the funnel spout, pull about 1 inch of the casing out and away from the spout and tie securely. (It is important to fill the spout before you tie the string, or the casing will inflate like a small balloon as the air in the funnel is forced along ahead of the meat.)

Holding the funnel while you force the meat through is a bit difficult, since you should also keep the thumb and forefinger of one hand on the casing to regulate its release as the meat is forced into it. The best way to do this is to hold the funnel against your body in the crook of your bent left arm (if you are left-handed, reverse these directions). With the thumb and forefinger of your left hand, release the casing on the spout against the pressure of the meat as it enters. With your right hand, spoon the meat into the funnel and tamp it down with the wooden spoon handle.

Stuff the casings rather loosely, since the filling expands when cooked.

### Filling Casings Using an Electric or Hand Grinder

A special sausagemaking attachment for mixer or meat grinder makes stuffing sausage quick and easy. Follow the manufacturer's directions for assembling the equipment. Slip the open end of the prepared casing (see above) over the outside of the stuffer tube. Slide the entire casing (whatever length is convenient) onto the funnel spout. Force some sausage meat through the machine until it is flush with the end of the funnel spout. Pull about 1 inch of the casing out and away from the spout and tie securely. (It is important to fill the spout before you tie the string, or the casing will inflate like a small balloon as the air in the funnel is forced along ahead of the meat.)

Fill the hopper with the meat mixture and grind for a few seconds, pressing the sausage mixture down evenly.

Keep the thumb and forefinger of one hand on the casing to regulate its release as the meat is forced into it. Release the casing on the spout against the pressure of the meat as it enters. If an air pocket develops in the middle of the casing, pierce the casing once or twice with a needle.

Hold the end of the casing with your right hand as it fills, easing the sausage gently away from the mouth of the tube. If the casing should tear, stop the grinder, tie off the sausage (see below) and then proceed. Stuff casings rather loosely, since the filling expands when cooked.

### Tying off the Sausages

Twist the casing several turns to form links at desired lengths, and/or tie off with heavy thread or light string.

### How to Cook Homemade Sausages

Homemade sausages need to be handled a bit more gently during cooking than the mass-produced kind. Since your sausages have not been made by an expert, there are bound to be a few overstuffed casings that will go *pop*! Never fear—these burst sausages will still taste delicious even though they look a bit untidy. The following instructions may help you to avoid mishaps:

· Before cooking, always prick each sausage in about 10 places with a needle. This will permit some of the juice and fat to ooze out and prevent pressure from building up inside the casing.

· Place the sausages 1 layer deep in a skillet just large enough to hold them without crowding.

· Add water until it reaches halfway up the sides of the sausages.

· Simmer the sausages, covered, for 5 minutes, then turn them, cover and simmer for 5 minutes longer.

· Pour off the water. Dry the pan with paper towels and add 2 to 3 tablespoons vegetable oil. Brown sausages on all sides over low heat until well done.

### How to Cook Homemade Sausage Patties

Homemade sausage patties need no special handling. Heat a small amount of vegetable oil in a heavy skillet, add the sausage patties and brown well on both sides until well done.

# ECONOMY SAUSAGES MADE WITH MEAT AND GRAIN

Anyone who is on a diet—or a budget—should definitely sample these superb sausages.

## Sausages with Oatmeal

*Your family will never know these are not 100 percent meat unless you let them in on the secret. I deliberately included very few spices in this recipe,\* since children seem to dislike any flavor that is too obvious*

(YIELD: 24 LINK SAUSAGES)

    2 Pounds pork tenderloin
    ½ Pound veal
    1½ Pounds fresh pork fat
    2 Cups rolled oats
    1 Cup water
    1 Tablespoon salt
    1 Teaspoon caraway seeds
    ⅛ Teaspoon each allspice and ginger

Chop the meat and fat into ¼-inch dice or force through the large disk of your grinder (see page 73).

Place the rolled oats and water in a saucepan and bring to a boil. Drain immediately and cool in the refrigerator for 15 minutes.

Mix the meat, fat, oats, salt, caraway seeds, allspice and ginger. Knead thoroughly with your fingers (see page 73), then form into patties or stuff into casings, using either funnel and spoon (see page 73) or a sausage attachment on your meat grinder or mixer (see page 74). Twist the casings to form links at desired length, or tie off with string. Refrigerate, freeze or cook immediately.

## *Italian-Style Sausage

To transform this recipe into spicy Italian-style sausages, omit the caraway seeds, allspice and ginger, and add to the meat mixture 10 large crushed garlic cloves, 2 teaspoons crushed red pepper, 2 teaspoons slightly crushed fennel, 1 teaspoon thyme leaves, 4 crumbled bay leaves, 1 tablespoon whole black pepper and ¼ teaspoon ground nutmeg.

## Sausages with Soybeans

*Soybeans give your sausages an interesting texture and fine nutty flavor.*

(YIELD: APPROXIMATELY 4 POUNDS SAUSAGE)

    2 Pounds pork tenderloin
    ½ Pound smoked pork butt
    1½ Pounds fresh pork fat
    1½ Cups dried soybeans
    1 Cup water
    1 Tablespoon salt
    ⅛ Teaspoon each nutmeg and allspice

Chop the meat and fat into ¼-inch dice or force through the large disk of your grinder (see page 73).

Place the soybeans in the water, bring to a boil and boil for 5 minutes. Drain the beans and grind or chop them into ⅛-inch pieces. Cool to room temperature. Use your fingers to knead together the meats, fat, beans, salt and spices (see page 73).

Form into patties or stuff into casings, using either a funnel and spoon (see page 73) or a sausage attachment on your meat grinder or mixer (see page 74). Twist the casings to form links at desired lengths or tie off with string.

Refrigerate, freeze or cook immediately.

## Gruetz Wurst

*These pork and beef sausages contain an absolute minimum of fat, and freeze extremely well.*

(YIELD: ABOUT 7 POUNDS)

    3½ Pounds pork shoulder, cut into
        1-inch pieces
    2½ Pounds lean beef or ground beef
    3 Cups uncooked oatmeal
    3 Onions, chopped
    2 Tablespoons butter

*½ Tablespoon each powdered thyme
and sage*
*¼ Teaspoon each allspice and nutmeg
Salt and pepper to taste*

Simmer the pork and beef in enough water to cover until very tender. Cook the oatmeal according to package directions until it is very thick. Sauté the chopped onions in the butter until transparent.

Grind the meats coarsely (see page 73), then combine them with the oatmeal and onions. Mix thoroughly. Add the thyme, sage, allspice and nutmeg, then season to taste with salt and pepper (see page 73).

Prepare the natural casings (see page 73) and use either funnel and spoon or grinder method to stuff them (see pages 73–74). Tie off in 5-inch lengths.

Put the sausages in a deep kettle, add water to cover, and bring to just under a boil. Simmer, covered, for about 40 minutes and drain well. Sausage must be quickly and properly stored to prevent spoilage.

## Ham and Chicken Sandwich Sausage

*This delicate, fine-textured sausage need not be stuffed into casings; merely wrap it in cheesecloth and cook in stock. (This sausage does not freeze well.)*

(YIELD: 1 SAUSAGE ABOUT 15 INCHES LONG)

1 *Pound boiled ham*
1½ *Pounds cooked white-meat chicken
Chicken bones (or 8 chicken
bouillon cubes)*
½ *Pound chicken livers*
7 *Eggs*
½ *Teaspoon salt*
⅛ *Teaspoon each thyme, nutmeg and
pepper*
2 *Tablespoons sherry or brandy
(optional)*
4 *Cups cracker crumbs*

Press the ham and chicken through the fine blade of your meat grinder. Make a stock by boiling the bones (or bouillon cubes) in 6 quarts water and 6 tablespoons salt. Boil the chicken livers for 6 minutes in water to cover, then drain

well and chop. In a large bowl beat 4 eggs, salt, thyme, nutmeg, pepper and brandy into the minced livers. Stir the ground meats into the liver and eggs along with enough cracker crumbs to make a sausage mixture firm enough to shape into a roll.

Shape the sausage mixture into a roll about 4 inches thick and 12 inches long. Roll the sausage in bread crumbs to cover (don't forget the ends of the sausage). Beat the remaining eggs in a baking dish long enough to hold the sausage. Roll the sausage in the beaten egg, then in cracker crumbs, egg, and cracker crumbs again. Wrap the sausage tightly in a piece of cheesecloth long enough to cover it at least three times. Tie off the ends with strong string (see page 000). Cook the sausage (in the cheesecloth) at a low boil for 1½ to 2 hours. Remove the sausage from cooking liquid and cool at room temperature for 8 hours. Refrigerate for 24 hours before using. Store in the refrigerator.

## Swedish Potato Sausage

*Potato sausage is a traditional Swedish sausage prepared in the province of Varmland. This unusual recipe helps you stretch your meat dollars in a particularly tasty way.*

(YIELD: 9 POUNDS SAUSAGE)

2 *Pounds round steak*
2 *Pounds pork shoulder*
8 *Large potatoes*
2 *Medium onions, peeled*
1½ *Tablespoons salt*
¾ *Teaspoon white pepper*
1½ *Teaspoons dry mustard*
¼ *Teaspoon ground allspice*
¼ *Teaspoon ground nutmeg
Cold water as needed
Natural pork casings*
1 *Tablespoon whole allspice (used in
boiling)*

Grind the beef and pork twice, separately, through the fine disk of grinder, or mince the meats with a sharp knife. Grind the meats together through the fine disk.

Peel and parboil the potatoes. Cool. Grind

potatoes and onions together using the fine disk of your grinder.

Mix the potatoes and onions with ground meat with large wooden spoon. Add seasonings and mix again, then add enough cold water to soften the mixture. Use your fingers to knead the mixture well (see page 73). Test consistency and taste by frying a small sample. Readjust seasonings if necessary.

Stuff casings rather loosely in 24-inch lengths (see pages 73–74). Prick with a large needle if any air bubbles form. Tie off the sausages (see page 74) and then tie the sausage ends together to form rings. Refrigerate portions to be used within a few days and freeze any surplus immediately.

To cook, boil for 45 minutes in a kettle large enough to avoid crowding. Add whole allspice to cooking water. Remove froth as it accumulates. Cut rings into 2-inch pieces and serve hot or cold.

# WINEMAKING

Given an accurate recipe, and providing you follow the necessary procedures without taking any shortcuts, it is nearly impossible to produce a bad wine. Winemaking has as much to do with patience as it does with perfection. Nothing good comes quickly—and something great takes even longer. If you can't bear to wait for your first wine to be ready to drink, make root beer in the meanwhile and drink that. Or set about making some cheese. If you are in an even greater hurry, make yogurt. Or butter. Or a cake or a loaf of bread. The time will pass quickly, and soon your wine will be pure gold, or ruby-red and mellow . . . resting on your shelf awaiting your pleasure.

It's easier and much more fascinating to tackle winemaking on a small scale at first, making one-gallon lots of several different wines and then moving up to five-gallon batches of the wines you like best.

I suggest that you make five or six wines over a period of a year. If you get impatient to taste your first wine, start a different one and watch it bubble. Rack *that* wine and store it, then begin another—and still another. If you can resist the temptation to sample your creations pre-

maturely, you should soon be on your way to a really superb collection.

## THE WINEMAKING PROCESS SIMPLIFIED

· Mix the basic ingredients as indicated in the wine recipe to prepare a "must" or primary mixture.

· Cover the must and allow it to ferment (Primary Fermentation).

· Rack the must by siphoning it into a clean jug, leaving any sediment behind (First Racking).

· Top off by filling the jug to its neck and sealing it with an air lock (Topping Off).

· Ferment this young wine in the jug until it is fairly clear (Secondary Fermentation).

· When the wine partially clears, siphon into another clean jug, top off and seal with an air lock (Second Racking).

· After 3 to 4 months, siphon the clearing wine into a third clean jug, then top off and seal once more (Third Racking).

· Store the wine in the jug until it clears completely.

· Before bottling, make certain the wine is clear by doing a candle test.

· If the wine proves clear, bottle and seal with corks.

· Allow the wine to age in the bottle until it is mellow enough to drink.

## WINEMAKING EQUIPMENT

If you have read this far, you are most likely intrigued with the idea of making your own wines and are wondering what you will need in the way of equipment and how much it will cost.

You may be surprised to learn that a good deal of winemaking equipment is already in your kitchen or can be purchased conveniently and inexpensively at your local hardware store.

### *Minimum Equipment*

PRIMARY FERMENTORS: For primary (first) fermentation, a plastic pail or trash can (without a lid) with a capacity slightly larger than the amount of wine you're making is your best bet. Two-gallon and 8-gallon containers of good-quality plastic are easiest to use. These are lightweight, unbreakable and easy to clean.

A plastic sheet (the kind the dry cleaner uses to cover your clothes) makes a fine cover. Cut this 5 inches larger than the container top and fasten down tightly with a string or a wide rubber band. The rising gas will find its way out without allowing fresh air in.

SECONDARY FERMENTORS: One-gallon, 2-gallon or 5-gallon glass, narrow-necked containers are necessary for the secondary fermentation of your musts. Buy glass jars or jugs or salvage glass cider jugs from supermarket shelves. Plastic containers are not recommended for the second fermentation, or for any prolonged storage of alcoholic beverages.

CASKS AND BARRELS: While aesthetically pleasing, these are not a wise investment unless you plan to make wine in batches of 30 gallons or more. These containers tend to leak and are difficult to clean.

AIR LOCK: Each of your secondary containers should be fitted with an air lock (also called "fermentation lock" or "trap") which allows fermentation gas to escape while preventing air from entering. Air locks are available in either glass or plastic and come complete with stopper (or bung). These should be the correct size to tightly fit the neck of your jars or jugs.

SIPHON HOSE: Since wine must be siphoned, or racked, from one container to another, you will need at least 5 feet of rubber or pliable plastic tubing not more than ½ inch in circumference. Your drugstore may stock this.

BOTTLES: Standard-sized wine bottles of pint, fifth or quart capacity are best. Their necks are especially designed to receive long, straight wine corks, and their uniform size makes them easy to store.

Red wines should go into either brown or dark green bottles to protect their color. For white wines, light green or even clear bottles are suitable.

Since wine should be enjoyed as soon as it's opened, half-gallon bottles are not recommended for the final bottling unless you have a wealth of thirsty friends. Avoid odd-shaped bottles for which closures may not be available. Collect previously used wine bottles from restaurants and friends as soon as you begin winemaking.

CORKS: You'll need to purchase new straight-sided (not tapered) corks. Ordinary household corks are not recommended.

CORKING DEVICE: A device of some sort, either hand-held or table-mounted, makes bottling a great deal easier.

### *Additional Equipment*

Other basic equipment generally found around the house:

PLASTIC FUNNELS.

PLASTIC GRAVY BASTER: For withdrawing wine samples.

WOODEN SPOONS: With extra-long handles for stirring musts.

PLASTIC OR GLASS MEASURING CUPS.

PLASTIC MEASURING SPOONS.

LONG-HANDLED NYLON BRUSHES: For scrubbing jugs.

WOVEN PLASTIC SPONGES: To loosen encrusted sediment in primary containers.

There are several pieces of basic equipment the beginner will need to buy specifically for winemaking. These are available at winemaking stores across the country or may be purchased by mail (see Sources of Supply, pages 273–74). One order and you're on your way.

SACCHAROMETER OR HYDROMETER, plus a cylindrical glass hydrometer jar for measuring the quantity of sugar in your must.

ACID TITRATION KIT: For measuring the total acid content of the must.

FLOATING WINE THERMOMETER (a new plastic or glass fish tank thermometer is perfect): to make sure your must is at the proper temperature for good fermentation.

CRUSHERS AND PRESSES: Unless you intend to enter into winemaking on a grand scale, don't buy expensive equipment. Small quantities of grapes or other fruits may be crushed by hand with a wooden masher, and their juices extracted by squeezing through a new nylon stocking or other strong mesh cloth.

## WINEMAKING INGREDIENTS

In addition to equipment, you will also need to have these basic winemaking ingredients on hand:

SODIUM OR POTASSIUM METABISULPHITE OR CAMP-DEN TABLETS: In powder or tablet form (food grade), for sterilizing equipment and musts.

SELF-STARTING WINE YEAST: Several packets of a good strain.

YEAST NUTRIENT: A blend of ammonium salts used to nourish the yeast and help it work actively.

BLENDS OF MIXED ACIDS: Or separate packets of *tartaric, citric* and *malic acids* for mixing your own blend (usually 2 parts tartaric and 2 parts citric to 1 part malic).

GRAPE TANNIN: To add to the flavor of all wines.

PECTIC ENZYMES: To remove excess pectin from wines made from pectin-rich stone fruits, such as peaches and nectarines.

ASCORBIC ACID (Vitamin C): To prevent excess oxidation or browning.

## CLEANING AND STERILIZING YOUR EQUIPMENT

### The Use of Metabisulphites

One of the most important processes in amateur winemaking is the protection of the wines from wild yeasts by sterilizing with the versatile chemical sulphur dioxide ($SO_2$).

Sold either as sodium metabisulphite or potassium metabisulphite and available in powder or tablet form (Campden tablets), sulphur dioxide is used to maintain scrupulous cleanliness, to inhibit growth of wild yeasts, to help prevent browning, to inhibit vinegar bacteria and to increase the storage life of all wines.

### Preparing a Stock Solution

Dissolve 2 ounces of metabisulphite crystals in a *glass* gallon bottle of warm water. Keep the bottle tightly capped when not in use. This sterile solution will last for months if handled carefully.

### Cleaning and Sterilizing

All equipment must be clean before you begin. Soak each piece in a strong mixture of hot water and sal soda (washing soda). Rinse several times under hot running water. Never use soap on winemaking equipment; soap leaves a film and gives an unpleasant taste to wines.

Pour about a pint or so of the sterile solution into your empty container. Rinse funnels, spoons, nylon pressing bags, thermometers, saccharometers or hydrometers, plastic basters, hydrometer jars and racking siphons in this solution. Fill air locks with 2 ounces of sterile solution (or about halfway full) to keep vinegar bacteria out of your musts or wines. Prepare corks for bottling by immersing them in a plastic dish filled with sterile solution. Weight corks down with a heavy glass plate. To sterilize bottles, pour the sterile solution from one bottle to another before returning it to the storage jar. Splash a bit of the sterile solution over the necks of secondary containers and bottles before racking wine into them. Drain all equipment thoroughly.

## ADDING METABISULPHITES TO MUSTS AND WINES

Campden tablets are usually added to musts to protect them from wild yeasts and spoilage organisms. A general rule of thumb is to use 1 tablet for 1 gallon or 4 tablets for 5 gallons of wine. Crush each tablet between two plastic measuring spoons, then mix with 1 ounce warm water and add to must or wine.

## USING THE SACCHAROMETER/ HYDROMETER

The saccharometer (literally "sugar-measurer") or hydrometer (literally "water-measurer") are essentially the same instrument—both tell the amount of sugar in the must. Sealed within each instrument is a printed scale bearing 2 columns of figures. The saccharometer or Balling scale measures the weight of the sugar in the must, with the potential alcohol content of each degree alongside. The hydrometer measures the Specific Gravity (or density) of the must, also with the potential alcohol content of each marking alongside. On the basis of the reading given by either of these, you will be able to adjust the sugar level of your must to coincide with the level recommended in your recipe.

Rinse saccharometer or hydrometer, hydrometer jar, plastic baster and wine thermometer in the stock metabisulphite solution. Combine the ingredients in your recipe, and before adding the yeast, draw off enough must with the baster to fill the hydrometer jar about three-quarters full. Strain the must sample if any pieces of fruit are present or the reading will be thrown off.

Cool, or warm, the must sample to about 59 degrees F. for an accurate reading. Set the filled hydrometer jar on a level surface, place the saccharometer/hydrometer in the must sample, spin it gently to dislodge any air bubble, and when it is still, take the reading at the lowest point where the must touches the stem.

As soon as you have taken the sugar reading, return the must sample to the primary container and proceed as directed in your recipe. It is possible, if you are following one of the recipes in this book, that your reading may be accurate the first time around. Most probably, though, since fruits differ in sugar content depending upon how and where they are grown, the reading may be off a bit in either direction. Additional sugar or extra water may be required to adjust the must. The readings given on page 85 are based on my experiences in adjusting sugar content. Follow this if you like or experiment by stirring a little more sugar or water thoroughly into the must and following up each addition with another test.

## THE ACID TEST

The next and equally important step before adding yeast is to determine the acid content of the must. Acid is present to a greater or lesser degree in all fruits; the acid content within even one variety of fruit will vary depending on the soil and climate where it was grown, the stage of ripeness, and so forth. Testing for acid content will enable you to discover quickly and easily, before fermentation is under way, whether your must will have the proper acid balance to assure you a finished wine of just the right tang and flavor. A correct proportion of acid means a healthy ferment, a must that is resistant to spoilage and a finished wine that will have good keeping qualities after bottling.

The best way to measure total acid content is

with a titration kit. This easy-to-use, inexpensive set of instruments and chemicals may be purchased or ordered from any wine supply house. The kit contains a graduated syringe, a testing vial, a bottle of sodium hydroxide or neutralizing solution, a small bottle of phenolphthalein or color solution and an eye dropper with which to measure the color solution.

Follow the instructions that come with your kit. The point at which the sample is neutralized is indicated by a complete color change in the sample. Red musts will change from red to brown to dark gray, while white musts will become brilliant clear pink. Always test for acids before adding yeast to your must. *Immediately discard the must sample in the testing vial! It is poisonous!*

If your must sample is short of acid—that is, if it requires only 4 cubic centimeters of sodium hydroxide to convert the color to pink or to gray—you can adjust this deficiency by thoroughly stirring in an acid blend. Usually ⅓ ounce of an acid blend (2 teaspoons) added to a gallon of must will raise the acid level by .03%, or 1 ounce (6 teaspoons) of the same blend will raise the acid level of 6 gallons by .015%.

After adding acid, don't become frustrated if you misjudge the first time around. Add a little more, and titrate as many times as necessary. Keep in mind that it's much easier to put acid into your must than it is to take excess acid out. If you miscalculate, reduce excess acid by diluting with water and readjusting the sugar balance if necessary.

Again, be sure to throw away must samples *after each titration* and thoroughly rinse all testing equipment. *Sodium hydroxide and phenolphthalein are poisons!* Cap these chemicals tightly; they deteriorate by exposure to the air. Refill bottles are available in most wine supply houses.

## ADDING YEAST

Now that the sugar and acid levels have been correctly adjusted, you're ready for the most pleasurable part of the winemaking process— adding the wine yeast that will begin fermenta-

tion and set to work converting the sugar in the must into alcohol.

Only true wine yeast will dependably launch and sustain the strong fermentation needed to produce *good* wine, time after time. The winemaker is primarily concerned with the production of alcohol. To increase the efficiency of this production, the proper nutrients must be added (see page 80) and the temperature should be brought to between 68 to 80 degrees F. Too cool temperatures may cause the fermentation to stick; hotter fermentation (over 80 F.) may make the wine bitter; and any temperature over 85 degrees F. may weaken the yeast.

Fortunately, there are superb self-starting wine yeasts available that can be sprinkled on top of the must, stirred in after 12 hours and just 24 hours later produce frenetic bubbling yeast activity. If all is proceeding as scheduled and alcohol is forming, a daily check on your must with the saccharometer/hydrometer will indicate the sugar content is dropping. Stir the must vigorously every day and keep the plastic cover tied down tight.

## RACKING YOUR WINES

The vigorous bubbling ferment that began after the yeast was introduced into your must will slow after a week or so, and daily checks with the saccharometer/hydrometer will indicate that your must is ready to be racked for the first time.

Racking consists of siphoning the must (or wine in subsequent rackings) from the dregs and yeast which have accumulated on the bottom of the container. This improves the quality of the wine and makes it clearer and more stable. If the must or wine were to be allowed to remain on its deposit or lees, the yeast would decompose and begin to feed on itself. This process, called "autolysis," renders the wine unstable and produces off-flavors.

### *Equipment Needed for Racking*

A clean 1-gallon or 5-gallon jar (depending on the amount of wine you're making).

A 5-foot length of plastic or surgical rubber tubing for siphoning.

Stock metabisulphite solution.

Air lock.

### First Racking

Rinse the equipment with the stock solution. Place the must in its primary container on a table or counter and set the clean jar on the floor underneath. Hold one end of the siphon beneath the surface of the must with one hand. Take the free end of the siphon into your mouth and start the siphoning with two strong pulls so that the wine won't back up in the siphon and disturb the lees. Pinch the sides of the siphon together at the top of the loop to cut off the flow for a moment, then lower the siphon into the clean jar.

In this first racking, allow the must to splash into the jar to aerate it a bit and free it of carbon dioxide. Fit with an air lock.

### Second and Third Rackings

Rinse the equipment with the stock metabisulphite solution.

In these subsequent rackings, keep aeration to a minimum by lowering the siphon to the bottom of the jar. Let the wine flow out gently without excess bubbling. Fit with an air lock.

### Topping Off Your Wines

Each time you siphon your wine from the accumulated yeast deposit into a clean jar, it will be clearer and more stable, but some wine will be left behind with the sediment. Since it is absolutely necessary to have as little as possible of the top surface of the wine exposed to the air in order to prevent spoilage, it is necessary to "top off."

TOPPING OFF WITH SURPLUS MUST: After the first racking there may be a bit of must left over. Place this surplus in a smaller sterile container and fit with an air lock. Store under the same conditions as the larger jar and use to top off in subsequent rackings. As the surplus diminishes, transfer to increasingly smaller jars, making sure to fit each with an air lock.

TOPPING OFF WITH SUGAR SYRUP: Top off with sugar syrup made with the same ratio of sugar to water as in the original recipe. If the must contained 2 pounds of sugar to 1 quart liquid, top off with 4 ounces sugar mixed with 2 cups of boiled water. Allow the syrup to cool, fill the jar to the bottom of the neck, and seal with an air lock. This syrup may also be used for topping off in secondary rackings if the wine seems weak.

TOPPING OFF WITH TAP WATER: Tepid tap water may be used for topping off if the wine seems too strong.

## WHEN AND HOW TO BOTTLE YOUR WINES

### Equipment Needed for Bottling

5 25-Ounce standard-sized wine bottles (or 4 25-ounce wine bottles and 2 half-bottles) for each gallon.

New straight-sided wine corks.

Corking device.

### When to Bottle

Although you are no doubt impatient to sample your wine, it is important to remember that good wine takes time to undergo secondary fermentation before being racked into bottles, and time to develop bouquet and flavor while aging in the bottles.

Bottling should never be rushed. Wine should be perfectly clear, with absolutely no suggestion of haziness, before you think of bottling. If wine appears even slightly hazy, rack it again and give it a few months longer to settle. Remember, if fermentation has not completely finished, the remaining yeast will decompose and cause renewed yeast activity and burst bottles.

Give wine a candle test to make sure it is ready to be bottled. In a dark room, set a lighted candle behind the jug of wine. The outline of the flame should shine through the wine as clearly defined and free from distortion as it would through a sheet of colored glass. When your wine passes this test it is ready to be bottled. Allow the wine to settle after the candle test and bring it to 60 to 65 degrees F. before you begin bottling.

### Fining

Most wines will clear by themselves to a hard, jewel-like clarity if racked at the recommended intervals and given enough time. When cloudiness persists, the wine may be fined or cleared with gelatin or pectic enzymes before bottling.

To fine with gelatin, add ⅛ teaspoon dissolved gelatin for each gallon of wine, but only if the wine has a natural high tannin content to begin with or tannin has been added prior to fermentation. Use pectic enzymes to fine cloudy wines according to manufacturer's directions. Rack all fined wines before bottling.

### Preparing Bottles, Corks and Closures

Bottles and closures should be clean before receiving the wine. Scrub each bottle with washing soda and hot water, rinse several times and drain thoroughly. Rinse by pouring stock metabisulphite solution from one to the other.

Sterilize corks by placing them in a plastic or glass bowl filled with stock solution. Set a heavy glass plate over them to weight them down, keeping them submerged for 20 minutes. Wipe dry with a cloth dipped in $SO_2$ solution.

## STORING WINES

Keep freshly corked bottles in an upright position for 2 or 3 days to permit corks to dry in shape, then inspect each to make sure they are airtight and leakproof. A professional touch at this point is to seal the corks with foil or viscose capsules, available at wine supply stores.

To store, lay bottles on their sides, to keep the corks from drying out. Provide a cool, dry storage spot, setting red wines on higher racks, white wines on lower ones.

## MISCELLANEOUS WINE TIPS

### "Stuck" Fermentations

Occasionally a complication arises during primary fermentation where the daily saccharometer/hydrometer check indicates that the readings are not dropping as predicted. When the Balling or Specific Gravity scales give identical readings for several days in a row, a "stuck" fermentation may have occurred. If your must drops less than one point in a week, ask yourself these questions: did you skimp on yeast nutrient; have you provided a sufficient amount of acid; did you add too much sugar, or too little; has the must temperature risen too high or fallen too low?

If temperatures are too high or too low, adjust by cooling or warming your storage place. Take a Balling or Specific Gravity reading. Dilute your must with water or fruit juice in an overly sugared must or, conversely, if the stuck must has insufficient sugar, add more as a cooled, boiled syrup. Stir the must for several minutes to aerate it and release carbon dioxide gas. Most musts will respond to any or all of these measures.

### Flavorings, Herbs and Spices

Weak wines may be improved by blending them with other wines or by adding wine flavorings, available at winemaking specialty stores. A true fruit extract such as blackberry, cherry, grape or peach may, if added judiciously, ameliorate a wine's flavor. Sherry, sauterne or port flavorings will add a mellow, smoother quality to a slightly bland wine.

There are also herbs and spices, sold in wine supply stores, that may be added to the primary fermentation to increase flavor. In addition to the more familiar aromatic herbs and spices— allspice, aniseed, cinnamon, ginger and nutmeg —there are more esoteric flavorings, such as waldmeister or woodruff (so pleasant in German May wines) and juniper berries. These are sold by weight or in preweighed and sealed packets.

### Winemaking à la Mode

Occasionally, in the course of racking two musts into their secondary fermentors, you may find yourself with a quantity of extra wine from each. Solve the problem by combining the two wines in one gallon jar, just to see what happens. Frequently the outcome is really exciting.

Never hesitate to experiment. Most combined wines will be drinkable, some will be excellent and at the very worst you will be provided with some interesting cooking wines.

### Sparkling Wines

Sparkling wines are wines that undergo a further fermentation in the bottle and, in the process, build up varying amounts of carbon dioxide gas. Making sparkling wines at home is, unfortunately, a tricky procedure not to be undertaken lightly by home winemakers, even if they have had some degree of experience. I do not make these wines myself and do not recommend that others do so, since it is absolutely imperative that the winemaker exert careful control over every step of the process, and even then burst bottles are a common problem.

### Conversion Table: Specific Gravity to Balling at 60 Degrees F.

The following is a chart based on readings taken from the musts and wines as we tested them. If your Specific Gravity reading is slightly off, either over or under (½ degree on Balling), it isn't important. Even if you make the same wine twice the results won't be precisely the same. Commercial wineries exert careful control over their wines, but even they have vintage years! So just relax and have fun making your wines.

#### Table for Adjusting Sugar in the Must

| Specific Gravity | Balling | Sugar in ounces to be added per gallon to raise must 1 point |
|---|---|---|
| 1.000 | 0 | |
| 1.004 | 1 | 31.5 |
| 1.008 | 2 | 30.0 |
| 1.012 | 3 | 28.5 |
| 1.015 | 4 | 27.0 |
| 1.020 | 5 | 25.5 |
| 1.023 | 6 | 24.0 |
| 1.026 | 7 | 22.5 |
| 1.030 | 8 | 21.0 |
| 1.034 | 9 | 19.5 |
| 1.038 | 10 | 18.0 |
| 1.042 | 11 | 16.5 |
| 1.046 | 12 | 15.0 |
| 1.050 | 13 | 13.5 |
| 1.055 | 14 | 12.0 |
| 1.059 | 15 | 10.5 |
| 1.063 | 16 | 9.0 |
| 1.067 | 17 | 7.5 |
| 1.072 | 18 | 6.0 |
| 1.076 | 19 | 4.5 |
| 1.080 | 20 | 3.0 |
| 1.084 | 21 | 1.5 |
| 1.088 | 22 | 0.0 |

## WINE RECIPES

### Dry Red Wine from Fresh Red Grapes

*If you grow your own, or if you live near an inexpensive source, you will probably want to try making wine from fresh grapes. Use equal quantities of high-sugar, low-acid vinifera grapes and low-sugar, high-acid hybrid varieties, or try your luck with any grapes available to you. It is absolutely necessary to test and correct the sugar and acid content of the must.*

(YIELD: 1 GALLON FIRST-RUN WINE AND 1 GALLON SECOND-RUN OR FALSE WINE)

PRIMARY FERMENTATION

7 *Pounds* vinifera *(or other) grapes*
7 *Pounds hybrid (or other) grapes*
*Acid blend as needed to adjust the acid content*
*Sugar and water as needed to adjust the sugar content*
1 *Campden tablet*
1 *Teaspoon yeast nutrient*
½ *Teaspoon pectic enzyme powder*
1 *Package self-starting all-purpose wine yeast*

ACID CONTENT: .65%
STARTING SPECIFIC GRAVITY: 1.088
(or *Balling*: 22.0)

Use the equipment as listed on page 79, plus a wooden mallet. Use your stock metabisulphite solution (see page 80) to sterilize all the equipment.

Stem the grapes and press a few at a time with your fingers until the skins snap. Drop the fruit into the primary container. Squeeze and pound the fruit with a wooden mallet to extract as much juice as possible. Mix in all the remaining ingredients except the yeast.

Withdraw a sample and test for sugar (see page 81). Withdraw another sample and titrate for acid content (see pages 81–82).

Set the primary container where it will undergo fermentation and sprinkle yeast over the surface of the must (do not stir the yeast in). Tie plastic sheeting down securely over the top of the container. After 12 hours remove the plastic sheet, stir well, re-cover and tie the top down tightly. Ferment to the color and body you prefer according to the following:

> Rosé wine—ferment for 12 hours.
> Light red wine—ferment for 2 days.
> Medium red wine—ferment for 3 days.
> Dark, robust red wine—ferment for 5 to 6 days.

Stir the must daily and re-cover the container each time. Do not stir the must for 12 hours prior to racking.

### FIRST RACKING

Use the equipment listed on page 82, plus a plastic funnel, a fine-mesh nylon bag (or new nylon stocking or cheesecloth) and a glass measuring cup with a handle. Sterilize all the equipment with stock metabisulphite solution (see page 80).

Set a glass jug alongside the primary container. Place a funnel lined with nylon bag, stocking or cheesecloth in the neck of the jug. Transfer the must, a cup at a time, leaving behind as much yeast sediment as possible. Squeeze the fruit in the cheesecloth to extract the juice. Save the skins for making second or false wine.

### SECOND RACKING

Use the equipment as listed on page 82. Sterilize the equipment with stock metabisulphite solution (see page 80).

Rack the wine off its heavy sediment (page 82). Do not top off at this point. Fit with a freshly filled air lock, set aside in a cool, dark place for 3 weeks, then top off with tepid tap water and refit the air lock.

### THIRD RACKING

> ½ Campden tablet
> 1 Tablespoon water

Use the equipment as listed on page 82. Sterilize the equipment with stock metabisulphite solution (see page 80).

Crush the ½ Campden tablet in the tablespoon of water and add to a sterile jug. Rack the wine off its sediment (see page 82) and top off with tepid tap water or with a sugar syrup (see page 83). Fit the jug with a freshly filled air lock and return to its storage place for 6 months.

### BOTTLING

> ¼ Campden tablet
> ¼ Tablet (100 milligrams) ascorbic
>    acid

For equipment, use 5 25-ounce wine bottles (or 4 25-ounce wine bottles and 2 half-bottles), a siphon hose and corks to fit. Sterilize all the equipment (see page 80). Chill the wine at about 40 degrees F. for several days prior to bottling to precipitate out tartrate crystals. Rack the wine into bottles as directed on pages 82–83.

Red grape wines should age in the bottle for at least 1 year. Age further if the wine tastes raw.

## Second or False Wine

*Double the volume of your wine by making "false wine" from the skins and partly fermented wine left behind in your container after the first racking. This wine is a bit lighter in body than first-run wine, but is every bit as good.*

(YIELD: 1 GALLON)

### PRIMARY FERMENTATION

1 Quart water
4 Cups granulated sugar
1 Tablespoon acid blend
1 Teaspoon yeast nutrient
⅛ Teaspoon grape tannin

Use the equipment as listed on page 79.

After racking the original red wine (see Dry Red Wine from Fresh Grapes, page 85), return the skins to the juice and yeasty sediment left behind in the container. Add water in equal amount to the wine you racked into the jug, then stir in the sugar, acid blend, yeast nutrient and grape tannin. Do not add yeast; there is enough left in the sediment to ferment the wine.

Cover tightly with plastic and set aside to ferment. Stir the must twice a day and make daily checks with hydrometer or saccharometer. As the Specific Gravity drops to 1.015 (Balling 4.0), follow the directions given on pages 82–83.

## Light-Bodied Apple Wine

*If you enjoy a delicate wine, one that is neither too sweet nor too dry, by all means try this delicious apple wine. It matures rapidly and should be ready to drink from 4 to 6 months after bottling.*

(YIELD: 1 GALLON)

### PRIMARY FERMENTATION

1 6-ounce can frozen apple juice concentrate*

* Other bottled or canned fruit juices—orange, cranberry, pear nectar, peach nectar—may be made into wines by following these basic directions.

3 Quarts cold water
1 Quart hot water
5 Cups granulated sugar
1 Campden tablet
1 Level teaspoon yeast nutrient
2 Tablespoons acid blend
¼ Teaspoon grape tannin
½ Teaspoon pectic enzyme powder (or 1 tablet, crushed in a little water)
1 Package self-starting all-purpose wine yeast

ACID CONTENT: .65%
STARTING SPECIFIC GRAVITY: 1.085
(or *Balling:* 21.0)

Use the equipment as listed on page 79, plus a can opener, a large stainless-steel or unchipped enamel saucepan and a wooden spoon. Sterilize all the equipment (see page 80), including the top of the concentrate can and the can opener.

Combine the apple juice concentrate and cold water in the primary container. Add the sugar to the hot water and stir over low heat until the sugar dissolves. Add the sugar syrup to the apple juice, then stir in all the remaining ingredients except the yeast.

Allow the must to cool to 75 degrees F. While the must cools, withdraw a sample and test for sugar with saccharometer or hydrometer (see page 81). Titrate another sample for acid content (see pages 81–82). Adjust for sugar or acid if necessary.

Set the primary container where it will undergo fermentation, and sprinkle the yeast over the must (do not stir in). Cover with plastic sheeting tied down tightly and allow the yeast to work for 12 hours. Remove the plastic sheeting, stir the yeast in thoroughly and re-cover tightly. Stir daily (re-covering each time) for 4 to 5 days, and take a sugar reading every day after the second day until Specific Gravity drops to 1.030 (Balling: 8.0). Now the must is ready for its first racking.

### FIRST RACKING

Sugar (or surplus wine) for topping off

Use the equipment as listed on pages 82–83. Sterilize the equipment with stock sterile solution (see page 80). Rack the must off its yeasty sediment (see pages 82–83). Top off with surplus wine or a sugar syrup prepared as directed on page 83, cooling the syrup before adding it to the must. Apply an air lock (see page 79) to the jug and allow the must to ferment for 3 weeks.

### SECOND RACKING

> ½ Campden tablet
> 3 Tablespoons water

Use the equipment as listed on page 82. Sterilize all the equipment with stock metabisulphite solution (see page 80). Crush the ½ Campden tablet with the 3 tablespoons water and pour into a clean jug. Rack the wine quietly off its sediment and into the jug (see page 82). No bubbles at this stage, please! Top off with tepid tap water if necessary. Seal with an air lock (see page 79) and set the jug in a cool, dark place for 3 months.

### THIRD RACKING

> ½ Campden tablet
> 3 Tablespoons water

Use the equipment as listed on page 82. Sterilize the equipment with stock sterile solution (see page 80). Add the ½ Campden tablet, crushed in the 3 tablespoons water, to the jug, then rack the wine, taking care to leave all sediment behind (see page 82). Attach a clean air lock (see page 79) to the jug. Return the wine to its cool, dark storage place for 4 to 6 months, or until clear enough to bottle (see pages 83–84).

### BOTTLING

Use the equipment as listed on page 83. When the wine has passed the candle test and no cloudiness or fermentation bubbles are present, it is time to bottle. Follow the directions given on pages 83–84).

Sample a little wine before applying appropriate closures. If not too raw, age wine no longer than 4 months before sampling a small bottle. This is a fairly mellow wine and should at this time be ready to drink. If the wine still tastes a bit raw, allow remaining bottles to age for 2 to 3 months longer. But do not wait too long before drinking this wine.

## Pineapple Wine

*Crushed pineapple from your grocer's shelves transforms into a tangy, pale amber, medium-bodied wine.*

(YIELD: 1 GALLON)

### PRIMARY FERMENTATION

> 3  Quarts water
> 4¾ Cups granulated sugar
> 2  20-ounce cans crushed pineapple in sugar syrup*
> 2  Teaspoons citric acid
> 1  Teaspoon yeast nutrient
> ½  Teaspoon grape tannin
> 1  Package self-starting all-purpose wine yeast

ACID CONTENT:  .60%
STARTING SPECIFIC GRAVITY:  1.095
(or *Balling*: 23.0)

Use the equipment as listed on page 79, plus a can opener, a large stainless steel or unchipped enamel saucepan and a wooden spoon. Sterilize the equipment, including the tops of the cans and the can opener (see page 80). In the large saucepan, bring the 3 quarts water and the sugar to a boil. Stir until the sugar is dissolved and set this syrup aside to cool.

Pour the undrained crushed pineapple and cooled sugar syrup into the primary container. Mix in the citric acid, yeast nutrient and grape tannin and stir until well blended.

Withdraw a sample of must and test for sugar content with saccharometer or hydrometer (see page 81), then test for acid content (see pages 81–82). Make necessary adjustments for sugar or acid.

As soon as the must temperature registers between 72 and 78 degrees F., set the primary container where it will undergo primary fermentation, sprinkle in the yeast (do not stir) and tie down the plastic sheeting. Allow the yeast to work for 12 hours, then stir in thoroughly and re-tie the plastic cover. Stir daily for 4 to 5 days,

---

* Other canned or frozen fruits—pears, peaches, strawberries, etc.—may be made into wine by following these basic directions. Reduce fruit to a pulp before beginning.

re-covering each time. Do a daily sugar test after the second day. When the Specific Gravity drops to 1.025 (Balling: 7.0), the must is ready for its first racking.

### FIRST RACKING

> ½ Campden tablet, crushed (¼ tablet extra, if necessary)
> 2 Tablespoons water

Use the equipment as listed on page 82, plus a fine mesh nylon bag (or clean nylon stocking), a plastic funnel, a small glass measuring cup with handle, and a smaller jug (if necessary). Sterilize all the equipment (see page 80). Because bits of pulp tend to clog the siphon hose, you must proceed a little differently when racking this wine. Place the clean jug alongside the primary container. Drape the fine nylon mesh bag or nylon stocking over the funnel, place the funnel in the neck of the jug, and pour the must through, a cupful at a time. Dip the must carefully from the primary container, leaving the yeasty sediment behind. As the bag or the toe of the stocking fills, squeeze out the juice and discard the pulp. Fill the jug to the neck, add the crushed ½ Campden tablet dissolved in the 2 tablespoons water, remove funnel and attach an air lock (see page 79). Transfer any surplus juice to a smaller glass container, add a crushed ¼ Campden tablet, and fit this small bottle with an air lock also. Use this extra juice for topping off at subsequent rackings. Allow the must to ferment, undisturbed, for 3 weeks.

### SECOND RACKING

> ½ Campden tablet
> 2 Tablespoons water

Use the equipment as listed on page 82. Sterilize the equipment (see page 80).

Crush the ½ Campden tablet with 2 tablespoons water and pour into the jug. Rack the wine off its sediment (see page 82). Top off with water or surplus must (see page 83). Apply a freshly filled air lock (see page 79) and place the jug in a cool, dark storage spot for 3 months.

### THIRD RACKING

> ½ Campden tablet
> ¼ Cup water

Use the equipment as listed on page 82. Clean and sterilize the equipment (see page 80).

Crush the ½ Campden tablet in ¼ cup water, then add to the jug. Rack the wine in slowly (see page 82). Apply an air lock filled with fresh metabisulphite solution (see page 81) and return the wine to its cool, dark storage place for 4 to 6 months, or until it passes a candle test (see When to Bottle, page 83).

Pineapple wine is frequently difficult to clear, and may need to be fined with pectic enzyme powder (see page 80). Fining should be used only when wine refuses to clear by itself within 9 months' time.

### BOTTLING

Use the equipment as listed on page 83.

Wines should be perfectly clear and show no evidence of further fermentation before they are bottled. As soon as your wine meets these requirements, bottle according to the directions given on pages 83–84. White (grape) wines, flower wines and fruit wines are usually ready to drink after 4 to 8 months in the bottle.

---

### *Red Wine from Frozen Grape Juice Concentrate*

*Frozen grape juice concentrate from your grocer's freezer may be transformed into a delicious, full-bodied sweet wine.*

(YIELD: 1 GALLON)

---

### PRIMARY FERMENTATION

> 54 Ounces frozen grape juice concentrate (9 6-ounce cans)
> 4 Quarts water
> 4 Cups granulated sugar
> 2 Teaspoons citric acid
> ½ Teaspoon yeast nutrient
> ½ Campden tablet
> 1 Package self-starting all-purpose wine yeast

ACID CONTENT: .60%
STARTING SPECIFIC GRAVITY: 1.095
(or *Balling:* 23.0)

Use the equipment as listed on page 79, plus a can opener, a large stainless-steel or unchipped enamel saucepan and a wooden spoon. Clean and sterilize all the equipment, including the tops of the cans and the can opener (see page 80). Make a sugar syrup by bringing 2 quarts water to a boil and stirring in the sugar until dissolved. While the syrup cools, open the cans of concentrate and pour into the primary container. Crush the ½ Campden tablet in 2 tablespoons of the water. Thoroughly stir in the remaining 2 quarts water, the crushed Campden tablet, the cooled sugar syrup, citric acid and yeast nutrient.

Withdraw a sample and test for sugar content with a saccharometer or hydrometer (see page 81). Take another sample and test for total acids (see pages 81–82). Make whatever adjustments are necessary to bring the must to proper levels of sugar and/or acid.

Set the container where it will undergo primary fermentation and take the temperature of the must. As soon as this registers between 72 and 78 degrees F., remove the thermometer and sprinkle in the yeast (do not stir it in). Tie the plastic tightly over the container, allow the yeast to work for 12 hours, then stir it in thoroughly. Re-tie the plastic covering. Stir daily for 4 to 5 days and take a sugar reading daily after the second day. As soon as the Specific Gravity drops to 1.030 (Balling: 8.0), the must is ready for its first racking.

### FIRST RACKING

> ½ Campden tablet
> Sugar syrup for topping off
> (see page 000)

Use the equipment as listed on page 82. Wash and sterilize equipment (see page 80).

Rack the must off its yeasty sediment (see Racking, page 82). Crush the ½ Campden tablet in the cooled sugar syrup and top off to proper level (see page 83). Attach the air lock (see page 79), and set aside in a cool, dark place to ferment for 3 months.

### SECOND RACKING

> ½ Campden tablet
> ¼ Cup water
> Tepid tap water for topping off, if necessary

Use the equipment as listed on page 82. Clean and sterilize the equipment (see page 80).

Crush the ½ Campden tablet in the ¼ cup water and pour into the jug. Rack the wine off its sediment (see page 82). Top off with tepid tap water if necessary (see page 83). Return the wine to its cool, dark storage place to ferment and clear, undisturbed, for 3 months.

### THIRD RACKING

> ½ Campden tablet
> ¼ Cup tepid tap water

Use the equipment as listed on page 82. Clean and sterilize the equipment (see page 80).

Crush the ½ Campden tablet in the ¼ cup water, add to the clean jug, then rack the wine quietly, leaving all sediment behind (see page 82). Attach the air lock (see page 79), store 3 months longer, then apply a candle test (see page 83). Should cloudiness persist, replace the stale metabisulphite solution in the air lock with fresh and allow the wine to clear completely.

### BOTTLING

Use the equipment as listed on page 83. Wines should be brilliantly clear and stable before bottling. Once your wine passes the candle test, follow the directions given on page 84.

Age the wine for 9 months, then sample a small bottle. If the wine still tastes a bit raw, age it several months more. Red grape wine generally requires about a year's aging in the bottle, but there are no hard and fast rules. Drink the wine when it suits your taste.

## IMPORTANT NOTE

Federal laws regulating the production of alcoholic beverages in the home are quite liberal. Heads of household may, upon filing duplicate copies of registration form 1541 with the Internal Revenue Service, make up to 200 tax-free gallons of wine per year for household consumption.

Obtain form 1541 simply by writing to the office of the Assistant Regional Commissioner, Alcohol and Tobacco Tax, in the district nearest your home. Winemaking may begin as soon as the forms are filed.

# MAKING
# LIQUEURS OR CORDIALS

These sweetened spirits can easily be prepared at home using only a bottle of vodka, one or two clean empty bottles, and your choice from the profusion of liqueur extracts available from wine suppliers. No aging is required. If you are looking for an experiment that offers instant satisfaction, as opposed to the months of involvement necessary to make wines, try making your own liqueurs.

What you get when you buy an extract is a scientifically blended concentration of the particular liqueur flavor and essential oils. The extracts themselves are inexpensive, and when one is added to an inexpensive bottle of brandy, vodka or other spirits, the end result is cheaper than its commercial counterpart.

Here is an abbreviated list of the flavors available as extracts:

| | |
|---|---|
| Anisette | Maraschino |
| Apricot | Orange |
| Banana | Peach |
| Blackberry | Pear |
| Black Raspberry | Pineapple |
| Chartreuse | Raspberry |
| Cherry Pit | Red Curaçao |
| Cherry Brandy | Sloe Gin |

| | |
|---|---|
| Crème de Cacao | Strega |
| Dry Gin | Tangerine |
| Green Mint | Triple Sec |
| Kirsch | Vanilla |
| Kümmel | White Mint |
| Latte de Vecchia | Yellow Convent |

In making liqueurs, it's always a good idea to follow the supplier's instructions, since bottles of extracts do come in different sizes. These generally call for 12 ounces of granulated sugar, 12 fluid ounces of alcohol (I use vodka or brandy) and one of their flavor extracts which come in ½-ounce bottles.

Dissolve the sugar in 1½ cups of boiling water. When the sugar mixture has cooled, pour it through a funnel into a bottle, add the brandy or vodka plus the flavor extract and shake thoroughly. Delicious!

Some liqueur extract suppliers do require a minimum order, so if you live in an area where there are no wine supply stores, you may find it more convenient (and economical) to make up an order among your friends.

A point to remember is that some extracts may contain a fractional amount of solids. Since your liqueurs will undoubtedly not be used all at once, you may find that a filmy deposit has formed during storage. All you need to do in this case is to siphon the liqueur into another bottle before using.

## Making Your Own Christmas Day Brandied Fruits with Mock Brandy

Here is an inexpensive method to brandy fruits without using brandy, and at the same time to transform rum into an exquisite brandy-like drink. These preserved fruits can be easily prepared at little cost. All you need is a sturdy crock with a lead-free glaze or a wide-mouthed glass jar, a few assorted berries and fruits, a quart of inexpensive rum and 6 months to Christmas.

Begin your preparations around the beginning of July, as spring turns into summer. Almost any whole fresh fruit or berry will do as long as these are ripe and absolutely unblemished. Strawberries, peaches, pears, plums, cherries, blueberries, grapes, raspberries or apricots are ideal. My favorite combination consists of peaches, dark cherries and grapes, but you may prefer a selection of fruits you pick from your own trees, bushes or vines.

The use of cheap rum brings down the cost of making these brandied fruits, but this is not the only reason for using it. Good-quality rum is characteristically smooth and mellow. Inexpensive rum may lack these characteristics, but it does possess the robust flavor essential to this recipe. Whatever the qualities inexpensive rum contributes to the fruit, the fruit returns, transforming the rum just in time for the holidays. Sterilize a crock or jar with metabisulphite sterile solution (see page 80) and pour in a quart of rum, light or dark. Rinse the fruit carefully. Remove all stems but leave the fruits whole. One or two peaches (or apricots), 1 cup of cherries (or strawberries) and 1½ cup of grapes (or blueberries) should be sufficient. Add the fruit to the crock or jar, cover the top loosely with a clean cloth, and store in a cool, dark spot for 6 months. Open the crock on Christmas Day, serve the fruit with the holiday bird and sip the "brandy" after dinner. The best things in life may not be free, but at least they can be inexpensive.

# CIDERMAKING

Refreshing and healthful cider is one of nature's finest drinks. I grew up in apple country (Pennsylvania), downwind of an orchard, and during late August, when the apples were ripening on the trees, I could barely control my longing for the first pressing of cider. We bought directly from the farmer weeks before cider was available on the stands for Halloween celebrations.

There was no need then for us to make our own, and I seldom now have the time, but the fresh taste of true cider is definitely worth the effort if you have an inexpensive source or your own home-grown apples that might otherwise go to waste. Cidermaking does require some special equipment if you want really excellent results, but you will save money in the long run. It might be wise to test out a gallon or two until you determine which combination of apples, apple concentrates, and so on, will give you the most delectable finished product.

Because of the availability of apples in the fall, cider is traditionally considered an autumn drink, but it can be prepared any time of the year if apples are available and inexpensive. True cider is actually fermented apple juice, an apple wine with a very low alcohol content.

This makes for both good news and bad news. The bad news is that cider does not have the keeping qualities of wine; the good news is that it is ready to drink much sooner than its temperamental sister.

## GENERAL DIRECTIONS FOR CIDERMAKING

Cidermaking follows the same basic procedure as winemaking. Apples are first reduced to a pulp by crushing, milling or mincing, and then pressure is applied to the pulp to extract the juices. After the expressed juice has been tested for sugar and acid content (see page 96), a suitable wine yeast is added, and the juice is allowed to ferment through to partial or complete dryness. At suitable intervals the juice is siphoned, or racked (see page 95), into different containers and allowed to clear and stabilize.

Late apples or winter varieties with their high sugar content and superb flavor make the best cider, but several different varieties can also be combined. Blend cooking or baking apples with dessert apples, or use a sweet variety in tandem with those of a tarter, more zesty fruit, until you have worked out the combination most pleasing to your taste. Even the cherubic crab apple makes fine cider when blended with other apples. Cider will tend to be sweet or dry, and will contain a higher or lower degree of acidity and astringency, depending on the type of apples you choose.

Apples for cider should be fully ripe. The more mellow the fruit, the more easily it gives up its juices. If you suspect that some of your picked apples have not yet reached the perfect degree of ripeness, wait a few days before beginning the cidermaking process. Each piece of fruit need not be absolutely perfect, but avoid using any with large bruises or soft spots.

### Puréeing the Fruit

Unless you have mountains of surplus apples and plan to make cider on a grand scale, you can probably get along very well without expensive pressing and crushing equipment. Enough apples for a gallon of juice can be prepared by cutting the fruit into the smallest possible pieces and crushing with a wooden masher. I use a long-handled pestlelike stick with a blunted end (inherited from a Pennsylvania Dutch relative, who also used it to subdue apples when making cider), or I use my food blender. If you own a blender, by all means put it to work to purée the fruit. The important thing to remember is that cider, like wine, is subject to metallic contamination, which produces a cloudiness in your beverage that is next to impossible to eradicate. All utensils used in preparing cider should be of glass, plastic, nylon or wood, and no metal other than stainless steel should ever come in contact with the fruit or the juice.

Juice yields will always vary according to the apple variety and the season of the year, but it's fairly safe to say that 18 to 20 pounds of apples will provide sufficient fresh juice for a gallon of cider. As you crush the apples, they must be protected from exposure to oxygen. Air causes fruit to brown and spoils the flavor of fresh juice almost immediately. Sulphur dioxide in the form of metabisulphites (page 80) and ascorbic acid (vitamin C) should be employed for protective

purposes, since both are effective in preventing undesired oxidation. Crush 1 Campden tablet and 1 100-gram ascorbic acid tablet for each 1 gallon of juice you plan to make. Stir in thoroughly.

Another extremely useful ingredient for cidermaking at this point is pectic enzyme powder (see page 80). Pectic enzymes prevent the cloudiness caused by the natural presence of pectin in all fruits (and thereby help to clarify cider as well as wines), but their chief virtue lies in their ability to make the crushed fruit yield its juices more readily when pressed. Add ½ teaspoon pectic enzyme powder to each 1 gallon of apple pulp. Sprinkle it directly over the fruit, or mix it first with a small amount of water. Either way it should be well stirred in.

### Extracting the Juice

The next important step is to extract from the puréed fruit as much of the juice as is possible. All this takes is a little patience and lots of muscle power. Work with small amounts of fruit for convenience and ease. Place the pulp in a finely meshed nylon bag, or use the foot end of a clean, new nylon stocking. Set the bag in a nylon mesh strainer or plastic funnel wide enough to be suspended over a plastic pail. Begin extraction of the juice by pressing the pulp between your fingers through the nylon. The juice will drip through the strainer and into the container. Finish by twisting and squeezing each bagful of pulp as dry as possible, then turn the stocking inside out, discard the wrung-out pulp, fill the bag again and continue until all of the juice has been extracted. As soon as you have a gallon of juice, cover the pail with a plastic sheet and tie down securely. Allow the juice to stand overnight to permit whatever solids still remain to settle to the bottom. The Campden tablet already added to the crushed fruit will effectively bar harmful bacteria from spoiling the juice.

### Siphoning Cider

Next day, the juice must be siphoned, or racked, off the accumulated sediment into another clean plastic pail to undergo primary fermentation. Racking procedures are described in some detail in the winemaking section (see page 82), but essentially the process consists of using a length of soft ½-inch rubber or plastic tubing to transfer the juice from one container to another. To do this, place one end of the siphon in the container holding the juice. (Take care not to disturb the settled solids at the bottom of the plastic pail; only the clearer juice should be racked into the fresh container.) Hold the other end of the siphon in your mouth and draw in to start the cider flowing. As juice fills the loop of the tubing, pinch it carefully about 6 inches below the free end to briefly halt the flow until you have lowered it into the second container. Unlike winemaking, where wine is splashed off its sediment during the first racking, racking in cidermaking should always be done as gently as possible in order to avoid oxidation. The free end of the siphon should rest on the container bottom while the juice passes smoothly without bubbling from one container to another, or, later on, from gallon jar to bottles.

## Testing Cider for Acid Content

It's usually a good idea to check the acid content of your juice before adding yeast to start the fermentation. Different varieties of apples will contain different amounts of acid, and soil and climate conditions may cause a variation of acidity within the same variety. Juice with a low acid content has little resistance to bacteria and is much more likely to oxidize. Too much acid, on the other hand, will keep fermentation from proceeding normally, and as a consequence the cider will require extra weeks to mature. If you have winemaking equipment I recommend that you make use of your acid titration kit (see Acid Test, page 81) to ensure that your juice will have sufficient acid content to carry it safely through fermentation.

Aim for an acid level of about .55 percent, although a percentage point off in either direction will not make too much difference. To increase the acid content of your juice, add acid blend (see page 82) by teaspoons or half teaspoons, depending upon how many degrees from ideal the acid level of the cider is off. Check for total acids after each addition until you reach the desired level.

If the acid content is too high to begin with, the problem is a bit more difficult. To achieve a pleasant, full-bodied, slightly acid cider, try blending in a reconstituted apple juice concentrate. Or, if you have no concentrate on hand, you may gradually stir in enough water to lower the acidity, and then add sugar syrup to raise the sugar content, a method that produces a beautifully light cider.

## Testing Cider for Sugar Content

Generally speaking, apples used in cidermaking should contain enough natural sugar for fermentation, but if you have any doubts and a saccharometer or hydrometer is handy, make a test for sugar content (see Using the Saccharometer/Hydrometer, page 81). A Specific Gravity of 1.060 (Balling: .15) is a good average. Add more sugar if necessary and test again.

## Adding Tannin to Cider

Tannin is another substance that is naturally present to a greater or lesser degree in apples, depending on the climate, variety and stage of ripeness. Tannin lends astringency and tang to cider as well as to wines. Among its other assets is the ability to assist wine or cider in clearing. There is really no way to test for tannin content in your apples, but you can taste the juice before setting it out to ferment, and add more tannin if the mixture seems lacking in character and tartness. The juice should have the bite of a well-flavored lemonade. About ¼ teaspoon of tannin should be just about right for a gallon of juice. Don't worry if on subsequent tasting your cider seems a bit too astringent. You can always add a bit of dissolved gelatin (see page 97) before bottling to clear the cider and to reduce the tannin content somewhat.

## Yeast Nutrient for Cider

Once your juice has been siphoned into the container where the first or primary fermentation will take place, tested for sugar and acid content and extra tannin has been added if necessary, all that remains is to add yeast nutrient (see page 80) for the yeast, plus the yeast itself.

The yeast nutrient mixed into the juice will supply the yeast with just the proper boost it needs to begin its work of turning your apple juice into clear, tangy cider.

## Yeast for Cider

While it is possible to ferment a cider of sorts using either baker's yeast or no yeast at all, depending solely upon the wild yeasts present in the air and on the fruit, only a true wine yeast or even a champagne yeast must be used to achieve an absolutely clear product. The easiest yeasts to use are the self-starting wine or champagne yeasts that may be sprinkled directly on the juice and stirred in 12 hours later. Within 24 hours a good strong ferment should be under way.

## Clearing or Fining Cider

Should your cider be less than crystal clear after fermentation, it will need to be fined, or cleared. Cloudiness in cider can often be effectively removed by adding ⅛ teaspoon dissolved gelatin, but only if tannin has been stirred in prior to fermentation.

## CIDERMAKING EQUIPMENT

Much of the equipment necessary for making cider can be found right in your own home, or may be purchased inexpensively in your neighborhood hardware store. Those of you who make your own wines should be pleased to discover that you already possess all the utensils you will need.

Cidermaking equipment is relatively simple. From the home or hardware store you'll need:

TWO HEAVY PLASTIC PAILS: One to receive the freshly pressed juice, and one for the first or primary fermentation.

CHEESECLOTH: A large bolt of it, a strong nylon mesh bag or an unused nylon stocking.

MASHING TOOL: One of hard wood, or a blender with a glass or plastic container and a stainless steel blade.

PLASTIC SHEETING: To cover the container of apple juice during the first stage of fermentation. Those that come from the dry cleaners are fine.

LONGHANDLED WOODEN SPOON: For stirring purposes.

SET OF PLASTIC SPOONS: For measuring ingredients.

PLASTIC OR RUBBER TUBING: About 5 feet long but not more than ½ inch in diameter, for siphoning the juice from one container to another.

PLASTIC GRAVY BASTER: If you plan on using a saccharometer or hydrometer for sugar control.

GLASS GALLON JARS: One or two, for the secondary stage of fermentation. Half-gallon jars or smaller bottles, plus suitable closures of plastic or cork, will be needed to receive the finished cider.

In addition, you will need to order or secure from a winemaking supply store;

CAMPDEN TABLETS and ASCORBIC ACID TABLETS: To prevent your crushed fruit and juice from browning.

PECTIC ENZYME POWDER: This assists the crushed fruit in yielding more of its juices.

GRAPE TANNIN: To supply just the right amount of bite to your cider.

ALL-PURPOSE WINE YEAST or CHAMPAGNE YEAST: Preferably the self-starting variety, to produce a strong, healthy ferment.

YEAST NUTRIENT: To nourish the yeast.

AIR LOCKS or FERMENTATION LOCKS: One for each gallon jar used for secondary fermentation. These locks, constructed of glass or plastic tubing inserted in a cork or plastic bung, perform an invaluable service in cidermaking as well as winemaking by allowing carbon dioxide gas to escape, and at the same time effectively prohibiting air and spoilage bacteria from entering. A sterile solution for the air lock can be prepared by dissolving ⅛ of a Campden tablet in 3 ounces of water.

CLOSURES: Such as corks, crown caps or plastic caps, for sealing finished cider.

Optional equipment includes:

SACCHAROMETER OR HYDROMETER, along with a hydrometer jar: For measuring the sugar content of your freshly pressed juice.

ACID TITRATION KIT: For measuring acid content.

CAPPING DEVICE: For applying crown caps.

A word about crushers and presses might be inserted here. You may have stumbled upon a marvelously cheap (and yearly) source of apples. In nearly every rural community there still exists a kindly farmer or two who will gladly rent his cidermaking equipment, or even crush and press your fruit for you. But if you plan to make cider on a grand scale, then sturdy, well-built crushing and pressing equipment will prove an excellent investment. Crushers especially designed for apples are available in both hand-powered and electric models. Electric crushers are cumbersome, however, and hard to move about. When purchasing a press, make sure that yours is rugged enough to handle apple pulp. A specialized cider press will withstand a lot of pressure. A well-preserved genuine antique crusher, if you can find one, will not only do the job but will appreciate in value as time goes on. Whenever possible I buy antique kitchen tools in preference to modern ones. These are generally beautifully designed, sturdy and a joy to look at and to hold.

## CIDER RECIPES

For consistently superior results cider should be made as carefully as wine. If you haven't the patience or if you feel like living dangerously, ignore the following instructions and simply press the juice, add the yeast and hope for the best. However, you will find, if you do take the care this recipe suggests, that the resulting clear, tangy cider is worth the extra effort involved.

### Apple Cider

(YIELD: 1 GALLON; MULTIPLY VARIOUS COMPONENTS BY THE NUMBER OF GALLONS YOU PLAN TO MAKE)

| | |
|---|---|
| 18 to 20 | Pounds fresh, ripe, sound apples |
| 1 | Campden tablet |
| | Additional sugar and water as needed |
| 1 | 100-gram ascorbic acid (vitamin C) tablet |
| ½ | Teaspoon pectic enzyme powder |
| ¾ | Teaspoon acid blend |
| ¼ | Teaspoon grape tannin |
| ¾ | Teaspoon yeast nutrient |
| 1 | Package self-starting all-purpose yeast or champagne yeast |

ACID CONTENT: .55%
SPECIFIC GRAVITY: 1.060
(or *Balling:* 15.0)

Use equipment as listed on pages 79–80. Wash all the equipment with sal soda and sterilize with metabisulphite (see page 80).

Wash the apples, removing any stems, and purée them (see page 95). Take care to protect your fruit from browning by stirring in the crushed Campden tablets, ascorbic acid tablets, pectic enzyme powder and grape tannin as soon as a small amount of the pulp has been prepared.

Extract the juice into a plastic pail (see page 95). Cover the juice in the pail with a piece of plastic sheeting, secured to the top of the container with string or a rubber band, and allow to stand overnight. Next day, use your siphon hose (see page 95) to transfer the juice. Add all the ingredients except the yeast to the racked juice and stir in thoroughly.

If you have at your disposal the equipment necessary for measuring the sugar and acid contents of your juice, this is the time to make these tests (see page 96). Specific Gravity should be 1.060, or 15.0 on the Balling scale. Add sugar if necessary. Titrate for total acids, and raise or lower the acid content as indicated in the general directions.

Stir in yeast nutrient and then sprinkle the yeast over the top of the juice (see page 97).

Re-tie the plastic sheeting securely over the top and allow the yeast to work for 12 hours in a fairly cool place (between 58 and 68 degrees F.). Remove the plastic sheet, stir the yeast thoroughly into the juice, then once more cover the pail tightly with the plastic and leave the juice to ferment for 3 to 5 days. Measure the progress of the fermentation with your sacchar-ometer or hydrometer. A Specific Gravity reading of 1.020, or 5.0 on the Balling scale indicates that the juice is ready to be siphoned into a secondary container. At this point you may allow the juice to undergo a secondary fermenta-tion, or if the juice is clear enough, you may rack directly into bottles. If you do decide to rack the juice again, carefully siphon the juice off any accumulated yeast deposit into a gallon jar, seal with an air lock, and allow the juice to ferment in a cool (60 to 65 degrees F.) spot for 3 to 4 weeks, when you may siphon it once more into another gallon jar and seal with an air lock. Add another ascorbic acid tablet at this point for good measure, to ensure that your cider will not brown. Fine the cider if it has failed to clear by this time (see page 97).

Bottle the cider as soon as it clears. To do this, simply siphon into bottles, avoiding any sediment, seal with appropriate closures and store in a cool place where the temperature will not exceed 50 degrees F. Age for 2 to 3 months before drinking.

## Apple Cider from Concentrates

Commercial concentrates made from pure, freshly pressed apples and vacuum-packed in handy containers are available at most winemaking supply stores. If you would like to make your own cider but have no apple trees, these con-centrates provide a convenient and economical source of apple juice.

You may follow the directions that come with your concentrate, but in general the process is as follows:

Reconstitute the concentrate by adding the amount of water called for. Add metabisulphites, ascorbic acid, pectic enzyme powder, yeast nutri-ent, and tannin if your concentrate recipe calls for it. Test for sugar content and for acid con-tent (see page 96). Adjust for sugar and acids if necessary.

Pour the apple juice into a glass jug, reserving some of the juice. Add a self-starting yeast and allow the juice to ferment. Seal with tightly wrapped plastic. When the first vigorous fer-mentation subsides, add the reserved juice and seal the jug with an air lock.

As soon as *all* fermentation ceases, carefully siphon the cider off the yeast sediment (see page 95) directly into bottles. Seal with appropriate closures and store in a cool (50 degrees F.) place.

# MAKING SOFT DRINKS, MOCK BEERS, TEAS & PUNCHES

Nowadays, not many people make their own soft drinks or brew their own mock beers. In fact, hardly anyone troubles enough to do much more than pick up a six-pack from the grocer's shelf. More's the pity. I remember with complete pleasure the barrel of root beer or birch beer, ginger beer or spruce beer our nearest neighbor always had cooling in the spring house. Her farm was on my way to and from the creek, and I could always count on a glass of one of these nippy drinks as I passed her door after swimming on a broiling summer's day. The floor of the spring house was cold and damp beneath my bare feet, the chill air against my swimming suit made me shiver even on the hottest day and the flavor of the "beer" was beyond description. The old-time customs left a legacy of memories, of thoughts and tastes, smells and feelings that new-time, now-time, easy-does-it customs just cannot provide. What do we offer our children in their place, I wonder?

Homemade soft drinks from commercial extracts are not at all difficult to brew, and they taste better than those from the supermarket. They also cost only a cent or so per ten-ounce bottle.

Mock beers are really wines with a very low alcohol content, so low in fact that most mothers do not prohibit their children from drinking them. These do have a bit of a bite, but that only adds to their refreshing quality.

Tea variations and punches are also not so often prepared as they were in Grandmother's day. The old-fashioned recipes have been lost or set aside. To remedy this oversight I have included several here. Serve these to your family instead of manufactured carbonated drinks. They are sure to remember you and your loving care long after they have forgotten the artificially flavored canned drinks you are serving them now.

NOTE: Any sparkling beverage is somewhat hazardous to handle after it is bottled. Take care to use pressure-proof bottles, to measure carefully and to follow directions precisely. Probably it is safest to stopper with corks so there is a built-in safety valve if pressure builds up in the bottles.

## Ginger Beer

(YIELD: ABOUT 1 GALLON)

1 Gallon water
1 Ounce ginger root, crushed (or candied ginger, finely chopped)
   Zest from 1 lemon, with none of the bitter white underskin
½ Pound granulated sugar
1 Teaspoon grape tannin
   Juice of 1 lemon
1 package self-starting wine yeast

Bring the water to a boil. Meanwhile, place the crushed ginger root (or candied ginger), lemon zest and sugar in a fermentation vessel (see wine-making equipment, page 79). Pour in the boiling water, stir well, and allow to cool slightly. Stir in the grape tannin (see page 80). When the mixture is lukewarm, add the lemon juice and sprinkle in the yeast but do not stir. Cover with plastic and let stand overnight. Next morning stir in the yeast and re-cover with plastic wrap, tied down.

Allow the beer, covered loosely with a plastic sheet, to ferment for 3 days, then rack the beer into a sterile container (see procedure on page 82), leaving behind the sediment. Cover with plastic sheeting and age for 3 weeks, then rack again. Drink the beer any time after it clears.

## Ginger Beer from Extract

*Here's a modern technique for making ginger beer. Note that ingredients must be measured carefully to prevent excess fermentation and exploding bottles.*

(YIELD: 5 GALLONS)

4¾ Gallons plus 1 cup lukewarm water
9 Cups granulated sugar
1 Bottle (2 fluid ounces) ginger beer extract
½ Package dry champagne yeast

Pour the 4¾ gallons lukewarm water into a large fermentation vessel (see Equipment, page 79). Stir in the sugar and mix until thoroughly

dissolved. Add the ginger beer extract. Sprinkle ½ package of champagne yeast (measure carefully!) over the 1 cup lukewarm water. Allow the yeast mixture to stand for 5 minutes, then pour it into the ginger beer mixture through several thicknesses of cheesecloth or a fine strainer. Stir the beer well, then rack into pressure-proof bottles. Top with corks or crown caps. Store the bottles upright in a warm place (68 to 70 degrees F.). Chill before serving.

## Grandmother's Ginger Beer

*This recipe is based on one from a cookbook written in the 1800s.*

(YIELD: 1 GALLON)

4 Quarts water
1 Pound light brown sugar
1½ Ounces "best ground Jamaica" ginger
1½ Ounces tartaric acid
2 Lemons, peeled and sliced
½ Teaspoon self-starting wine yeast

Bring the water to a boil. Place the sugar, ginger, tartaric acid and lemon slices in a large fermentation vessel (see Equipment, page 79). Pour in the boiling water, stir well, and allow the mixture to cool. When lukewarm, sprinkle the yeast on the surface of the "must." Set the beer aside for 12 to 24 hours, then stir in the yeast. Allow the beer to ferment for 2 weeks, when it will be ready for use.

## Root Beer (from Extract)

*Root beer must be fermented and stored in pressure-proof bottles (commercial soft-drink bottles are fine).*

(YIELD: 5 GALLONS)

4 Pounds granulated sugar
3 Ounces root beer extract
4¾ Gallons plus 1 cup lukewarm water
   Scant ½ teaspoon dry active yeast

Place the sugar in a plastic fermenting vessel (see Equipment, page 79). Shake the extract well and pour it over the sugar. Add the water and stir until the sugar is thoroughly dissolved.

Measure the yeast very carefully (take care not to use one bit more than recommended). Sprinkle the yeast over the 1 cup of lukewarm water. Allow to stand for 5 minutes, then stir it carefully. Strain the yeast through cheesecloth into the root beer mixture and stir until the yeast is thoroughly mixed in.

Use a cup and funnel to pour the root beer mixture into pressure-proof bottles. Seal with crown caps, then store the bottles on their sides in a warm, draft-free place until the root beer becomes effervescent (this should take about 5 to 10 days). When the root beer is sparkling, store the bottles where the temperature will be fairly cool and even. Chill before opening and drinking.

If the finished beer is not sweet enough for your taste, stir a teaspoon of brown sugar into every glass before drinking or serving.

### Old-Fashioned Natural Root Beer

*This is an old-time recipe I have just discovered. I haven't tested it yet, but it looks interesting.*

(YIELD: ABOUT 5 GALLIONS)

1½ Pounds burdock roots
½ Cup corn kernels, roasted until well browned
2 Ounces dried sassafras or sassafras roots
2 Ounces hops
About 5 gallons water
2½ Pounds white or brown sugar
1 Package self-starting wine yeast
Yeast nutrient

Burdock is a big-leafed plant that grows abundantly in the country or in vacant city lots, but digging its roots will require a strong back. Dig about 1½ pounds of roots, rinsing them thoroughly so that no dirt remains (discard the leaves). Cut the roots into pieces. Place the pieces in a large pot, together with the corn kernels and sassafras. Add the hops and cover with 3 gallons of water.

Bring the mixture to a boil, cover the pot and allow the mixture to boil for 20 minutes. Strain into a large fermenting vessel, then add enough additional water to make 5 gallons of liquid. Add about ½ pound of either white or brown sugar, or a combination of white or brown sugar, for each gallon of liquid. If this recipe follows others I have tested, starting Specific Gravity of the liquid should be 1.025 (6.5 Balling), which will give you the desired 3 percent alcohol suitable for root beer. For instructions on how to find Specific Gravity or Balling degrees, see Using the Saccharometer/Hydrometer, page 81.

When the temperature of the liquid reaches 70 degrees F., stir in the yeast nutrient and sprinkle the yeast over, but do not stir it in. Cover and let stand overnight.

Stir the yeast in, re-cover the fermenting vessel and allow the mixture to ferment for 2 days before chilling and drinking. The beer will probably not be clear by this time, but it should be sparkling and delicious.

### Orangeade

(YIELD: ENOUGH TO SERVE 8)

6 Cups fresh orange juice
¼ Cup lime juice
¼ Cup granulated sugar
Club soda
8 Orange slices
8 Lime slices

Mix the juices and sugar in a tall pitcher. Divide the mixture into 8 ice-filled glasses, add club soda to the brim and garnish each glass with an orange and a lime slice.

### Lemonade

(YIELD: ENOUGH TO SERVE 8)

10 Cups water
7 Lemons
1½ Cups granulated sugar (or to suit your taste)
Club soda or ginger ale
8 Lemon slices

Bring 4 cups of the water to a boil. Squeeze the lemons and add the juice to the boiling water. Stir in the sugar and boil a minute or two longer. Remove from the heat and add the remaining cups of water. Chill.

To serve, strain the lemon mixture into ice-filled glasses and add soda to the brim. Garnish with lemon slices.

## Lemon-Limeade

(YIELD: ENOUGH TO SERVE 8)

6 Cups water
4 Limes
4 Lemons
1¼ Cups granulated sugar (or to suit your taste)
Lime-flavored soda

Bring 3 cups of water to a boil. Squeeze the lemons and limes and add the juice to the boiling water, then stir in the sugar. Boil for 3 minutes. Remove from the heat and add the remaining water. Chill thoroughly.

To serve, pour over ice in 8 glasses. Fill each to the brim with lime soda.

## Old Fashioned Lemon Syrup

*Try this old-fashioned recipe for lemonade or any drink where lemon flavoring is called for.*

(YIELD: 1½ CUPS)

1 Pound granulated sugar
1 Cup lemon juice

Place the sugar in a jar or bowl, add the lemon juice and stir with a spoon (a silver one is stipulated in the original recipe). Allow the mixture to stand for 24 hours, stirring it frequently during your waking hours. When the sugar is completely dissolved, dip a heavy cotton cloth into hot water, wring very dry, then strain the syrup through into bottles. With its heavy sugar content, this syrup will keep a very long time.

## Wintergreen Tea

(YIELD: ENOUGH TO SERVE 8)

1½ Cups crushed teaberry leaves
12 Cups boiling water
Granulated sugar or honey (optional)

Place the teaberry leaves in a glass or enamel pot and cover with the boiling water. Steep for 3 minutes before pouring into cups. Sweeten to taste if desired.

## Spice and Posy Tea

(YIELD: ENOUGH TO SERVE 8)

1 Cup dried rose petals
1 Cup dried lavender
1 Cup dried elder flowers
1 Cup dried camomile
1 Cup ground sassafras root
1 Teaspoon whole (or ¼ teaspoon ground) allspice
1 Teaspoon whole (or ¼ teaspoon ground) cloves
¼ Teaspoon ground nutmeg

Mix all the ingredients carefully and store in an airtight glass jar. To use, place 2 teaspoonfuls in each cup, add boiling water and stir.

## Spice-Mint Tea

(YIELD: ENOUGH TO SERVE 8)

2 Whole cinnamon sticks
10 Whole cloves
10 Whole allspice, coarsely crushed
12 Cups water
3 Cups mint leaves
Granulated sugar to taste (optional)

Place the cinnamon sticks and spices in a glass or enamel saucepan, cover with the water and bring to a boil. Boil for 2 minutes, then add the mint leaves. Remove the tea from the heat. Allow to steep 1 minute before straining into cups. Sweeten to taste if desired.

## Minted Orange Tea

(YIELD: ENOUGH TO SERVE 8)

 6 Tea bags
1½ Cups mint leaves (packed tight)
 12 Cups boiling water
 3 Cups fresh orange juice
 Granulated sugar
 Mint sprigs for garnish (optional)

Place the tea bags and mint leaves in an unchipped enamel pan. Cover with the boiling water and allow to steep for 5 minutes. Remove the tea bags and add the orange juice and sugar to taste. Chill well.

To serve, fill 8 tall glasses with ice and pour the chilled mixture over each. Garnish with mint sprigs if desired.

## Iced Tea Punch

(YIELD: ENOUGH TO SERVE 8)

12 Lemons
 8 Cups strong tea
 2 Cups granulated sugar
 Rum

Wash the lemons, then carefully peel off the zest, or thin yellow outer skin, of each; take care not to include any of the bitter white underskin. Place the strips of zest in a large pitcher and cover with the hot tea.

Cut and squeeze the lemons. Mix the lemon juice and sugar together. Allow to stand 1 hour, then combine with the tea. Add rum to suit your fancy. Pour over ice in a punch bowl.

# THREE

## MoneySaving

## Recipes

*THE time has unfortunately passed when the country
store with its minimum of staples and maximum
of wholesome, individually produced country specialties was
located "just down the road apiece." Now we have to
fend—and find these items—for ourselves. This book,
hopefully, has provided in the preceding chapters an
interesting and helpful guide for anyone interested in self-
sustenance. If you choose, you can now make your own
mixes, staples, cheeses and sausages, butter and yogurt. You
can fill your freezer to advantage with moneysaving
meats, fish, soup stocks, leftovers and almost anything else
that suits your needs. The remainder of this section provides
recipes for by-passing the supermarket and utilizing these
homemade edibles and other economy foods in the most
interesting and tasty ways possible.*

# LEAN-MEAT & ONE-DISH MEALS

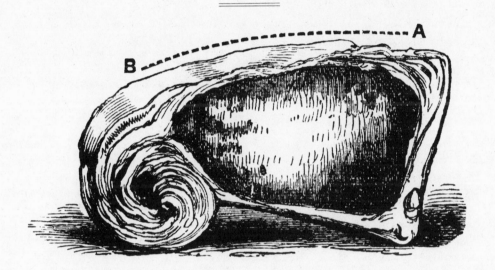

## Corned Beef or Tongue and Cabbage

*Meat is less expensive when you corn it yourself. Wait until there is a special on tongue, brisket, flanken or rump and follow directions below.*

Wipe the beef well and use an ice pick or carving fork to pierce it through and through so that the brine can penetrate it. Stir 2½ cups each rock salt and dark brown sugar into 1 gallon of water. Add 2 teaspoons bicarbonate of soda, 2 teaspoons whole allspice, 1 teaspoon whole peppercorns, and 4 teaspoons sodium nitrate (saltpeter, available in most drugstores).

Place the meat in a large glass or unchipped enamel container. Cover the meat with a weighted board and pour in enough brine to reach at least 1 inch over the top. (It may be necessary to make a second gallon of the brine.) Refrigerate the meat for 1 to 1½ weeks. Use this same method for corning tongue.

(YIELD: ENOUGH TO SERVE 8)

> Corned beef or tongue (see above)
> 1 Teaspoon whole cloves
> 1 Large bay leaf
> 1 Teaspoon peppercorns
> 3 Cloves garlic, peeled and minced
> 8 Turnips, peeled
> 8 Small white onions, peeled
> 2 Small heads cabbage
> 10 to 12 New potatoes in their skins, well washed
> 8 Beets
> 8 Small carrots, scraped
> Mustard with Beer (see page 29)
> Butter

Rinse the corned beef or tongue in cold water, discarding the brine. Place the meat in a large pot of cold water along with the whole cloves, bay leaf, peppercorns and minced garlic. Bring to a boil, then lower the heat and simmer for 3 hours. Add the turnips and onions and cook for 30 minutes longer.

Meanwhile, cut the cabbage into quarters, discarding the cores. In separate pots, cook the potatoes in their skins until tender, and cook and peel the beets.

Add the carrots and cabbage to the meat pot and cook for 20 minutes, or until the carrots are tender. Place the meat on a serving platter and surround with all of the hot vegetables. Serve with beer mustard and a sauceboat of the broth mixed with butter.

## Tongue with Currants and Jelly Sauce

(YIELD: ENOUGH TO SERVE 6)

1 Beef tongue, smoked
4 Cloves garlic, peeled and sliced
1 Teaspoon whole cloves
1 Large bay leaf
1 Teaspoon peppercorns
2 Tablespoons butter
1 Cup Beef Consommé (see page 147)
¼ Cup sherry or Madeira
½ Cup currant jelly
½ Cup currants
1½ Tablespoons cornstarch
½ Cup cold water

Place the tongue in a deep kettle. Add the garlic, whole cloves, bay leaf, peppercorns and water to cover. Bring to a boil and cook at medium heat for 5 minutes, skimming off and discarding any foam that rises to the surface. Reduce the heat, cover and simmer for 3 hours. Remove the tongue from the broth and set aside to cool, then trim and skin.

Heat the butter in a large, heavy skillet. Add the consommé, sherry, jelly and currants. Mix the cornstarch with the cold water, stir into the sauce and cook, stirring constantly, until thick and clear. Cut the meat into thin slices and reheat briefly in the sauce. Serve hot, with a side dish of sauce.

## Flank Steak with Stuffing

(YIELD: ENOUGH TO SERVE 6)

1 2½-Pound flank steak
3 Stalks celery, trimmed and coarsely chopped
2 Medium onions, peeled and finely chopped
3 Tablespoons butter, more if necessary
3 Tablespoons vegetable oil, more if necessary
3 Cups soft bread crumbs
2 Tablespoons minced fresh parsley
1 Teaspoon each salt, sage and thyme
⅓ Cup hot water
1 Egg
2 Cups Basic Beef Stock (see page 145) or canned beef broth

Use a sharp knife to score one side of the steak in ¼-inch-deep diagonal slices against the grain of the meat.

Sauté the celery and onion in the butter and oil until the onion is transparent. Stir in the bread crumbs, parsley, salt, sage, thyme and hot water. Add the egg and mix the stuffing well.

Arrange the stuffing over half the unscored side of the steak. Fold the other half over and sew the ends together, using a needle and strong thread. Add more butter and oil to the skillet if necessary and brown the steak on both sides, turning once. Reduce the heat, add the stock, then cover and cook for 2 hours, turning once. Slice against the grain and serve hot.

## Sauerbraten

(YIELD: ENOUGH TO SERVE 8)

4 Pounds rump or beef chuck
½ Teaspoon salt
¼ Teaspoon black pepper
4 Bay leaves
10 Whole cloves
10 Peppercorns
1½ Cups white vinegar
2 Tablespoons vegetable oil

6 Medium carrots, scraped
6 Medium onions, peeled
3 Tablespoons dark brown sugar
14 Gingersnaps

Rinse the meat, pat it dry, then sprinkle with the salt and pepper. Knead the seasonings in with your knuckles so that as much as possible adheres to the surface of the meat. Place the meat, bay leaves, whole cloves and peppercorns in a deep earthenware, glass or enamel dish. Add the vinegar and enough water to cover. Set the dish, covered, in the refrigerator to marinate for 6 days.

Remove the meat from the marinade, reserving the liquid. Heat the oil in a large kettle. Wipe the meat dry and brown it on all sides. Slice the carrots and onions and add to the kettle, along with 1 tablespoon of the brown sugar and 1 cup of the reserved marinade. Cover and cook over very low heat for 4 hours. Remove the meat from the kettle, set it aside and keep it warm.

There should be about 4 cups liquid remaining in the kettle. If not, bring the amount to 4 cups by adding enough of the reserved marinade. Boil the 4 cups liquid until it is reduced and has begun to thicken. Crush the gingersnaps and stir them in with the 2 remaining tablespoons of sugar. Correct the seasonings, slice the meat and serve topped with the hot gravy and vegetables.

### Beef Shank Pot Roast

*Try this out-of-the-ordinary pot roast next time your supermarket has a special on shanks of beef.*

(YIELD: ENOUGH TO SERVE 8)

4 Meaty center-cut beef shanks, at least ½ pound each and 1 inch thick
Paprika
Sage
Black pepper
4 Tablespoons vegetable oil
2 Large onions, peeled and sliced
1 6-Ounce can tomato paste
3 Large tomatoes, peeled and seeded (optional)

1½ Cups Basic Beef Stock (see page 145) or canned beef broth
All-purpose flour, if necessary
6 Large sweet potatoes
2 Tablespoons butter or margarine
2 Tablespoons minced fresh parsley

Dredge the meat with a liberal sprinkling of paprika to give it a deep red color, then season with sage and pepper. Heat the oil in a heavy skillet and brown the shanks on all sides. Add the onions, tomato paste, tomatoes and stock. Cover and simmer the shanks, stirring occasionally, for 1½ to 2 hours, or until tender. Thicken the gravy with a little flour and water if necessary.

Meanwhile, scrub the sweet potatoes and cook them in their jackets until tender. Cool a bit before peeling.

To serve, cut the meat into pieces and slice the sweet potatoes. Arrange on a serving plate; top with bits of butter and gravy. Garnish with the parsley.

### Stuffed Beef Heart

*Beef heart is not always available, but when it does appear it is usually quite inexpensive, since so few people know how to prepare it. Now that you have a recipe, why not try it and take advantage of the savings?*

(YIELD: ENOUGH TO SERVE 6)

1 3 to 4 pound beef heart (ask the butcher to clean it for you)
Milk to cover
Cornbread Stuffing Mix (see page 6)
½ Teaspoon leaf thyme
Melted butter or margarine
1½ Cups dry bread crumbs
Mustard with Beer (see page 29)

Soak the cleaned heart in the milk overnight, turning it occasionally. Discard the milk.

Prepare the stuffing as directed, using the ½ teaspoon additional thyme. Stuff the heart and sew it together with heavy string, then tie it in cheesecloth and wrap it in aluminum foil. Place in a kettle and cover completely with cold water. Bring to a boil and boil for 10 minutes, skimming off any scum that may form, then cover the kettle and simmer for 2½ hours. Remove the heart from the pot and discard the cooking water. Unwrap the heart and pat it with paper towels to remove surface moisture.

Preheat the oven to 375 degrees F.

Brush the heart with melted butter or margarine, roll it in the bread crumbs and place in a shallow roasting pan. Bake for 30 minutes, basting with butter or margarine after 15 minutes. Slice the heart and serve it hot, with beer mustard.

## Oxtail Ragout

*Oxtail ragout may not sound like the perfect answer to inflation, but it is so rich and delicious, so utterly satisfying, you are sure to add it to your list of inexpensive luxury meals.*

(YIELD: ENOUGH TO SERVE 8)

| | |
|---|---|
| 7 or 8 | Pounds oxtails, cut in pieces |
| | All-purpose flour |
| 4 | Slices bacon, minced |
| 3 | Tablespoons vegetable oil |
| 3 | Cloves garlic, peeled |
| 4 | Large onions, peeled |
| 8 | Small carrots, scraped |
| 3 | Tomatoes, peeled and seeded (or 1 tablespoon tomato paste) |
| 1 | Cup wine (red is best) |
| | Beef Stock (see page 145) or water |
| 2 | Tablespoons minced fresh parsley |
| 1½ | Teaspoons each leaf thyme and freshly ground black pepper |
| ⅛ | Teaspoon ground cloves |
| 1 | Tablespoon salt |
| 8 | Potatoes, well washed |

Rinse the meat, dry well and dredge in flour. Fry the bacon bits until crisp in a large, heavy pot, then remove with a slotted spoon and set aside. Heat the oil with the bacon fat and brown the meat, a few pieces at a time, setting the browned pieces aside on paper towels.

Mince the garlic, chop the onions and slice the carrots. Sauté the vegetables until the onions begin to take on color. Chop the tomatoes and add them to the pot; stir over medium heat for 5 minutes.

Return the meat pieces to the pot containing the vegetables. Add the wine and broth or water to cover and bring to a boil. Boil for 10 minutes, skimming off any froth that rises to the top. Add the parsley, thyme, pepper, cloves and salt. Cover and simmer for several hours, or until the meat is tender. Skim off and discard as much fat as possible, then thicken the ragout with flour and water if necessary.

Meanwhile, boil the potatoes in their skins.

Serve the ragout hot, with the peeled potatoes sprinkled with the reserved bacon bits.

## Marrow Beans with Lamb Neck

(YIELD: ENOUGH TO SERVE 8)

| | |
|---|---|
| 1½ | Pounds dried white marrow beans |
| | Water |
| 1 | Tablespoon salt |
| ⅓ | Cup vegetable oil |
| 2¼ | Pounds lamb neck, cut in small pieces |
| | Salt and pepper |
| 2 | Large onions, peeled |
| 4 | Large tomatoes |
| 6 | Carrots, scraped |
| 3 | Cloves garlic, peeled |
| 1 | Bay leaf |
| ¾ | Teaspoon leaf thyme |
| 1 | Teaspoon dried red pepper |

Wash and pick over the beans. Cover them with water and leave in a cool place to soak overnight. In the morning drain the beans, add fresh water to cover and the 1 tablespoon of salt and cook over low heat, partially covered, for about 2 hours, or until the beans are tender but still a bit crunchy.

Meanwhile, heat the oil in a heavy skillet. Dry the lamb pieces on paper towels and brown on all sides in the hot oil. Remove from the heat and season the meat to taste with salt and pepper, then arrange it in the bottom of a large, heavy casserole. Slice the onions, tomatoes and carrots, and mince the garlic. Return the skillet to the heat and stir in the vegetables, bay leaf, thyme and dried red pepper, scraping with your spoon to mix in any remaining bits of meat and juice. Stir constantly while the mixture simmers briefly, then remove from the heat and set aside.

Preheat the oven to 325 degrees F.

Drain the beans, reserving the liquid. Pour the beans over the lamb pieces and mix gently. Cover with the vegetable-spice mixture, adding enough of the reserved bean liquid if necessary to completely cover the beans. Cover the casserole and bake for 1¼ hours, or until the beans have absorbed most of the liquid.

## Poor Man's Paella

*Here the chopped clams, clam juice and filé powder provide the fish flavor that normally comes from expensive seafood.*

(YIELD: ENOUGH TO SERVE 6 TO 8)

2 2½-Pound chickens, cut in parts
1 Pound kielbasa (or other highly flavored sausage)
3 Large onions, peeled
¼ Cup cooking oil, more if necessary
1¾ Cups uncooked long-grain rice
⅛ Teaspoon each saffron or turmeric, thyme, coarsely ground black pepper and filé powder
1½ Cups (or 1 10¾-ounce can) chicken broth
1 8-Ounce bottle clam juice
1 8-Ounce can chopped clams
1¾ Cups fresh (or 1 10-ounce package frozen) peas
¼ Cup pimiento squares

Rinse the chicken pieces and pat dry. Cut the sausage in ¼-inch-thick slices. Cut the onions into coarse dice.

In a large, heavy Dutch oven or skillet sauté the chicken pieces in the hot oil until lightly browned on all sides. Remove and set aside.

Fry the sausage slices and onion in the oil in the pan until the onion is transparent. Set aside with the chicken. Add the uncooked rice to the pan and stir over medium heat for 5 minutes (add more oil if necessary to coat the rice). Stir in the spices.

Return the chicken and sausage to the pot.

Add the chicken broth, clam juice and chopped clams (take care to spoon the clams and juice carefully into the pot so as not to disturb any sand that may be on the bottom of the can). Add enough water to just cover the ingredients in the pot. Cover and bring to just under a boil. Lower the heat and simmer, covered, for 15 minutes. Stir in the peas and pimiento, cover and simmer 15 to 20 minutes longer, or until the rice tests done. Serve hot.

## Goulash

*Rump, chuck, stew meat, veal or pork will serve in this most popular and economical dish. A very special way to utilize supermarket specials.*

(YIELD: ENOUGH TO SERVE 8)

3 Pounds rump, chuck, veal or pork, cut into 1½-inch cubes
5 Tablespoons vegetable oil (not olive oil)
7 Large onions, peeled and sliced
4 Cloves garlic, peeled and minced
3 Tablespoons Hungarian sweet paprika
3 Tablespoons vinegar
2 Teaspoons leaf thyme
1 Tablespoon tomato paste
¾ Teaspoon each salt and freshly ground black pepper
3 Tablespoons all-purpose flour
3 Cups beef broth, more if necessary
1 Lemon
2 Teaspoons caraway seeds
¼ Cup minced fresh parsley
  Hot, cooked noodles or dumplings
  Cold sour cream

Lightly brown the meat in the oil in a heavy pot. Add the onions and garlic and sauté until golden. Stir in the paprika, vinegar, thyme, tomato paste, salt, pepper and flour and cook, stirring, for 3 minutes. Add the broth and stir constantly until the gravy is smooth, then cover the pot and simmer for 2 hours, or until the meat is tender. Add a little broth or water if necessary as the meat cooks.

Grate the zest (the thin, yellow outer skin with none of the bitter white underskin included) from the lemon. Whirl the caraway seeds in your blender.

Transfer the goulash into a serving dish. Sprinkle the top with the lemon zest, caraway seeds and minced parsley. Serve with noodles or dumplings and a sauceboat of cold sour cream.

## Hungarian Chicken

(YIELD: ENOUGH TO SERVE 6)

2 Tablespoons butter
¼ Cup vegetable oil
1½ Tablespoons Hungarian sweet paprika
2 Frying chickens, cut into quarters
3 Large onions, finely chopped
6 Tablespoons tomato paste
1 Teaspoon granulated sugar
½ Cup chicken broth or water
   Salt
2 Cups sour cream
3 Tablespoons all-purpose flour
   Hot, cooked noodles

Heat the butter and oil together in a large skillet. Stir in the paprika and continue to cook, stirring constantly, until well blended. Add the chicken pieces and sauté until golden brown, turning frequently.

Add the onions to the skillet and cook until translucent. Mix the tomato paste with the broth and sugar and stir into the skillet, then season to taste with salt, cover and simmer over low heat until the chicken is tender. Transfer the chicken to a serving platter and keep warm in the oven. Combine the sour cream and flour and stir the mixture into the sauce. Cook, stirring constantly, only long enough to heat through. Pour the sauce over the chicken and serve at once over hot noodles.

## Meatball and Sauerkraut Goulash

(YIELD: ENOUGH TO SERVE 6)

1½ Pounds ground beef
1½ Pounds ground pork

½ Teaspoon sage
¼ Teaspoon each salt, freshly ground black pepper and caraway seeds
1 Cup soft bread crumbs
¼ Cup milk
1 16-ounce can sauerkraut
¼ Cup vegetable oil
4 Medium onions, chopped
2 Green peppers, seeded and chopped
1 Tablespoon Hungarian sweet paprika
4 Fresh tomatoes, peeled, seeded and chopped (or 2 cups canned tomatoes)
½ Cup Basic Beef Stock (see page 145) or water
1 Bay leaf
1 Cup sour cream
   Hot, cooked noodles

Combine the ground meats and spices. Soak the bread crumbs in milk. Drain ½ cup of the sauerkraut well and mince it with a sharp knife. Squeeze the bread crumbs dry and discard the milk. Stir the minced sauerkraut and bread crumbs quickly into the meat mixture and shape into meatballs; do not overwork the meat. Sauté the meatballs in the oil until brown on all sides. Add the onions, peppers and paprika and continue to cook until the vegetables wilt.

Drain the remaining sauerkraut, rinse under running water, then drain again and add to the meatballs and vegetables, along with the tomatoes, stock and bay leaf.

Cover and simmer the goulash over low heat for 40 minutes. Adjust seasonings to taste. Stir in the sour cream and serve immediately over hot noodles.

## Meatballs and Spaghetti

(YIELD: ENOUGH TO SERVE 6)

1 Cup crushed stale bread (or Herb Stuffing Mix, see page 5)
¼ Cup milk
2½ Pounds ground beef
3 Tablespoons catsup
2 Tablespoons prepared mustard
⅛ Teaspoon each thyme and sage

3 Tablespoons cooking oil
5 Cups tomato sauce (or 2 10¾-ounce cans tomato soup)
1 Cup water
¼ Teaspoon fennel seeds
⅛ Teaspoon each powdered cloves and oregano
1 Tablespoon granulated sugar
¼ Cup red wine (optional)
1 16-Ounce package spaghetti
Freshly grated Parmesan cheese (optional)

Soak the bread crumbs in the milk for 5 minutes. Pour off any excess milk.

Mix the meat, moistened bread, catsup, mustard, thyme and sage lightly with your fingers only until the ingredients are well incorporated. Shape into meatballs and fry in the hot oil until brown on all sides.

Add the tomato sauce, water, fennel, cloves, oregano, sugar and wine and bring to a boil. Lower the heat and simmer, covered, for 30 minutes, stirring occasionally.

Meanwhile, cook the spaghetti according to package directions. Serve the meatballs and sauce over the hot spaghetti, with a side dish of grated Parmesan cheese, if desired.

## Salisbury Steak

(YIELD: ENOUGH TO SERVE 6)

2 Pounds lean ground beef
1 Small onion, peeled and minced
1½ Tablespoons minced green pepper
1 Tablespoon minced fresh parsley
⅛ Teaspoon thyme
Salt and pepper
Paprika
All-purpose flour
Vegetable oil
4 Tablespoons butter
½ Cup catsup
1½ Tablespoons lemon juice
1½ Teaspoons each Worcestershire sauce and prepared mustard
Dash Tabasco
3 Tablespoons sherry

Combine the ground beef with the onion, green pepper and parsley. Add the thyme and salt and pepper to taste. Mix well and shape into 6 large patties about 1 inch thick. Sprinkle both sides of the patties with paprika mixed with a little flour and brush lightly with oil. Arrange on the broiler rack about 4 inches from the heat and broil to the desired degree of doneness, turning once.

Meanwhile, heat the butter, catsup, lemon juice, Worcestershire, mustard, and Tabasco over a low flame. Stir well to blend all the ingredients. Season to taste with salt and pepper, mix in the sherry, and bring to just under a boil. Serve the patties hot, topped with a spoonful of the sauce.

## Hamburger Steak with Sautéed Potatoes

*When is hamburger not really hamburger? When it's shaped like a steak, striped with mustard and catsup, and baked with sautéed potatoes.*

(YIELD: ENOUGH TO SERVE 8)

3 Slices white bread, crumbled
⅓ Cup milk
2½ Pounds ground beef
8 Tablespoons catsup
4 Tablespoons prepared mustard
¾ Teaspoon each oregano and tarragon
1 Teaspoon garlic salt
2 Large onions, peeled
¼ Cup grated Parmesan, Swiss or Cheddar cheese
3 Tablespoons vegetable oil
8 Large potatoes, peeled

Soak the bread in the milk and squeeze dry, discarding the milk. In a large bowl, mix the milk-soaked bread, ground beef, 5 tablespoons of the catsup, 2 tablespoons of the mustard, the oregano, tarragon and garlic salt.

Divide the mixture into equal parts. Pat each half into a round shape about ¾ inch thick. Grate one of the onions and spread it in the center of one half of the meat. Sprinkle the cheese over the onion. Place the second half of the meat on the first half, pinching the edges to seal the cheese and onion inside.

Preheat the oven to 325 degrees F.

Heat the oil in a fairly large roasting pan. Slice the potatoes and remaining onion and sauté them to a very light brown in the roasting pan. Push these partially cooked vegetable slices toward the outside of the pan to make room for the hamburger steak and slide the meat into the pan without breaking it. Decorate the hamburger steak with alternate stripes of the remaining catsup and mustard. Bake for 40 minutes.

Raise the oven temperature to 375 degrees F. Turn the potato slices with a spatula and continue baking for 20 minutes more, or until the meat is well done.

## Deep-Fried Pies with Savory Fillings

*These savory meat pies are the perfect vehicle for using bits of leftover meat.*

(YIELD: ENOUGH TO SERVE 6)

Prepare a double recipe Instant Pie Crust (see page 48); mix as directed. Roll out to medium thickness and cut into 6-inch squares. Place 2 to 3 tablespoons of any filling listed below on one side of each square. Wet the inside edges of the squares with a bit of water. Fold over to make a triangular pie, and press the edges together with thumb and forefinger or make a decorative edge with the prongs of a fork. Fry in hot oil until golden brown on both sides, turning once. Drain briefly on paper towels and serve piping hot.

### Ham and Cheese Filling

2 Cups minced leftover cooked ham
1 Cup grated Cheddar cheese
1 Medium tomato, coarsely chopped
¼ Teaspoon thyme

Combine all ingredients and mix well.

### Sausage and Mushroom Filling

2 Cups cooked and crumbled homemade sausage meat (see pages 75–77)
⅛ Teaspoon sage
½ Pound mushrooms, thinly sliced
1½ Tablespoons butter or oil

½ Cup Basic White Sauce (see page 171), at room temperature

Prepare the sausage according to directions, then set the meat aside with a slotted spoon. Stir the sage and mushrooms into the pan drippings. Add 1½ tablespoons of butter or oil if necessary and sauté until the mushrooms are tender. Drain well and bind with the white sauce.

### Lamb Curry Filling

2 Tablespoons butter
1 Medium onion, coarsely chopped
1 Medium apple, peeled, cored and coarsely chopped
2½ Cups minced, cooked lamb
1 Teaspoon curry powder
1 Tablespoon all-purpose flour
½ Cup milk
2 Teaspoons currants

Heat the butter in a large skillet and lightly sauté the onion for 2 to 3 minutes. Add the apple and lamb, sprinkle with curry powder, then sauté together for 5 minutes, stirring occasionally. Blend in the flour. Add the milk and continue to cook, stirring constantly, until the sauce is thick and smooth. Stir in the currants.

### Bacon and Egg Filling

6 Strips bacon
1 Medium onion, coarsely chopped
6 Hard-cooked eggs, peeled and coarsely chopped
½ Teaspoon prepared mustard
2 Tablespoons milk

Fry the bacon until crisp, then remove and drain on paper towels. Lightly sauté the onion in the bacon drippings. Crumble the bacon and return to the skillet, along with the chopped eggs. Stir in the mustard and milk.

## Sausages with Red and Green Peppers

*Serve this colorful Italian dish with polenta
for a really filling economy meal.
Remember, though, polenta takes about 2 hours
to cook, so plan ahead.*

(YIELD: ENOUGH TO SERVE 6)

3 Pounds homemade (or other)
  sausages (see pages 75–77)
5 Tablespoons olive oil
3 Medium sweet green peppers, cut
  into ½-inch strips
3 Medium sweet red peppers, cut
  into ½-inch strips
3 Large onions, peeled and sliced
2 Cloves garlic, peeled and minced
1 Teaspoon oregano
  Salt and coarsely ground fresh
  pepper
1 Tablespoon wine vinegar
  Polenta (see page 117)

Cover the sausages with water and cook at a low
boil for 5 minutes, turning occasionally. Drain
the sausages and brown evenly over low heat in
2 tablespoons of the oil. Turn frequently to
brown evenly.

Heat the remaining oil in another large skillet
and sauté the peppers, onions and garlic until
the peppers are barely tender. Season with the
oregano and salt and pepper to taste. Just before
serving, sprinkle the peppers with the vinegar
and stir in the sausages. Serve hot over the
polenta.

## Old-Fashioned Boiled Dinner

*Here's a robust family meal that is lovely to look
at, has good old-fashioned flavor and cooks all
in one pot! Fresh vegetables and homemade
sausage combine for stick-to-the-ribs goodness.*

(YIELD: ENOUGH TO SERVE 8)

2½ Pounds kielbasa sausage
 2 Pounds new potatoes, washed
   Salt
12 Carrots, scraped

1 Pound fresh asparagus, trimmed
  Pepper

Place the sausage and new potatoes in a large
dutch oven with salted water to cover. Cover and
bring to a boil; reduce the heat to a simmer.
Simmer 20 minutes, or until the potatoes are
almost done.

Add the carrots and cook, covered, for 10
minutes. Add the asparagus and cook, covered,
another 5 minutes. Drain.

Arrange the sausage links in circles on a large
platter and fill the center with potatoes. Arrange
the carrots and asparagus in spoke fashion
around the sausage and serve immediately.

## Sausage and Garden Vegetable Dinner

(YIELD: ENOUGH TO SERVE 8)

3 Pounds homemade sausage—
  Italian-style is best (see page 75)
  About 3 tablespoons olive oil
1 Large onion, peeled and sliced
2 Sweet green peppers, seeded
2 Sweet red peppers, seeded
2 or 3 Small white turnips, peeled
  and sliced
2 Medium (or 3 to 4 small) zucchini
  Salt and pepper
⅓ Cup water or beef broth

Pierce the sausage all over with a large needle.
Fry on all sides in the oil in a skillet over
medium heat until almost thoroughly cooked
(about 15 minutes). Remove and keep warm. In
the same skillet, lightly fry the sliced onion,
peppers and turnips. Cover and cook 8 to 10
minutes, stirring occasionally to prevent sticking.

Wash the zucchini and cut into ½-inch-thick
strips. Add the zucchini to the pan and season
with salt and pepper to taste. Cook, stirring,
another minute or two. Arrange the sausage with
the vegetables in the pan. Add the water, cover
and cook for 15 minutes. Serve hot.

### Sausage with Savoy Cabbage in Brown Sauce

(YIELD: ENOUGH TO SERVE 8)

2 Rather small heads savoy cabbage
3 Cups water
  Salt
2 Tablespoons butter
2 Small onions, finely chopped
3 Tablespoons all-purpose flour
  Pepper
  Vinegar
16 Lengths sausage

Remove the tough outer leaves from the cabbage, then quarter and remove the center stalk. Trim any tough ribs.

Bring 3 cups of water to a boil in a large pot. Add salt to taste and the cabbage. Cover and simmer about 8 to 10 minutes, or until tender. Drain the cabbage well, reserving the stock. Chop the cabbage and drain again.

Heat the butter in a 1½-quart saucepan. When hot and bubbling, add the onion; sauté until golden brown. Stir in the flour and continue to sauté over low heat until the flour turns brown (be careful not to burn the onion or blacken the flour). Slowly add 2 cups of the reserved cabbage liquid, beating smooth with a wire whip or wooden spoon. Season with salt, pepper and a dash of vinegar to taste. Cook until thickened and smooth (about 3 minutes), stirring constantly. Add the chopped cabbage, cover and simmer about 5 minutes.

Fry the sausage (see page 74) and serve hot on a platter with the cabbage.

### Jamaican Red Peas and Rice

*This is usually served along with meat and fried bananas, but in this case the meat, beans and rice are cooked together to save you work.*

(YIELD: ENOUGH TO SERVE 8)

1½ Pounds dried red or pink beans
1½ Tablespoons salt
4 Medium onions, peeled
3 Cloves garlic, peeled

3 Tablespoons olive oil
1½ Pounds lean beef, either stew meat, spareribs or even chopped chuck
2½ Tablespoons chili powder
1½ Tablespoons ground cumin
2 Teaspoons leaf thyme
½ Teaspoon nutmeg
1 Teaspoon dried red pepper (optional)
5 Cups Basic Beef Stock (see page 145) or canned beef broth
8 Cups cooked rice

Wash and pick over the beans. Soak them overnight in water to cover, then drain and place in a large pot. Add fresh water to cover, mix in 1½ tablespoons salt, and bring to a boil. Simmer the beans, partially covered, for about 2 hours, checking occasionally to make sure that the liquid covers them at all times. Add more water during the cooking if necessary.

Chop the onions and mince the garlic. Heat the oil in a heavy saucepan and sauté the onions, garlic and beef for 10 minutes. Stir in the chili powder, cumin, thyme, nutmeg and red pepper. Cook for a few minutes more, then add the stock. As soon as the mixture returns to simmering, remove from the heat and set aside.

When the beans are tender but not mushy, pour them and their liquid into a large casserole. Gently stir in the meat mixture, taking care not to mash the beans too much as you mix. Before covering the casserole, check to make sure that the level of the bean liquid is at least ½ inch above the beans. If not, adjust the level with boiling water.

Cover the beans and set them on the middle rack of an oven preheated to 325 degrees F. Bake for 2 hours, or until the beans are very tender. Stir the cooked rice carefully into the beans and return to the oven for 5 minutes. Serve hot.

### Spanish Casserole with Rice

(YIELD: ENOUGH TO SERVE 6)

⅔ Cup uncooked rice
2 Tablespoons butter
1 Medium onion, peeled and chopped

2 to 3 Cups leftover chopped meat
¾ Teaspoon salt
¼ Teaspoon paprika
2 Stalks celery, trimmed and chopped
½ Green pepper, chopped
1 10¾-Ounce can tomato soup

Prepare the rice according to package directions. Meanwhile, heat the butter and sauté the onion until golden brown. Remove from the heat and stir in the meat, salt and paprika.

Preheat the oven to 350 degrees F.

Arrange one-third of the rice in the bottom of a greased deep casserole. Arrange half of the meat mixture over the rice and top with half of the chopped celery and green pepper. Build successive layers with another third of the rice, the remaining meat mixture and the rest of the celery and pepper. Top with the remaining rice. Pour the tomato soup over the casserole and bake, covered, for 30 minutes.

## Rice Ring

(YIELD: ENOUGH TO SERVE 6)

1 Cup uncooked rice
3 Tablespoons melted butter
⅛ Teaspoon nutmeg
1 Tablespoon minced fresh parsley
  (or 1 teaspoon parsley flakes)

Cook the rice according to package directions. Stir the butter, nutmeg and parsley flakes into the hot, cooked rice, then firmly pack the hot mixture into a well-greased Teflon ring mold. Set the mold in a pan of hot water and bake in an oven preheated to 350 degrees F. for 10 to 15 minutes.

Let stand for about 5 minutes after removing from the oven, then loosen and invert onto a serving platter. Fill center with any one of the combinations listed below.

### Fillings

Cooked fish with Mushroom Sauce (see page 172)
Cooked turkey with Hard-Cooked Egg Sauce with Capers (see page 172)
Cooked lamb with Curry Sauce (see page 172)

Cooked ham with Mixed Vegetable Sauce (see page 172)
Cooked chicken with À la King Sauce (see page 172)
Tuna with Mushroom Sauce (see page 172)
Shellfish with Newburg Sauce (see page 172)
Chipped beef creamed with Hard-Cooked Egg Sauce (see page 172)

## Cheese Rice Ring

(YIELD: ENOUGH TO SERVE 6)

½ Cup rice
¼ Cup milk
⅓ Cup grated Cheddar cheese
2 Tablespoons minced fresh parsley
2 Tablespoons melted butter
2 Tablespoons grated onion
¼ Teaspoon salt
1 Egg, beaten

Cook the rice according to package directions. Remove from the heat and stir in the milk, grated Cheddar cheese, parsley, melted butter, grated onion, salt and beaten egg.

Pack the mixture firmly into a well-greased Teflon ring mold. Set the mold in a pan of hot water and bake for 45 minutes in an oven preheated to 350 degrees F. After removing from the oven, loosen and invert on a serving platter. Fill the center with any of the combinations mentioned in the recipe for Rice Ring (see above), or with peas or mixed vegetables.

## Polenta

*Polenta provides an inexpensive, nutritious substitute for potatoes, rice or noodles.*

(YIELD: ENOUGH TO SERVE 6)

6 Cups water
2 Teaspoons salt
1½ Cups cornmeal

Bring the water and salt to a hard boil in the top of a double boiler. Gradually add the cornmeal, a little at a time, stirring constantly until all the cornmeal is incorporated. Cook only long enough to thicken the mixture slightly, then place over boiling water and allow to simmer for 1 to 1½ hours. Spoon the mixture into a flat rectangular dish and let stand until firm. Cut into squares and serve warm or at room temperature.

### Cheese Polenta

Prepare the polenta as directed (see above). Stir 3 tablespoons butter and 6 tablespoons grated Parmesan cheese into the mixture just before spooning into a flat dish. If desired, sprinkle with additional cheese just before serving and warm in the oven or under the broiler.

### Polenta with Sausages and Peppers

Prepare the polenta as directed (see above). Fry 1 pound thinly sliced homemade sausages, 1 cup green peppers cut in ½-inch dice and 1 clove minced garlic in 2 tablespoons olive oil until the sausage pieces are browned on both sides. Arrange the sausage and pepper mixture in the bottom of rectangular baking dish, spoon the polenta on top and dot with butter. Sprinkle with grated Parmesan cheese and bake in an oven preheated to 375 degrees for about 15 minutes, or until the top of the polenta is golden brown.

### Fried Polenta

To serve leftover polenta, cut into thin slices, dip in beaten egg and sauté in 2 tablespoons butter until golden brown on both sides, turning once. Serve as a substitute for rice or potatoes.

### Meatless Stuffed Green Peppers

(YIELD: ENOUGH TO SERVE 6)

6 Large green peppers
6 Stalks celery
3 Large onions, peeled
3 Tablespoons bacon drippings, butter or cooking oil
4 Cups crushed stale bread (or stuffing mix, see pages 5–6)
3 Tablespoons soy sauce
½ Cup catsup
1 Large egg, lightly beaten
1 Cup tomato sauce

Prepare the peppers by cutting the stem tops into lids. Remove the seeds and white pith from the peppers, then wash tops and bottoms and pat dry. Cut the celery and onions into ¼-inch diagonal slices and sauté in the oil until the onion is transparent. Add the stale bread, soy sauce, catsup and egg and stir until well mixed.

Stuff the peppers, set the lids on top, and place upright in a shallow ovenproof dish. Pour 1 cup water around the base of the peppers and cover with aluminum foil so steam does not escape.

Bake in an oven preheated to 350 degrees F. for 45 minutes, then remove the aluminum foil and baste the tops and sides of the peppers with tomato sauce. Raise the heat to 375 degrees F. and bake for 20 minutes more. Serve immediately.

### Cabbage au Gratin

(YIELD: ENOUGH TO SERVE 6)

1 Large head cabbage
5 Cups Basic Beef Stock (see page 145) or canned beef broth
3 Cloves garlic, peeled and crushed
1 Bay leaf
  Pinch of ground cloves
1 Cup Basic White Sauce (see page 171) or Curry Sauce (see page 172)
1 Cup leftover minced meat
⅓ Cup grated Parmesan cheese
¼ Cup fine bread crumbs

Remove the limp outer leaves and cut the cabbage into quarters. Remove the hard core, then shred the vegetable and place in a large saucepan. Add the stock, garlic, bay leaf and cloves; cover and cook over medium heat until tender.

Drain the cabbage and return to the saucepan. Stir in the white sauce (or curry sauce) and meat. Turn the cabbage mixture into a large, buttered ovenproof casserole. Top with the grated cheese and bread crumbs and bake in an oven preheated to 350 degrees F. for 20 minutes, or until the top is nicely browned. Serve hot.

# ECONOMY MEALS
# FROM THE ORIENT

### Stir-Fried Beef

*The best way I can think of to eat rich and pay poor is by cooking Chinese meals. Variations on these two recipes should keep you busy more than a month of Sundays.*

(YIELD: ENOUGH TO SERVE 8)

1 Pound flank steak or other lean beef, partially frozen
2 Tablespoons sherry
2 Tablespoons cornstarch
2 Tablespoons soy sauce
1 Teaspoon granulated sugar
2 Pounds vegetables (see Vegetable Combinations for Stir-Fried Beef, below)
3 Slices fresh ginger root
1/3 Cup vegetable oil
1 Teaspoon salt
1 Cup Basic Beef Stock (see page 145) or canned beef broth
3 to 4 Cups hot, fluffy rice

Using a very sharp knife, slice the beef very thinly *across* the grain while it is still partially frozen.

Place the sherry, cornstarch, soy sauce and sugar in a bowl and stir to blend thoroughly. Add the meat and toss lightly to coat all surfaces. Allow to stand for 15 minutes, stirring occasionally.

Meanwhile, prepare your vegetables by cutting them into even-sized pieces. Slice the ginger root, following the pattern of the vertically running fibers. Mince the ginger slices.

Heat a large skillet over medium heat until hot enough for a drop of water to sizzle over the surface. Add half the oil, then add the beef and stir-fry for a minute or two; the meat should be cooked only long enough for it to lose its red color. Remove the meat from the pan and add the remaining oil, the salt and the minced ginger root. Stir-fry a few seconds, then add the vegetables and continue to stir-fry. Allow the vegetables to heat a bit and become coated with the oil, then stir in the stock. Cover and cook over medium heat until the vegetables are nearly done. Return the beef to the skillet and stir-fry for 1 minute. Serve immediately over the hot, fluffy rice.

### Vegetable Combinations for Stir-Fried Beef

The vegetables that accompany stir-fried beef should always arrive at the table crisp, crunchy and at the height of their color and flavor. The secret lies in proper preparation and cooking technique.

Begin by slicing or shredding your vegetables into nearly equal shape and thickness. Soft vegetables may be sliced vertically, while harder ones like broccoli, carrots, cauliflower and green beans should be cut on the diagonal. All vegetables will retain their original freshness if you cut them just before cooking.

Some vegetables, particularly the harder ones, benefit from a brief parboiling or blanching, which shortens the time needed for stir-frying. To parboil, cook green vegetables in boiling water until they turn bright green, nongreen vegetables until they are slightly soft yet still crisp. To blanch vegetables, cover them quickly with boiling water, drain immediately, then rinse with cold running water. Take care that all vegetables are perfectly dry before adding them to the oil in the skillet.

Vegetables should be added to the stir-fry pan after the meat has been stir-fried and removed, since vegetables usually need less heat and more cooking time. Coarse vegetables, unless parboiled or blanched beforehand, require more cooking than their tender relatives, so add them first. Slide your vegetables by handfuls into the hot oil, stirring as you go and coating each piece with oil. Stir-frying action should be quick but gentle; take care not to crush the vegetables or crowd them together. Add the stock, then cover and cook until the vegetables take on a bright color or are heated through. Overcooking will make them soggy and limp.

Use your imagination and make up your own combinations, using any of the following vegetables. They all taste good when stir-fried and provide the basis for interesting contrasts in color and texture.

ASPARAGUS: Cut the stalks diagonally into 1- to 1½-inch pieces. Parboil thick stalks; blanch tender ones but avoid blanching the tips.

BROCCOLI: Separate into small florets, trim, then slice diagonally into 1-inch lengths. Cut thicker stalks in half before slicing. Parboil.

CABBAGE: Shred or cut tender leaves in ¼-inch strips, slice thicker parts into wedges or chunks and parboil.

CARROTS: Scrape and slice diagonally. Parboil.

CAULIFLOWER: Separate into florets. Cut thick stems diagonally. Parboil.

CELERY: Trim leaves and ends, cut diagonally in 1-inch lengths. Blanch.

GREEN BEANS: Trim and cut in 1-inch lengths. Parboil.

LETTUCE: Separate and tear well-washed (and dried) leaves into bite-sized pieces.

MUSHROOMS: If you feel like treating your family, these are a wonderful addition to Chinese food. Wipe with a damp cloth, then trim the tough stem ends. Leave small mushrooms whole, slice large ones vertically.

ONIONS: Peel and slice very thin.

PEAS: Shell and blanch.

PEPPERS: Seed, then cut in strips or 1-inch squares.

POTATOES: Peel and dice. Parboil.

SNOW PEAS: These are usually available frozen. To use, thaw first and separate. Dry thoroughly on paper towels.

SPINACH: Wash thoroughly and shake dry. Trim tough stems, then tear or leave whole.

SUMMER SQUASH OR ZUCCHINI: Peel and cut in ¼-inch slices.

If Chinese groceries are available in your area, pick up one or two exotic ingredients to make your Chinese meals even more interesting.

TREE EARS: A favorite of mine because they have an interesting, chewy texture, expand when presoaked in warm water and last indefinitely on your pantry shelf.

GINKO NUTS: These come in cans and look and taste like little hard-cooked egg yolks. They are quite decorative, and I am sure they are extremely nutritious as well.

CHINESE CABBAGE: Much more subtle and delicious than our American garden variety. To my mind it is worth the few extra pennies it may cost.

### Stir-Fried Curried Beef

(YIELD: ENOUGH TO SERVE 8)

1 Pound lean beef (flank steak is best), partially frozen
2 Teaspoons granulated sugar
2 Tablespoons each cornstarch and curry powder
¼ Cup sherry
3 Medium onions, peeled
3 Slices fresh ginger root
¼ Cup vegetable oil
1 Cup Basic Beef Stock (see page 145) or canned beef broth
3 to 4 Cups hot, fluffy rice

Trim off all fat and gristle, then cut the beef into paper-thin slices, slicing *against* the grain. If your slices turn out slightly thicker than anticipated, pound them with the flat side of your knife (this also helps to tenderize a not-so-tender cut of meat). Work the sugar, cornstarch, curry powder and sherry into the meat and marinate for ½ hour.

Slice the onions as thinly as possible. Mince the ginger root slices.

Heat a large, heavy skillet, dutch oven or wok until a droplet of water splashed onto it skates across the surface, then add the oil. As soon as it heats, add the onion slices and stir-fry until soft but not brown. Stir in the ginger root and continue to stir for 2 minutes. Add the beef and stir-fry only long enough for all of the slices to lose their red color (about 1 or 2 minutes). Stir in the stock. Bring the ingredients to a low boil, then cover and cook for 2 minutes more. Serve immediately over the hot, fluffy rice.

### Piquant Beef Slices with Vegetables

(YIELD: ENOUGH TO SERVE 6)

1½ Pounds flank steak
4 Tablespoons vegetable oil

5 Medium green peppers, cut into 1-inch strips
4 Medium onions, peeled and thinly sliced
4 Medium tomatoes, thinly sliced
2 Cloves garlic, peeled and crushed
2¼ Cups Basic Beef Stock (see page 145) or canned beef broth
¼ Cup each cider vinegar and soy sauce
¼ Cup granulated sugar
¾ Teaspoon ground ginger
2 Tablespoons cornstarch
⅓ Cup water
3 to 4 Cups hot, cooked rice

Cutting against the grain, slice the flank steak ¼ inch thick (partial freezing beforehand makes slicing easier). Heat 3 tablespoons of the oil in a large skillet and stir-fry the vegetables for 5 minutes, then remove vegetables from the pan and set aside. Add the remaining 1 tablespoon oil, the crushed garlic and the meat and stir-fry until the slices are brown on the outside but still slightly pink on the inside; take care not to overcook! Remove the meat from the skillet and set aside.

Return the vegetables to the pan, add the stock, vinegar, soy sauce, sugar and ginger and bring to a boil over high heat. Mix the cornstarch and water until smooth and stir quickly into the vegetable mixture. Continue stirring rapidly until the sauce is clear and thick. Add the meat, stir 1 minute more, then serve immediately over the hot rice.

### Chop Suey

(YIELD: ENOUGH TO SERVE 8)

3 Tablespoons vegetable oil
2 Pounds shredded, uncooked pork, chicken, veal or any combination of these
6 Stalks celery
3 Large onions, peeled and sliced
10 Mushrooms, well-washed and sliced (optional)
1 8-Ounce can water chestnuts, drained and sliced

1 15-Ounce can bean sprouts, drained,
   or 2 cups fresh
2 10¾-Ounce cans condensed chicken
   broth or 3 cups stock
¼ Cup soy sauce
1 Tablespoon sherry (optional)
2½ Tablespoons cornstarch
3 to 4 Cups hot, cooked rice

Heat the oil to smoking in a wok or large frying pan. Stir-fry the meat for 2 minutes.

Trim the celery and cut into diagonal pieces about ¼ inch wide. Bring the celery pieces just to a boil in a small pan. Drain well.

Cut the onion slices into quarters and add, along with the celery, mushrooms, water chestnut slices and bean sprouts, to the meat. Stir-fry for 5 minutes over medium-high heat.

Mix until smooth the condensed chicken broth, soy sauce, sherry and cornstarch. Add this to the meat-vegetable mixture and stir constantly until the sauce is smooth and thick. Serve hot, over the rice.

## Deep-Fried Sparerib Squares with Sweet and Sour Sauce

(YIELD: ENOUGH TO SERVE 6)

INGREDIENTS FOR THE FRIED RIBS

2 Pounds pork spareribs
3 Tablespoons soy sauce
2 Tablespoons sherry
   Cooking oil for deep-frying
2 Eggs
   Cornstarch

INGREDIENTS FOR THE SAUCE

2 Large onions
2 Tablespoons cooking oil
1½ Cups Basic Chicken Stock (see page
   146) or 1 10¾-ounce can chicken
   broth
⅓ Cup catsup
¼ Cup soy sauce
3 Tablespoons granulated sugar
¼ Cup vinegar
1 Tablespoon cornstarch
¼ Cup cold water

3 to 4 Cups hot, cooked rice
2 Scallions, trimmed and chopped

Trim excess fat from the ribs and cut them apart, then chop into 1-inch pieces with a cleaver. Place the rib pieces in a shallow bowl and cover with the soy sauce and sherry. Toss once or twice to cover all surfaces. Allow to stand at least 1 hour, turning occasionally.

Heat the oil to smoking hot. Beat the eggs lightly. Dip the rib pieces first in egg, then in cornstarch. Fry, a few at a time, to a crisp golden brown. Drain on paper towels.

Sauté the onions in the cooking oil for 2 minutes. Add the chicken stock, catsup, soy sauce, sugar, vinegar and fried pork squares and stir over medium heat for 8 minutes. Mix the cornstarch with the cold water until smooth. Add to the sauce and stir constantly until thick and clear. Serve immediately over the rice, garnished with chopped scallions.

## Braised Spareribs with Pineapple

(YIELD: ENOUGH TO SERVE 6)

2 Pounds pork spareribs
⅓ Cup soy sauce
1 20-ounce can pineapple chunks
½ Cup vinegar
½ Cup granulated sugar
1¼ Cups water
2 Tablespoons vegetable oil
1 Tablespoon all-purpose flour
½ Teaspoon salt
2 Tablespoons cornstarch
3 Cups hot, cooked rice

Trim the excess fat from the ribs and cut them apart, then use a cleaver to chop the ribs into 2-inch sections. Place in a shallow bowl. Pour the soy sauce over the ribs and refrigerate for 45 minutes, turning occasionally. Drain the ribs and discard the soy sauce.

Drain the canned pineapple, reserving the juice. Measure ½ cup of the juice and mix with the vinegar, sugar and 1 cup of the water. Set the pineapple chunks aside.

Heat the oil in a heavy skillet. Stir in the ribs and brown for 4 minutes.

Sprinkle the ribs with the flour and pour the pineapple-vinegar-sugar mixture over. Bring to a boil, stirring constantly, then lower the heat and simmer, covered, until the ribs are tender (about 45 minutes).

Add the pineapple chunks and salt. Mix the cornstarch and ¼ cup water to a smooth paste. Add to the sauce and stir constantly until thick and clear. Serve immediately over the rice.

### Paper-Thin Pork Chops with Apples and Apricots

(YIELD: ENOUGH TO SERVE 6)

10 to 12 Very thin pork chops
3 Tablespoons cooking oil
5 Apples
12 Dried apricots
¼ Cup soy sauce
5 Tablespoons light brown sugar
¼ Cup sherry or fruit juice

Fry the pork chops in the oil until they are nicely browned on both sides.

Peel and core the apples and cut them into eighths. Arrange the apple slices and apricots in a 9- by 13-inch ovenproof glass baking dish, top with the pork chops and sprinkle with the soy sauce, sugar and sherry (or fruit juice).

Bake in an oven preheated to 350 degrees F. for 35 minutes. Serve hot.

### Spicy Oriental Chicken Wings

(YIELD: ENOUGH TO SERVE 4 AS A MAIN COURSE OR 8 AS AN HORS D'OEUVRE)

25 Chicken wings
⅓ Cup vegetable oil (not olive oil)
½ Cup sherry or rum
½ Cup soy sauce
½ Cup honey
¼ Teaspoon each aniseed and ground ginger
⅛ Teaspoon ground cloves
3 to 4 Cups hot, cooked rice

Wash the chicken wings and pat dry with paper towels. Strip the skin from the wings; cut off and discard the bony wing tips.

Bring water to a boil in a large saucepan and drop in the wings. As soon as the water comes to a second boil, remove the saucepan from the heat and drain off the liquid. Arrange the wings on paper towels to dry.

Heat the oil in a large skillet and brown the wings on both sides, turning once. Pour off the excess oil. Return the skillet to the heat and add the sherry, soy sauce, honey and spices. Cook over medium heat, stirring occasionally, until the sauce is thick and the wings are well coated. Serve hot with rice.

### Soy Fried Chicken with Lemon-Soy Sauce

(YIELD: ENOUGH TO SERVE 6)

4 Chicken breasts, boned
½ Cup soy sauce
¼ Cup lemon juice
3 Tablespoons granulated sugar
Vegetable oil for deep-frying
5 Tablespoons cornstarch
2 Large onions, peeled and sliced
2½ Cups Basic Chicken Stock (see page 146) or canned chicken broth
⅓ Cup cold water
3 to 4 Cups hot, cooked rice

Cut the chicken into 2-inch sections and place in a flat, shallow bowl. Combine the soy sauce, lemon juice and sugar and pour over the chicken pieces. Marinate for at least 1 hour, turning the pieces occasionally. Remove the chicken from the marinade and pat dry, reserving the marinade. Work 3 tablespoons of the cornstarch into the chicken pieces with your fingers. Fry the chicken in 1 inch of hot oil until brown on both sides, turning once. Drain and set aside.

In a separate skillet, sauté the onions for 3 minutes in 3 tablespoons of oil, stirring frequently. Add the reserved marinade and the chicken stock and bring to a boil over high heat. Mix the remaining 2 tablespoons cornstarch with the ⅓ cup cold water, add to the sauce and stir constantly over medium-high heat until the sauce is thick and clear. Add the chicken pieces and cook for 1 minute more.

Serve immediately over the hot rice, with additional soy sauce if desired.

## Deep-Fried Chicken Balls with Peach Sauce

(YIELD: ENOUGH TO SERVE 6)

2 Large chicken breasts, boned
12 Water chestnuts
2 Scallions, with 3 inches of green top
5 Tablespoons soy sauce
2 Tablespoons cornstarch
1 Egg white
    Vegetable oil for deep-frying
1 16-Ounce can sliced peaches
3 Tablespoons sherry
3 Cups hot, cooked rice

Remove and discard the skin from the chicken. Mince the raw chicken, water chestnuts and scallions. Mix in 2 tablespoons of the soy sauce, 1 tablespoon of the cornstarch and the egg white. Form the chicken mixture into 1½-inch balls (add a bit more cornstarch if necessary to hold the balls together) and deep-fry in 1 inch of hot oil, turning once, until golden brown on all sides. Drain on paper towels.

Drain the peach slices, reserving the syrup. Combine the peach syrup, sherry and remaining 3 tablespoons soy sauce. Mix in 1 tablespoon cornstarch until smooth, then stir constantly over medium-high heat until the sauce is thick and clear. Add the peach slices and chicken balls and stir for a minute or two to heat. Serve immediately over the hot rice.

## Fried Rice with Chicken

(YIELD: 4 TO 6 SERVINGS)

6 Tablespoons vegetable oil
2 Eggs
½ Teaspoon salt
4 Cups leftover cooked rice
2 Medium onions, peeled, sliced and then cut in half

¼ Cup chopped, cooked chicken
2 Tablespoons chopped, cooked ham
2 Tablespoons chopped, cooked shrimp
½ Chinese sausage, chopped
12 Fresh mushrooms, sliced
½ Cup fresh (or frozen) green peas
1 Small Chinese cabbage (or 8 to 10 leaves)
2 Teaspoons soy sauce

Heat 1 tablespoon of the oil in a small skillet. Beat the eggs lightly and cook until set, turning once. Remove the omelet from the pan, cut into strips 1 inch by ¼-inch and set aside.

Heat 2 tablespoons of the oil with the salt. As soon as the oil is very hot, add the rice. Sauté for 5 minutes, stirring constantly, then remove from the pan and set aside. Add another 2 tablespoons oil to the pan, stir in the onion and sauté until lightly browned. Add the chicken, ham, shrimp, sausage and remaining vegetables. Sauté together for 3 minutes, adding more oil if necessary to keep the ingredients from sticking to pan. Gradually stir in the rice. When the mixture is hot, stir in the soy sauce and omelet strips. Cook only long enough to heat, then remove from heat and serve at once.

## Chinese Stewed Chicken

(YIELD: ENOUGH TO SERVE 6)

1 3½-Pound chicken
2½ Cups boiling water
1½ Cups Basic Chicken Stock (see page 146) or 1 10¾-ounce can chicken broth
1 Small head Chinese cabbage (or 1 head lettuce)
1 Cup sliced mushrooms
1 8-Ounce can water chestnuts
3 Large onions, peeled
2½ Tablespoons cornstarch
3 Cups hot, cooked rice

Rinse the chicken and dry well (remove the skin if you prefer). Chop the chicken into 2-inch sections with a meat cleaver. Pick over and discard any small slivers of bone.

Arrange the chicken in a large, heavy skillet or saucepan. Pour the boiling water and chicken stock over the chicken pieces and bring the liquid to a boil. Lower the heat, cover and simmer for 30 minutes.

Meanwhile, wash the vegetables and cut in 1-inch-wide diagonal slices. Add to the hot chicken mixture, cover and simmer over low heat for 30 minutes more.

Just before serving, mix the cornstarch with a little cold water. Stir into the hot chicken mixture, continuing to stir until the sauce is thick and clear. Serve immediately over the hot rice.

## Red-Pepper Chicken

*These tender young chickens are cooked in a fiery red pepper and fennel sauce.*

(YIELD: ENOUGH TO SERVE 6)

2 2½-Pound chickens
1 Teaspoon aniseed
1 Teaspoon dried red pepper
½ Stick cinnamon
¾ Cup soy sauce
⅓ Cup each cooking oil and sherry
7 Scallions, with 5 inches of green top
1 Tablespoon granulated sugar
1 Small head lettuce, shredded
3 to 4 Cups hot, fluffy rice (optional)

Rinse the chickens and dry with paper towels. Place the aniseed, red pepper and cinnamon stick on a square of cheesecloth, then tie the ends to form a spice bag.

Heat the soy sauce, oil and sherry in a large, heavy pan. Chop 3 scallions. Add the chickens to the pan, sprinkle with the scallion pieces and set the spice bag alongside. Simmer, covered, for 50 minutes, turning the chickens from time to time and pressing the spice bag occasionally to extract all flavor.

Chop the remaining scallions, sprinkle over the chickens, then stir in the sugar and simmer 10 minutes more. Discard the spice bag.

Arrange the shredded lettuce on a serving platter. Top with the chickens and spoon the sauce over. Serve with hot fluffy rice if desired.

## Madras Egg Curry

*No curry tastes better than this one.*

(YIELD: ENOUGH TO SERVE 6)

1 Cup uncooked rice
2 Small onions, peeled and coarsely chopped
1 Small garlic clove, peeled and crushed
2 Tablespoons butter
2 Teaspoons curry powder
1 Large tomato, chopped
1 Tablespoon tomato paste
1½ Cups Basic Chicken Stock (see page 146) or 1 10¾-ounce can chicken broth
1 Tablespoon granulated sugar
1½ Tablespoons all-purpose flour
⅓ Cup water
6 Hard-cooked eggs

Cook the rice according to package directions.

Sauté the onions and garlic in the butter for 3 to 4 minutes. Stir in the curry powder and cook for 3 minutes more. Add the tomato, tomato paste, chicken stock and sugar, then lower the heat and simmer the mixture for 10 minutes. Mix the flour and water together; add to the curry mixture, stirring until slightly thick. Slice the eggs and add to the curry mixture, cooking only long enough to heat. Serve at once over the rice.

## Banana Curry

(YIELD: ENOUGH TO SERVE 4 TO 6)

INGREDIENTS FOR COOKING
THE BANANAS

3 Large, slightly green bananas
1 Tablespoon butter
½ Teaspoon each caraway seeds, chili powder, ground cinnamon and ground turmeric
Pinch each ground cloves and coriander (optional)

INGREDIENTS FOR COOKING
THE CURRY

    2  Tablespoons butter
    2  Very large onions, peeled and very
       coarsely chopped
    ¼  Pound finely minced leftover
       cooked meat (or ¼ pound uncooked
       ground beef or lamb)
    2  Teaspoons curry powder
    ½  Teaspoon caraway seeds
 1½  Cups Basic Chicken Stock (see page
       146) or 1 10¾-ounce can chicken
       broth
    2  Tablespoons milk
    1  Tablespoon lemon juice
 1½  Tablespoons flour
    ¼  Cup water
    2  Hard-cooked eggs, very coarsely
       chopped
    3  Cups hot, cooked rice

DIRECTIONS FOR COOKING
THE BANANAS

Peel the bananas and cut into 1-inch sections.
Heat the butter in a large, heavy skillet, add the
spices and sauté for 2 minutes. Add the banana
pieces and stir over medium heat for 3 minutes,
or until all surfaces are covered with the spice
mixture. Remove the bananas from the skillet
and set aside. (Bananas prepared in this fashion
are frequently used as a garnish in other curry
dishes.)

DIRECTIONS FOR COOKING
THE CURRY

Using the same skillet, heat the butter and sauté
the onions for 3 minutes, stirring occasionally.
Add the meat and cook, stirring constantly, until
brown. Sprinkle the meat with the curry powder
and caraway seeds. Stir over medium heat for 1
minute, then add the stock, milk and lemon
juice. Bring to a boil and cook at a low boil for
5 minutes. Combine the flour and water and

stir in thoroughly. Cook over medium heat, stirring constantly until the sauce thickens.

Lower the heat, add the reserved bananas and
chopped eggs and cook only until steaming hot.
Serve over the rice.

## Pakistani Spiced Peas and Potatoes

*Exotic recipes like this one add interesting
variety to meatless meals.*

(YIELD: ENOUGH TO SERVE 4 TO 6)

    2  Pounds potatoes, peeled and cut in
       ½-inch cubes
    3  Tablespoons butter
    3  Tablespoons vegetable oil
    1  Clove garlic, peeled and crushed
 1½  Cups fresh green peas (or 1
       10-ounce package frozen)
    ¾  Teaspoon chili powder
    ½  Teaspoon each ground cumin,
       turmeric and ginger
 1½  Teaspoons salt
    2  Medium tomatoes, chopped
4 to 6  Eggs
    3  Scallions, with 3 inches of green top,
       minced

Sauté the potato cubes in 2 tablespoons each of
the butter and oil, to which has been added the
crushed garlic. Cook, stirring frequently, until
the potatoes are fork-tender. Add the peas and
cook for 3 minutes more, then spoon the vegetables onto a large plate and set aside.

Add the remaining butter and oil to the skillet,
along with the spices and salt. Stir in the tomatoes, cooked potatoes and peas and cook over low
heat until piping hot.

Meanwhile, fry the eggs as you like them.

Arrange the vegetables on serving plates, top
with the fried eggs, sprinkle with the scallions
and serve at once.

# EGG & CHEESE MEALS

## Omelets

*The art of omelet making seems a bit tricky at first, but once you have mastered the basic technique you are sure to enjoy serving them in endless varieties. Try preparing small, rather than large, omelets in the beginning—they are much, much easier to cope with.*

(YIELD: ENOUGH TO MAKE 1 OMELET
TO SERVE 2)

4 *Eggs*
2 *Tablespoons water or milk*
*Salt and pepper*
1 *Teaspoon butter*

Beat the eggs and liquid together and season with salt and pepper to taste.

Heat the butter in a skillet over a medium flame. As soon as the butter is sizzling but before it browns, pour the egg mixture into the pan and stir for 30 seconds with a fork, using a rapid circular motion. Lift the cooked part of the omelet so that the uncooked egg can run under-neath. As soon as the eggs are set on the bottom but still soft and creamy on top, press the skillet handle down and let the omelet slide toward you and partway up the side of the pan. Now flip the omelet over toward the center of the pan. Quickly tilt the pan in the opposite direc-tion and allow the omelet to slide partially out of the pan on the side away from the handle. Holding a plate under this side, raise the pan handle so that the omelet flips over and out onto the waiting plate.

Now you should have a perfectly shaped oval omelet quite adequate for 2 people. If you are serving more than 2, proceed in the same manner and make a succession of small omelets.

Omelets are quite delicious "as is," but they are exceedingly versatile and will accept an al-most limitless number of fillings, either prepared from scratch or left over from previous meals. Just remember to cut or chop your additions very fine and have them warm or at room tem-perature. Spread your filling across the center of the omelet as soon as the eggs are set but are still soft and creamy.

Here is a beginner's list of omelet variations, but please don't hesitate to concoct your own.

Anything that tastes good to you is a suitable variation.

### Filling Variations

CHEESES:  Freshly grated Cheddar, Swiss, Parmesan, Gruyère or jack
Cottage cheese
Cream cheese

MEATS:  Crumbled bacon
Cooked and minced ham, chicken or veal

FISH:  Flaked, cooked or canned fish
Minced shrimp, lobster or crab

VEGETABLES:  Almost any cooked vegetable will be suitable, fried, sautéed or in a cream sauce, or try fresh vegetables like tomatoes or scallions.

HERBS:  Fresh are best but dried are fine, too. Use them alone or with other ingredients.

In addition, many interesting main-course omelets can be made by topping a filled omelet with an appropriate sauce.

### Spinach Omelet with Mornay Sauce

Mix a little white sauce with cooked and well-drained spinach. Fill the omelet with the creamed spinach and top with Mornay Sauce (see page 172).

### Zucchini Omelet with Mushroom Sauce

Fill the omelet with sliced, sautéed zucchini. Top with Mushroom Sauce (see page 172).

### Mediterranean Omelet

Sauté coarsely chopped zucchini, onion and tomato in butter. Season with oregano, salt and pepper. Fill the omelet with the well-drained vegetables sprinkled with a bit of grated Parmesan cheese.

### Bacon Omelet with Vegetable Sauce

Fill the omelet with crumbled fried bacon. Top with a bit of Mixed Vegetable Sauce (see page 172).

### Ham and Scallion Omelet

Fill the omelet with finely chopped scallion and leftover ham.

### Curried Lamb Omelet with Herb Sauce

Fill the omelet with leftover ground lamb sprinkled with curry powder. Top with a bit of Herb Sauce (see page 172).

### Sausage Omelet with Fresh Basil

Fill the omelet with fried crumbled sausage and minced fresh basil.

### Turkey Omelet with Fresh Sage

Mix minced leftover turkey with a little Basic White Sauce (see page 171). Fill the omelet with the creamed turkey and sprinkle with minced fresh sage.

### Mushroom Omelet with Crumbled Bacon

Fill the omelet with sautéed minced mushrooms mixed with a little Basic White Sauce (see page 171). Sprinkle with crumbled crisp-fried bacon.

### Tomato Omelet with Fresh Herbs

Sauté chopped tomato and onion in butter. Drain well and use the mixture to fill the omelet. Sprinkle the filling with mixed minced fresh herbs.

### Sour Cream and Anchovy Omelet

Fill the omelet with cold sour cream and bits of chopped anchovy.

### Lettuce Omelet

Sauté finely chopped lettuce and chives in butter. Fill the omelet with the warm vegetables and a dollop of cold sour cream.

## Basic Scrambled Eggs

*If you dress up the dinner with a satisfying soup, a green salad and an outstanding dessert, scrambled eggs (with variations) make a perfectly satisfying meal.*

(YIELD: ENOUGH TO SERVE 6)

3 Tablespoons butter
12 Eggs
2 Tablespoons milk or water (optional)
Salt and white pepper

In a heavy skillet, melt the butter over very low heat. Break the eggs into a large bowl, add milk or water if desired, and stir only long enough to blend the yolks and whites. Season with salt and pepper to taste.

As soon as the butter is hot but not bubbly, cover the bottom of the skillet with the egg mixture. The eggs will firm on the bottom and sides first. Push these parts toward the center of the pan, allowing the liquid egg mixture that remains to flow underneath and cook. When all the egg mixture is set but still creamy and custardlike, remove the skillet from the heat and scramble quickly with a fork. Serve immediately.

### Scrambled Eggs with Ham

Increase the butter by 1 tablespoon. Heat the butter in a large, heavy skillet and lightly sauté 1 cup finely diced leftover cooked ham. Beat 8 eggs together lightly and season to taste with salt and white pepper. Reduce the heat, pour the egg mixture over the sautéed ham and cook as directed. Remove from the heat, add 1 teaspoon minced fresh parsley, then scramble and serve at once.

### Scrambled Eggs with Tomato Sauce

Heat 1½ cups tomato sauce in a small saucepan. Prepare Basic Scrambled Eggs as directed (see above) and divide among serving plates. Spoon the warm tomato sauce over each portion, then garnish with minced scallions and a sprinkling of grated cheese. Serve at once.

### Scrambled Eggs with Asparagus

Trim any thick, woody stems from 1 pound asparagus and cook, covered, in a little boiling salted water over very low heat until tender (about 12 to 15 minutes). Prepare Basic Scrambled Eggs as directed (see above). Drain the asparagus and arrange over the eggs just before serving. Top with Mornay Sauce (see page 172) if desired.

## Luncheon Eggs

(YIELD: ENOUGH TO SERVE 4 TO 6)

2 Tablespoons butter or margarine
4 Scallions, with 4 inches of green top, chopped
1 Cup dried chipped beef
9 Eggs
2 Ounces cream cheese
Freshly ground black pepper
Buttered toast triangles
2 Tablespoons minced fresh parsley

Melt the butter in a large skillet. Add the scallions; sauté for 2 minutes over medium heat. Stir in the chipped beef. Beat the eggs and stir into the beef and scallions. Add the cream cheese and cook, stirring frequently, until the eggs are soft-set. Season to taste with pepper and spoon onto buttered toast triangles. Serve immediately, garnished with the minced parsley.

## Woodcock

(YIELD: ENOUGH TO SERVE 4)

2 Tablespoons butter
8 Egg yolks
1 Cup light cream
¼ Teaspoon each salt and black pepper
4 Slices bread
1½ Tablespoons anchovy paste
1 Tablespoon minced fresh parsley

Heat the butter in the top of a double boiler over medium heat. Blend the egg yolks, cream and seasonings together until well mixed. Scramble the egg mixture in butter until set to custard-like consistency.

Meanwhile, toast the bread and spread each slice with anchovy paste. Heap the eggs on top, garnish each serving with minced parsley and serve at once.

### Basic Poached Eggs

Use your egg poacher to prepare eggs in this style; it's the easiest way by far. However, if you haven't a poacher, try this method of preparation:

Bring 5 parts water to 1 part vinegar to a boil in a fairly shallow pan (the pan should be deep enough so that the eggs will not stick to its bottom). Break 1 egg into a cup or small bowl. Bring the water to just below the boiling point and slide the egg in. Poach the egg for 2 or 3 minutes, or until the white is firm. If you're *very* careful, and provided the pan is large enough, you can prepare several eggs at one time.

Keep poached eggs hot by slipping them into warm salted water until ready to serve.

Poached eggs may also be poached in clear broth or consommé and served as a garnish in the hot soup.

#### Poached Eggs with Spinach and Mornay Sauce

Prepare 2 eggs for each serving, according to directions above. Cook frozen spinach according to package directions, or prepare fresh spinach. Drain and chop the spinach, then toss with butter.

Place the spinach on a heatproof serving platter. Arrange the poached eggs on the spinach and cover with Mornay Sauce (see page 172). Sprinkle the sauce with grated Parmesan cheese and broil 5 inches from the heat until the cheese melts and browns slightly. Serve immediately.

#### Eggs Benedict

Split and toast 1 English muffin for each serving. Sauté 1 slice baked ham or Canadian bacon for each muffin half. Place the meat slices on the split muffins and arrange a poached egg (see above) on top of each. Cover the eggs with hollandaise sauce or Mornay Sauce (see page 172). Serve hot.

#### Poached Eggs Orient

Allow 2 poached eggs (see above) for each serving. Place each egg on a slice of hot toast, sprinkle liberally with soy sauce to taste and garnish with minced scallions.

#### Poached Eggs with Bacon

Allow 2 strips bacon for each egg, poached as per directions above. Fry the bacon to a crisp golden brown. Drain briefly on paper towels and place on hot, buttered toast. Top with a poached egg and serve at once.

#### Poached Eggs with Tomato Sauce

Prepare 2 poached eggs (see above) for each serving. Place on hot, buttered toast and top with hot tomato sauce. Serve immediately.

#### Poached Eggs with Dried Chipped Beef

Soak 2 cups dried chipped beef in cool water for 15 minutes to remove excess salt. Drain thoroughly and stir into 3 cups Basic White Sauce (see page 171). Spoon over hot toast triangles and top each serving with 2 poached eggs (see above). Serve hot.

### Sportsman's Eggs

(YIELD: ENOUGH TO SERVE 4)

　2 Tablespoons butter
　1 Pound chicken livers
½ Cup minced onion
　2 Tablespoons minced green pepper
¼ Cup tomato paste
　1 Cup beef stock or broth
½ Cup dry white wine
　4 Eggs
　　Salt
　4 Slices bread, toasted and cut into triangles

Heat the butter in a large skillet and sauté the chicken livers, onion and green pepper until lightly browned. Mix the tomato paste into the stock and add to the skillet. Simmer for 5 minutes, then add the wine and simmer for 5 minutes more.

Break the eggs, one at a time, into the simmering liquid, taking care not to break the yolks. Cover the skillet and cook until the egg whites are set. Season to taste with salt.

Allow 1 egg and 4 chicken livers per serving, and arrange on buttered toast triangles.

## Stuffed Eggs

(YIELD: ENOUGH TO SERVE 8)

Add flavor and nutrition to this egg dish with distinctive fillings utilizing bits of leftover meats. Serve the stuffed eggs cold for lunch, or top with white sauce or curry sauce and bring them forth hot from the oven as a main course for supper.

To prepare, cut 12 hard-boiled eggs in half lengthwise. Separate the whites and yolks. Mash the yolks together and add your choice of the following fillings. Spoon the mixture into the egg whites.

Chill and serve cold, or arrange the stuffed halves in an ovenproof dish, cover with 2 cups of Basic White Sauce (see page 171) or Curry Sauce (see page 172) and bake for 20 minutes in an oven preheated to 350 degrees F.

### Chicken and Walnut Stuffing

Mash the egg yolks with ½ cup cooked, minced chicken, 3 tablespoons chopped walnuts and ⅛ teaspoon nutmeg. Bind with 2½ tablespoons sour cream or a bit of Basic White Sauce (see page 171) or Curry Sauce (see page 172).

### Ham and Mushroom Stuffing

Combine the mashed egg yolks with ½ cup cooked and minced ham, ¼ cup sautéed mushrooms, ¼ teaspoon powdered thyme and 2½ tablespoons sour cream.

### Bacon and Celery Stuffing

Sauté 6 strips bacon until crispy brown. Drain briefly, then crumble and set aside. Add ¼ cup chopped celery to the hot bacon drippings and cook until tender. Mix the bacon bits, chopped celery and mashed egg yolks together. Bind with 2½ tablespoons sour cream or Basic White Sauce (see page 171).

### Zucchini and Lamb Stuffing

Cook ¾ cup chopped zucchini in 2 tablespoons vegetable oil until tender. Toss with ½ cup minced, cooked lamb, then add to the mashed egg yolks. Season with a dash of garlic salt and bind with 2½ tablespoons sour cream.

## Eggs on Toast Norway

(YIELD: ENOUGH TO SERVE 4 TO 6)

8 to 10  Hard-cooked eggs
1  Large onion, peeled
2  Tablespoons butter
8  Flat anchovy fillets, finely chopped
   Freshly ground black pepper
   Buttered toast triangles

Shell and chop the hard-cooked eggs and set aside. Chop the onion, then lightly sauté in butter until golden. Stir in the anchovies and eggs. Season the mixture to taste with pepper and cook only long enough to heat through. Heap onto buttered toast triangles and serve at once.

## Eggs Mimosa

(YIELD: ENOUGH TO SERVE 6)

2  Cups Basic White Sauce (see page 171)
   Salt and black pepper
   Cayenne pepper
8  Hard-cooked eggs
1  Cup cooked peas
1  Cup cubed, cooked ham, cut into ½-inch squares

½ Cup pimiento, cut into
½-inch squares
Toast triangles

Prepare the white sauce as directed and season
with salt, black pepper and cayenne pepper to
taste. Shell the eggs, separating the whites from
the yolks. Set the yolks aside and chop the whites
coarsely. Stir the egg whites, peas, ham and
pimiento into the white sauce and cook only
long enough to heat through.

Press the egg yolks through a fine sieve with
the back of a spoon. Heap the hot white sauce
mixture over hot toast triangles and garnish each
serving with sieved egg yolk.

## Scotch Eggs

(YIELD: ENOUGH TO SERVE 6)

3 Cups cooked and crumbled
homemade sausage meat (see pages
75–77)
2 Cups soft bread crumbs
2 to 3 Raw eggs
1 Cup fine, dry bread crumbs
6 Hard-cooked eggs
Vegetable oil for deep frying
6 Slices toast, buttered and cut into
triangles

Combine the sausage meat with the bread
crumbs. Bind with 1 or 2 of the raw eggs to a
fairly moist consistency. Shell the hard-cooked
eggs, then press the sausage mixture evenly
around each.

Beat the remaining raw egg lightly. Dip the
coated eggs first in raw egg, then roll in the dry
bread crumbs and fry in hot oil until golden
brown on all sides. Serve on the buttered toast
triangles.

## French Toast

*Slightly stale bread is best for this popular
breakfast treat.
French toast can also double as a lunch or supper
dish when topped with one of the savory sauces
mentioned on pages 171–72.
Don't forget, French toast freezes well if kept
for short periods of time.*

(YIELD: ENOUGH TO SERVE 8)

4 Eggs
⅔ Cup milk
5 Tablespoons butter or margarine
16 Slices day-old bread

Beat the eggs lightly with the milk in a wide,
shallow bowl. Heat the butter in a skillet. Dip
the bread slices briefly into the egg and milk
mixture to coat both sides. Fry the bread until
golden brown on both sides, turning once. Serve
hot with Brown Sugar Syrup (see page 23), cinnamon sugar, jam or jelly.

## Cheese Toast

*Cheese toasts and salad make an unusually tasty
lunch.*

(YIELD: ENOUGH TO SERVE 6)

12 Slices partially dry leftover bread
2 Tablespoons butter
¼ Cup olive oil
2 Large cloves garlic, peeled
1 Pound Swiss cheese, cut into
very thin slices

Trim crusts from the leftover bread. Heat the
butter and oil in a large skillet with the garlic
and fry the bread to a golden brown on both
sides, turning once.

Arrange the bread on an ovenproof serving
platter and top each slice with cheese. Place
in an oven preheated to 400 degrees F. or broil
on a rack several inches from the heat until the
cheese bubbles and browns. Serve at once.

### Cheese Toast with Anchovies

Prepare bread slices as directed above and arrange on an ovenproof serving platter. Place 3 well-drained flat anchovy fillets on each piece of toast, top with cheese slices and proceed as directed.

### Cheese Toast with Stuffed Olives and Bacon

Sauté 24 strips bacon until crispy brown. Drain and set aside. Prepare bread slices as directed above and arrange on an ovenproof serving platter. Cover with bacon and then with sliced cheese. Cut stuffed olives into slices, arrange over the cheese and bake or broil until the cheese is bubbly hot.

### Cheese Toast with Tomatoes

Prepare bread as directed above, arrange on an ovenproof platter and cover with cheese slices. Top each serving with 2 tomato slices. Bake or broil until the cheese melts and bubbles.

### Basic Welsh Rabbit

*Another standby when meat is not on the menu is smooth, delicious Welsh rabbit. For more interesting meals, sample the variations until you find your favorite.*

(YIELD: ENOUGH TO SERVE 6)

1 Tablespoon butter
1¼ Pounds Cheddar cheese, grated
¾ Cup plus 1 tablespoon flat beer, at room temperature
1 Tablespoon dry mustard
Salt and cayenne pepper to taste
2 Teaspoons Worcestershire sauce
1 Egg
12 Slices toast, buttered and cut into triangles

Melt the butter in a large, heavy skillet over low heat. Sprinkle in the cheese, stirring constantly with a wooden spoon. While the cheese is melting, add the ¾ cup beer, a bit at a time, and stir until the mixture is smooth and free from lumps. Combine the mustard, Worcestershire sauce,

salt and cayenne; add the 1 tablespoon beer and mix to a smooth paste. Blend this into the cheese mixture. Beat in the egg until it disappears into the cheese, spoon over the buttered toast triangles and serve at once.

### Welsh Rabbit with Green Pepper

Sauté ¼ cup finely chopped green pepper in the melted butter. Stir in the cheese and continue as directed above. Serve with bacon slices if desired.

### Mushroom Welsh Rabbit

Increase the butter by 2 tablespoons. Sauté ½ cup coarsely chopped mushrooms in the melting butter, then stir in the cheese and proceed as directed above.

### Welsh Rabbit with Ham

Prepare Welsh rabbit as directed above. As soon as the egg is well mixed into the cheese mixture, add ½ cup chopped, leftover cooked ham. Cook only long enough to heat through.

### Welsh Rabbit with Bacon and Pimiento

Prepare Welsh rabbit as directed above. As soon as the egg is stirred in, add 4 slices bacon, fried and crumbled, and 2 tablespoons chopped pimiento. Cook only long enough to heat through. Garnish with minced scallions.

### Welsh Rabbit with Sardines

After preparing Welsh rabbit as directed above, drain a 2-ounce can of sardines, arrange on hot toast triangles and spoon the cheese mixture over. Garnish with minced scallions if desired.

### Welsh Rabbit with Broiled Tomato Slices

Set toast on a large heatproof serving platter. Spoon the hot cheese mixture over the toast and top each serving with 2 tomato slices. Broil for 1 minute and serve immediately.

### South of the Border Rabbit

Increase the butter by 1 tablespoon and sauté ½ cup finely chopped onion with ¼ cup finely chopped green pepper. Stir in the cheese, beer and mustard mixture. As soon as the egg is mixed in, add 1 cup well-drained stewed or canned tomatoes and ½ teaspoon chili powder. Heat through and serve at once.

### Welsh Rabbit with Grilled Tomatoes

Cut the stem end from 6 medium tomatoes. Cut each tomato in half, shake a bit to remove some of the seeds, then drain, cut side down, for 5 minutes. Meanwhile, prepare Welsh rabbit as directed above.

Arrange the tomatoes, cut side up, on a broiling rack. Sprinkle bread crumbs on top and dot with butter. Broil the tomatoes, about 5 inches from the flame, for 5 minutes, or until the tops turn golden brown. Place 2 grilled tomatoes on each toast slice and cover with rabbit. Serve hot.

# SOUFFLÉS & CRÊPES

### The Basic Main Dish Soufflé

*The soufflé has long been considered a frivolous dish, one that is at home only in gourmet restaurants. Suddenly, since meat has become something of a luxury, the protein-rich soufflé has found favor with the penny-wise consumer. Little wonder! You can fold almost any finely chopped or puréed leftover into a soufflé and end up with a dish fit for your own special family.*

(YIELD: ENOUGH TO SERVE 4 TO 6)

2 Tablespoons butter
2 Tablespoons all-purpose flour
¾ Cup cold milk
  Salt
4 Egg yolks
5 Egg whites

Melt the butter in a heavy pan set directly over medium heat. Blend in the flour, then stir in the cold milk and season to taste with salt. Cook, stirring constantly, until the sauce thickens slightly.

Remove the pan from the heat and fold in 1½ cups of one of the ingredients listed below. Beat in the egg yolks, one at a time. When all the ingredients are well blended, allow the mixture to cool slightly.

Beat the egg whites until they stand in stiff peaks and fold them into the mixture. Turn at once into a buttered soufflé dish or other deep baking dish. Bake in an oven preheated to 350 degrees F. for 30 minutes, or until the soufflé is puffy and browned on top.

If you prefer your soufflé less crusty, set the dish in a pan of hot, not boiling, water while it bakes.

### Cheese Soufflé

Fold in 1½ cups grated natural cheese.

### Vegetable Soufflés

Fold in 1½ cups of any of the following cooked and puréed vegetables:

Asparagus
Broccoli
Spinach

*Zucchini*
*Mixed vegetables*

Or try using:

*Finely chopped and sautéed*
*mushrooms*
*Finely chopped and sautéed*
*onions*

### Meat, Poultry or Fish Soufflés

Soufflés make unique use of your leftover meats, poultry and seafood. Fold in 1½ cups of any of the following:

*Cooked, minced ham*
*Cooked, minced chicken*
*Cooked, minced turkey*
*Cooked, flaked fish*
*Finely chopped seafood*

### Basic Crêpe Batter

*By far the most elegant way to use leftovers is the "serve-them-rolled-in-a-crêpe" plan. These paper-thin pancakes magically transform yesterday's "bits and pieces" of meats, seafood or vegetables into appetizing and inexpensive entrées.*
*Use the recipes that follow as a starting point and then let your imagination and/or the contents of your refrigerator be your guide to delicious, moneysaving meals.*

(YIELD: 16 TO 20 CRÊPES)

3 *Tablespoons butter*
6 *Eggs*
1½ *Cups sifted all-purpose flour*
¼ *Teaspoon salt*
2 *Cups milk*

Rub the inside surface of a 6-inch skillet with ½ teaspoon of the butter, set over low heat for a minute, then remove and wipe the pan. Add another ½ teaspoon and repeat the process. (This seasons the skillet so your crêpes won't stick.)

Beat the eggs lightly, then continue to beat as you add the flour and salt. When the mixture is smooth, beat in the milk until the batter is well blended and free from any lumps. Refrigerate the batter for an hour or two.

Preheat your skillet with ¼ teaspoon butter, tilting it back and forth to coat the bottom and sides evenly. Stir the cold crêpe batter. For each crêpe, pour 3 tablespoons batter all at once into the pan, rotating it quickly so the mixture spreads over the surface. As soon as bubbles appear on the top of the crêpe, loosen it with a spatula, then turn to lightly brown the other side. Use about ⅛ teaspoon butter to brown each additional crêpe, preparing them all in the same manner.

Stack the crêpes as you finish each one, and keep them warm until serving time.

### Ham and Mushroom Crêpes

(YIELD: ENOUGH TO SERVE 8)

2½ *Cups finely chopped, cooked ham*
2 *Cups sliced mushrooms*
1 *Sweet green (or sweet red) pepper, minced*
3 *Tablespoons margarine*
¼ *Teaspoon oregano*
½ *Teaspoon salt*
3 *Cups Basic White Sauce (see page 171)*
*Basic Crêpe Batter (see above)*
¼ *Cup grated Swiss or Parmesan (or 2 tablespoons of each)*
*Paprika*

Place the ham in a large bowl. Sauté the mushrooms and sweet pepper in the margarine until the vegetables are tender. Add the cooked vegetables, the oregano and ½ cup white sauce to the meat and mix well.

Prepare the crêpes as directed. Spread about 6 tablespoons of the ham mixture and 1 tablespoon white sauce down the center of each crêpe. Fold the sides of the crêpes over the filling. Place the stuffed crêpes in an ovenproof glass baking dish, pour the remaining sauce down the center and sprinkle with cheese and paprika. Bake for 20 minutes in an oven preheated to 375 degrees F.) and serve immediately.

## Meatless Crêpes à la King

*Eggs taste marvelous when used as crêpe fillers.*

(YIELD: ENOUGH TO SERVE 8)

Basic Crêpe Batter (see page 136)
8 Hard-cooked eggs, shelled
6 Scallions, trimmed and chopped
1¼ Cups diced celery
1½ Cups fresh (or frozen) peas
¼ Cup pimiento, cut into ¼-inch squares
3 Cups Basic White Sauce (see page 171)
16 Strips pimiento

Prepare the crêpes and keep them warm.

Coarsely chop the eggs. Sauté the scallions and celery until tender; cook the peas.

Mix the eggs, scallions, celery, peas, pimiento squares and 1 cup of the white sauce. Spread some of the hot egg mixture down the center of each crêpe and fold the edges over. Place 2 or 3 crêpes on each plate, spoon a little hot white sauce over and decorate with strips of pimiento. Serve immediately.

## Crêpes with Curried Egg Filling

(YIELD: ENOUGH TO SERVE 8)

Basic Crêpe Batter (see page 136)
8 Hard-cooked eggs, shelled
1½ Cups fresh (or frozen) peas
1½ Cups diced celery
1 Tablespoon margarine
3 Cups Basic White Sauce (see page 171)
1½ Teaspoons curry powder
1 Cup toasted, slivered almonds
16 Tablespoons chutney (see page 25), optional

Prepare the crêpes and keep them warm.

Coarsely chop the eggs. Cook the peas. Sauté the celery in the margarine. Heat the white sauce, add the curry powder and blend well.

Mix the eggs, peas, celery, almonds and 1 cup of the curry sauce. Spread the center of each crêpe with the curried egg filling and fold the edges over. Place 2 crêpes on each plate and spoon the hot curry sauce over. Top with chutney if desired.

## Cheese Crêpes

*Float these crêpes in steaming hot beef broth, serve with a tossed salad and some fresh-baked Italian bread and enjoy an unusual—and inexpensive—all-in-one protein meal.*

(YIELD: ENOUGH TO SERVE 8)

9 Eggs
¾ Teaspoon salt
3 Cups all-purpose flour
3½ Cups grated Parmesan cheese
Nutmeg
8 Cups Basic Beef Stock (see page 145) or other beef broth
¼ Cup each finely chopped parsley and scallions

Beat the eggs and salt together and add the flour, a little at a time, until the batter reaches the consistency of smooth cream. Add a little water if the mixture seems too thick.

Spoon 3 tablespoons of batter into a greased, preheated 6- to 8-inch skillet. Keep the crêpes very thin by tilting and rotating the pan. Cook to a light brown, then loosen and turn to brown the other side. Repeat with the remaining batter, stacking the crêpes as each is finished and keeping them all warm.

While the stock heats, heap 1 tablespoon of the cheese in the center of each crêpe, top with a sprinkle of nutmeg and roll up. Divide the crêpes among 8 soup plates, ladle a cup of hot soup into each, and garnish with the parsley and scallions. Serve immediately.

## Quick Blini Appetizers

(YIELD: ENOUGH TO SERVE 8 TO 12)

6 Medium potatoes, peeled
5 Tablespoons milk
⅓ Cup all-purpose flour

¾  *Teaspoon salt*
5  *Eggs*
6  *Tablespoons heavy cream*
  *Sour cream*
4  *Tablespoons butter*
  *Flat anchovy fillets or capers*
  *Minced chives*

Slice and cook the potatoes. When tender, force them through a fine sieve with the back of a spoon. Mix the milk, flour and salt into the potato purée, then add the eggs, one at a time, working each thoroughly into the mixture before adding the next. Add the heavy cream and 2 tablespoons sour cream and stir until the batter is smooth.

Melt some of the butter on a large griddle. Drop the batter by tablespoonfuls into the hot butter, turning each blini once to brown lightly on both sides. Stack the blinis as they finish browning and keep them warm. Add more butter to the griddle for each batch of blinis you cook.

To serve, top the blinis with a dollop of sour cream and a piece of anchovy fillet or a few capers. Sprinkle with minced chives.

# THE SALAD MEAL

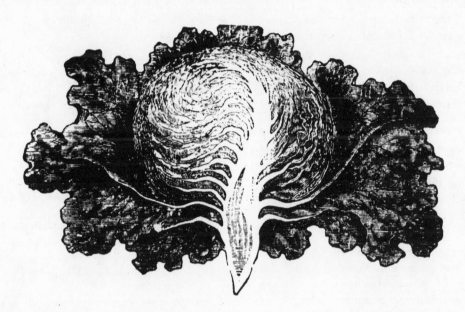

One of the best ways to save money in these times of outrageous prices is to find filling, nutritious and delicious substitutes for, or ways to extend, the main-course meat or fish dish. The main course salad fills this function admirably. It makes good sense (and is more healthful too) to eat only four meat or fish dinners every week, substituting a salad for one night's dinner, waffles or crêpes for another, and perhaps finishing off the week with a main-course egg dish.

The salad meal is more interesting (and satisfying) when served with a soup, a crusty home-baked bread and a glamorous dessert—dessert crêpes would be perfect here (see pages 159–60). Serve summer's tender, fresh greens as satisfying entrées (or as an accompaniment to other meals). Create your own combinations of greens and vegetables; heighten flavors with aromatic herbs; add bits of cooked meats, flaked fish, chopped seafood, sliced or chopped hard-cooked eggs, plain or savory croutons, strips or cubes of cheese, then complement your creation with a piquant homemade dressing. With a bit of imagination you can concoct enough variations in ingredients and dressings so that no two salads need ever be the same.

## Fixings for Your Salads

LETTUCE: Try some of the loose-leafed varieties like butterhead or Bibb, romaine and leaf lettuce as well as the more compact head varieties. Grow your own if you have the space (see page 178)—or even if you think you haven't (see page 184)—and by all means include those flavorful lettuce substitutes, endive and escarole, occasionally. Whatever type of lettuce you select for your salads, be sure to choose only the freshest and most perfect leaves. Wash them thoroughly in cold water or set them into a bowl of ice and water to crisp, then drain in a colander or lettuce basket and pat with a dry towel; no water should be left on the leaves to dilute the dressing. Tear, rather than cut, your greens into bite-sized pieces. Refrigerate if not used immediately. Lettuce should always be served fresh, crisp, dry and well chilled.

OTHER GREENS: Choose young, tender leaves of fresh leafy vegetables like spinach, watercress, collards, Swiss chard and kale. Young leaves of such root vegetables as beets and turnips make nutrition-filled and tasty additions to salads.

Slightly bitter dandelion leaves may also be included in this group; pick these young and tender in spring from any pollution-free area. Also gather peppery nasturtium leaves to perk up almost any salad. Use the flowers themselves as an unusual decoration.

VEGETABLES: Tomatoes, carrots, radishes, sweet peppers, scallions and cucumbers are the traditional components of summer salads, but don't limit yourself to these. Many vegetables that are ordinarily served cooked are really delightful raw. Try young snap beans, small yellow or zucchini squash thinly sliced, edible pea pods and tiny cauliflower and broccoli florets. Cooked and cooled, vegetables like beets, asparagus, peas and leeks are always a welcome treat, and add unique flavors and textures to salads. Protein-rich beans—chick-peas, soybeans—make a nice change-of-pace filler, and crunchy bean sprouts can't be beat.

HERBS: Fresh chives, chervil, mint, parsley and tarragon are the most popular salad herbs, but don't neglect the possibilities of anise, borage, sweet marjoram, dill and summer savory. Fresh herbs make delicious additions to salad dressings, too.

## Chef's Salad Bowl

(YIELD: ENOUGH TO SERVE 6)

2 Quarts salad greens
2 Cups cooked turkey, cut into thin strips
2 Cups cooked ham, cut into thin strips
2 Cups Gruyère or Swiss cheese, cut into thin strips
2 Green peppers, cut into thin strips
1 Large sweet onion, peeled and very thinly sliced
1 Medium cucumber, very thinly sliced (well-washed young cucumbers from your garden need not be peeled)
12 Cherry tomatoes
 Blue Cheese French Dressing (see page 168) or Vinaigrette Dressing (see page 168) or any other dressing of your choice

Crisp the salad greens in ice water, drain and blot dry. Select 6 to 8 of the largest leaves and use to line the bottom and sides of a large salad bowl. Tear the remaining greens into bite-sized pieces and place in the bowl. Arrange the meat, cheese and fresh vegetables attractively over the greens. Serve cold, accompanied by the dressing of your choice.

## Salade Niçoise

(YIELD: ENOUGH TO SERVE 8)

6 Potatoes, boiled
1 Head Bibb lettuce or small head romaine
1 Large sweet onion, peeled and thinly sliced
2 Tablespoons minced fresh parsley
1 Tablespoon minced fresh basil (or 1 teaspoon dried)
1 Cup Basic French Dressing I (see page 167)
1 6½-Ounce can chunk tuna
3 Large tomatoes, cut into eighths
3 Hard-cooked eggs, shelled and cut into quarters
1 2-Ounce can flat anchovy fillets, halved
18 Black olives

Peel and slice the potatoes. Crisp the lettuce in ice water; drain and blot dry. Tear the lettuce into bite-sized pieces and arrange around the bottom and sides of a large salad bowl. Combine the potato slices, onion, parsley and basil and gently toss with the dressing. Arrange over the salad greens and garnish with the tuna, tomatoes, eggs, anchovies and olives.

## Summer Supper Salad Bowl

(YIELD: ENOUGH TO SERVE 8)

2 Quarts lettuce, romaine or other greens
2 Sweet green peppers, seeded and sliced into rings
2 Sweet red peppers, seeded and sliced into rings

10 Radishes, sliced
5 Small carrots, scraped and shredded
½ Pound cooked ham, cut in thin strips
½ Pound American cheese, cut in thin strips
8 Hard-cooked eggs, peeled and quartered
4 Ripe tomatoes, cut in wedges
1½ Cups Catsup French Dressing (see page 168)
2 Tablespoons grated onion

Wash the lettuce or greens well, drain and dry carefully. Chill to crisp if desired, then break into bite-sized pieces and place in a large salad bowl. Arrange the peppers in overlapping rings on the lettuce, along with the radishes and carrots. Arrange the ham and cheese strips, egg quarters and tomato wedges around the top. Shake the dressing with the grated onion, pour over the salad, toss and serve immediately.

## Country Garden Salad Bowl

(YIELD: ENOUGH TO SERVE 8)

2 Heads Bibb lettuce
2 Small heads escarole
2 Cups fresh spinach leaves
2 Cups fresh cauliflower florets
2 Small zucchini, thinly sliced
8 Small carrots, scraped and cut in thin strips
4 Ripe tomatoes, cut in wedges
½ Pound cheese of your choice, cut in thin strips
Garlic French Dressing (see page 168) or Herb French Dressing (see page 168)

Separate and wash the lettuce and escarole leaves, left whole. Drain well, then dry between 2 dish towels. Arrange over the bottom and sides of a large salad bowl. Rinse and dry the spinach, then place, along with the cauliflower florets, zucchini slices, carrot strips, tomatoes and cheese strips, over the greens, in groups. Chill thoroughly. At table toss gently with the dressing until well coated.

## Summer Festival Salad

(YIELD: ENOUGH TO SERVE 8)

1 Quart head lettuce leaves, torn into pieces
2 Small zucchini, thinly sliced
2 Small cucumbers, peeled and thinly sliced
6 Small carrots, scraped and diced
12 Radishes, thinly sliced
8 Scallions, with 3 inches of green top, chopped
8 Tomatoes, sliced
14 Sprigs fresh parsley
8 Hard-cooked eggs, quartered
Basic French Dressing II (see page 167) or Creamy French Dressing (see page 168)

Wash and dry the lettuce. Arrange the leaves in a salad bowl, then add the zucchini, cucumbers, carrots, radishes and scallions. Arrange the tomato slices, parsley sprigs and quartered eggs attractively on top and refrigerate until very cold. Toss the salad with the dressing at the table.

## Waldorf Salad Deluxe

For a luncheon salad that really holds its own, increase the nuts and add more cubes of cheese to this all-American salad.

(YIELD: ENOUGH TO SERVE 8)

4 Cups diced apples
3 Cups diced celery
1½ Cups broken walnut halves
2 Cups cubed mild Cheddar cheese
1½ Cups Mayonnaise (see page 169) or commercially prepared mayonnaise
16 Large whole lettuce leaves

Place the apples, celery, walnuts and cheese cubes in a bowl and toss with the mayonnaise. Chill well. Arrange 2 crisp, whole lettuce leaves on each of 8 salad plates. Top with equal portions of the salad and serve.

## Fresh Herb Salad

(YIELD: ENOUGH TO SERVE 8)

2 *Heads Bibb lettuce*
6 *Tablespoons salad oil*
2 *Tablespoons tarragon vinegar*
1 *Teaspoon granulated sugar*
½ *Teaspoon salt*
2 *Cloves garlic, peeled and crushed*
¼ *Cup each minced fresh chives, minced fresh dill and minced fresh parsley*
2 *Teaspoons fresh thyme leaves*
1 *Pound leftover cooked turkey, chicken or ham*
2 *Small cucumbers, very thinly sliced (well-washed young cucumbers from your garden need not be peeled)*
18 *Cherry tomatoes, halved*

Pull the leaves gently from the lettuce and crisp them in ice water for a few minutes. Pat dry with paper towels and chill well.

Place the oil, vinegar, sugar, salt and garlic in a screwtop jar, shake vigorously to mix, then refrigerate until very cold.

Just before serving, tear the lettuce leaves into bite-sized pieces and place in the salad bowl. Add the fresh herbs and toss lightly. Arrange the meat, cucumber slices and tomatoes over the top. Shake the dressing once more, then pour over the salad. Toss at table until each leaf glistens with dressing. Serve immediately.

## Cottage Cheese Salad Bowl

(YIELD: ENOUGH TO SERVE 8)

4 *Cups cold Cottage Cheese (see page 59) or commercially prepared cottage cheese*
2 *Tablespoons minced chives or scallions*
1½ *Cups slivered nuts*
2 *Heads each leaf lettuce and romaine*
8 *Ripe peaches*
  *Basic French Dressing I (see page 167) or Thousand Islands Dressing (see page 170) or Chutney French Dressing (see page 168)*

Mix the cottage cheese with the chives and nuts. Tear well-washed and dried lettuce and romaine leaves into bite-sized pieces and arrange in a shallow salad bowl. Chill the cheese and greens separately until serving time.

Heap the cottage cheese mixture in the center of the greens and surround with the peaches, sliced. Pour the dressing on the greens and serve immediately.

## Avocados with Cottage Cheese

*If you can find avocados on special sale, this salad is a treat.*

(YIELD: ENOUGH TO SERVE 8)

4 *Cups Large-Curd Cottage Cheese (see page 60) or commercially prepared cottage cheese*
5 *Scallions, with 3 inches of green top, minced*
  *Freshly ground black pepper*
½ *Cup Mayonnaise (see page 169)*
1½ *Tablespoons lemon juice*
  *Salt*
2 *Ripe avocados*
2 *Small heads Bibb lettuce*
2 *Medium tomatoes, peeled, seeded and chopped*
1½ *Cups Thousand Islands Dressing (see page 170)*

Place the cottage cheese in a large bowl. Add the minced scallions, pepper, mayonnaise and 1 tablespoon of the lemon juice. Season with salt to taste and mix thoroughly, then cover and refrigerate for 1 hour.

Just before serving, cut the avocados in half lengthwise, peel, pit them and cut into slices. Sprinkle with the remaining lemon juice.

Wash, crisp and dry the lettuce leaves and arrange them on a large serving plate. Mound the chilled cottage cheese in the center. Spoon the chopped tomatoes in a circle around the bottom of the cheese and arrange the avocado slices in a spiral on the lettuce leaves. Serve immediately, with the dressing in a side dish.

## Tossed Tuna and Greens Salad

(YIELD: ENOUGH TO SERVE 8)

2 Quarts mixed lettuce or other salad
  greens
2 Cups drained canned tuna
⅔ Cup Chili Sauce French Dressing
  (see page 168)
¼ Cup minced fresh chervil, chives,
  parsley or other herbs

Tear the washed, dried and chilled greens into bite-sized pieces and place in a bowl. Top with the tuna and toss with the dressing, then sprinkle the herbs over the top and serve.

## Fish and Mushroom Salad

(YIELD: ENOUGH TO SERVE 8)

2 Heads leaf lettuce
2 Small heads romaine
½ Pound fresh mushrooms
3 Cups flaked fish
¾ Cup Vinaigrette Dressing,
  prepared with lemon juice instead
  of vinegar (see page 168)

Wash and dry the leaf lettuce and romaine, then tear into bite-sized pieces. Chill the greens. Wipe the mushrooms, trim the ends and slice on top of the greens. Add the fish, toss with the dressing and serve.

## Tomato and Sweet Onion Salad

A super-easy salad that will enliven almost any meal, this is an ideal way to use the bounty of a summer garden.

(YIELD: ENOUGH TO SERVE 8)

8 Large, ripe tomatoes
2 Large sweet onions
1½ Cups Fines Herbes Dressing
  (see page 170)

Peel and slice the tomatoes and onions and arrange in alternate slices on 8 salad plates. Cover with the dressing.

## Rice Salad

(YIELD: ENOUGH TO SERVE 6)

3 Cups Freezer Rice (see page 46),
  or cold, cooked rice
1½ to 2 Cups leftover ham or turkey,
  cut into thin strips
2 Green peppers, seeded and cut into
  thin rings
1 Large Bermuda onion, peeled and
  thinly sliced
12 Large pimiento-stuffed olives, sliced
12 Large pitted black olives, sliced
  Curry French Dressing (see page
  168) or Garlic French Dressing
  (see page 168)
6 Crisp lettuce leaves
2 Tablespoons minced fresh Italian
  parsley
3 Medium tomatoes, cut in eighths
3 Hard-cooked eggs, peeled and cut
  in quarters

Combine the rice, meat, peppers, onion and olive slices in a large bowl. Toss gently with the dressing. Arrange the lettuce leaves in a large salad bowl and heap the rice mixture in the center. Sprinkle with the parsley. Serve cold, garnished with the tomato wedges and eggs.

## Beef and Potato Salad

(YIELD: ENOUGH TO SERVE 6)

3 Potatoes, boiled
3 to 4 Cups leftover roast, boiled or
  corned beef, cut into ½-inch cubes
1 Cup diced celery
8 Scallions, with 3 inches of green
  stem, chopped
1 Sweet red and 1 sweet green pepper,
  seeded and cut into thin strips
¼ Cup minced fresh parsley

 1½  Cups Catsup French Dressing
       (see page 168) or Vinaigrette
       Dressing (see page 168)
       Crisp lettuce leaves
       Tomato wedges

Cool, peel and cut the potatoes into ½-inch cubes. Combine the beef, potatoes, celery, scallions, red and green peppers and parsley. Toss gently with the dressing and refrigerate until well chilled. Serve cold on a bed of crisp lettuce leaves garnished with tomato wedges.

## Parslied Ham

*Chill leftover ham, vegetables and a generous portion of fresh parsley in gelatin for a gourmet summer supper.*

(YIELD: ENOUGH TO SERVE 6)

 3  Cups leftover ham, cubed
 3  Cups cooked vegetables (carrots,
       peas, etc.)

 2  Envelopes unflavored gelatin
 ¾  Cup cold water
 3  Cups Beef Consommé (see page
       147) or canned consommé
 ½  Cup white wine
 ¼  Cup tarragon vinegar
 ¾  Cup minced fresh parsley
 1  Tablespoon chopped fresh tarragon
       or 1 teaspoon dried

Place the ham and vegetables in a large glass loaf pan or attractive mold. Sprinkle the gelatin over ½ cup of the cold water in separate large bowl, and set aside to soak.

Meanwhile, combine the remaining cold water, the consommé, wine and vinegar in a saucepan. Heat to just under a boil and add to the gelatin, then stir until the gelatin dissolves. Cool the gelatin mixture to lukewarm, then stir in the parsley and tarragon. Pour over the ham and vegetables, taking care that all are completely immersed. Chill for at least 4 hours, or until the gelatin mixture is completely set. Unmold and cut into thin slices before serving cold.

# SUPER SOUPS

One of the most satisfying meals I can think of is one that includes a thick, hearty soup, a crusty bread, a crispy salad, dessert, coffee—and nothing else. This menu has become a trend in gourmet dining, and it is one you can adopt with great success and very little expense.

Soup stock—rich and hearty, brimful of simmered flavor and nourishment—is the base for a dazzling array of super soups. This is a perfect way to utilize inexpensive cuts of meat, bones trimmed from cuts prepared for your freezer, or those leftover meat and vegetable scraps and nutrition-filled vegetable cooking liquids. Soup stocks on hand in refrigerator or freezer provide fingertip convenience when preparing soups, sauces or main dishes. Remember that stock, broth and bouillon are basically the same, and this recipe may be used interchangeably for all of these.

### Basic Beef Stock

(YIELD: 2 TO 3 QUARTS)

1½ Pounds lean beef
2 Pounds beef bones
1 Pound veal bones
   Leftover scraps of meat
1 Roast chicken carcass or 4 chicken feet, cleaned and skinned
4 Quarts water or a combination of vegetable liquids and water
3 Medium onions
2 Stalks celery with leaves
3 Medium carrots
4 Sprigs fresh parsley
   Raw vegetable scraps or leftover vegetables
6 Peppercorns
2 Teaspoons salt

Arrange the beef and bones in a large soup kettle and cover with the liquid. Bring slowly to a boil over low heat, removing any scum which rises to the surface. When no more scum appears, add

145

the vegetables, peppercorns and salt. Cover the kettle loosely; too tight a fit may cause your stock to cloud. Simmer over low heat for 2 to 2½ hours, or until the meat is tender.

Cool the stock a bit, then strain it through a fine sieve or cheesecloth. Discard the meat, bones and vegetables (their flavor and nutrition have already passed into the stock). Divide the stock into pint or quart jars, cool further, then cover tightly and refrigerate, removing any fat that rises to the surface. Refrigerated stock keeps well, but bring it to a boil every 3 or 4 days to keep it fresh if not used immediately.

Frozen stock will remain at peak quality for several weeks when stored at 0 degrees F. or below. However, when preparing stock for the freezer, omit the peppercorns and salt. Spices behave unpredictably when frozen. Pour the chilled and thoroughly skimmed stock into plastic pint or quart freezer containers, allowing 1 inch of headspace for expansion during freezing. Seal tightly and freeze. Thaw slightly in the refrigerator before reheating slowly over low heat. Season with salt and pepper to taste just before serving.

### Basic Chicken Stock

*If you plan to freeze your chicken stock, omit the garlic and pappercorns.*

(YIELD: 2 TO 3 QUARTS)

1 *3-Pound chicken*
1 *Roast chicken carcass*
8 *Chicken necks*
4 *Chicken feet, cleaned and skinned*
1 *Veal knuckle*
4 *Quarts water or any combination of vegetable liquids and water*
3 *Stalks celery with leaves*
3 *Medium carrots*
  *Raw vegetable scraps or leftover vegetables*
1 *Clove garlic, peeled*
⅛ *Teaspoon thyme*
8 *Peppercorns*

Place the chicken, chicken carcass, chicken necks and feet and veal knuckle in a kettle and cover

with the water. Bring slowly to a boil over low heat and simmer for 1 hour, skimming off any foam that appears on the surface. Add the celery, carrots, vegetable scraps, garlic, thyme and peppercorns. Cover the kettle loosely—too tight a fit may result in a cloudy stock—and continue to simmer for 1½ to 2 hours. Remove the cooked chicken and reserve for Chicken Hash (see page 156). Strain the stock through a fine sieve and cool quickly, then chill. Skim off any surface fat and reheat to use, or keep in refrigerator storage until needed. Refrigerated stock keeps well, but bring it to a boil every 3 or 4 days to maintain freshness.

To freeze chicken stock, pour the cold and skimmed liquid into conveniently sized plastic freezer containers, seal tightly and store at 0 degrees F. or below. Frozen stock will remain at peak quality for several weeks in proper freezer storage conditions. To use, thaw slightly in the refrigerator before reheating slowly over low heat. Season to taste with salt and pepper before serving.

### Clarified Stock

*Cloudy soup stock may be clarified easily in this way.*

2½ to 3 *Quarts well-skimmed beef or chicken stock*
2 *Egg whites*
2 *Egg shells*

Bring the stock to a boil in a large kettle. Beat the egg whites to a froth and add them, along with the egg shells, to the boiling stock, stirring constantly. Reduce the heat and continue to stir while the stock simmers at a low boil for 10 minutes. Remove from the heat. Allow the egg particles to settle, then strain the stock through several layers of cheesecloth. Refrigerate or freeze as directed above, and use when clear soups or sauces are called for.

## Beef or Chicken Consommé

(YIELD: ABOUT 2 QUARTS)

3 Quarts Basic Beef Stock (see page 145) or Basic Chicken Stock (see page 146)
1½ Pounds lean chopped beef or chicken (optional)
2 Egg whites
2 Egg shells

Pour the stock into a large kettle, add the meat, egg whites and egg shells, and bring slowly to *just under a boil*, stirring constantly. Simmer slowly for 2 hours, until the stock is reduced and the flavor becomes quite concentrated. Remove from the heat, allow the particles to settle, then strain through several layers of cheesecloth. Serve immediately, reheating over a low flame if necessary. Otherwise, cool quickly and refrigerate or freeze.

### Consommé Variations

The rich bouquet and subtle flavor of consommé combine to make it the perfect way to begin a meal. Heighten its nourishing goodness with any number of variations. Dice or cut small amounts of raw vegetables into thin strips and cook them directly in the soup, or add spoonfuls of raw or leftover cooked vegetables just before serving. Embellish your consommé with freshly cut herbs, or add a dash of wine or sherry for a distinctive touch. Try little dumplings, small amounts of vermicelli, rice or noodles, plain or savory croutons, or even poached eggs—versatile consommé will enhance them all.

## Chinese Egg Drop Soup

*Nothing could be easier to prepare than this never-fail Chinese soup.*

(YIELD: ENOUGH TO SERVE 6)

2 Cups raw ground meat
2 Tablespoons soy sauce
2 Tablespoons vegetable oil
6 to 8 Cups Basic Chicken Stock (see page 146) or canned chicken broth
1 Cup chopped fresh spinach
4 Eggs
4 Teaspoons water

Mix the ground meat with the soy sauce until well blended. Heat the oil, add the meat and stir over medium heat for 3 minutes. Add the stock or broth and simmer for 5 minutes. Stir in the spinach, bring the soup to a boil, and cook for 3 minutes.

Beat the eggs and water together in a small bowl. Remove the soup from the heat and beat in the eggs in a steady stream. Return the soup to low heat and simmer for 3 minutes longer. Serve immediately.

## Curried Egg and Tomato Soup

(YIELD: ENOUGH TO SERVE 6 TO 8)

2 Tablespoons butter
2 Small onions, peeled and coarsely chopped
1 Small clove garlic, peeled and crushed
2 Teaspoons curry powder
1 Large tomato, chopped
1 Tablespoon tomato paste
1 Tablespoon granulated sugar
5 Cups Basic Chicken Stock (see page 146) or 2 10¾-ounce cans chicken broth plus 1 can water
1½ Tablespoons all-purpose flour
⅓ Cup water
2 Hard-cooked eggs, chopped

Heat the butter in a deep kettle and sauté the onions and garlic for 3 minutes. Add the curry powder and sauté for 2 minutes more. Stir in the chopped tomato, tomato paste and sugar. Cover with the stock and bring to a boil. Lower the heat, cover the kettle and simmer for 10 minutes.

Blend the flour and ⅓ cup water to a smooth paste and add to the soup. Stir constantly until the soup thickens slightly. Serve hot, garnished with the chopped egg.

## Onion Soup

(YIELD: ENOUGH TO SERVE 8)

8 *Medium onions, peeled*
5 *Tablespoons butter or margarine*
¼ *Cup all-purpose flour*
2½ *Quarts Beef Consommé (see page
      147) or 2 10½-ounce cans beef
      consommé plus 1 soup can water*
3 *Tablespoons olive or vegetable oil*
2 *Cloves garlic, peeled and minced*
8 *Slices French bread*
2 *Cups grated Swiss cheese*

Cut the onions into thin slices and sauté them in
the butter until transparent, stirring occasionally
to keep them from browning. Stir in the flour and
blend well. Add the consommé and bring the
soup to a boil, stirring constantly. Boil for 1 minute.

Heat the oil in a large skillet and sauté the
garlic for 2 minutes. Fry the bread slices to a
golden brown on both sides, turning once. Remove and drain the bread briefly on paper towels,
then place one slice in each of 8 soup bowls.
Ladle the hot soup over the bread and serve
immediately, with a bowl of grated cheese on the
side.

## Corn Clam Chowder

(YIELD: ENOUGH TO SERVE 8)

1 *Clove garlic, peeled*
8 *Strips bacon*
2 *Cups thin Basic White Sauce
   (see page 171)*
2 *10-Ounce packages your own frozen
   corn or 2 1-pound cans creamed
   corn*
2 *8-Ounce cans minced clams
   Milk or light cream*
4 *Tablespoons butter or margarine
   Paprika
   Seasoned Croutons (see page 28),
   optional*

Mince the garlic and cut the bacon into 1-inch
pieces. Place both in a large, heavy kettle and
sauté over medium heat until the bacon is crisp.
Remove the kettle from the heat, stir in the
white sauce and corn and spoon in the clams and
juice, taking care not to include any sandy bits
that may be in the bottom of the can. If the soup
seems too thick, add a little milk or light cream
until it reaches the consistency you prefer.

Simmer the soup over medium heat for 15 minutes, stirring occasionally; do not allow to boil.
Pour into soup bowls and top each portion with
a piece of butter and a dash of paprika. Serve
hot, garnished with croutons if desired.

## New England Clam Chowder

*If you live near an area where you can do your own
clamming, this filling chowder should cost you
next to nothing.*

(YIELD: ENOUGH TO SERVE 8)

25 to 30 *Clams in their shells
          A handful of cornmeal*
4 *Slices bacon, minced*
2 *Large onions, peeled and coarsely
   chopped*
5 *Large potatoes, peeled*
2½ *Cups cold water*
3½ *Cups milk*
1 *Cup heavy cream
   Salt and freshly ground black
   pepper*

Scrub the clam shells well and place in a
bucket of cold water. Throw the handful of
cornmeal into the bucket and let the clams
stand for one hour to disgorge their sand. Rinse
the clams in fresh, cold water.

Sauté the bacon and onions for 3 minutes in a
large, heavy kettle. Cut the potatoes into ½-inch
cubes, add them to the kettle and sauté for 3
minutes more, stirring constantly.

Arrange the clams in a large kettle and add the
2½ cups cold water. Cover the kettle and simmer
until the clams open. Remove the clams from the
kettle, reserving the meat and discarding the
shells. Carefully (so as not to include any sand
from the bottom) ladle the clam liquid into the

kettle containing the bacon and vegetables. Simmer, covered, for 35 minutes.

Mince the clams and add them to the vegetables, along with the milk and cream. Add salt and pepper to taste and slowly bring the chowder just to a boil. Serve steaming hot with a crusty bread and a crunchy salad.

## Poached Egg Chowder

(YIELD: ENOUGH TO SERVE 4)

2 Medium onions, peeled
4 Medium potatoes, peeled
2 Tablespoons vegetable oil
3 Cups Basic Chicken Stock (see page 146) or canned chicken broth
1½ Cups fresh (or frozen) lima beans
Salt
Pinch of sweet marjoram
4 Eggs
Fried Bread Croutons (see page 28)
Dash of paprika
2 Tablespoons minced scallions

Chop the onions and cut the potatoes into ½-inch slices. Sauté the onions in the oil until soft and transparent, then add the potato slices and cook briefly on each side. Pour the broth over the vegetables. Stir in the lima beans, salt and marjoram. Cover and cook over medium heat for 15 to 18 minutes, or until the beans are tender but not mushy.

Push the vegetables to one side and crack one of the eggs into the broth. Continue one at a time with the remaining eggs, making room for each by pushing the vegetables aside. Cook only long enough for the eggs to poach.

To serve, place fried bread croutons in each bowl. Carefully set an egg on top and sprinkle with a dash of paprika. Ladle the soup and vegetables into each bowl around the eggs and garnish with the minced scallions. Serve hot.

## Tart Vegetable Soup

*Short ribs of beef turn this hearty vegetable soup into a meal. If today is meatless Tuesday in your house, substitute tomato juice for the water, leave out the meat and sprinkle the hot soup with grated cheese and croutons just before serving!*

(YIELD: ENOUGH TO SERVE 8)

1½ Pounds short ribs of beef
A leftover ham bone, if one is available
5 Large onions, peeled
5 Carrots, scraped
1 Bunch celery, with the leaves, well washed
⅓ Cup granulated sugar (more if desired)
3 Tablespoons lemon juice (more if desired)
3 Tablespoons Worcestershire sauce
2 Teaspoons peppercorns, coarsely crushed
1 Teaspoon each rosemary and caraway seeds
½ Teaspoon ground cloves
¾ Teaspoon salt
½ 6-Ounce can tomato paste
Sour cream
2 Large tomatoes, chopped
6 Scallions, with 3 inches of green top, trimmed and chopped
2 Green peppers, seeded and chopped
1 Tablespoon chopped fresh dill

Place the meat and bones in a large soup kettle. Chop the onions, carrots and celery and add them, along with the sugar, lemon juice, Worcestershire sauce, peppercorns, rosemary, caraway seeds, cloves and salt. Mix the tomato paste with enough water to cover the meat, bones and vegetables. Cover the kettle and bring the liquid to a boil, then lower the heat and simmer the soup for 3 hours, adding more water if necessary to maintain the level of the liquid.

Add sugar and lemon juice until the soup is as sweet and tart as you like it, then serve the soup hot, with a dollop of sour cream. Pass the fresh chopped tomatoes, scallions, green peppers and dill in a bowl on the side.

## Cold Buttermilk Soup

(YIELD: ENOUGH TO SERVE 6)

1½  Cups chopped cooked chicken or
    turkey
 6  Cups Basic Chicken Stock (see page
    146) or canned chicken broth
 4  Egg yolks
1½  Cups buttermilk
1½  Teaspoons curry powder
 3  Tablespoons chopped fresh parsley

Heat the chicken and stock together in a large
saucepan. Place the egg yolks, buttermilk and
curry powder in a small bowl and beat until well
blended. Stir into the stock, over low heat, until
the soup is thick and creamy (take care not to
boil the soup or the eggs will curdle). Allow the
soup to cool, then refrigerate for at least 4 hours.
Serve cold, garnished with the chopped parsley.

## Quick Cold Buttermilk Soup

*This exquisite summer soup can be stirred
together in less than 3 minutes if you hurry.*

(YIELD: ENOUGH TO SERVE 6)

6 to 8  Cups cold buttermilk
    4   Hard-cooked eggs, peeled and
        chopped
    2   Cups chopped leftover cold meat
    6   Scallions, with 3 inches of green
        top, chopped
    2   Large tomatoes, seeded and
        chopped
    2   Tablespoons minced fresh dill
    1   Tablespoon chopped fresh fennel,
        rosemary or thyme
        Salt and freshly ground coarse
        black pepper to taste

Stir all the ingredients together and serve immediately, ladled over ice cubes, or refrigerate
overnight. Serve topped with additional freshly
ground black pepper.

## Eggplant Soup with Chicken Slices

*This is a unique soup from start to finish. It is also
one of my favorite ways to dress up leftover meat
and turn it into a gourmet treat.*

(YIELD: ENOUGH TO SERVE 8)

 ½  Cup dry-roasted peanuts
 4  Cloves garlic, peeled and minced
12  Scallions, with 3 inches of green
    top, trimmed
1½  Cups thin slices leftover chicken
    (or turkey)
 6  Tablespoons vegetable oil (not
    olive oil), more if necessary
 1  Large eggplant, peeled
 8  Tablespoons all-purpose flour
 4  Eggs, beaten
2½  Quarts Basic Chicken Stock
    (see page 146) or canned
    chicken broth
 8  Tablespoons soy sauce

Pound the peanuts to a powder using a mortar
and pestle.

Mix the garlic, scallions and chicken slices;
sauté them for 2 minutes in 2 tablespoons of the
oil. Using a slotted spoon, remove the sautéed
garlic-chicken mixture from the oil in the pan
and set it aside in a bowl.

Add the remaining oil to the pan. Cut the
eggplant into sticks about 2 inches long and ½
inch thick. Dip the eggplant pieces in flour and
then in the beaten egg. Fry the eggplant in the
hot oil until golden brown on all sides, adding
more oil if necessary.

Meanwhile, heat the chicken stock. When the
broth is steaming hot, stir in the garlic-chicken
mixture and the soy sauce. Divide the hot, fried
eggplant sticks into 8 soup plates, ladle the soup
over and sprinkle with the powdered peanuts.
Serve immediately.

## Kentucky Burgoo

*Thick, spicy burgoo is a breeze if you prepare the meat and broth ahead of time and freeze at o degrees F. When ready to serve, thaw the broth, add leftover meat, the vegetables and seasonings and continue the cooking.*

(YIELD: ENOUGH TO SERVE 8 GENEROUSLY)

3 Pounds soup bones
1 Pound lean lamb
1 Turkey carcass
2 Cups leftover cooked chicken or turkey
3 Quarts water
3 Large onions, peeled and diced
3 Large potatoes, peeled and diced
4 Medium carrots, scraped and diced
1 Sweet green pepper, chopped
1 Sweet red pepper, chopped
1 Small head cabbage, coarsely shredded
1½ Cups chopped celery, with leaves
1 Cup chopped okra
2 Cups fresh (or frozen) whole corn kernels
2 Cups fresh (or frozen) lima beans
2 Cups tomato purée (or 4 cups peeled, seeded and chopped tomatoes)
Salt
Cayenne pepper
Worcestershire sauce
A-1 Sauce
Tabasco Sauce
½ Cup minced fresh parsley

Place the bones, lamb and turkey carcass in a large kettle, cover with the water, and bring to just under a boil. Skim off the froth and simmer the broth, covered, over low heat until the meat is very tender (about 2 hours). Remove from the heat and cool quickly. Strain the broth and freeze it if desired.

To continue the cooking, chop the meat and chicken and add it to the hot broth along with the onions, potatoes, carrots, peppers, cabbage, celery, okra, corn, lima beans and tomato purée. Mix in the seasonings with a light hand, keeping

in mind that their flavor increases during cooking.

Cover the burgoo and cook over very low heat for 3 or 4 hours, stirring occasionally at first, then more frequently as the mixture thickens. Adjust the seasonings to taste just before serving hot, garnished with the minced parsley.

## Hearty Louisiana Gumbo

*Freeze your cooked meat bits until you have assembled enough, then prepare this rich, nourishing meal-in-itself. Although crabmeat is usually included in the soup, its price is so exorbitant that seafood flavor has been attained by adding lobster shell to the broth. The result is not quite the same, but it is still delicious.*

(YIELD: ENOUGH TO SERVE 8 GENEROUSLY)

1 Chicken carcass
1 Fresh lobster shell (ask your seafood store owner when you buy the shrimp)
½ Pound uncooked shrimp, peeled and shells reserved
4 Strips bacon, chopped
2 Large onions, peeled and finely chopped
2 Cups well-washed and chopped celery, with leaves
1 Sweet green pepper, chopped
1 Sweet red pepper, chopped
1 Cup chopped okra
4 Cloves garlic, peeled and finely chopped
1 Pound leftover cooked beef, cubed
1 Pound leftover cooked pork, cubed
1 Pound leftover cooked ham, cubed
4 Medium tomatoes, peeled, seeded and chopped
1 6-Ounce can tomato paste
1 Bay leaf, crumbled
½ Teaspoon leaf thyme
Salt and pepper to taste
¼ Cup minced fresh parsley
1 Tablespoon filé powder
10 Okra pods, halved
2 Cups hot cooked rice

Cover the chicken carcass and lobster shell with water, add the shrimp shells and bring to a boil.

Boil for 10 minutes, skimming off any froth that accumulates. Lower the heat and simmer the broth, covered, for 2 hours. Strain the broth.

In a large kettle, sauté the bacon for 3 minutes. Add the onions, celery, peppers, okra and garlic. Sauté until the onions are transparent and the okra is lightly browned. Add the cubed leftover meats, chopped tomatoes and enough of the broth to bring the liquid level at least 1 inch above the vegetables and meats. Stir in the tomato paste, bay leaf, thyme, salt and pepper.

Simmer the gumbo, covered, for a half hour, adding more broth or water if the mixture seems too thick. Add the okra pods and shrimp and simmer a half hour longer. Adjust the seasonings. Remove from the heat and stir in the parsley and filé powder. Spoon some cooked rice into each soup bowl and ladle the gumbo over. Serve hot.

## Bread Casserole Soup

*Cheese makes this satisfying bread soup a protein-rich meal.*

(YIELD: ENOUGH TO SERVE 8)

    8  Medium onions, peeled
   12  Stalks celery, with leaves, well
        washed
    4  Tablespoons butter or margarine
    2  Teaspoons peppercorns
   ½   Teaspoon leaf thyme
   ¼   Teaspoon oregano
    2  Bay leaves
  2½   Quarts Basic Beef Stock (see page
        145) or canned beef broth
   ½   Pound Swiss cheese, grated
   ¼   Pound Parmesan cheese, grated
   15  Slices leftover white or French bread

Slice the onions and cut the celery into 1-inch pieces. Heat the butter in a large saucepan and sauté the onions, celery and spices. As soon as the onions are transparent, add the stock or broth and simmer, covered, over low heat for 1 hour.

Combine the grated Swiss and Parmesan cheeses and arrange alternative layers of bread and cheese in 2 deep ovenproof dishes. Strain

the broth, divide between the 2 dishes, then cover and bake for 1 hour in an oven preheated to 375 degrees F. Serve hot.

## Beef Bone and Bean Soup

*When the cupboard is really bare, hustle on down to the supermarket and then rustle up some beef bone and dried bean soup. If you have a dollar or two to spare, add a few short ribs for a soup that can easily pinch-hit for dinner.*

(YIELD: ENOUGH TO SERVE 8 GENEROUSLY)

    3  Pounds beef bones (or 2 pounds
        beef bones and 1½ pounds
        short ribs)
  2½   Quarts cold water
   ¾   Cup dried black-eyed peas
    1  Cup dried pinto beans
   ½   Teaspoon dried red pepper
    1  Tablespoon salt
    2  Large onions, peeled
    2  Large potatoes, peeled
    2  Large carrots, scraped
    3  Cloves garlic, peeled
    2  Teaspoons chili powder
    1  Bay leaf
   ¼   Teaspoon black pepper
        Fried Bread Croutons (see page 28)

Rinse the bones, place them in a soup kettle and cover with the cold water. Cover the kettle and bring the water to a boil, then lower the heat and simmer for 2 hours, skimming any foam from the surface as it rises.

Add the peas, beans, red pepper and salt and simmer for 3 hours longer, or until the peas and beans are fairly tender.

Coarsely chop the onions, potatoes and carrots. Mince the garlic. Add these vegetables to the soup, along with the chili, bay leaf and black pepper. Simmer for 1 hour longer. Correct the seasonings if necessary and serve piping hot with the croutons.

## Sauerkraut Soup

(YIELD: ENOUGH TO SERVE 8)

2 1-Pound cans sauerkraut
2½ Quarts Basic Beef Stock (see page 145) or canned beef broth
½ Pound bratwurst sausage or kielbasa
3 Large onions, peeled
2 Tablespoons butter or vegetable oil
4 Medium potatoes, peeled
1 Tablespoon each catsup and prepared mustard
½ Teaspoon each caraway seeds and fennel seeds
1 Teaspoon paprika
½ Teaspoon salt
½ Cup leftover diced cooked meat (optional)

Minced fresh chives or parsley
Seasoned Croutons (see page 28), optional

Drain the sauerkraut, rinse well with water, then drain thoroughly again. Place the stock in a large kettle, add the drained sauerkraut and the bratwurst or kielbasa and simmer for 30 minutes.

Chop the onions. Heat the butter in a separate skillet and sauté the onions until tender and transparent. Grate the potatoes, soak them in cold water for 5 minutes, then drain them well. Add the onions, potatoes, catsup, caraway seeds, fennel seeds, paprika and salt to the mixture in the kettle. Remove the bratwurst from the kettle; slice and return it to the soup. Cover the kettle and simmer gently for 30 minutes more. Ten minutes before serving, stir in the diced leftover meat. Serve hot, garnished with minced chives or parsley and croutons.

# THE BIG BIRD
# & BIG-BIRD RECIPES

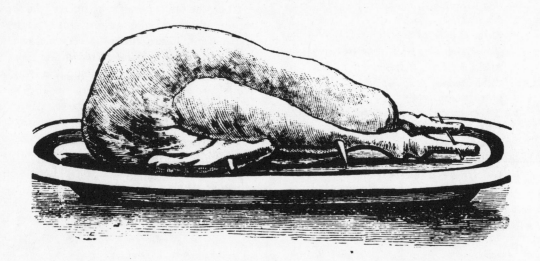

### How to Roast Turkey

*A whole turkey, fresh or frozen, offers one of the best supermarket buys when figured in cost per serving. Turkey reheats without tasting "leftover," and adapts admirably to recipes from all over the world.*

To roast a whole turkey, begin by rubbing the cavity lightly with salt. Add stuffing of your choice (see pages 5–6) just prior to roasting. Cream together several tablespoons softened butter, 1 teaspoon poultry seasoning and ½ teaspoon garlic salt (optional). Rub the seasoned butter over the skin of the bird. Truss the turkey and set, breast side down, on a rack in a roasting pan.

Loosely cover the bird with a tent of aluminum foil and cook at 325 degrees F. for one hour. Turn the turkey breast side up and continue to cook until the bird tests done, figuring about 20 minutes per pound. Lift the aluminum foil at frequent intervals during the cooking time and brush the skin with pan drippings. If the breast skin browns excessively before the bird is thoroughly cooked, flatten the aluminum foil directly against the skin.

To test for doneness, gently move one drumstick up and down, or use a fork to pierce the skin where the drumstick meets the breast. If the turkey is ready for carving, the drumstick will move easily, or the juices will run clear (not pink) when the bird is pierced. Allow the turkey to stand at room temperature at least 10 minutes before carving.

### Turkey Pot Pie

(YIELD: ENOUGH TO SERVE 6)

4 Cups leftover turkey, cut into
  ½-inch dice
2 Cups potatoes, boiled and cut into
  ½-inch dice
3 Cups Mushroom Sauce (see page
  172)
  Salt and black pepper to taste
  Nutmeg

Pot Pie Noodles (see page 27)
Instant Pie Crust for single-crust
pie (see page 48)

Combine the turkey and potatoes with the sauce and pour into a deep ovenproof casserole. Season with salt, pepper and nutmeg. Roll out and cut the noodles. Arrange over the turkey mixture, taking care the noodles do not overlap. Top with the pie crust, slashed in several places to allow steam to escape. Bake in an oven preheated to 450 degrees F. for 15 minutes, then reduce the heat to 350 degrees F. and bake for 25 minutes more. Serve hot.

## Far East Turkey (or Chicken) Pie

(YIELD: ENOUGH TO SERVE 6)

Instant Pie Crust for 1 double-crust
pie (see page 48)
2 Medium onions, chopped
3 Tablespoons butter
2 Cups diced fresh (or frozen) carrots
1 Teaspoon salt
¼ Teaspoon black pepper
2 Tablespoons all-purpose flour
1 10¾-Ounce can condensed chicken broth
3½ Cups chopped cooked turkey or chicken
1½ Cups fresh (or frozen) peas
2 Tablespoons capers
4 Hard-cooked eggs
1 Egg white, lightly beaten

Prepare the pie crust as directed and divide the dough in thirds. Combine 2 of the dough pieces and roll out to a ¼-inch thick circle. Line a 10-inch pie plate with this crust. Roll out the smaller piece of pie dough and cut into ½-inch-wide strips. Reserve these for a lattice top.

Sauté the onions in the butter until golden brown. Stir in the carrots, salt, pepper and flour. Add the broth and bring to a boil, stirring constantly, then lower the heat and simmer for 15 minutes. Add the turkey and peas. Cool to room temperature.

Preheat the oven to 375 degrees F.

Using a slotted spoon, transfer the turkey mixture to the pastry-lined pie plate. Add the capers and enough sauce to barely cover the turkey and vegetables. Shell and slice the eggs; arrange over the mixture. Top with a latticework of the reserved pastry strips, brush the top lightly with the egg white and bake for 40 to 50 minutes, or until the crust is golden brown. Serve immediately.

## Turkey Tetrazzini

(YIELD: ENOUGH TO SERVE 6)

1 16-Ounce package spaghetti
½ Pound mushrooms, sliced
2 Tablespoons butter
4 Cups Basic White Sauce (see page 171)
    Salt and white pepper to taste
⅛ Teaspoon nutmeg
3 Tablespoons sherry
3½ Cups cooked turkey, cut in julienne strips
½ Cup grated Parmesan cheese

Cook the spaghetti according to package directions. Sauté the mushrooms in the butter and set aside.

Meanwhile, prepare the white sauce and season with salt and pepper. Stir in the nutmeg and sherry.

Drain the spaghetti; combine with the mushrooms and 2 cups of the white sauce. Place the spaghetti mixture in a well-buttered baking dish. Stir the turkey strips into remaining white sauce. Make a well in the center of the spaghetti and pour in the turkey mixture. Sprinkle the cheese over the top and bake in an oven preheated to 350 degrees F. for 10 to 15 minutes, or until the top bubbles and browns slightly. Serve hot.

## Turkey Divan

(YIELD: ENOUGH TO SERVE 6)

6 Slices white bread
Butter

3 Cups thinly sliced cooked
white-meat turkey

2 10-Ounce packages frozen broccoli
spears, cooked

3 to 4 Cups Mornay Sauce (or other
savory sauce; see page 172)

¼ Cup grated Parmesan cheese

Preheat the oven to 350 degrees F.

Toast the bread, spread lightly with butter and arrange in a large, buttered rectangular baking dish. Arrange the turkey slices over the toast and top with broccoli spears. Cover with the Mornay sauce and sprinkle with the cheese. Bake at 350 degrees F. for 20 minutes, or until the top bubbles and browns lightly.

## Turkey-Noodle Casserole

(YIELD: ENOUGH TO SERVE 6)

1 12-Ounce package noodles

3 Tablespoons butter

½ Pound fresh mushrooms, sliced

1 Medium onion, chopped

3 to 4 Cups chopped leftover turkey

2 Cups fresh (or frozen) peas

¼ Cup pimiento squares

3 Cups Basic White Sauce (see page
171)

⅛ Teaspoon nutmeg

¾ Cup soft bread crumbs

2 Tablespoons melted butter

Cook the noodles according to package directions. Meanwhile, heat 2 tablespoons of the butter and sauté the mushrooms and onions for 3 minutes.

Drain the noodles and arrange half of them in the bottom of a deep casserole. Add the turkey, sautéed vegetables, peas and pimiento. Mix the nutmeg into the white sauce and pour into the casserole. Arrange the remaining noodles over the sauce and dot with the remaining 1 tablespoon butter. Mix the crumbs with the melted butter and sprinkle over the top. Bake, covered, for 20 minutes in an oven preheated to 350 degrees F., then uncover and bake for 10 minutes longer, or until the top is nicely browned. Serve at once.

## Turkey Casserole with Rice

This recipe, based on a Near East dish, is slightly more expensive but equally delicious when made with chicken.

(YIELD: ENOUGH TO SERVE 6)

2 Tablespoons butter

1 Tablespoon vegetable oil

3 Cups cooked turkey breast, cut in
strips 3 inches by ½ inch

3 Medium onions, coarsely chopped

1 Cup chopped dried apricots

1 Cup raisins

1½ Teaspoons salt

½ Teaspoon black pepper

2 Cups uncooked rice

5 Cups Basic Chicken Stock (see page
146) or canned chicken broth

3 Tablespoons tomato paste

1½ Tablespoons granulated sugar

½ Stick cinnamon
Generous pinch of allspice
Curry Sauce (see page 172)
Super-Spicy Peach Chutney (see
page 25)

Heat the butter and oil in a large skillet and sauté the turkey strips, onions, apricots and raisins for 5 minutes. Stir in the salt and pepper.

Place the rice in the bottom of a large casserole. Mix together the stock, tomato paste, sugar, cinnamon stick and allspice, then pour over the rice. Stir in the turkey mixture. Seal the casserole tightly with aluminum foil and bake in an oven preheated to 300 degrees F. for 1 hour and 40 minutes, or until the rice is tender and the liquid has been absorbed. Serve hot with a boat of the curry sauce and a dish of the chutney on the side.

## Turkey (or Chicken) Hash

(YIELD: ENOUGH TO SERVE 8)

4 Cups minced leftover turkey (or
chicken)

4 Cups coarsely chopped boiled
  potatoes
1 Large onion, finely chopped
⅛ Teaspoon each nutmeg and sage
  Salt and pepper
2 Cups Basic White Sauce (see page
  171)
4 Tablespoons butter or margarine

Combine the turkey, potatoes and onion; add the spices and salt and pepper to taste. Stir in ⅓ cup of the white sauce.

Heat the butter in a large skillet and cook the hash over medium heat for about 15 minutes on each side, turning once. As soon as the hash is crusty and golden brown, remove it from the heat. Set a serving plate over the skillet top. Quickly invert both pan and plate so that the hash turns out in one piece. Cut into wedges. Serve hot, with the remaining white sauce in a sauceboat.

## Oriental Chicken or Turkey Crêpes

(YIELD: ENOUGH TO SERVE 8)

2½ Cups finely chopped cooked
   chicken or turkey
⅔ Cup finely chopped water chestnuts
⅔ Cup thinly sliced, cooked celery
3 Cups Basic White Sauce (see page
  171)
½ Teaspoon salt
1 Recipe Basic Crêpe Batter (see page
  136)
½ Cup sour cream
½ Cup toasted blanched, slivered
  almonds
¼ Cup soy sauce

Put the chicken, water chestnuts and cooked celery in a large bowl. Sprinkle with salt, then bind together with ½ cup of the white sauce.

Prepare the crêpes as directed. Spread about 6 tablespoons of the chicken mixture and one tablespoon white sauce down the center of each crêpe. Fold the sides of the crêpes over their fillings and set them, seam side down, in a shallow, well-buttered baking dish.

Mix the sour cream with the white sauce and

spoon over the crêpes. Bake in an oven preheated to 375 degrees F. for 20 minutes, or until both crêpes and sauce are heated through. Garnish with the almonds and soy sauce and serve piping hot.

## Turkey Croquettes

*A superb way to use leftover turkey is to make crunchy turkey croquettes. Serve these with a creamy savory sauce (see pages 171–72) and a spoonful of leftover cranberry sauce.*

(YIELD: ENOUGH TO SERVE 6)

2½ Cups finely minced leftover turkey
3 Hard-cooked eggs, finely minced
1½ Cups Homemade Bread Crumbs
   (see page 6) or stuffing mix (see
   pages 5–6)
¼ Teaspoon sage or thyme
  Salt and black pepper
⅔ Cup thick Basic White Sauce
  (see page 171)
1 Egg, lightly beaten
  Vegetable oil for deep frying

Combine the turkey and hard-cooked eggs with ½ cup of the bread crumbs. Season with sage and salt and pepper to taste. Bind the mixture with the white sauce and refrigerate for at least 2 hours.

Heat 1 inch of oil in a large skillet. Shape the turkey mixture into 1-inch-thick patties. Dip each patty first in lightly beaten egg, then in the remaining bread crumbs. Fry until golden brown on both sides, turning once. Drain briefly on paper towels and serve hot.

## Turkey à la King

(YIELD: ENOUGH TO SERVE 6)

Prepare a double amount of À la King Sauce (see page 172). Stir in 3 to 4 cups cubed leftover turkey and serve hot over toast triangles, rice or noodles.

### Turkey Curry

(YIELD: ENOUGH TO SERVE 6)

Substitute 4 cups coarsely chopped leftover turkey for the hard-cooked eggs in Madras Egg Curry (see page 125) or stir the same amount of turkey into a double portion of Curry Sauce (see page 172). Serve hot over rice.

### Waldorf Turkey Salad

(YIELD: ENOUGH TO SERVE 6)

4 Cups diced leftover turkey
1 Cup diced celery
½ Cup walnut pieces
2 Cups diced unpeeled apples
1 Cup Mayonnaise (see page 169) or prepared mayonnaise
½ Cup sour cream
2 Tablespoons lemon juice
2 Tablespoons minced fresh parsley
  Crisp lettuce leaves

Combine the turkey, celery, walnuts and apples. Mix together the mayonnaise, sour cream, lemon juice and parsley and gently toss with the turkey mixture. Arrange on crisp lettuce leaves. Serve cold.

### Three-Bean Turkey Salad

(YIELD: ENOUGH TO SERVE 6)

1 16-Ounce can red kidney beans, rinsed and drained
1 20-Ounce can chick-peas, rinsed and drained
1 Cup leftover green beans (or 1 15½-ounce can green beans, drained)
1 Sweet red onion, very thinly sliced
3 Cups diced leftover turkey
2 Cups Sweet Vinegar Dressing (see page 169)
3 Hard-cooked eggs, cut in quarters

Combine the kidney beans, chick-peas, green beans, onions, turkey and dressing. Toss gently until well coated. Refrigerate and serve cold, garnish with the hard-cooked eggs.

# SWEETS

## DESSERT CRÊPES

Add sugar to the Basic Crêpe Batter (see page 136), spread the crêpes with sweetened fruit, whipped cream and/or a silky sauce *et voilà!* an unusual and elegant dessert.

### *French Apple Crêpes*

*If the brandy in this recipe is beyond your budget, substitute orange juice and add it along with the corn syrup. Simmer the sauce 1 minute and then proceed with the recipe.*

(YIELD: ENOUGH TO SERVE 8)

 *Basic Crêpe Batter (see page 136), plus 1 tablespoon granulated sugar*
4 *Cups peeled, cored and thinly sliced tart apples*
4 *Tablespoons butter*
6 *Tablespoons light brown sugar*
¼ *Teaspoon ground cinnamon*
¼ *Cup light corn syrup*

¼ *Cup apple brandy or liqueur*
1 *Cup heavy cream, whipped*

Prepare the crêpes as directed, adding the 1 tablespoon sugar along with the flour and salt. Stack the crêpes and keep them warm.

Lightly sauté the apple slices in 2 tablespoons of the butter, sprinkle with the sugar and cinnamon, then cover and cook until tender. Take care not to overcook; the apples should still have a bit of crunch to them.

Remove from the heat and spread a few tablespoons of the apple mixture down the center of each crêpe. Roll up and set aside.

Heat the remaining butter in a large skillet or chafing dish, add the crêpes and top with the corn syrup. As soon as the crêpes are heated through, sprinkle with the brandy and ignite. Serve hot, with a bowl of whipped cream on the side for guests to help themselves.

## Make-Ahead Strawberry Crêpes

(YIELD: ENOUGH TO SERVE 8)

Basic Crêpe Batter (see page 136),
plus 1 tablespoon granulated sugar
3 Cups sliced strawberries
6 Tablespoons granulated sugar
2 Cups sour cream
1½ Tablespoons orange liqueur (or
orange juice)
3 Tablespoons butter
Confectioners' sugar

Prepare the crêpes as directed, adding 1 tablespoon sugar to the basic batter at the same time you mix the flour and salt into the eggs. Stack the crêpes and keep warm..

Arrange the strawberries in a shallow bowl and sprinkle with 3 tablespoons of the sugar. Mix the 3 remaining tablespoons sugar into the sour cream along with the orange liqueur or juice.

Spread equal amounts of the sour cream over one side of each crêpe, spoon some strawberries in the center, then roll up and place the crêpes, seam side down, in shallow dish. Chill thoroughly until ready to serve.

Place the butter in a large skillet and heat the crêpes briefly. Serve topped with a few sprinkles of confectioners' sugar.

## DESSERT SOUFFLÉS AND OMELETS

If your entree has been light and simple and not overladen with protein, give your family a special treat with a delectable protein-rich dessert soufflé or omelet.

## Basic Vanilla Soufflé

(YIELD: ENOUGH TO SERVE 4 TO 6)

2 Tablespoons butter
1½ Tablespoons all-purpose flour
½ Cup milk
½ Teaspoon vanilla extract
5 Egg yolks
4 Tablespoons granulated sugar
6 Egg whites

Melt the butter in a saucepan, blend in the flour and cook, stirring constantly. Meanwhile, scald the milk in a separate saucepan. As soon as the butter and flour mixture begins to take on a golden color, add the scalded milk. Continue to stir the sauce until thick, then cook, stirring, for an additional 5 minutes. Remove from the heat and stir in the vanilla extract.

Beat the egg yolks together with 3 tablespoons of the sugar until well blended and mix these into the sauce. Beat the egg whites until they stand in stiff peaks, sprinkle them with the remaining tablespoon of sugar and continue to beat until the sugar has been absorbed. Fold one-third of the egg whites carefully into the egg yolk mixture with your spatula. As soon as this has been thoroughly incorporated, fold in the rest of the egg whites.

Sprinkle a light coating of sugar over the bottom and sides of a buttered soufflé or baking dish. Gently pour in the soufflé mixture and bake in an oven preheated to 350 degrees F. for 35 to 40 minutes. Serve hot.

### Chocolate Soufflé

Make the Basic Vanilla Soufflé as directed above, adding 1½ 1-ounce squares grated semisweet chocolate to the scalded milk before adding it to the butter-flour mixture. When beating the egg yolks, add another 3 tablespoons sugar.

### Lemon Soufflé

Prepare the Basic Vanilla Soufflé as directed above, but omit the vanilla. Just before folding in the egg whites, add the grated zest and juice of ½ lemon to the thickened egg yolk mixture.

### Orange Soufflé

Prepare the Basic Vanilla Soufflé as directed above, omitting the vanilla. Add the grated zest of 1 small orange and 2 tablespoons orange juice to the thickened egg yolk mixture. Fold in the egg whites and proceed as directed.

### Nut Soufflé

Heat the butter, blend in the flour and add the scalded milk as directed in Basic Vanilla Soufflé (see above). After removing the mixture from the heat, add ½ teaspoon almond extract instead of the vanilla, then stir in ½ cup finely ground blanched almonds or other nuts. Proceed as directed.

### Dessert Omelet with Fresh Fruit

Sprinkle sliced apples, bananas, peaches, strawberries or any other berries or fruit you prefer with sugar and a little lemon juice. Set aside for 1 hour.

Prepare the basic Omelet as directed on page 127. Before folding each omelet over, arrange ½ cup of the fruit down the center. Fold the omelet over, allow to finish setting, then slide from the pan to the plate and sprinkle with confectioners' sugar.

Ignite the omelets if you wish with 2 to 3 tablespoons flaming rum or kirsch, or top with any fruit sauce included on pages 173–74. Serve immediately.

### Flaming Dessert Omelet with Jam Filling

Follow directions for preparing the basic Omelet as given on page 127. Just before folding each omelet over, spread 2 tablespoons jam down the center. Fold over the omelet, allow it to finish setting, then slide from pan and sprinkle with confectioners' sugar. Pour 2 or 3 tablespoons flaming rum or kirsch over each omelet. Serve immediately.

### Dessert Omelet with Chopped Nuts

Prepare the basic Omelet as directed on page 127. Before folding each omelet over, arrange 2 tablespoons finely chopped nuts down the center. Sprinkle with sugar and cinnamon to taste. Fold the omelet over and finish cooking, then slide from the pan and top with a sprinkle of cinnamon and sugar. Serve immediately.

### Dessert Omelets Topped with Fruit Sauce

Prepare the basic Omelet as directed on page 127. After sliding each omelet from the pan, top with any fruit sauce included on pages 173–74. Serve hot.

## DESSERT WAFFLE COMBINATIONS

These are only a few of an almost endless number of possibilities. Dream up some to suit your own tastes.

### Apricot Waffles with Flaming Rum Sauce

Top Apricot Waffles (see page 7) with Vanilla Ice Cream (see page 163) and cover with Flaming Rum Sauce (see page 173).

### Orange Waffles with Blueberry Sauce

Top Orange Waffles (see page 8) with Vanilla Ice Cream (see page 163) and spoon over Blueberry Sauce (see page 173).

### Chocolate Chip Waffles with Hot Fudge Sauce

Top Chocolate Chip Waffles (see page 7) with Vanilla Ice Cream (see page 163) or coffee ice cream and cover with Hot Fudge Sauce (see page 173).

### Pineapple Waffles with Pineapple Sauce

Top Pineapple Waffles with Peach Ice Cream (see page 163) and Pineapple Sauce (see page 173).

### Nut Waffles with Apple Cinnamon Sauce

Top Nut Waffles (see page 7) with Rum-Raisin Ice Cream (see page 164) and Apple-Cinnamon Sauce (see page 173).

### Nut Waffles with Hot Fudge Sauce

Top Nut Waffles (see page 7) with chocolate ice cream and Hot Fudge Sauce (see page 173).

### Nut Waffles with Fruit and Brown Sugar Syrup

Top Nut Waffles (see page 7) with Vanilla Ice Cream (see page 163), fresh peach slices sprinkled with lemon juice and Brown Sugar Syrup (see page 23).

### Butterscotch Waffles with Nut Sauce

Top Butterscotch Waffles (see page 7) with coffee ice cream and Nut Sauce (see page 173).

### Coconut Waffles with Strawberries

Top Coconut Waffles (see page 7) with sweetened whipped cream and strawberry slices.

### Pineapple Waffles with Peachy-Pineapple Sauce

Top Pineapple Waffles (see page 8) with sweetened whipped cream and room-temperature Peachy-Pineapple Sauce (see page 173).

### Chocolate Chip Waffles with Nut Sauce

Top Chocolate Chip Waffles (see page 7) with unsweetened whipped cream and room-temperature Nut Sauce (see page 173).

### Plain Waffles with Fruit and Blueberry Sauce

Top plain waffles (see page 7) with sweetened whipped cream, sliced strawberries and room-temperature Blueberry Sauce (see page 173).

### Coconut Waffles with Fruit and Raspberry Sauce

Top Coconut Waffles (see page 7) with sweetened whipped cream, sliced fresh peaches and a dollop of Raspberry Sauce (see page 174).

### Banana-Split Waffles

Top Cherry Waffles (see page 8) with chocolate and vanilla ice cream, banana slices, room-temperature Fudge Sauce (see page 173), a dollop of whipped cream and a cherry.

## ICE CREAMS AND ICES

### How to Churn Your Own Ice Cream

Homemade ice cream—pure, thick and creamy—is fun to make and delicious to eat. Compared to it, the artificially flavored, chemically preserved supermarket variety pales into insignificance. If you have your own livestock or some other good source of surplus milk and cream, or even if you want to splurge once in a while, this is a treat you must try. You may not actually save any money, but you will get velvety old-fashioned flavor and extremely high quality. Better still, you will know your dessert is additive-free.

You will need either a hand-operated or an

electric 2-quart freezer. The recipes that follow make about 1½ quarts each, enough to fill the churn's metal freezer can about two-thirds full before the ice cream expands during freezing. Be sure to have on hand plenty of cracked ice and rock or kosher salt, too, before you start.

Prepare your ice cream mixture according to any of the recipes below, drape a large strainer with cheesecloth and pour the mixture through into the metal freezer can. Top the can with its cover and set into the freezer tub. Arrange the cracked ice and salt in alternating layers around the sides of the can, using 4 or 5 parts ice to 1 part salt. Be sure to pack the tub right to the top for faster freezing.

If yours is an electric churn, simply follow manufacturer's directions for churning. With a hand-operated churn, connect the crank to the dasher and have your family take turns revolving the crank in a rhythmic motion. As the cranking becomes more difficult, enlist the aid of a strong helper to speed the turning. When full resistance is felt, the cream is probably thick enough. Disconnect the crank and remove the cover of the can, but take care that no salt water seeps into the freezer can.

The cream at this stage will be delicious and custardlike. If you prefer a stiffer cream, remove and scrape the dasher, then add any additional ingredients and pack the mixture down with a spoon.

Tuck a sheet of aluminum foil tightly over the top of the freezer can. Wipe the inside of the can cover dry, insert a cork or some crushed aluminum foil in the opening, and fit the cover securely on the can. Pour off as much of the melted ice in the tub as possible and repack with fresh ice and salt in the same ratio as before. Insulate the tub with newspapers and allow the ice cream to stand about 2 hours to harden to the desired consistency. If you must check on the progress of your cream, be sure to hold the metal freezer can down in the tub while removing the cover, or ice may slip underneath and make your freezer impossible to reclose.

### Vanilla Ice Cream

(YIELD: ABOUT 1½ QUARTS)

2½ Cups heavy cream
3 Cups milk
2½ Teaspoons vanilla extract
8 Egg yolks
1 Cup granulated sugar

Pour the cream and milk into a heavy saucepan and heat only long enough to scald the mixture. Beat the egg yolks and sugar together until creamy, then add the hot cream and milk a little at a time, beating constantly until well blended.

Place the mixture in the top of a double boiler over hot water and heat, stirring constantly, over a fairly low flame. If the water in the bottom of the double boiler boils too violently, the mixture may curdle. As soon as the mixture thickens, remove it from the heat and stir in the vanilla extract. Set a large strainer over the metal freezer can and carefully pour the mixture through. Chill quickly, then prepare to churn (see page 162).

### Strawberry Ice Cream

Prepare the mixture for Vanilla Ice Cream as directed above and chill it quickly. Wash, hull and dry 1 quart of strawberries, then arrange in a bowl and sprinkle with ½ cup granulated sugar. Mash with a fork and set aside while you pack the freezer tub and churn the ice cream (see page 162). Stir in the strawberries after removing the dasher and crank. Continue as directed.

### Peach Ice Cream

While preparing your mixture for Vanilla Ice Cream (see above), peel and slice 3 pounds of very ripe peaches. Sprinkle them with ½ cup granulated sugar and set aside for 30 minutes, then mash to a pulp and let stand for an additional 30 minutes. Stir the fruit into the ice cream after removing the dasher and crank. Proceed to freeze.

### Tutti-Frutti Ice Cream

Heat the mixture for Vanilla Ice Cream (see above) until it thickens, remove from the heat and strain into the metal freezer can. Purée 4 ripe bananas by pressing them through a fine strainer. Stir the banana purée into the thickened cream and chill quickly. Churn as directed on page 162.

After removing the dasher and crank, whip 1 cup heavy cream and blend into the ice cream, along with 2 cups coarsely chopped nuts, 2 cups sliced strawberries and ½ cup chopped maraschino cherries. Pack the mixture down firmly and freeze as directed.

### Rum-Raisin Ice Cream

Prepare the mixture for Vanilla Ice Cream as directed above. While the cream is churning (see page 162), place 2 cups chopped raisins in a bowl and stir in ½ cup rum. Whip 1 cup heavy cream and set aside. Remove the dasher and crank, fold the rum-soaked raisins and whipped cream into the ice cream, pack down and proceed as directed.

### Peppermint-Stick Ice Cream

Prepare and churn Vanilla Ice Cream as directed above. Add ¾ pound finely crushed peppermint sticks after removing the dasher and crank, then pack down firmly and freeze as directed.

## Orange Ice

(YIELD: ABOUT 2 QUARTS)

2½ Cups granulated sugar
4 Cups water
2 Cups orange juice
¼ Cup lemon juice
2 Egg whites (optional)

Bring the sugar and water to a boil over medium heat and cook for 5 minutes. Remove from the heat and cool. Mix in the orange and lemon juice, then pour the mixture through a strainer lined with cheesecloth into the metal freezer can. Chill quickly and follow the churning and freezing instructions indicated on pages 162–63.

If a creamier sherbet is desired, beat 2 egg whites until stiff and fold into the mixture after removing the dasher and churn. Continue as directed.

## Raspberry Ice

*If you are fortunate enough to grow quantities of these wonderful berries and happen to have a surplus supply, by all means use puréed fresh berries; otherwise frozen berries may be substituted.*

(YIELD: ABOUT 1½ QUARTS)

Fresh or frozen raspberries (enough to make 2½ cups purée
1½ to 2 Cups granulated sugar
1 Cup water
2 Tablespoons lemon juice
2 Egg whites (optional)

To prepare raspberry purée from fresh berries, force enough raspberries through a fine sieve to measure 2 cups. Set aside. Bring 2 cups of sugar and the water to a boil over medium heat and cook for 5 minutes, then remove and allow to cool. Add the respberry purée and lemon juice and stir thoroughly.

To prepare frozen berries, follow the directions given above but reduce the sugar to 1½ cups.

Pour the mixture through a strainer lined with cheesecloth into the metal freezer can of your churn. Chill in the refrigerator or freezer, then continue according to directions on pages 162–63. Should you wish a more fluffy ice, beat 2 egg whites until they stand in stiff peaks and fold into the raspberry mixture after removing the dasher and churn. Continue as directed.

### Other Fruit Flavors

Strawberry, peach, blueberry or apricot ices can be made by substituting 2 cups of any of these puréed fruits for the raspberry purée.

## MISCELLANEOUS SWEETS

### Bread Pudding

(YIELD: ENOUGH TO SERVE 8)

20 Slices day-old bread
 4 Tablespoons butter or margarine
 5 Eggs
3½ Cups milk
 1 Cup granulated sugar
 1 Cup currants or raisins
 ½ Cup chopped candied fruits,
    rinsed and drained
 1 Teaspoon vanilla extract
 1 Teaspoon ground cinnamon
 ½ Teaspoon nutmeg

You may leave the crusts on the bread if you prefer, or remove them and use the trimmings to make bread crumbs (see page 6).

Lightly butter each slice of bread and cut into 1-inch cubes. Grease a deep baking dish lightly with butter. Arrange the bread cubes in the dish.

Combine the remaining ingredients and beat thoroughly. Pour the mixture over the bread. Stir once, then bake the bread in an oven preheated to 350 degrees F. for about 1 hour, or until it is firm and golden brown on top. Serve warm or at room temperature.

### Lollipops

(YIELD: ABOUT 2 POUNDS)

4 Cups granulated sugar
1 Cup light corn syrup
1 Cup water
  Food coloring
  Flavoring

Mix the sugar, corn syrup and water in a heavy saucepan. Cook without stirring until a candy thermometer shows a reading of 300 degrees F.

For different coloring and flavoring, pour the hot syrup into separate warm pans. Stir in the coloring and flavoring only long enough to mix. Arrange wooden sticks in buttered gem pans, candy molds or tiny paper pill cups. Pour a little syrup into each. Cool, then wrap each pop in waxed paper or plastic wrap.

### Popcorn Balls

Popcorn balls are fun to make and may be used to decorate a Christmas tree. Tie these plastic-wrapped balls, as well as cookies, nuts, gumdrops, candy canes and homemade candies to the branches of the tree and nibble the decorations during the twelve days of Christmas.

(YIELD: ABOUT 3 DOZEN)

1½ Cups light corn syrup
1½ Cups water
 6 Cups superfine granulated sugar
1½ Tablespoons vanilla extract
   Red food coloring (optional)
12 Quarts lightly salted popcorn

Place the syrup, water and sugar in a saucepan and bring the mixture to a boil. Remove any loose sugar crystals that may form along the sides of the pan. Cook the syrup at a full boil until it reaches 238 degrees F. on a candy thermometer or forms a pliable ball when a bit is dropped into a cup of cold water. Remove the syrup from the heat; stir in the vanilla and coloring.

Cool until the syrup is still warm but cool enough to handle, then pour it over the popcorn. Stir until all popcorn is well coated. Spread butter generously over your hands and shape the popcorn into 3-inch balls. Cool on a well-greased cookie sheet, then cover each ball in plastic wrap, leaving several inches of wrap on either end to be twisted and tied in candy-kiss fashion with Christmas ribbon.

## Apple Marmalade

*This marmalade is superb with meats and curry.*

(YIELD: 6 8-OUNCE JARS)

6 Pounds hard, tart apples
2 Lemons
2 Ounces preserved ginger (or a
  1-ounce piece of fresh ginger root)
3 Pounds granulated sugar
⅛ Teaspoon cayenne pepper
¼ Cup water

Wash and core the apples and cut into thin slices. Peel the zest (the thin yellow outer skin of the lemon, with none of the bitter white underskin included) from the lemon and cut into thin strips. Chop the ginger.

Put the apples, lemon zest, ginger, sugar, cayenne pepper and water in a heavy pot. Squeeze in the juice from the lemons and bring to a boil over medium heat. Lower the heat and cook at a low boil until the syrup is thick, stirring frequently to prevent scorching. Place in hot, sterile jars and seal.

# DRESSINGS & SAUCES

## DRESSINGS AND MARINADES

### Basic French Dressing I

(YIELD: ABOUT 2 CUPS)

½ Cup wine (or cider) vinegar
1 Teaspoon salt
Freshly ground black pepper
1½ Cups olive oil (or other salad oil)

Place the vinegar in a shallow bowl. Sprinkle with the salt and pepper and beat in with a fork. Continuing to beat, add the oil slowly. Pour into a covered jar and chill. Shake well before using.

To make a milder dressing, substitute lemon juice for the vinegar.

### Basic French Dressing II

*This makes a spicy addition to any salad.*

(YIELD: ABOUT 1⅓ CUPS)

¼ Cup wine (or cider or tarragon) vinegar
1 Teaspoon salt
½ Teaspoon each granulated sugar and dry mustard
¼ Teaspoon paprika
Freshly ground black pepper
1 Cup olive oil (or other salad oil)

Place the vinegar in a screwtop jar, add the seasonings, cover and shake well. Pour in the oil, cover and shake again. Chill, then shake once more just before using.

### Anchovy French Dressing

Mix 1 tablespoon anchovy paste, 1 tablespoon minced fresh parsley and 1 teaspoon minced onion with ½ cup French Dressing I or II (see above). Shake well and serve with mixed greens or egg salad.

### Blue Cheese French Dressing

Add 2 tablespoons crumbled blue cheese to ½ cup French Dressing I or II (see above). Serve with tomatoes and greens or fruit salad.

### Catsup French Dressing

Add 1 or 2 tablespoons catsup to each cup of French Dressing I or II (see above). Mix vigorously before serving on greens or meats. If you prefer a spicier flavor, try adding ½ teaspoon Worcestershire sauce along with the catsup.

### Chili Sauce French Dressing

Blend 2 tablespoons chili sauce into ½ cup French Dressing I. Serve with cold meat, fish, or vegetable salads.

### Chutney French Dressing

Add 1 tablespoon chutney (see page 25) and ¼ teaspoon curry powder to ½ cup French Dressing I or II (see above). Serve with cold meats.

### Creamy French Dressing

Substitute lemon juice for the vinegar when preparing French Dressing I or II (see above). To each ½ cup dressing, gradually add ⅓ cup light cream, a bit at a time, beating well after each addition until the mixture is creamy and thick. Serve with chicken, potato or fruit salads.

### Curry French Dressing

Add ½ to 1 teaspoon curry powder, depending on your taste, to ½ cup French Dressing I or II (see above). Shake the mixture thoroughly before using with mixed greens, fish or meat salads.

### Garlic French Dressing

Peel 1 clove garlic and drop into French Dressing I or II (see above) before chilling in the re-frigerator. Remove the garlic before serving over any green salad.

### Herb French Dressing

Mince 2 tablespoons fresh basil, chervil, chives, tarragon, thyme or other herbs, singly or in combination, with 1 cup French Dressing I or II (see above). When using dried herbs, reduce the total amount to about 1 teaspoon. Serve with any greens.

### Mint French Dressing

Use lemon juice instead of vinegar when preparing French Dressing I or II (see above). Add 2 tablespoons finely chopped mint leaves to each cup of dressing. Use with fruit salads.

## Vinaigrette Dressing

(YIELD: ABOUT 1 CUP)

    6 Tablespoons wine vinegar
    ½ Teaspoon salt
      Freshly ground black pepper
    ½ Teaspoon dry mustard (optional)
    ⅔ Cup olive oil (or other salad oil,
      or a combination)
    ¼ Cup finely minced fresh chervil,
      parsley or tarragon, singly or
      in combination

Beat the vinegar with the seasonings until well mixed, then add the oil and beat again. Add the herbs to the dressing just before serving, or sprinkle them directly on the salad after tossing with the dressing. Use with mixed greens, or as a sauce for meat, chicken or vegetables.

### Variations

Add any or all of the following for subtle changes in flavor:

    1 Hard-cooked egg, grated
    1 Tablespoon minced pickle
    1 Tablespoon minced fresh chives
    1 Tablespoon minced green pepper
    1 Tablespoon chopped capers

### Italian Dressing

(YIELD: ABOUT 1 CUP)

¼ Cup wine (or tarragon) vinegar
2 Anchovy fillets, mashed
  Freshly ground black pepper
¾ Cup olive oil

Place the vinegar in a shallow bowl and add the bits of anchovy and the pepper. Stir until well blended, then slowly beat in the oil. Refrigerate before shaking again and serving over mixed salads.

### Sweet Vinegar Dressing

(YIELD: ABOUT 1 CUP)

¼ Cup salad oil
¼ Cup wine (or cider) vinegar
¼ Cup granulated sugar
¼ Cup catsup
¼ Teaspoon onion salt

Place all the ingredients in a screwtop jar and shake to mix thoroughly. Chill well. Shake again and serve with lettuce or other mixed greens.

### Mayonnaise

(YIELD: ABOUT 2 CUPS)

2 Egg yolks, at room temperature
1 Tablespoon Dijon mustard
1 Tablespoon hot vinegar or lemon
  juice
¾ Cup each olive oil and vegetable oil
  Salt
  Pepper

Rinse a small bowl with hot water and wipe dry. Put the egg yolks, mustard and 1 teaspoon of the vinegar into the warmed bowl and beat with a wire whisk or an electric mixer at low speed until smooth. Mix the oils together and grad-

ually beat into the egg yolk mixture, ½ teaspoonful at a time, beating continuously and waiting until the previous addition has been thoroughly incorporated and the mixture is creamy before adding more.

When one-third to one-half of the oil has been used, beat in the rest of the hot vinegar until the mixture seems clear and creamy, then gradually add the remaining oil in small amounts as before, beating constantly after each addition. When all the oil has been absorbed, season to taste with salt and pepper. Chill thoroughly before using.

### Green Mayonnaise

To 2 cups Mayonnaise (see above), add 1½ tablespoons each finely minced fresh chervil, chives and parsley and 1 teaspoon lemon juice if desired. Mix until well blended. Serve cold with vegetable salads, hard-cooked eggs, fish or seafood.

### Quick Aïoli (Garlic Mayonnaise)

*There are some gourmet treats that turn everyday foods into something really special. This highly seasoned sauce transforms boiled beef, poached fish or vegetables (cooked or raw) into a meal to remember.*

(YIELD: ABOUT 1 CUP)

2 Tablespoons bread crumbs
3 Cloves garlic, peeled
1 Tablespoon lemon juice
2 Large egg yolks
⅛ Teaspoon each salt and freshly
  ground black pepper
¾ Cup olive oil
  About 1 tablespoon boiling water

Whirl the bread crumbs in a blender at high speed for about 5 seconds. Coarsely chop the garlic and add, along with the lemon juice, to the blender jar. Blend at high speed until smooth, then add the egg yolks and seasonings. The mixture should be quite stiff.

Turn the blender on high once more and gradually add the oil, a few drops at a time at first, then slowly increase the amount until it runs in a thin steady stream. When half the oil has been incorporated, add 1 teaspoon boiling water to thin the mixture a bit. Continue adding the remaining oil while blending at high speed, stopping the action and adding another teaspoon or so of boiling water only if the mixture becomes too thick for the blender to turn easily.

When all the oil has been incorporated, the sauce will be very thick. Scrape from the jar with a rubber spatula and turn into a bowl. Chill before using.

### Fines Herbes Dressing

(YIELD: ABOUT 1½ CUPS)

1 Cup olive oil (or other salad oil)
¼ Cup tarragon vinegar
2 Tablespoons dry red wine
¾ Teaspoon salt
½ Teaspoon paprika
¼ Teaspoon dry mustard
  Freshly ground black pepper
2 Tablespoons each fresh minced basil and parsley
1 Tablespoon minced fresh thyme

Combine all ingredients in a screwtop jar and shake well. Use over sliced tomatoes, cucumbers or mixed greens.

### Thousand Islands Dressing

(YIELD: ABOUT 1½ CUPS)

1 Cup Mayonnaise (see page 169) or commercially prepared mayonnaise
3 Tablespoons chili sauce
1 Tablespoon each cider vinegar and cream
3 Tablespoons finely chopped celery
2 Tablespoons minced green pepper
1 Hard-cooked egg, grated
½ Teaspoon paprika
  Salt to taste

Combine all the ingredients and mix very thoroughly. Keep chilled until serving time.

### Piquant Boiled Dressing

*This dressing is a delicious topping for lettuce wedges, fish or shellfish. Or, if you like, mash it with hard-cooked egg yolks for superior stuffed eggs.*

(YIELD: SLIGHTLY OVER 1 CUP)

2 Teaspoons butter
⅓ Cup lemon juice
4 Teaspoons all-purpose flour
1 Cup sour cream
3 Tablespoons light brown sugar
2 Egg yolks
2 Teaspoons each prepared mustard and salt
  Generous pinch of cayenne pepper

Melt the butter in the top of a double boiler over hot water. Add the lemon juice, then stir in the flour until smooth. Add the remaining ingredients in order and cook, stirring constantly, until the dressing is thick and smooth. Cool and store in a small jar.

This dressing will keep, refrigerated, for 2 weeks.

### Peanut-Cream Dressing

(YIELD: 1½ CUPS)

¾ Cup light cream
½ Cup peanut butter
5 Tablespoons honey
¼ Teaspoon salt

Mix the cream, peanut butter and honey together until well blended. Season with the salt, then mix again and serve with fruit salad.

### Wine Marinade for Beef or Lamb

(YIELD: 2 CUPS)

1 Cup vegetable oil
½ Cup red wine
¼ Cup each wine vinegar and
  tomato juice
3 Cloves garlic, peeled and minced
1 Bay leaf, crumbled
1 Tablespoon minced fresh sweet basil
  or 1 teaspoon dried
1 Tablespoon minced fresh oregano
  or 1 teaspoon dried

Place all the ingredients in a saucepan, mix well, then bring to a boil. Remove from the heat and stir thoroughly. Cool before pouring over beef or lamb. Marinate the meat overnight in the refrigerator, turning once.

### Fruit Juice Marinade

(YIELD: ABOUT 1 CUP)

¼ Cup each lemon juice, lime juice
  and orange juice
¼ Cup soy sauce
1 Teaspoon dry mustard
4 Cloves garlic, peeled and minced
1½ Tablespoons vegetable oil

Combine the fruit juices, soy sauce, mustard and minced garlic in a small bowl. Gradually beat in the oil, ½ teaspoon at a time, taking care to incorporate each addition well before adding the next. Pour over beef, chicken or lamb and marinate for 2 to 3 hours, turning the meat several times.

### South Seas Marinade

(YIELD: 1½ CUPS)

½ Cup each vegetable oil and soy
  sauce
¼ Cup dry sherry

4 Cloves garlic, peeled and minced
1 Teaspoon chili powder
⅛ Teaspoon black pepper
1 Cup canned crushed pineapple,
  plus 1 cup pineapple syrup from
  the can

Mix all ingredients except the pineapple and syrup in a jar, shake to blend and pour over beef, pork or chicken. Marinate 2 to 3 hours.

Mix the marinade with the pineapple and pineapple juice. Boil over medium heat for 15 minutes, stirring occasionally. Serve hot with the broiled meat.

## SAVORY SAUCES

These sauces, all of which are based on the Basic White Sauce that is given below, may be spooned over waffles or English muffins or served as fillings for crêpes or omelets.

### Basic White Sauce

(YIELD: 2 CUPS)

4 Tablespoons butter
¼ Cup all-purpose flour
2 Cups milk
½ Teaspoon salt
  White pepper

In a heavy saucepan, melt the butter over medium heat and stir in the flour. When the mixture is smooth, remove from the heat and add the cold milk all at once, stirring until the mixture is well blended and free from lumps. Return to medium heat and cook, stirring constantly, until creamy and thick. Season with salt and white pepper.

Should you desire a thinner white sauce, increase the amount of milk by ½ cup. To make a thicker product, reduce the quantity of milk to 1¼ cups.

### Mixed Vegetable Sauce

Stir 1½ cups mixed, cooked leftover vegetables (cut peas, carrots, celery, lima beans, green beans, zucchini, etc.) into Basic White Sauce (see page 171). Reheat if necessary.

### Curry Sauce

Melt the amount of butter called for in Basic White Sauce (see page 171) in a large saucepan. Stir in the flour and 1 teaspoon curry powder, then proceed as directed.

### Hard-Cooked Egg Sauce

Stir 2 coarsely chopped hard-cooked eggs into Basic White Sauce (see page 171) along with a little extra salt and freshly ground pepper.

#### Hard-Cooked Egg Sauce with Olives

Add ½ cup green stuffed olives, sliced, to Basic White Sauce (see page 171) along with the hard-cooked eggs.

#### Hard-Cooked Egg Sauce with Capers

Add 1 tablespoon well-drained capers to Basic White Sauce (see page 171) along with hard-cooked eggs.

#### Hard-Cooked Egg Sauce with Peas

Add one cup cooked peas to Basic White Sauce (see page 171) along with the hard-cooked eggs.

#### Hard-Cooked Egg Sauce with Pimiento

Add ¼ cup diced, well-drained pimiento to Basic White Sauce (see page 171) along with the hard-cooked eggs.

### À la King Sauce

Stir ¾ cup cooked, diced chicken or turkey, ½ cup cooked peas and 2 tablespoons diced, well-drained pimiento into Basic White Sauce (see page 171) along with a little extra salt and freshly ground black pepper.

### American Cheese Sauce

Add 1½ cups grated American cheese to hot Basic White Sauce (see page 171). Stir over low heat until the cheese melts.

### Mornay Sauce

Add ½ cup grated Swiss cheese and ⅓ cup grated Parmesan cheese to hot Basic White Sauce (see page 171). Stir over low heat until the cheeses melt.

### Herb Sauce

Stir 2 tablespoons mixed fresh herbs (thyme, chervil, marjoram) or ½ teaspoon dried herbs into Basic White Sauce (see page 171).

### Newburg Sauce

Add 1½ cups flaked or chopped crab or lobster to Basic White Sauce (see page 171). Stir for 5 to 10 minutes, or until the sauce is piping hot. Remove from the heat and beat in 1 beaten egg yolk and 1 to 2 tablespoons sherry.

### Mushroom Sauce

Add 1 cup cooked, sliced mushrooms to Basic White Sauce (see page 171). Stir over low heat until the sauce is piping hot.

## SWEET SAUCES

### Pineapple Sauce

(YIELD: ABOUT 2 CUPS)

1 8½-Ounce can crushed pineapple
1 Cup light corn syrup
2 Tablespoons granulated sugar
1 Tablespoon lemon juice

Drain the pineapple and reserve the juice. Mix the pineapple juice, corn syrup and sugar in a small heavy saucepan. Boil over medium heat until the mixture is thick and syrupy, then stir in the reserved pineapple and the lemon juice. Serve hot or at room temperature.

### Peachy-Pineapple Sauce

Follow the recipe for Pineapple Sauce (see above), but fold in 1 cup peeled, pitted and chopped ripe peach pulp along with the pineapple and lemon juice. Serve hot or at room temperature.

### Blueberry Sauce

(YIELD: ABOUT 4 CUPS)

2 Tablespoons cornstarch
¾ Cup cold water
1½ Cups granulated sugar
2 Tablespoons lemon juice
3½ Cups fresh blueberries

In a small, heavy saucepan, mix the cornstarch into the cold water until the mixture is free from lumps. Stir in the sugar, lemon juice and blueberries. Bring to a boil over medium heat, stirring constantly until the syrup is thick. Serve hot.

### Cherry Sauce

Follow the directions for Blueberry Sauce (see above), but substitute 3½ cups pitted, chopped dark sweet cherries for the blueberries.

### Apple-Cinnamon Sauce

Follow the directions for Blueberry Sauce (see above), but substitute 3½ cups peeled, cored and sliced apples for the blueberries and add ½ teaspoon ground cinnamon.

### Nut Sauce

Follow the recipe for Brown Sugar Syrup (see page 23), then stir in 1½ cups chopped nuts. Serve hot or at room temperature.

### Flaming Rum Sauce

Add a touch of drama to your desserts—flame them with this scrumptious sauce.

(YIELD: ABOUT 2 CUPS)

1 12-Ounce jar of your favorite jam or jelly (raspberry, strawberry, apricot, peach, cherry, etc.)
¼ Cup orange juice
¼ Cup rum

Mix the jelly and orange juice in a small heavy pan or skillet. Stir over low heat until well mixed, then remove the pan from the heat and pour the rum carefully over the top of the sauce. Allow to stand for a minute to warm the rum, then ignite with a match. When the flame dies, stir the sauce once and spoon it over waffles or crêpes.

### Hot Fudge Sauce

(YIELD: ABOUT 2 CUPS)

4 1-Ounce squares unsweetened chocolate
2 Tablespoons butter or margarine
1½ Tablespoons instant nonfat dry milk
1 Cup milk
1 Cup sugar
1 Teaspoon vanilla extract

Melt the chocolate and butter together in a heavy saucepan over low heat. Stir the instant nonfat dry milk into the milk, then combine with the sugar. Add the milk and sugar mixture to the melted chocolate and butter. Stir over medium heat until the sauce reaches the boiling point, then reduce the heat and cook, stirring frequently, until the sauce thickens slightly. Remove from the heat and stir in the vanilla. Serve hot.

### Raspberry Sauce

*If you are fortunate enough to grow your own raspberries, by all means use them. Otherwise you will have to rely on the less expensive frozen variety.*

(YIELD: ABOUT 2 CUPS)

3 Cups fresh (or 2 10-ounce packages frozen) raspberries
⅓ Cup seedless raspberry jelly

Rub the fresh or defrosted frozen berries through a fine sieve to produce a purée. Heat the jelly slightly to melt it, then stir it into the purée until smooth. Serve cold over fresh, frozen or canned fruits or vanilla ice cream.

# FOUR

## Growing Things

*THERE was a time, and not too long ago, when folks bought only those things they couldn't grow. They gardened, canned, pickled and raised their own animals for eggs and meat. Whatever land they had they put to good use. It seems to me it is time for us to do the same. The surest way to free yourself from supermarket tyranny is to somehow eliminate all but the most important trips to those bulging aisles and supplement your store-bought foods with home grown and produced ones.*

*If you have a yard or garden, even one no bigger than a bathtub, plant a salad garden. If your property is larger and zoning permits, consider raising your own animals. The sooner we learn to think of supermarket buying as a last resort rather than a way of life, the sooner we will break free from the supermarket habit.*

# SALAD BOWL GARDENS

Why just a salad garden?

If your growing area is just a small backyard (or even less space), and a full-scale garden is out of the question, the salad bowl garden may be the perfect answer for you. Salads can provide the basis for many a light, nutritious meal all spring and summer long. Nothing beats the high cost of food like home-grown vegetables. A few dollars invested in seeds can save you up to a hundred dollars in grocery bills if you plan your summer menus around the salad meal. Serve a bowl of tossed mixed greens with egg wedges and tuna fish, or a chef's salad with strips of meat and cheese, or try tomatoes stuffed with meat, chicken, fish or eggs. (See the Index for recipes.) Just start your meal with a chunky soup, add a loaf of home-baked bread (or some rolls) and a dessert, and you have a meal that is inexpensive and delicious.

The anti-inflation value of salad gardening is only the first of many rewards. Salad vegetables grown at home taste better and are more wholesome as well. Why settle for mealy, inedible tomatoes (picked green and ripened en route to your grocery), lifeless, plastic-packed radishes and carrots, heavily waxed cucumbers and limp let-

tuce? It is a sad commentary on modern life that today's commercial produce growers have, in many instances, bred out the flavor that nature so carefully bred in, in order to grow produce that will withstand rough handling. As a salad garden gardener you can take a stand against tasteless vegetables and refuse to buy the store-bought kind until they put back the flavor. In the meantime, you can so easily grow your own and, with a little planning, stagger your plantings and reap the benefits of a summer-long harvest.

Salad vegetables need little space; even a fairly small garden will produce an abundant yield. In addition, many crops are extremely accommodating—lettuce grows beautifully tucked away in odd corners of your flowerbed, where the partial shade the flowers afford protect the maturing heads from the hot midsummer sun. Fast-growing radishes can be set among rows of slower-growing lettuce. You can usually harvest two crops of radishes before the lettuce needs its full amount of space. Leaf lettuce and herbs make attractive and practical borders for flower gardens. The lush, dark green foliage of the pepper plant is as beautiful as any ornamental shrub, and you can dine on its smooth red and green fruits. If you are really pressed for space, barrels, boxes or planters filled with seedlings set in rich loamy earth can be attractively arranged on porch, patio or balcony. Even a fire escape or sunny window sill will provide you with a good-sized yield.

Salad vegetables come in multiple varieties. You can choose from four different lettuce types; early, midseason and late tomatoes of every size; mild early and sharp winter radishes. All are delicious.

Plant the salad ingredients you like best— anything from the commonplace to the exotic. It is best to start with the basics—lettuce, tomatoes, carrots, radishes, peppers—then add a row or two of green onions, or a combination of herbs. You might also try those interesting and flavorful pinch hitters for lettuce—endive and escarole. If you have a little room to expand or a fence to extend your garden vertically, try a sprawling vegetable like cucumbers.

## GENERAL DIRECTIONS FOR GARDENING

### Where to Put the Salad Garden

Most vegetables will thrive anywhere they can receive six or more hours of daily sunshine, whether in the garden, on a porch or patio, or on a sunny windowsill. Tomatoes, radishes, carrots, peppers—any vegetable that sends forth edible fruits or roots—demand direct sun. But lesser amounts of open sun are not critical for foliage plants like lettuce, which can be set in partial shade if necessary.

Do not crowd your vegetables. As seedlings and as mature plants they must compete with each other for moisture and nutrients. It is best to keep them away from shrubs and tree roots for this same reason. Dig up and remove any rocks or stones from your garden plot—unless you are partial to crooked carrots or radishes.

Arrange rows according to the height the mature plants will reach so that they all receive uniform sun. Some will surprise you with their rangy heights, so make sure one does not shade the other.

### What Kind Of Soil?

Vegetables will generally grow in almost any kind of soil. Best conditions for your salad gardening are found in deep, fine, sandy or silt loams with good drainage, but it is also possible to upgrade less-than-ideal soils.

Resuscitate heavy clay soils with compost or humus worked deeply in, or rejuvenate tired soil with judicious applications of fertilizer. Soil will occasionally have a pH count that is out of kilter. The pH scale indicates the degree to which a soil is acid or alkaline. Figuring pH 7.0 as neutral, yours may have a lower count and be too acid, or higher and be too alkaline. Since most vegetables do well in a slightly acid soil, if you have soil problems, a soil test is a good idea. You can do this test yourself with a soil-test kit available at many garden centers, or, if you prefer, ask your local garden supply store to do it for you. Your state agricultural station or state university will also do the test for you if you send them a soil sample. Such services are often free, although occasionally there will be a nominal charge. The test is well worth the price, however, since you will probably also get advice on remedying the soil condition. Generally, finely ground limestone restores an acid soil to productivity, while moderately alkaline soils respond to compost.

### Feeding Your Soil

Fertilizer is good for any soil, and compost is undoubtedly the cheapest kind. A compost heap is a do-it-yourself project that gratefully accepts all organic matter: grass clippings, dead leaves, healthy green plants and such cast-offs from your kitchen as vegetable peelings, egg shells, fruit skins and coffee grounds. Simply select an out-of-the-way corner for your collected goodies, mix with manure or a commercially prepared compost starter, sprinkle with bone meal and then wet down with water. It may take up to a year before total decomposition sets in. For this reason it is generally advisable to begin your compost pile in the spring, but you can speed the process somewhat by turning the pile over occasionally to admit air. Compost is doubly beneficial, serving as both fertilizer and soil builder.

When building a compost heap is totally out of the question, a salad gardener can turn to other types of fertilizers. Organic fertilizers derived from animals and plants, and inorganic fertilizers prepared from minerals or mineral by-products, are available commercially at very low cost. Your garden supply store can advise you which is best for your needs.

## When to Plant

Let dry, workable soil, not calendar date, be your guide. Climate differs in each area of the country, so planting times differ, too. Try this simple experiment to discover when it is safe to put seeds into the ground: lightly squeeze a handful of soil; if it compresses into a soggy ball, wait a week or so and try again. When the ball of soil crumbles with the light tap of a finger, get out your garden tools and start digging.

## How to Plant

Dig a shallow trench about a foot deep where your garden is to go. Note where the color of the earth changes. This color line marks the division between topsoil and subsoil. Confine your digging to the topsoil only. Keep at least 2 inches above, and do not disturb, the subsoil.

Remove any rocks you find and break up big clods of earth as you go. Rake or sift the soil until it is fine and even. Mark off your rows with sticks and string, and plant with sufficient space between rows to allow ample room for the vegetables you have chosen.

Consult your seed packet for planting instructions. Some of the hardier seeds can go directly into the ground in the spring as soon as the soil can be worked and all danger from frost is past. Other seeds require early summer planting for fall harvest, and still others need a long growing season and should be started indoors in late winter or early spring.

Follow the packet instructions carefully, especially when planting directly into the ground. A good rule of thumb is this: shallow planting in early spring, deeper seeding in warm weather.

Space the seeds as uniformly as possible. Overcrowding wastes seed and makes thinning difficult. Cut a shallow trench for each row with a long, pointed stick and carefully shake the seeds out of the packet. Try placing a few seeds at a time in folded paper for easier distribution; let them slide into the trench a few at a time as you draw the paper along. Sift fine soil lightly over the seeds through your fingers or a sieve and tamp it down firmly with the heel of your hand. Keep the soil moist to speed germination.

Growing seeds indoors gives you a jump on the season. Tomatoes and peppers need a head start in areas where spring arrives late. So does lettuce if you expect to harvest tender young leaves ahead of their usual season.

Growing seeds for future transplant to garden is easy, provided you have a warm and sunny spot or adequate artificial lighting indoors. Sow according to package directions in any kind of container with good drainage. Peat pots or peat pellets are excellent for starting seeds, and they cost just a few pennies apiece. You can plant them, pot and all, when the weather warms up. Many gardeners prefer them because there is less handling of plants involved. Or you can utilize your empty milk cartons, egg boxes or bleach bottles. A coffee can with drainage holes punched in the bottom makes a miniature greenhouse when capped with its plastic top. Punch a few holes in the cover for good ventilation. You can also remove both ends of the can and set the ventilated plastic top on the bottom of the can. Then just take off the plastic when transplanting and push the root ball directly into its prepared hole. Another unique and interesting method for starting seeds is to fill halves of egg shells with soil.

Fill your containers with disease- and weed-free potting soil, or use a lightweight planting mixture of sand and peat moss. You can save money by sterilizing your own ordinary garden soil. Sift it well and set in a shallow pan in an oven preheated to 160 to 170 degrees F. for 30 minutes on 2 successive days. Prepare a potting mix by combining equal amounts of sterilized soil, peat moss and vermiculite.

Start your seedlings about 6 to 8 weeks before you figure it is safe enough to plant them in the garden. Healthy growth is most certain when they can go outdoors shortly after developing their second set of true leaves.

## Transplanting

Continue regular watering until about a week before transplanting time, then cut back on moisture. Give the plants a few hours of partially shaded outdoor exposure each day to gradually acclimatize them to cooler temperatures. This hardening off cushions the tender seedlings against transplant shock.

Pick a cloudy day to do your transplanting, or supply the newly planted seedlings with a little light shade for a few days after planting to help them adjust quickly and establish sturdy growth. Fertilize the garden about a week prior to transplanting if you feel it is necessary, but forget about fertilizer when you set the seedlings in. They have all they can do to adjust to new growing conditions. About a week later give them a boost with a weak, water-soluble fertilizer.

If you prefer not to fuss with indoor planting, you can usually buy inexpensive seedlings that are already started. These fill the bill for gardening enthusiasts who lack time, space or a sunny south window, and nursery transplants need no hardening off. You may find, however, that you are limited to the varieties your nurseryman chooses to grow.

## Water, Water ...

You can usually count on normal rainfall to provide enough moisture for young vegetables until late spring, but you should establish a regular pattern of watering as soon as the onset of summer brings dry, searing heat and subsequent wilting. Watering the garden once for every two times you water the lawn is a good rule to follow.

Water should penetrate the soil to a depth of at least 3 inches. Shallow watering will force roots to the surface in their search for moisture. Use a perforated hose, which blankets the soil in heavy mist, or water by sprinkler in the morning to give the foilage a chance to dry out by nightfall.

## Pick a Mulch

You can conserve moisture and keep weeds down by applying a layer of some kind of organic material between the rows once the seedlings have been thinned and are well established. Use grass clippings or last year's residue of leaves for a good, economical mulch that will also add vital nutrients to the soil as it decays. One or 2 inches of either of these is enough because they both tend to mat a bit. Peat moss, buckwheat hulls or straw also work very well.

# WHAT TO PLANT

Salad vegetables are easy to grow, but it is always a good bet to start with the best seed obtainable. Study the seed catalogues, and select only named varieties whether you are buying seeds or transplants. Be sure that the varieties you choose are high-quality and disease-resistant.

Cultivate very carefully at all times—roots are often close to the surface and can easily be injured. Better still, forget the weeding and apply a mulch when the seedlings are thinned. This keeps weeds down and conserves moisture. Fertilize at regular intervals once seedlings are off to a good start. Healthy and vigorous plants can usually resist whatever diseases or pests may come their way.

## Lettuce

The most basic salad vegetable, lettuce, grows best during cooler weather. For earlier harvest, start some seed indoors in late winter and transplant to cold frame or garden when the weather warms up. Seed can be planted directly in the garden as soon as the soil is workable and a bit on the dry side. Make successive plantings two weeks apart until June, then wait until late summer to resume sowing for your fall crop. Lettuce tends to bolt or go to seed when it is exposed to blazing midsummer sun, but if you can provide it with a cooler, partially shaded area, you will have good pickings even in hot weather.

Lettuce is available in four main types:

CRISPHEADS: Compact and heavy, with rich green heads. Ithaca (Improved Iceberg) is a good early variety. Great Lakes and Imperial stand up well to heat, while hardy Evergreen is vigorous even in cold weather.

BUTTERHEAD OR BIBB: These varieties are distinguished by their delicate flavor and loosely folded green outer leaves encompassing a buttery yellow and compact center. Try heat-tolerant Buttercrunch or Butter King.

LEAF LETTUCE: This is my favorite. It matures more quickly than the other types and is easy to grow even where summers are hot. Leaf varieties usually have crisp, frilled leaves that grow in clusters, making the heads particularly attractive as decorative borders. Black Seeded Simpson and Prizehead are good, dependable early varieties, or you may prefer tender, sweet Salad Bowl or heat-tolerant Grand Rapids. Ruby's bright green leaves, prominently tinged with red, make this variety especially appealing.

COS OR ROMAINE: A tall and cylindrical lettuce with stiff, crisp, elongated leaves and a tart, distinctive flavor. Try Paris White, Valmaine or Parris Island Cos.

### GENERAL DIRECTIONS

Sow lettuce seed ¼ inch deep in rows 1½ feet apart, then thin according to instructions. Give crispheads plenty of room by spacing them about 1 foot apart. Space butterheads and cos types 8 to 10 inches from each other, leaf varieties 6 to 8 inches apart. Use all pulled seedlings as salad greens.

The different types mature at different rates, but plan on picking leaves from any of the loose-heading or loose-leafed varieties throughout the growing season to incorporate in summer salads.

## Tomatoes

Tomatoes outdistance every other vegetable for popularity among home gardeners. Plant a combination of early, midseason and late varieties—try different sizes, shapes and colors, too—for a multitude of delectable additions to your salad bowl all season long.

Try Valiant, Springset, New Yorker or Fireball for an early crop; Heinz 1350, Big Boy, Wonder Boy, Royal Ace or Viceroy for midseason harvest and Beefmaster for your late-summer meals. Small Fry produces enormous clusters of round, red one-inch tomatoes, and Tiny Tim's mini-sized bush bears lots of miniature fruit. Roma is a good pear-shaped red variety, or if you enjoy orange tomatoes, try full-sized Sunray or pear-shaped Yellow Pear.

Sow tomato seeds indoors about 6 to 8 weeks prior to planting out of doors. Harden off before setting the seedlings out. Space 2 to 3 feet apart.

Gardeners are of two minds regarding whether or not to stake their plants. Some argue that staking results in fewer tomatoes, while staking proponents hold that staked plants are less subject to blossom-end rot. If you do stake your plants, insert the stakes soon after transplanting and use strips of cloth rather than wire twists to hold the delicate growing stem to the stake.

Mulch your plants to conserve moisture, and prune them once a week to remove the small shoots that appear at the point where the leaf stem joins the main stem. Fertilize every 3 to 4 weeks after fruits reach 1-inch size.

Leave your tomatoes on the vine until red and ripe for maximum good eating. Keep mature fruit picked to increase yield. When severe frost threatens, gather the remaining green tomatoes and store in a dark, cool place. When needed, ripen on a warm window sill out of direct sunlight. Some of your unripe tomatoes may be used for making relishes or other green tomato recipes (see page 26).

## Carrots

Carrots are usually characterized by shape and length, so choose a variety suited to your soil. Long, slim-tapered Imperator or Gold Pak do well in light, sandy soils. Choose Royal Chantenay, Danvers Half-Long or Oxheart if your soil is heavy or somewhat rocky.

Sow seeds as soon as the soil can be worked because carrots do their best growing in cooler conditions. Arrange the seed thinly ½ inch deep in rows 1 foot apart, thinning the early varieties 2 inches apart, later ones 3 inches apart. Use the thinnings in your salads for an unusual treat. Follow with successive plantings 3 weeks apart until midsummer for a continuous harvest.

Carrots germinate slowly, so mark their rows with fast-growing radishes. Use them as soon as they reach edible size. Should you find yourself with a good-sized late crop, dig them up before the first frost and trim the tops to ½ inch from the root crown. Store in a cool place until needed.

### Radishes

Quick, dependable radishes can be planted anywhere in the garden. They mature so fast you can have a steady supply most of the season. Varieties come in all sizes, shapes and even a few different colors. Cherry Belle or Champion are traditional round red types; French Breakfast is an oval red. For white radishes, choose round Comet or tapering White Icicle. Sparkler is round and scarlet with a white tip. Black Spanish or pink-skinned China Rose are good winter varieties.

Begin succession plantings of the early radish types every 2 weeks as soon as the ground is workable, sowing the seed ½ inch deep in rows 10 to 12 inches apart. Thin to stand 1 inch apart as soon as the first growth appears. Use in salads as soon as they mature; they tend to grow bitter with age and heat. Discontinue planting during the height of the summer, then set out winter varieties at the end of August.

### Peppers

There are two main classes of peppers—the sweet, mild kind and the pungent, hot types. For salad purposes the mild variety is best, although you may still select from different shapes and colors. Some are blocky or heart-shaped, others resemble tomatoes. You can pick and use them green, or allow them to ripen to red or yellow. Bell Boy Hybrid, Yolo Wonder and Ace Hybrid are good varieties. Hybrid Peter Piper is an extra-early bearer, while Calwonder will ripen to bright yellow.

Sow seed indoors about 8 to 10 weeks before the weather warms up. Figure about 3 plants per family member to be sure of a summer-long supply. Wait for warm, humid days to arrive before transplanting. Pepper plants often abort and drop their fruit if the air is too hot and dry. Set the seedlings 18 to 24 inches apart in rows 2 feet apart.

Harvest the fruit at any stage, green or color-ripened, but let it grow to mature size first. Keep the plants well picked so they keep producing.

### Scallions

These are the green or bunching onions, so called because of their bulbless, tender green shoots. Evergreen Bunching, Beltsville Bunching and Hardy White Bunching are all good varieties.

Start successive plantings of scallions from seed in spring for continuous summer harvest or, if your winters are not too severe, in the fall for an early spring crop. Pull the clusters of tender green shoots that sprout from each seed as needed.

### Endive and Escarole

These flavorful substitutes for lettuce prefer cooler temperatures for growing. Plant them in the early spring as soon as frost danger is past, or sow a fall crop in mid-August. Endive has curly or fringed leaves. Try Salad King or Green Curled Endive. Escarole, of which Broad-Leaved Batavian is a good variety, has broad, lettucelike leaves.

Sow the seed directly in the garden as soon as the ground can be worked, planting ¼ inch deep in rows set 1½ to 2 feet apart. Thin to 10 or 12 inches apart when the seedlings are 2 or 3 inches tall. Pick as needed after blanching and before hot weather sets in, then use the same rows for a fall crop by sowing again in late August.

Both endive and escarole must be blanched to reduce their slightly bitter flavor. Simply pick a day when the leaves are perfectly dry, tie the side leaves up over the center leaves with string or rubber bands and leave for 4 to 5 days in warm weather, 10 to 14 days when the temperature is cooler.

## Cucumbers

Cucumbers like lots of living space, so if you can give them room to sprawl, or a fence or trellis to climb up on, by all means include them in your salad bowl garden. You can grow pickling varieties if you prefer, but the slicing cucumbers are best for salads. Try Victory or Spartan Valor, both early and constant producers, or Burpless Hybrid. Burpless Hybrid or Sweet Slice are perfect for those salad devotees who do not get along too well with the regular varieties. There is even a dwarf, bushlike variety, Hybrid Patio Pik, that fits neatly into a small garden or even a good-sized patio planter.

Sow cucumber seed directly in the garden once frost danger has passed. Set groups of 6 to 8 seeds about 4 to 5 feet apart along a trellis or fence, thinning each group to the strongest 3 or 4 seedlings as soon as they reach 6 inches in height. Train the vines to climb as they grow, but be careful not to tear them. Both vines and blossoms are easily injured.

Pick the ripe fruit often by rolling the vines over carefully and cutting the stem with a sharp knife. Regular harvesting encourages longer and more abundant production.

# SALAD BOWL
# MINIGARDENS IN A POT

Even city-dwellers can enjoy the summer savings and delectable freshness of own-grown salad vegetables as long as a balcony, fire escape, doorstep—or even a sunny window sill—is available. Container gardening can satisfy even the most frustrated gardeners—and at a price nearly anyone can afford.

Basic materials are cheap. All you really need to get your minigardening under way are some containers, lots of soil (either synthetic or the real thing), the seeds of your choice and a sunny location where your plants can soak up about six hours of sunshine daily.

## CONTAINERS

Almost any kind of container will do. Use whatever you have on hand—pails, plastic buckets, bushel or wire baskets, wooden crates or boxes, clay or plastic pots. Readymade planters of wood, clay, metal or plastic are ideal if you have them or can scrounge them up from the cellars or garages of your suburban relatives or neighbors. Large plastic trash cans or even plastic laundry

baskets make inexpensive, lightweight and practical receptacles for minigardens. Your choice of containers can be as far out as your imagination, but there is one important consideration—the size of the plant when it's fully grown.

Safeguard any new wood containers from wear and tear by painting them inside and out with a suitable wood preservative. Solid plastic containers will need some kind of drainage facilities. Drill 4 to 6 small, evenly spaced holes along the sides about 1 to 2 inches above the container bottom. Line the bottom with a 1-inch layer of gravel, stones or shards from smashed clay pots. Laundry or bushel baskets whose open sides will not contain the soil properly may be lined with plastic sheeting before filling. Punch a few holes in the plastic for drainage.

## SOIL

Finding suitable soil to fill your planters may present a problem to city gardeners. Vegetables, particularly those grown in containers, insist upon rich, friable, light soils. The least expensive soil is what you get from your country friends. You can make sure it is disease-free by sterilizing it in your oven. Simply bake it on foil-lined baking sheets at 160 to 170 degrees F. for 30 minutes on 2 successive days. Then mix it with a few handfuls of vermiculite and sand.

If carting home several cubic yards of earth makes you weary just to think about it, try buying one of the soil substitutes sold at garden supply centers. This is synthetic soil, composed of vermiculite, peat moss and fertilizer. The initial expense may be a bit high, but you will find synthetic soils have several advantages over Mother Nature's own. First, they are weed- and disease-free. In addition, they hold moisture and plant nutrients very well, and they are lightweight and portable, a point to keep in mind in case you have to tug large containers around to keep up with the sun.

Preparing your own soil substitute may save you some money if you're planning to fill lots of large containers. Combine 1 bushel of vermiculite with 1 bushel of shredded peat moss. Add 1½ cups of crushed limestone (the dolomitic kind, which contains magnesium), 1 cup of 5-10-5 fertilizer, and ½ cup of 20 percent superphosphate. Sprinkle with a bit of water to minimize dust reaction while you're elbow deep, and mix these ingredients thoroughly.

## LIGHT

Vegetables require lots of direct sunlight, and those grown in minigardens are no exception. A good rule of thumb to follow is to place your tomatoes and peppers and other fruit-bearing vegetable plants where they will get the most sun. Your root vegetables will tolerate a little partial shade, and leafy vegetables like lettuce actually produce better if you keep them very lightly shaded, especially in hot weather.

## HOW DOES YOUR MINIGARDEN GROW?

Choosing seeds for your containers should present no problems, since most salad vegetables respond with enthusiasm if given ample room.

Any salad vegetable that grows successfully in the garden—lettuce, tomatoes, carrots, radishes, peppers, herbs and even cucumbers—will also thrive in suitably sized containers. Select any of the varieties listed in the Salad Bowl Garden section along with their planting instructions on pages 180–83. Or study seed catalogues on your own to see what's new and recommended. Buy only fresh, named and disease-resistant seeds for best results.

You may want to try some varieties especially bred for patio or porch and thus ideal for minigardening. These include:

· Small Fry, Pixie, Patio or Tiny Tim tomatoes. The last-named, an exquisite small cherry tomato, bears beautifully even when set on a sunny window sill.

· Short'n Sweet, Scarlet Nantes, Royal Chantenay or Nantes Half Long carrot varieties, all of which grow short and tender and do well in a shallowly prepared bed.

· Patio Pik, a multipurpose cucumber that yields quantities of fruit in a confined growing area.

Treat the vegetables for your minigarden with the same respect you would give to any vegetable planted out of doors. Most salad vegetables may be planted directly in their containers outdoors as soon as all danger from frost is gone. Others, like tomatoes or peppers, may need a jump on the growing season because of the time they take to reach maturity. If you live in an area where spring arrives late, start these fruit-bearing plants indoors in late winter, transplanting to outside conditions when the weather warms up. Follow the same general instructions for seeding indoors and transplanting as directed in the Salad Bowl Garden section on pages 179–80.

Lettuce may be started indoors by seeding en masse in large pans or flats. Transplant the healthier plants to their growing rows in wide containers out of doors. Tomatoes and peppers are best grown individually in peat pellets or pots. Set 2 or 3 seeds in each pellet, moisten with water, then place in a plastic bag and secure the top with a wire twist. As soon as the seedlings emerge, pull out all but the most vigorous. Transplant seedling and pellet to a larger container after the first true leaves develop. Transplanting is easy from then on, since root disturbance is minimal.

For a successful harvest, vegetables should be planted or transplanted out of doors as soon as frost-free days (and nights) arrive. Consult the planting dates for your particular area as shown on the seed packet. Temperatures vary from place to place, but it is a fairly safe bet that if you are a city-dweller you will find that you can set your plants out a week or two earlier than your cousins in the country.

Early crops started indoors will need to be hardened, or accustomed to outdoor living, before moving outside. Begin hardening them off by cutting back on moisture a week or two before you plan to set them out. Give them an outing for a few hours each day during this period, too, but protect them from the sun's burning rays with a little light shade.

Once your minigarden vegetables are established and settled into their permanent homes, begin a regular routine of watering, fertilizing, and cultivating. Since most vegetables are about 90 percent moisture, they need a weekly water supply equal to about 1 inch of rain during their outdoor growing season. Controlling moisture in container gardening is easy. Water the plants each time the soil feels dry to your touch about ½ inch beneath the surface. Be careful not to overwater, since wet feet will slowly kill your plants. Make sure that your containers have adequate drainage; gravel or other similar material should line the bottom of each. In exceptionally hot weather, water as often as needed, but keep water off the plant foliage if possible, especially when watering late in the evening. Wet leaves encourage disease.

Begin a fertilizing program about three weeks after your seedlings grow their first two true leaves, then continue at three-week intervals for rapid growth and good production. About 1 level teaspoon of 5-10-5 fertilizer per square foot of soil is a good average. Mix well into the top ½ inch of soil and water thoroughly. As an alternative you may prefer a good water-soluble fertilizer, which minimizes the chance of burning tender roots. Follow manufacturer's directions.

Airborne weeds often turn up in the unlikeliest places. Should weeds appear in your minigarden, it is easy to pull them up by hand. Some porch and patio gardeners like to use a small hand weeder, but I cannot recommend it; tender roots are injured too easily. It is also a good idea to turn over the surface soil occasionally while the plants are growing. An old tablespoon and/or fork is fine for this, but again, take care. Apply a mulch (see page 180) once plants are established to conserve water and keep the soil cool.

# HERBS
# FOR YOUR SOUL
# & YOUR SALAD BOWL

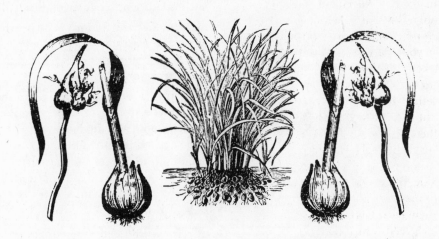

Growing herbs should be your rest from work, your pleasure, the present you give yourself for other work you must do. There is no avocation so gratifying, no crop so satisfying—none that takes so little trouble and gives so many rewards—as the planting, growing, harvesting and using of herbs.

These aromatic plants descended from hardy weed ancestors—and revered by generations of gardeners from Roman times (and before)—make gardening foolproof even for the novice. Sow a few varieties here and there in the garden, tuck them into borders, hang them in planters, grow them in pots on a sunny window sill, or plan and plant a whole garden just of herbs. They will reward you in more ways than you can imagine.

Fresh herbs will grace your table in foods or as fragrant additions to flower arrangements. Dry your herbs and keep or sell them. Make herb-rich aromatic potpourri for gifts (see page 190). You can use your herbs to flavor vinegar or pickles or even to make a bouquet. However you use them, herbs will give you back more pleasure leaf for leaf than any other garden inhabitant.

Herbs in general are hardy, easy-to-grow plants that need virtually no attention once established in an old-fashioned herb garden, set among flowers or vegetables or in 6-inch pots. Most prefer those two fundamentals of good gardening—sun and well-drained soil. But some will thrive in partial shade, and soil for herbs needs no special nutrients or enrichment. Should you forget to water them, they'll still survive. In fact, herbs usually increase their production of aromatic oils during drier summers.

## GROWING HERBS INDOORS

Indoor herb gardeners will find sweet basil, chives, marjoram, mint, parsley, sage, savory and thyme most suitable for a sunny window sill, since most of the others grow too tall. Start them from seeds in late winter or early spring in 6-inch pots. Use a packaged potting soil well mixed with sand. Good drainage is a must for herbs, which cannot abide perpetually wet feet. Set small pebbles or bits of charcoal on the bottom of each pot before filling it with soil. To speed germination you may soak the seeds overnight in water or place the unopened packets in your vegetable crisper for a few days before planting. If you have no time for fuss or bother, you may sow the seeds directly on top of the soil without further ado. In either case, moisten the soil before planting and sow the seed sparingly. Cover the pots loosely with plastic wrap while they germinate. Keep the plants well watered until they are established, but do not overdo.

Allow the top surface to dry out before watering again, and water preferably from the bottom. Indoor herbs also welcome an occasional misting. Since house plants do need feeding, a small amount of fertilizer will be necessary for indoor growth, but limit its application to half strength, or your herbs will overgrow and lose fragrance.

## GROWING HERBS OUTDOORS

Sow the seeds directly in a sunny, well-drained location as soon as the weather is dependably warm. Dig up the soil to a depth of 8 inches, rake it smooth and sift the top ¼ inch. Set the herb seeds on top of the soil and cover them very lightly with soil dusted through a sieve. Pat the soil down a bit with your hands before watering, and keep the seeds fairly moist until they germinate. Thin when at least 4 true leaves have developed on each plant.

Herbs are usually classified for garden growing according to whether they are annuals, perennials or biennials. Since most have the endearing habit of reappearing each subsequent spring no matter how they are classified, herb enthusiasts need mainly to know the size each of their favorites reaches at maturity for easier placement in the garden, plus some harvesting tips and culinary uses.

ANISE: Sow this 18-inch annual directly in the garden when the weather warms up. Use the green leaves in salads, pull the gray seeds off the heads when ripe and use for flavoring in cakes, bread, applesauce, soups and stews.

BASIL (SWEET): This quick-growing 12- to 18-inch annual with leaves ranging from green to purple should be planted after the last frost. Thin the seedlings to stand 1 foot apart and pinch the stems to promote bushier growth. Gather the leaves before the tiny white flowers bloom. Use fresh or dried to season salads, vinegars, meat, fish, poultry and sauces.

BASIL (LEMON): This lemon-scented offshoot is a 2-foot annual. Plant when the weather is dependably warm; keep the soil moist until the seedlings appear. Thin to stand 1 foot apart. Delicious with salads and fresh vegetables.

BORAGE: Sow this 18-inch faintly aromatic annual when the weather is dependably warm. Use the star-shaped flowers or leaf sprigs to flavor summer drinks or salads.

CHERVIL is a delicate, fernlike annual similar in appearance and flavor to parsley. Plant it directly in rich, moist soil in shade, or allow it to nestle under taller plants. This herb, which reaches a height of 18 inches at maturity, loses much of its flavor when dried, so use it fresh—in salads, omelets, spinach, with poultry or veal dishes or as a garnish.

CHIVES: A mild, onion-flavored hardy perennial that grows in tall, spiky grasslike clumps. Plant seeds thickly in early spring. Showy lavender blossoms emerge in early summer. Divide clumps and pot for indoor use during winter. Snip leaves for use in soups, salads and vegetables.

CARAWAY: Plant this attractive 2-foot biennial one year and harvest the seeds the following June. Use the young leaves and shoots to season salads, the seeds to flavor pastry, cakes, cheese and sauces.

CATNIP: A 2- to 3-foot perennial with gray heart-shaped leaves. Sow on top of the ground in spring or early fall. Use leaves green or dried as seasoning or for preparing catnip tea.

DILL: The lacy, light-green leaves of this 2- to 3-foot annual add delightful flavor to salads, soups, lamb dishes and sauces. Use the pungent dried leaves, stems and seeds for pickling. Make successive plantings until early summer; harvest seeds when ripe, brown and flat.

FENNEL: This 2½-foot licorice-flavored herb is similar to dill but somewhat more difficult to grow. Pinch off the top leaves to try to shape the plant and promote new growth. Grows as a perennial in mild climates but only annually where winters are cold. Florence fennel develops celerylike bulbous stalks that may be eaten raw or boiled.

HOREHOUND: This decorative 14- to 18-inch perennial grows in sprawling clumps. Set the seeds in sandy soil in spring, thin to stand 1 foot apart as a border. Use the wrinkled gray leaves for flower arrangements, or boil to extract flavor for medicinal candy.

LAVENDER: This is a 2-foot compact perennial that bears masses of blue flowers. Dry the leaves and flowers to use in sachets and potpourris.

MARJORAM (SWEET): This aromatic 1- to 2-foot plant grows as a perennial in mild climates, but must be replanted each year where cold winters prevail, or potted and brought indoors for fresh leaves in winter. Sow on top of the ground in spring, tamp down a bit and keep moist with a fine spray until seedlings appear. Keep the top leaves picked to prevent flowering and to promote new growth. Use fresh or dried to complement salads, vegetables, sauces and meat dishes or to flavor vinegars and marinades.

MINT: Start this quick-growing 2-foot perennial from seeds or cuttings in sun or shade—and stand back! Keep vigorously confined so that it doesn't take over the garden. Try several of the different flavors. Use the leaves fresh for garnishes or in salads and fruit desserts, crushed for flavoring teas and lemonade. Or dry the leaves for winter teas.

OREGANO: This 2½-foot perennial is a pungent cousin to sweet marjoram. Sow the seeds where they will get lots of sunshine and moderate amounts of water. Snip fresh or use dry in Italian foods, meat and vegetable dishes and sauces.

PARSLEY: Sow this popular garnish from seed in sun or partial shade when the weather is dependably warm. Choose from such varieties as Champion Moss Curled, Extra Triple Curled or the strong-flavored Dark Green Italian. Soak the seeds overnight in warm water to speed germination. Parsley will often grow a second year if allowed to go to seed. Use the refreshing flavor of fresh parsley in salads, vegetables and sauces, in addition to using it as a garnish. Dry the mature leaves before the flowers bloom to secure fine year-round flavoring for your meals. Parsley is rich in vitamins A and C.

ROSEMARY grows as a perennial where winters are mild, and as an annual in colder areas. It is one of the very few herbs difficult to establish in the herb garden. Start this 3- to 4-foot plant from seeds, soaking them well beforehand, or from cuttings. Choose a dry, sunny location, and keep the spiky tips pinched back to encourage growth. Rosemary, fresh or dried, is particularly delicious with lamb, chicken or veal.

SAGE is a very fragrant perennial that reaches 1 to 2 feet in height. With its gray leaves and attractive blue flowers it makes both an ornamental and useful border for any garden. Thin the young plants to stand 15 inches apart and give lots of water—sage is probably the thirstiest of the herbs. Pick leaves from the top first to encourage growth, then use the 3 or 4 largest on the bottom. Use fresh or dried with poultry, stuffing, fish, sauces or in herb breads.

SUMMER SAVORY: Seeds for this 1-foot, narrow-leaved annual should be sown directly in the garden when the weather is suitably warm. Thin seedlings to stand 12 inches apart and watch for masses of pink-hued blossoms in August. Use the leaves fresh or dried for flavoring salads, salad dressings, gravies and stew.

TARRAGON: The delicate flavor of this perennial herb is a favorite and welcome addition to salads, soups, baked fish and vinegar, but it often proves temperamental when set out in the garden. Try it from transplants to ensure success.

THYME: This short, shrublike perennial reaches about 12 inches in height. Start indoors from seed and transplant, or sow directly on top of well-prepared soil, thinning to stand 8 inches apart. Don't overwater the seeds—they prefer drier conditions. Keep the plants well-shaped, clipping off the small top leaves to prevent formation of the small lavender or pink flowers. Use the pungent leaves and stems for flavoring soups, stews, poultry, meat loaf and sauces.

## HARVESTING HERBS

Herbs used fresh from the garden are marvelously pungent, but you will need about 1 tablespoon of any variety to equal the potency of a teaspoonful of its dried counterpart. Snip tender young leaves fresh as needed—the plants will be more shapely and you'll have fewer tangles and drooping stems. Crush or chop fresh herbs to extract maximum flavor, or soak dried herbs a bit in vinegar or oil to extract their concentrated fragrance.

The best time to harvest your herbs for drying is shortly before the flowers open, when the concentration of oils is at its peak. Select a warm, dry day and make midmorning cuttings to assure that the stems and leaves will be free from early dew. Snip off the stems at the base, leaving a few stalks behind to ensure next year's supply.

## DRYING HERBS

The prime requisite for drying herbs is a cool, dry, well-ventilated area. Spread them out on window screens or paper towels, or place them in loosely tied bunches of 3 or 4 stalks and hang them upside down. Hang the stalks in large paper bags if you wish, but take care that the sides of the bag do not brush against the leaves.

Herbs will generally dry in 3 to 4 days if the weather is not humid. If humid conditions hinder drying, set the herbs on a cookie sheet in a warm oven just long enough to dry out any leftover moisture. Handle carefully when preparing for storage—you'll find the stalks and leaves are quite brittle when dry. Spread several dishtowels out on a flat surface, hold the stalks a few inches above, then gently strip the leaves from the stems. Sort out and discard any bits of stem. Shake the edges of the towels to gather the leaves and store in airtight jars or bottles. If you've hung your herbs to dry in paper bags, stripping them is simply a matter of rubbing the sides of the bag between your hands until the leaves drop off. Remove the woody stalks from the bag and pick off any bits of remaining leaves. Discard the stalks and store the crumbled leaves in clean, airtight jars.

Label and date the jars or bottles for easy reference and store tightly capped in a cool, dry place. Dried herbs quickly lose their flavor when exposed to heat or sun.

## FREEZING HERBS

For year-round fresh flavor, freeze part of your crop of herbs. Harvest the stems and leaves as usual before the flowers bloom, wash and dry well, then pack into small containers or bags and store in the freezer. Frozen herbs require no time at all to thaw. Their appearance after thawing may be somewhat less than perfect, but their flavor will still be superb. Frozen herbs generally have the same strength as fresh.

### *How to Make Gift Potpourris*

You can easily turn your herbs and flowers into lovely and practical gifts if you grow and dry some of the more fragrant varieties. Among the most popular pleasant and spicy scents are those from:

| | |
|---|---|
| Lemon balm | Rose geranium |
| Lemon geranium | Rosemary |
| Lemon verbena | Tarragon |
| Lemon thyme | Lavender flowers |
| Orange mint | |

Dry all according to the directions above. Fill flat sachets of organdy, silk or other fancy materials left over from sewing. Small glazed pots filled with a bouquet of mixed dried herbs add a welcome touch to any room. A tiny antique sewing basket filled with this mixture makes a marvelous gift.

### *Pomander Balls*

Pomander balls are another easy make-it-yourself gift. Simply stud some apples or oranges all over with cloves, roll them in powdered allspice and cover with fine nylon net. Dress them up a bit with ribbons and touches of dried flowers.

## MAKING MONEY FROM HERBS

Herb growing can be a very profitable sideline or even a highly profitable fulltime business.

Herbs may be packaged in quarter-ounce quantities in small heat-sealed plastic envelopes, which may then be neatly stapled to an 11- by 14-inch card in, say, 4 rows of 10 each.

If your herbs retail for $.30 per packet, the retail value of each card will be $12. The retail dealer normally expects to make around 40 percent profit on merchandise of this type, which means you sell him your card for $7.20. One acre of herbs should yield enough to fill at least a thousand cards, and if you can sell that many cards you gross over $7,000! Deduct around $2,500 for expenses—the cost of planting, labor, packaging materials and so on—and you still have $5,000 profit to show for your efforts!

Packaging a full acre of herbs may be somewhat ambitious, but there is no reason why you cannot do proportionately well with a smaller area. There definitely is a market for fresh, flavorful, home-grown herbs. Supermarkets, groceries, food specialty stores, health food stores and the like are all good potential outlets.

. . . and just think of the pleasure of living downwind of an acre of herbs!

# SIMPLE HOME TREE SURGERY

Simple tree surgery is an uncomplicated, bloodless art that may be practiced by any tree owner who has a small degree of mechanical skill. Since this is exacting work where neatness counts, it does help if you have some interest in, and knowledge of, general woodworking.

Decay must be removed thoroughly and completely if your tree is to survive. For this, use general woodworking tools—a saw, mallet and a few sharp gouges of various sizes. For filling and finishing you will need some stiff-bristled brushes, shellac, creosote, tar (and a means for melting it) and, if the holes are fairly large ones, a three-to-one concrete mixture, some reinforcing wire and perhaps a piece or two of tar paper.

Trim off all dead, broken or rotted limbs. Be sure you make your cut behind the diseased area, in good healthy wood. Shellac the edges of the bark and the sap wood, and creosote the sawn edge to keep fungus from attacking the freshly cut wood. Finally, coat the cut neatly with hot tar to reseal and protect it.

If you have the misfortune to run into an area of decayed wood in the trunk or a heavy limb, your job will be somewhat more complicated. In this case all decayed wood should be gouged away down to fresh, healthy wood. Paint this well with creosote and then coat the entire area with melted tar. If the resulting cavity is fairly substantial in size and in a location where water or debris might accumulate, the cavity should, if at all possible, be filled with concrete. (Concrete work high up on the trunk or on a high limb can be difficult and dangerous, and is best left to professionals.)

Just before you trowel in your concrete, which should be a fairly stiff, dry mix, apply a heavy coating of melted tar. This will act as an expansion joint and keep your concrete from cracking. If the hole is over six inches in diameter and if you have had no experience with concrete, it would be best to have a professional do the job. Should this be out of the question for any reason, proceed as follows.

First, span the back of the hole with reinforcing wire. Build your concrete up in layers about 6 inches deep and separate each layer with a piece of heavy roofing tar paper. This will make for a more flexible cavity and will allow for a bit more expansion. After the concrete has hardened, use a sharp knife (a linoleum knife works well) to cut away any tar paper that may be sticking out. Flush over with more concrete.

These basics should be helpful provided you stick to simple, basic repairs. Actually tree surgery is an art as well as a science, and there is a great deal more involved than the mere lopping off of limbs and the filling of holes. Tree surgery includes the diagnosis of disease, feeding and caring for sick trees and the rescue of those that have been struck by lightning, hit by cars or otherwise victimized by accidents of man and nature.

# RAISING EARTHWORMS FOR FUN & PROFIT

If you garden, and if you have the space you should, you probably realize how helpful worms are for aerating your soil. What you might not be aware of is that you can raise your own earthworms, not only to increase your garden's yield, but to make money as well. Have you ever noticed those small magazine ads urging you to make your fortune raising worms? Amazingly enough, earthworms are really big business. They are apparently in great demand, not only by fishermen—and there are millions of those—but by other organic gardeners.

While I have never had a great deal of interaction with worms, except for growing them in the mulch for my garden, they are evidently easy to raise in great quantities with very little effort if you follow a few simple rules.

Worms demand little in the way of attention, since they are not overly sensitive and all they require in equipment is a large bottomless box about 3 or 4 feet wide and 8 feet long. Make this from any old lumber you might have lying about, paint it to keep it from rotting and cover up the cracks in the sides. If you live in a cold climate, dig a pit about 3 feet deep, set your box in it and fill it with a rich compost mixture.

(Manure, well-soaked sawdust, garden soil and bits of garbage make a pretty good combination.) Water the compost and let it stand for a few days. Once it has heated and then cooled off, it is time to plant your little tenants.

Of course, you will have to feed your worms. Chicken mash mixed with water and sprinkled evenly on the surface of their bed will do fine. All that remains is to wet down the bed every couple of days to keep it damp but not soggy and to turn the compost every 3 or 4 weeks with a pitch fork. When winter rolls around, fill up the pit with old leaves, straw or old burlap to keep your worms from freezing, and restart the bed from scratch once every year. Aside from these basics, the worms are pretty much on their own.

If you are also raising rabbits, all your problems are solved. Rabbit raisers can place worm boxes right underneath the hutches. The excess rabbit food and droppings fall into the worm box and feeding and compost problems are solved automatically.

With earthworms selling at around four to five dollars per thousand, they can be a fairly profitable venture. If you happen to live in an area where there is good fishing, a sign on the front lawn will probably bring you some business. Or you might sell to a nearby nursery or organic garden center. Most worm tycoons apparently conduct their business via the mails, using containers and bags especially made for shipping by worm-container manufacturers. That will give you some conception of the scope of the business!

Now we get down to the real nitty-gritty—who does the harvesting? From here on in, my friend, you are on your own.

If you want more information, the U.S. Department of Agriculture (or your public library) can fill in the details.

# RAISING
# YOUR OWN FISH

Here is an interesting way to keep your freezer filled with free fish. If you have an acre of land to spare, some source of water and a sufficient annual rainfall, try raising fish in your own pond. The best method, according to government sources, is to excavate a low area and use runoff from surrounding areas to keep it filled. Of course, if you happen to have a stream or a spring on your property, by all means incorporate it into your pond area and your water problems will be over.

Various types of fish can be kept—bull heads, pickerel, and so on—but the easiest to raise and the most delicious to eat are sunfish and bass. You can obtain fingerlings for nothing (or next to it) from state hatcheries or the U.S. Fish and Wild Life Service. The experts have worked out an ingenious system that works like a charm. Bulldoze your 1-acre pond from 6 to 12 feet deep to keep your fish from freezing in winter and suffering the effects of drought in summer. Fill the pond, or allow it to fill, then add about 100 pounds of 8-8-4 crop fertilizer. This gets the cycle started by promoting the growth of algae. Next, in the spring or fall, stock the pond with about 800 sunfish and 100 bass fingerlings—and stand back! The baby sunfish eat the algae, the baby bass eat the sunfish, and you eat the adults of both varieties. The cycle continues year after year, provided you keep fertilizing the pond and keep your hook and line busy. If you get lazy and fall behind on your fishing, the sunfish population will soon finish off the available algae and that in turn will finish off your pond.

A 1-acre pond will normally yield around 40 to 50 1-pound bass and 700 sunfish every year.

If this sounds like your pond of fish, check with your U.S. Fish and Wild Life Service for pond-building details, and so on.

# RAISING LIVESTOCK
# IN A SMALL SPACE

If you have an acre or two of land (and a farmer or friend who will take over the milking and feeding for you if you cannot be at home 365 days a year), raising your own livestock is a lovely thing to do. True, you must have patience and be an early riser, or willing to become one. A cow cannot wait to be milked just because you have had a late night. But think of the pleasures of having between 3,000 and 6,000 quarts of milk a year per cow! Think of all the butter and cheese! Of freezers full of meat! Of home-picked eggs that taste the way eggs used to taste—with no drugs or pesticides included in the meager price! Think of furry nuzzlings and lowings in the night. And never needing a lawn mower—or fertilizer.

There *is* responsibility involved. Newcomers to farming and raising livestock should not undertake too much too soon. This, in all probability, will exclude breeding and the tender loving care needed by any newborn animal. But omitting this experience, it is possible and practical to raise young animals to producing and/or slaughtering age.

Livestock animals do require a vigilant eye, and someone to take care of them on a daily basis. But as anyone who has had the experience will tell you, there are few pleasures like watching your own healthy animal grow day by day. Meat from animals you have raised yourself tastes much more delicious than any you can buy in the supermarket or butcher's shop, and it costs about one-third as much per pound.

Raising livestock on a commercial level is a science that requires patience and many technical skills. Most professional producers acquire much of their know-how by growing up around animals and then further their knowledge by studying animal husbandry at an agricultural college. To attempt to raise any animal without first having some knowledge of its character, diet, diseases and daily requirements is foolish and inhumane. But if you study the subject and follow the advice of experienced neighbors and state and county agricultural agencies, it is possible to raise your own animals successfully.

Livestock animals can be purchased either from an individual farmer or rancher, or at a livestock auction. For those who are not trained to pick out the most desirable characteristics from a distance, the best way to buy your animals is from a trustworthy neighbor. If your "small space" is new and you have not met your neighbors yet, take the time to knock on their doors, introduce yourself and explain your desire to raise your own meat. The country is not the city, and more than likely you will find someone who will suggest a good person to buy an animal from, or a knowledgeable veteran who will be able to give you advice while you are raising one. If all else fails, look under livestock sales in the classified advertisements in your community newspaper. Remember that it is always best to see and touch your animals before you buy them. In a business where prices fluctuate on a daily basis and there are so many producers, the cardinal rule is "Let the buyer beware." Ask around about prices before you buy, from as many people in your area as possible. If there is a livestock auction nearby, sit through a few sale days and figure the average price for the kind of animal you plan to buy. Try to get out and see as many different kinds and breeds as possible, and take the time to read as much as possible about your animal. After doing this, you should have an idea of a good price to offer when you are finally standing in the barn, pen or corral, ready to make a deal. Keep in mind that you are making an investment in something you will have to live with for a least a season.

## RAISING CHICKENS

If you own half an acre or so of land, or even if you claim a large yard as your domain, you should be able to raise chickens with little trouble and a substantial savings in money. Be aware, though, that many suburban areas have zoning restrictions on the raising of poultry, so make sure to check into your local ordinances before you dash out and buy yourself a handsome flock. There are many breeds and crosses of chickens that are excellent for a small flock, whether for eggs or meat or both. If fresh eggs are your passion, White Leghorns or crossbred strains are known for their productivity. A good all-purpose bird, for both meat and eggs, is the Rhode Island Red. Your best bet again, since there are so many breeds of chickens, is to ask farmers in your area what breeds they have found best suited to family production. If you like the "country" look of brown eggs and are interested in keeping a variety of nice-looking, colorful birds, check into the off-beat breeds. You will probably find almost any kind or combination of colors you want! The most desirable aspect of raising chickens for someone who has not done much living down on the farm is the ease with which they may be raised in small numbers.

To get an idea of the size of a flock to suit your needs, calculate the number of eggs you and your family consume per day and multiply by 2½.

## How to Buy Your Chickens

One way to start a flock is to buy day-old chicks. Although baby chicks are appealing, for the inexperienced flock owner they are generally not a good investment because of their need for constant care (and a heated brooder house) and their high mortality rate. For a small family flock, it is probably best to buy older chickens—ready-to-lay pullets, or hens that have completed one year of production before you buy them. Pullets can be bought from a commercial pullet raiser and yearling hens from a commercial egg producer. Yearling hens are usually removed from commercial flocks after 12 to 15 months of laying and are replaced by pullets. In either case, there are some general guidelines to look for on the bird itself in order to determine its laying capacity before you buy it.

The first place to look is at the comb and wattles (the red crown and the pouches under the beak). A good egg-layer should have a large, smooth comb and wattles, a nonlayer has a dry, small and shriveled comb and wattles. Next look at the "vent" under the tail, and the pubic bones supporting the vent. Hold the hen head downward, cupping the head with your hand, resting it against your forearm, with a couple of free fingers on your holding hand to prevent the legs from scratching. Lift the tail up with your other hand so that the vent shows, pressing up against the vent with your fingers. A good egg-layer will have wide pubic bones and a large vent. On a good egg-layer, you should be able to fit at least two and, better yet, three of your fingers between the pubic bones, pressing up against the vent. On a nonlayer, you will not be able to do this. Also check the vent for color—a yellow color indicates that a hen is not laying, whereas a pink, white or bluish-white vent indicates that it is a good layer.

To buy chickens exclusively for meat, get chicks that can be put on "range"—old enough to run freely outside of a brooder house, or about 6 to 8 weeks old. Give them about another 10 to 16 weeks to grow, and they are ready for your frying pan.

A general and most important rule is to buy your chickens only from a reputable dealer. Be sure each has been tested for and found free of pullorum and typhoid diseases. Always ask about what disease prevention measures have gone into the chickens you are buying, and make sure to buy only from vaccinated flocks. At the same time, check for mites, lice and other parasites, using your fingertips to press back the feathers, so you can see that the down and skin are insect-free.

## How to Feed Your Chickens

For small, family-size, noncommercial flocks, the "hunt and peck" method is the most convenient and inexpensive. Chickens need very little in the way of housing when they are given adequate space, and you will find that when they are allowed to roam in a farmyard they will supplement their diets with insects, seeds and other chicken delights. The yolks of the eggs from "hunt and peck" hens will be darker in color, richer-tasting and better for you, too. Supplement your chickens' diet with grains (corn, wheat, oats and barley) or commercially prepared feeds and mashes. Chickens lay eggs in larger numbers when they are fed laying mash or laying mash and grain as the major portion of their diet, so keep a shallow trough of these in the yard. A laying hen will eat about 90 pounds of feed in a year, or about 7 to 9 pounds of feed each month.

A good feed should consist of 4 parts wheat, oats or barley to 1 part protein supplement (available at your local feed store), or 3 parts corn to 1 part protein supplement. Give laying hens oystershell, or a calcium supplement (not very much is needed) for good, strong egg shells. If you are feeding whole corn, provide grit along with it.

Your chickens will appreciate your fresh kitchen scraps in addition to their regular food. Vegetable peelings (only cooked potato peelings, please), green tops (not onions) and surplus milk are best. Be especially careful not to include any spoiled meat, fruit peelings, onions or any food leftovers with a strong taste, as they can pass on their unpleasant flavors to eggs and meat. Give only the amount that the hens can finish eating in 5 or 10 minutes, and never feed scraps out of a galvanized container.

Always make sure your hens have enough clean, fresh water. Keep the water where it will not spill and get the chickens' feet wet. Clean the waterer at least once every 2 days.

## How to House Your Chickens and Keep Them Clean

Although this book recommends the easy and convenient "hunt and peck" system where the chickens run loose in a yard or small space, and lay their eggs wherever the spirit moves them, it does save effort on the part of the egg gatherer if the chickens are provided with some shelter and a place to nest and lay their eggs. You can remodel or build a small structure for your laying flock, or convert a part of a larger building. If this cannot be conveniently done, you can provide your chickens with a low, watertight roof, preferably closed in on 3 sides, as shelter from bad weather. I have known people who provided only orange crates covered with tar paper and lined with fresh straw. This casual approach does, however, expose the chickens to parasites and diseases.

If you decide to build a chicken coop, or if you have a suitable structure already available, make sure it is dry and well ventilated, but also free from drafts. To provide comfortable space, each hen should be given at least 2½ square feet in order to prevent cannibalism. If you intend to use a wooden floor for the coop, build it at least one foot off the ground in order to prevent termite damage and reduce rotting. Concrete floors are best, and the easiest to keep clean.

If you provide nests for your flock, you will have cleaner eggs and fewer broken ones. A community nest is the easiest to build and less expensive than individual nests. The United States Department of Agriculture recommends a community nest 48 inches wide and 24 inches deep for a flock of 30 hens. Build it almost like a closed box, with a sloping lid to keep birds from perching on the top. Cut 2-inch ventilation holes at the back or sides. Make sure to leave an opening approximately 1-foot square for easy entrance and exit. Raise the box about 20 inches off the floor, with a projecting platform or series of slat perches along the side of the box where the entrance is, so the hens can jump up onto it and enter the nest. If you prefer individual nests, provide one for every 4 hens. Build them at least 14 inches high, 14 inches wide and 12 inches deep. Good nesting material to put in either individual or community nests is fine wood shavings, sawdust or straw. These should be replaced with fresh material when it becomes dirty, clotted with droppings or very damp.

Before you put your hens in any chicken house or shelter, make sure it is thoroughly clean, then disinfect the inside. Put litter on the floor—clean wood shavings, sawdust, ground corncobs, chopped straw, or other material that soaks up moisture. Start with a 3- to 4-inch layer. Add fresh litter over the top of that until it builds up to 6 to 8 inches. Stir the litter every few days, and remove any caked or extremely wet spots. Use the same built-up layer of litter as long as you keep the same flock of hens. Replace all litter, after cleaning and disinfecting the house, when you replace your flock.

Clean your trough or feeder 2 or 3 times a week, and your waterer daily or once every 2 days.

The United States Department of Agriculture advises that hens are healthier when they are kept confined in the chicken house at all times, that there is a lower rate of mortality and egg loss. However, for those who go along with the "hunt and peck" method of raising them, providing good nesting facilities is recommended, and it is a good idea to keep the hens confined in the chicken house, if you have one, until about midday, and to close the chicken house when the hens have returned for the night. For the highest rate of productivity, hens should get 14 hours of light each day. If you are going to keep your hens in a chicken house, be sure to install a light (a 40-watt bulb with a reflector is adequate), and keep it on for 14 hours each day. A time clock or a hand-wound alarm clock can be rigged up to turn the lights on automatically.

### Keep an Eye Out for Disease

Always check your flock every day (when you feed them or gather eggs is usually a good time) for signs of disease. The signs of an outbreak are coughing, sneezing, difficulty in breathing, watery eyes, a sudden drop in the consumption of feed, droopiness and abnormal droppings. Whenever you suspect sickness in a bird, immediately isolate it from the rest of the flock. Call your local veterinarian or county agent to get a reliable diagnosis and start treatments as soon as possible. Kill very sick birds, and burn or bury their remains in order to prevent the disease from spreading.

### Collecting and Storing Your Eggs

Try to gather your eggs twice a day, once in the morning and once in the evening. If you leave eggs too long, some will probably be broken and the hens will eat them, and from this they can develop the bad habit of breaking their own eggs for food. Clean soiled eggs, washing them if they are very dirty. For your own protection, use cracked eggs only in foods that are cooked well. The best temperature for egg storage is between 45 and 55 degrees F., in a refrigerator or cool cellar. Don't freeze your eggs.

### General Advice

If you ever have any questions as to the health of your flock, or if you have other questions about how to give better care, do not hesitate to contact the United States Department of Agriculture or your county agent, who will be glad to help you do it yourself and save money.

## RAISING DAIRY CATTLE

If you have at least 2 or 3 acres of good pasture land, you might want to try raising a calf for beef (see page 212) or a dairy cow. It is possible to raise your own beef at about one-third the cost per pound that you pay in the supermarket, and a dairy cow will give you from 3,000 to 6,000 quarts of milk per year. But raising cattle requires care, hard work and patience. To decide whether or not this enterprise would be practical for you, you must, of course, figure the savings in family food bills against the cost of buying and feeding the animal. Once you have seen the financial picture, let your more aesthetic side take over and consider the pleasures, rare in this day and age, of working with one of the largest, most beautiful and most gentle of the domesticated animals.

Owning and keeping a cow in your "small

space" is practical only if ample pasture and hay are available, a comfortable, sanitary cow shelter can be provided and someone (either you, a relative or a friend) has the time and can be on hand *every day* to feed, water and milk the cow. There must also be an obliging bull somewhere in the neighborhood. Keep in mind that a cow will eat 20 to 25 pounds of hay each day, or 3 to 4 tons a year, if no pasture is available. In addition to this, she will need from 1 to 2 tons of a good grain or concentrate feed mix, and about 1,000 pounds of straw will be needed for adequate bedding. The cost of raising a cow will vary according to which region of the country you live in, and from year to year according to the availability of feed. In this age of rising prices, it would be pointless to speculate here on cost, since a figure quoted to-day would be obsolete tomorrow.

To best calculate the total cost of raising a dairy cow in your area, first check around to determine the price of a good cow (see pages 197–98). Telephone your county agricultural agent and ask him the going price for a ton of hay, and your local feed and grain store for the price of a ton of good concentrate feed. Try to get your county agent to take a look at your pasture land (you have already paid for this service by paying your taxes), and give you an estimate on how many months it would be suited to the grazing of a dairy cow. You can usually reduce the amount of feed you need to purchase by improving your pastures, and you should discuss possible improvements with your county agent. After accumulating these facts, you should be able to come up with a good idea of the expense involved.

### Buying a Dairy Cow

There are five principal breeds of dairy cows in the United States—Ayrshire, Brown Swiss, Guernsey, Holstein-Friesian or Jersey. Jerseys and Guernseys are the cows most often used for family milk production because they are smaller, eat less, do not produce great quantities of milk and the milk they do produce is richer in butterfat than that of most of the other breeds. The best age at which to buy a milk cow is 4 or 5 years, or a cow that has had her second or third

calf, because she will be young enough to have a good 6 to 10 years of production ahead of her, and she will have already proven herself as a milk-producer.

The cow you select for family production should be sound and healthy, easy to milk and, above all (especially if you have children, or are not agile enough to dodge flying hooves), it should be gentle and free of bad habits. There are several things to look for when you buy your cow. First, examine the cow's udder. Squeeze it gently and feel around to make sure it has no lumps or hardened tissue, and no open sores. Make sure the cow has good-sized teats—at least 3 inches long. Avoid buying cows with very large and meaty udders that do not shrink after milking.

Next, sit down to milk the cow yourself a few times. (If you have never done this, you will not find it easy. Get the cow seller to demonstrate how to do it. Milking a cow is both a gentle pulling and squeezing motion, holding the teat between your palm and fingertips, like making a soft fist and pulling downward at the same time. If you are not used to the exercise, you should feel the strain as much in your forearms as in your hands.) Examine the milk by letting the first milk drawn out of each teat stream onto a stretched piece of dark cloth, or close-woven dark cloth stretched over a tin cup or "strip cup" especially designed for examining milk. Make sure that the milk contains no clots, flakes, strings or blood.

Do not buy a cow that kicks, butts at you or continually moves around nervously, or one that "jumps" and is frightened by your slow, gentle movements and jostling of bucket and stool. Do not buy a cow that wears a yoke, muzzle or nosepiece, because they are sure signs she has had bad habits such as breaking through fences or self-sucking. And last, but extremely important, make sure the cow you buy is free from tuberculosis, brucellosis and leptospirosis—diseases which can be transmitted to man. Make the seller show you results of tests by a veterinarian within 30 days of the time you complete the sale.

## How to Take Care of Your Cow

Make a policy to move slowly and quietly around your cow. Always let her know where you are and where you are going when you are close to her, by going about your work steadily. Handle her gently. Many dairymen even talk to their cows, and if she seems a little upset, try a long, low "Soooooo . . ." several times, like saying "Whoa . . ." to a horse. Make sure that all fences around your pasture land are strong and well constructed, so she will not get into the habit of breaking through fences to that greener pasture on the other side. A "cow-tight" fence is generally 4½ feet high and made with at least 4 barbed wires, which should be tightly stretched and fastened to good, strong posts 8 feet apart.

Keep your cow clean by brushing her every day with a good wire brush or curry comb, being especially sure to get caked manure off her flanks and thighs. This not only keeps her clean, but keeps her gentle; and as anyone would, she will take pleasure in a good, daily back-scratching.

Milk your cow twice a day, early in the morning and evening. Try to be as regular about milking times as possible. If you leave her unmilked, even for a few hours after the regular milking time, her teats will start to swell and her udder will tighten, making her very uncomfortable. Before you milk, make sure the udder and flanks are clean and free of dirt that might fall into the milk pail. Always wipe the udder and flanks with a clean, damp cloth before you milk. Use a small-top milk pail, and milk with both hands, quickly and gently. Keep your fingernails short and take off any rings or obtrusive jewelry. Never put anything, straw or milking straws, up into the teats.

Your family cow should be provided with a sunny, comfortable shelter, both to protect her from bad weather and to set a regular place for milking. She will have a good deal of freedom to move around in a box stall about 10 feet square, or she can be confined in a smaller stall if she is held with a stanchion, chain, rope or halter. Try to provide a feeding trough and a stable source of water (do not put water in anything she can kick over) in her stall. It is recommended, for both ease and a savings in milk that might be kicked over unintentionally, to have a stanchion in the stall for use at milking time. It is a good idea to provide a feedbox in front of the stanchion, to help keep her happy when she is constrained. There should also be a gutter at one end of the stall for easy manure removal. The stall should be kept clean and provided with a good layer of bedding. A window at the front or back of the stall (depending on the prevailing winds), or an open space in the roof, should be built into the stall to provide sunlight and ventilation.

## How to Feed Your Dairy Cow

The best feed for your cow is good, green pasture for grazing, with an added ration of grain. The best pasture mix is alfalfa or clover, with brome, wheat grass or other high-protein grasses. This kind of pasture does not drop in production during the hot summer months, but has the disadvantage that it must be reseeded every 5 years. Ask your county agricultural agent to look at your pasture and recommend improvements, and advise you about the durability of your grasses. Most permanent pastures drop in feed production over the summer, and must be supplemented with some hay. Remember that the better your pasture is, the less you will have to spend on feed.

A good feeding practice is to let your cow out to pasture right after milking in the morning, and to feed her about 3 to 6 pounds of a good grain or grain concentrate after milking in the evening. Keep her in the stall or shelter overnight, providing her with a little hay. This practice helps avoid possible problems with overgrazing, and you will only have to herd the cow into the milking area once a day, most likely without much difficulty, because a reward in good grain awaits her in the stall. There are farmers, however, who recommend that pasture grazing should be done at night, since some animals do not eat as much under a hot sun and start losing weight and milk production. If you live in a particularly hot area, you might consider grazing your cow at night, and keeping her in the stall during the day.

In winter, when snow prohibits grazing, feed your cow 20 to 25 pounds of good hay a day, with an added 3 to 6 pounds of grain or grain concentrate. The balance of hay and grain a cow needs varies with each animal, and usually depends on how much milk she is producing. Different kinds of grains can be fed—barley, wheat, oats or ground corn and wheat bran. Rolled grains are usually easier to feed and easier for her to eat. Check the prices of all these grains in your area. A good practice is to vary the grain according to the fluctuating prices —if wheat costs a lot this year, buy barley instead, or corn, or whatever is cheapest. Ask your feed store salesman about the relative nutritional content of each grain, and balance different quantities of grains fed according to their nutritional content.

Caution: Don't ever leave large quantities of grain within reach of your cow, or even in any area she might break into, because of the possibilities of "foundering." Some animals become very sick when they eat too much grain, and can even die. Also, a word about alfalfa: if there is too much alfalfa hayland in your area, make sure your fences are very tight and your cow cannot break into a field that is made up of alfalfa growing without any other grasses. Occasionally cows eat enough straight alfalfa so that they "bloat" on gases in one or more of their four stomachs. This, if left unreleased by a veterinarian within a few hours, can kill your animal.

Try to feed a good alfalfa hay (straight *dry* alfalfa does not cause bloat), or a good brome, or high-protein grass hay. When cutting bales open to feed to your cow (about half a bale or a third of a bale, if they are large, heavy bales, is the usual ration per day), make sure that all baling wire is taken out of the hay fed to your cow, since cows sometimes eat baling wire along with their hay by accident, and become sick with intestinal obstructions. In general, be careful to keep all loose wires or pieces of wire, or other small pieces of metal, out of range of your cow. If you can, buy bales held together by twine, in order to avoid baling wire in the feed.

Last, but also very important, provide your cow with a block of trace mineralized salt, or add loose salt to her feed at the rate of about 1 pound of salt for every 100 pounds of feed. Most farmers leave a salt block in a wooden box in the open pasture, near the source of clean, fresh water.

## Sanitation and Pasteurization

As soon as you have finished milking, strain your milk through a clean cloth. Single-use strainer cloths are the best, but if you want to reuse strainer cloths, wash and boil them after each use. All raw milk should be pasteurized. Heat the milk to 142 degrees F. and hold it at that temperature for 30 minutes, or heat it to 161 degrees F. and hold it there for 15 seconds. Do not boil or drastically overheat your milk. A good, small electric home pasteurizer can be bought for about $65.

After you pasteurize your milk, cool it rapidly to 50 degrees F. or lower. Keep it in a refrigerator, or a very cool place, until you are ready to use it. Let your milk stand in a deep container until the cream rises to the top, and skim the cream about 24 hours later. The cream can be used in making butter and some rich cheeses, and the skim milk (usually much higher in butterfat content than the skim milk you buy in cartons in the store) can be used for the table, cheese-making and for cottage cheese (see pages 59–60).

Keep all your milk utensils clean by rinsing them in cold water as soon as they have been used. Then wash them in very hot water with a detergent, scrubbing them well. Rinse the utensils, then scald them with boiling water. Store your milk containers and utensils in a clean place, open to fresh air, without covering them. Use only utensils that are seamless, so the milk will not crust up in the seams and increase the rate of souring.

## How to Freshen Your Cow

A cow should be allowed to calve and freshen her milk production at about 12-month intervals. Ask your county agricultural agent about a breeding service in your area. If there is no bull available, or if it would be difficult to transport the cow to the bull and still keep milking her, or vice versa, artificial insemination will be best. A cow's period of gestation is about the same as it is for people—9 months, so the breeding should be done about 3 months after she has had her last calf. It is a good idea to let the cow go dry for a month to 6 weeks before she calves. Doing this will result in greater milk production after she has had her calf, and is generally considered healthier for her. Cows can be made to go dry by gradually reducing their feed and discontinuing to milk them, milking them a little less each day for a few weeks until they are dry.

Cows usually do not have much trouble giving birth to their calves, but if you see that there is a prolonged and difficult labor lasting more than several hours, you should contact your local veterinarian. In cold weather, the cow should be provided with a warm stall and lots of good bedding at calving time. After calving, you should not drink her milk for about a week and a half, since it will contain substances designed to increase the calf's resistance to disease, and will be different in color and texture than regular milk. After about 2 weeks, "wean" the calf from the mother, and feed it from a bucket or bottle out of the milk you get from the mother. A newborn calf can generally be sold, but if you raise it to about 3 months old it will bring a higher price.

## RAISING DAIRY GOATS

It might be more convenient and less expensive to raise a dairy goat rather than a dairy cow. Goat's milk is more easily digested than cow's milk, and is often better for infants and invalids who cannot drink cow's milk. A good dairy goat will give about 2 quarts of milk per day for 8 to 10 months of the year, and it can be fed for about one-sixth the cost of feeding a cow. The price of a dairy goat is lowest of all the commercial milk-producing animals, and a doe with a good record of production and of a good breed will probably cost you no more than $100. Make sure that any goat you buy is from a herd free of tuberculosis and brucellosis, diseases which can be transmitted to man.

### How to Feed Your Dairy Goat

A dairy goat should be fed all the clover, alfalfa or mixed hay she will eat, along with available root crops such as turnips, carrots, beets or parsnips (in place of root crops a good-quality silage can be fed). In summer, keep your goat on good pasture in between milking times, and in addition to this, feed her 1½ pounds of root crops or silage and 1 to 2 pounds of grain per day. In winter, feed her 2 to 4 pounds of alfalfa or clover hay in place of natural pasture. Goats on pasture usually need less grain and concentrate feeds. While your doe is pregnant, feed her all the roughage (good hay) she can eat throughout the fall and winter, along with 1 pound of root crops and ½ to 1 pound of grain. Strongly flavored feeds, such as turnips and silage, should be fed only after milking so that the milk will

not take on any strong flavors. Keep rock salt available to your goat at all times, and mix a small quantity of fine salt in with the grain mixture. If you cannot feed your goat alfalfa or clover hay, she will need additional calcium and phosphorus supplements. Make sure there is plenty of fresh water available at all times.

## Housing

Goats are very hardy, climbing animals and do not need any special kind of housing, but they should be provided with a simple shed or lean-to structure to protect them from extreme weather. Because goats are natural climbers, they will tend to climb up on anything low enough for them to reach unless they are tethered. Try to be extremely clean and sanitary in handling your dairy goat. Remove concentrations of manure regularly, and wipe the flanks and teats with a clean, damp cloth before you milk. Bucks, or male goats, are the ones with the infamous odor, and if breeding service is offered in your area, you will not want to keep one. Make sure the fencing on your small space is made of woven wire topped with 2 strands of barbed wire, or 8 strands of barbed wire stretched tightly and fastened to posts 8 to 10 feet apart, with intervening wire or wooden stays. Goats are very good at finding their way through small spaces, so be careful to keep your fences sound and tight all year round.

## Milking

You will find it difficult to milk your goat without some kind of a milking stand or structure. The milking stand should be built about 15 inches off the ground, and should be a wooden platform on which the goat can stand, with a stanchion on one end and a seat for the milker on one side. Young does are usually quite rambunctious when they are being trained to milk, and a stanchion and milking stand will help to confine them. Grain put in a box in front of the stanchion, within easy reach of the goat at milking time, also has a quieting effect. After a few milkings your goat will probably become accustomed to the stanchion and stand, and will jump up into them voluntarily. Although most does need to be milked only twice a day, if a doe is a particularly heavy producer she may need to be milked 3 times a day after freshening. It is usually best to milk your goat once in the morning and again in the evening.

## Freshening Your Goat

Does should be allowed to freshen at least once a year. They will come into heat regularly between September and January, and after this they usually cannot be bred again until late in August. They generally stay in heat 1 to 2 days, with a period of about 20 days between heats.

Try to find a buck in your area to run with your goat for at least 2 periods of heat. After a period of gestation of about 150 days (5 months), your doe will give birth. Your goat will probably go dry on its own, after about 8 months of milking, and should be milked again about a week to 10 days after giving birth. Does usually have litters of 2 kids, but will sometimes have triplets or quadruplets. Kids can be raised for sale or meat with little difficulty. Start feeding them cow or goat's milk from a bottle until they learn to drink from a pan or trough. You can start to feed them grain and small quantities of good hay and root crops at about 20 days of age, gradually increasing the amount of solid feed as you decrease the amount of milk you give them until they are "weaned," and ready for sale or further feeding for meat, which tastes somewhat like lamb and is called "chevron."

### General Advice

A good dairy goat should produce milk for at least 8 months before she naturally goes dry before her period of gestation. A goat that gives milk for less than 6 months is usually a poor producer and not worth what it costs to feed her.

## RAISING SHEEP

In many ways, sheep are the ideal livestock. They are inexpensive to buy, are relatively low-risk and require little effort and attention.

Before you actually buy sheep, check around your area to find out whether or not there is a large sheep rancher within driving distance. During the lambing months, usually the winter months or very early spring, depending on the severity of the weather in your area, sheep ranchers often are left with "bum" lambs, or lambs whose mothers have either died at birth or have rejected them soon after birth. Most ranchers do not find it profitable to take the time to raise "bum" lambs, so they are usually disposed of or left to die. It is possible to get free "bum" lambs during the winter months by talking to a sheep rancher.

You can raise these lambs fairly easily, although they have a very high mortality rate. Feed them milk out of a bottle and feed them grain or "creep" feeds at about 20 days of age, and put them out to pasture gradually as you decrease the amount of milk you feed them. They should be weaned at about 120 days of age, and are ready to be marketed or butchered when they weigh between 70 and 100 pounds. If you want to be certain of a prospering flock, start with good, proven ewes, rather than with "bum" lambs.

The best age to buy ewes is when they are a year and a few months old. They should be bred to have their first lambs at about 2 years of age, following a period of gestation of about 150 days (5 months). Ewes usually come into heat in late summer or early fall, and should be bred as soon as possible so that they have their lambs in winter, when the cold will keep down parasites that might be a problem to you in warmer weather. Try to find a ram from a rancher or local breeding service for your ewes, to avoid the expense of buying and keeping one of your own. Most good young ewes are marketed in late summer or early fall.

### How to Feed and Care for Your Sheep

Sheep do best on a pasture of alfalfa and mixed grasses, although they have a phenomenal ability to eat almost any kind of grass and even some weeds. (Let them run on that overgrown corner of your small space, and they will have it under control in no time at all.) If your pasture is good, your animals will not need any additional feed other than a mineral-salt block kept near a source of clean, fresh water. Avoid putting sheep on pasture that is *exclusively* alfalfa or other legumes. Sheep, like cattle, are susceptible to bloat due to overfeeding of legumes, and can die if not treated immediately after you see them listless and with a swollen stomach. If you see that your sheep are losing weight on your pasture, or if they are in poor condition when you buy them, you should add a little grain to their diets. In winter, when no pasture is available, you should feed your ewes 3 to 4 pounds of alfalfa or alfalfa-mix hay per day.

For a month before your ewes are due to

lamb, add about ½ pound of grain in with their daily hay ration. For lambing time, see that your ewes are provided with a weather-tight shed, with a separate pen for each ewe and plenty of bedding. Try to find someone with experience to help out at lambing time, or be ready to call in your veterinarian if your ewes show signs of difficult birth. After your lambs are born, you should start feeding them as soon as possible, or about 10 to 16 days after birth. Fix up a small pen or creep feeder for the lambs. A good creep feeder can be built by putting upright slats about 3 feet in height and 9 to 12 inches apart around a trough, to keep the ewes from eating the grain. Feed your lambs ground or rolled grain until they are weaned or ready to be marketed at between 70 to 120 pounds. It is also a good idea to keep a scale around to keep close track of your lambs' rates of growth and to weigh your fleeces at shearing time.

If you are a true "do-it-yourselfer," you will need additional equipment at lambing time. Try to find someone with experience who can show you how to use docking* and castrating tools. Personally I prefer to see a good movie while a professional takes care of these less than pleasant chores.

### Shearing Your Sheep

Sheep should be sheared in late spring or early summer, usually after lambing. Shearing is a skill that requires much practice, and is hard for a novice to do without ruining the quality of the wool. Try to find someone with experience to show you how to shear, or hire a custom shearer to take care of your small flock. Wool brings very good prices in today's market, and the chances are that your wool sales will pay much of the costs of your winter feed. Or you can card it, spin it and use it yourself, though making yarn from wool is a very time-consuming process.

---

* Docking is the cutting of the long tails from the lambs at about 2 weeks of age.

### General Advice

Raising sheep is usually very easy, if you have the available pasture and fencing. But before you try it, contact your county agricultural agent and have him take a look at your place and tell you about possible problems, which will vary according to the area in which you live.

## RAISING YOUR OWN DUCKS

Raising ducks commercially is a complex and risky business, but for either meat or eggs they are relatively easy to raise in small numbers. If chicken every Sunday sounds like a luxury to you, duck every Sunday is sure to please you even more.

Ducks require a plentiful source of clean, fresh water for swimming and also to avoid choking on dry feeds. They should be provided with a small shelter for brooding that is warm, dry and free of drafts. It is not recommended that you try to raise more than about 20 ducks at a time if you have no commercial aspirations. Most ducks that are good for meat are not good egg producers, and most egg-producing breeds are small and mature late, so they are not as good for meat. The standard meat-producing breeds are Pekin and Aylesbury, which can average about 150 eggs per year if treated properly. The best egg-producing breeds are the Khaki Campbell and the Indian Runner, both nice-looking birds to have around, with egg-production levels close to and sometimes better than that of chickens, or about 280 to 300 eggs per year. You should decide what you need from a small number of ducks before you buy them—either eggs, meat or both—and check into available breeds.

### Raising Ducks for Eggs

The best kind of ducks to buy for small egg production are ducks of the good egg-laying breeds. Find a duck farm in your area and try to buy breeding stock that is about 7 months of age, or ready to go into production. Or if you want to take a chance on lower productivity and spend less money, find ducks that have gone through one cycle of egg production and have decreased in productivity. Most duck farmers will be ready to sell these ducks for meat anyway, and you will be able to buy them at less than normal breeder prices. These birds will have to be put through a "forced moulting," and then kept 8 to 10 weeks before bringing them back into egg production.

Provide your ducks with a small breeder house—a small shed or part of a larger structure that is provided with a row of individual nests 12 inches wide, 18 inches deep and 12 inches high, set close to the floor. Ducks lay their eggs almost exclusively at night, so they may be let out to run in a small space with available water for swimming and feeding during the day, and herded back into the breeder house to be locked up for the night. It is a good idea to keep water in the breeder house, making sure it is set over a screened drain or wire floor, in order to avoid wetness throughout the breeder house. Keep a good layer of litter on the floor, starting with 4 inches, add to it gradually until it reaches 6 to 8 inches, and stir it frequently. Keep a light bulb in the breeder house in order to extend the daylight hours to provide the total of 14 hours of light per day needed for maximum egg production.

Gather your duck eggs after 7 or 8 A.M., check-

ing the nests again a little later for eggs from your lazier ducks. Let the breeding stock out of the house when you make the first collection.

Ducks can eat a variety of different feeds. There are commercially prepared pellets available through most feed stores, but if this seems too expensive, grain mashes and concentrate mixtures suitable for chickens are good enough for small production. Feed about ½ pound of pellets or mash per bird, in 2 daily feedings, scattering the feed pellets over the yard ground, near the available supply of water, or feeding the mash twice a day in shallow troughs or pans, making sure there is enough room at the trough so that all your ducks get their daily requirements. To ensure good egg-shell quality, provide oystershell or a calcium supplement in the diet.

After about 5 months of production, most "meat" breeds start to lose their egg-producing ability, whereas with the "egg" breeds, the ability should not lag for about 8 to 10 months. If you have bought birds that have already been through one egg-producing cycle, it will not be practical to try to force-moult them for a third cycle, and they should be used for meat. If your birds have been through only one egg-producing cycle, force-moult them by reducing their feed and keeping them out of the light as much as possible. After moulting, allow them to rest 8 to 10 weeks before putting them back into full production.

## Raising a Small Number of Ducks for Meat

If you want to get into limited meat production, keep 1 drake for every 6 ducks in your flock. The best breeds to raise are the Pekin and Aylesbury, because the ducklings reach a good market weight—about 8 or 9 pounds—in 8 weeks.

Build yourself a home incubator or use a small commercial incubator for chicken eggs. After you gather your eggs, wash any soiled ones with great care in water about 110 to 115 degrees F. Be careful not to use water even slightly colder than the eggs, because this increases the chances of bacteria getting drawn through the pores in the egg shell. Do not save any cracked, misshapen or excessively small eggs for incubation. Store perfect eggs at a temperature of 55 degrees F. and a relative humidity of 75 percent until you have enough to fill your incubator. Turn the eggs daily after the first week of storage, and store for no longer than 2 weeks. Once the eggs are ready for the incubator, allow them to warm for 5 or 6 hours, then put them in, small end down. The eggs should be turned in the incubator at least 3 or 4 times a day for the 28 days required for incubation.

Candle the eggs after a week by passing them over a small hand candler. The living embryo of a fertile egg will appear as a dark spot near the large end of the egg, and you will be able to see spiderweb-like blood vessels radiating from the spot. A dead embryo will appear as a dark spot stuck to the shell membranes, with no blood vessel radiation, or a dark ring of blood will be clearly visible. Eggs that are totally infertile will show no spots at all. Remove the infertile, dead and otherwise unsuitable eggs from the incubator. Candle the eggs again after 25 days of incubation. You will be able to see the formed bills of the ducklings within the air cells of the eggs, and there will be a lot of movement of the duckling ready to hatch.

After all the eggs in the incubator have hatched or been removed, move the ducklings to a brooder facility. Beware of chills and overcrowding when you move them. Your brooder facility should be a tightly enclosed space of at least 1 square foot per duckling. It should be provided with an artificial source of heat for at least 4 weeks (an electric space-heater, pro-

tected from contact with flammable materials, will do nicely for a small brooder space). Maintain a temperature between 85 and 90 degrees F. the first week, reducing the temperature 5 degrees F. per week until the required 4 weeks have passed. By the fourth week of age, the ducklings will have enough feathers to be let outdoors in all but extremely cold weather. Ducklings need clean drinking water at all times. The brooder house should be provided with a source of water set over a screened drain in such a way that it will not spill over the litter and cause wet spots.

To feed your ducklings, start them with a commercially prepared "starter" diet for the first 2 weeks and replace it with a "grower" diet thereafter. If these diets are not available in your area, you can approximate the "starter" diet by mixing three-fifths cornmeal and one-fifth soybean oil meal, with alfalfa meal and protein concentrates making up the other one-fifth, with vitamins added. The "grower" diet has a higher proportion of cornmeal. For smaller production, however, a good, mashed grain meal will do just as well, provided it is very high in protein concentrates. Feed your ducklings the "grower" diet or mash until they are 8 weeks of age, when they will have reached their prime market weight of between 8 and 9 pounds.

## General Advice

Ducks are extremely susceptible to many diseases, and they should be watched carefully for droopiness, irregular feces, poor motor coordination and coughing. If any of these symptoms develop, isolate the sick birds from the rest of the flock and call a veterinarian or your county agricultural agent to check out the disease. In general, the key word in avoiding sickness is to keep your breeder house, brooder house and yard as clean as possible. Clean all facilities before introducing new birds. Try to avoid exposing your ducks to stagnant water, or to any rotting materials. If you have any doubts about health, it is almost always best to call someone in than to run the risk of having your entire flock wiped out by a plague.

## RAISING YOUR OWN GEESE

Geese are easier to raise than ducks, because they don't require housing. When your pasture is green, they will not need additional feed, but they will grow faster if they are raised on a grain or "grower" diet. There are several different breeds of many sizes, some more colorful than others, and you should check around your area to see what breeds are readily available. Good breeds for meat production (it probably will not pay you to try to raise geese for their eggs), are the Tolouse or the Emden, which reach between 20 and 25 pounds as their normal adult weight.

### *How to Care for Your Geese*

Most geese are very good at mating and hatching their eggs. They should be provided with open wooden boxes, or shallow barrels, with some protection from the rain, and litter in them for their nesting needs. The nests may be scattered around your yard or pasture. In general, it is a good idea to have 1 gander for every 5 geese.

Geese usually start laying their eggs in February and March and often continue to lay until early summer. During the winter, they should be fed a pelleted winter "breeder" ration, or grain mash similar to that fed to ducks and chickens. Provide oystershell or other calcium supplements to ensure good egg-shell quality. If you plan to breed your geese for as many offspring as they will produce, gather the eggs twice daily and follow the incubation procedure described for ducks (see page 210), with the exception that goose eggs require from 29 to 31 days of incubation. Many goose breeders prefer to use a setting chicken, turkey or duck to hatch their goose eggs. Mark the eggs before placing them in the nests and turn them daily by hand. Sprinkle the eggs with water 3 or 4 times a day in order to provide the moisture goose eggs need to hatch.

If you wish to brood your goslings apart from the setting goose, in order to keep her laying eggs, provide a small brooder house or corner of a building protected from the weather and predators similar to that described for ducks. Set the temperature between 85 and 90 degrees F., and reduce it 5 to 10 degrees F. per week until 70 degrees F. is reached. Your goslings' behavior will show you how comfortable they are. If they huddle together near the source of heat, they are too cold. Conversely, if they move away from the heat source, they are too warm. In warm weather, you can let your goslings outside as early as 2 weeks after they hatch, but watch them carefully and herd them back into the coop, or brooder area, whenever it rains, until they learn to do this themselves.

After geese are 6 to 8 weeks old, they should need no brooding facilities. Feed your goslings a "starter" or "grower" feed, or grain mash, and provide them with plenty of water. After geese are 5 to 6 weeks old, the larger portion of their feed can be pasture, but give them additional

grain until about 8 to 10 weeks of age in order to promote rapid growth and good health. An acre of good pasture should support about 20 to 40 birds. In making the transition from pellets or grain to pasture, the geese should be offered grain or pellets in a pan or trough in the pasture on a free-choice basis. Be sure your pasture areas and green feed have not been treated with chemicals harmful to the birds.

Good feeds to fatten your geese or to use as a supplementary diet if your pasture starts to give out are wheat, oats, barley, corn or mixtures of these grains in either rolled or whole form.

### Geese as Natural Weeders

Geese are very selective about what they eat, and are generally more partial to the weeds surrounding the plants you may be raising than to the plants themselves! As a consequence, they are frequently used as weeders for such crops as strawberries, sugar beets, corn, cotton and ornamental plants, as well as in orchards and vineyards. For the best weeding results, start with 6-week-old goslings and provide them with shade and waterers throughout the field. Keep the weeder goslings hungry, feeding them only a little additional grain each evening.

### How to Kill and Pluck Your Ducks and Geese

Most newcomers to farming enjoy the care and feeding of the animals, but have not yet inured themselves to the slaughtering that is a natural part of farm life. Some, and I am included in this group, never grow accustomed to it. Even as a child I was always elsewhere when time for slaughtering arrived (although I must confess I never missed the feasts that followed). Farmers, born and bred, generally consider this "city" trait either amusing or hypocritical or both. They are perhaps right and we are perhaps wrong, but when it is time for slaughtering I am still numbered among the absent. If you are less squeamish and prefer to take over the perfectly natural task of slaughtering the birds you have raised to that end, here are directions given to me by a trustworthy friend.

Before you slaughter your birds, keep them away from feed for 8 to 12 hours, but allow them access to plenty of fresh water. Hang the birds by their feet and take a long, sharp knife and cut across the outside of the throat high up on the neck, just under the lower bill. This will sever the jugular vein and ensure swift, complete bleeding of the carcass. Birds that are not bled well before eating will have a stronger taste than is usually desirable.

There are two ways to pick your bird once it has stopped bleeding—dry picking or scalding. Dry picking is a very time-consuming, tedious task, but it results in a better-looking carcass than scalding. If you dry-pick your birds, you must be careful not to tear their skin. To scald them, put the birds in hot water (140 degrees F.) for 3 minutes. Start plucking them immediately after scalding, pulling pinfeathers out by grasping them between your thumb and the edge of a dull knife.

If you find it very difficult to remove pinfeathers and down, try dipping the rough-picked carcasses in molten wax. Dip your bird, then plunge it into cold water in order to harden the wax, and continue dipping it until a thick layer of wax has formed all over the body. Peel the wax layer off the carcass. Most pinfeathers and down should come off with the wax. This wax can be remelted, strained, and used to clean pinfeathers from other birds.

After they have been plucked, you can eviscerate your birds immediately, or you can store them in slush-ice or crushed ice overnight, but not much longer. It is a common practice to keep giblets and hearts with the carcasses for use in stuffings, soups and sauces.

## RAISING YOUR OWN BEEF

Of all the foods that have risen in price in the last few years, beef seems to have taken the biggest bite out of the family budget. If you are not too squeamish about the idea of raising an animal, working with it every day, then having it butchered for your table, you might want to try raising a calf or an older animal for a year-round supply of beef.

A beef animal should be kept at least 6 months to get the maximum benefit from your initial investment for the price of the animal and its feed. As with your dairy cow, a beef animal needs daily care, so do not contemplate raising one unless you are prepared to make the necessary sacrifices. Keep in mind that the profit you will be making can be measured only in amount of weight gained during the time you own the animal, so if you do not have at least 2 acres of good pastureland, feeding costs may make it impractical to raise one. Figure the costs, which will vary according to the costs of feed in your area, before you saddle yourself with the expense and risk. It is usually a good practice also, if the initial capital outlay is hard on the family budget, to insure your animal at least for the amount of purchase.

Cattle reach about 85 percent of their final adult weight by the end of the first year of growth. Younger animals produce the most tender meat, but the quality of the meat does vary according to the quality of the animal you purchase. What age animal you buy will depend on how much time you will be able to keep it and pay for its feed. In the beef business, most ranchers try to time the calving of their cows to early spring. They keep a calf over the summer months, through the fall, and usually they sell them with the first snow in winter or when they'll have to start feeding them hay. The calves are usually sold to owners of feed lots, who take them off a diet of grasses, and start "fat feeding" them with grains and grain mixed with beet pulp, soybean meal, molasses, and other fattening feeds, combined with hay or "roughage." The feed-lot owner will usually keep his animals four or five months, sometimes longer, selling them when they reach a prime market weight, which varies according to the animal but is usually between 800 and 1,200 pounds at between 1 year and 18 months of age. Unless you can do "fat feeding" on a major scale (and thus have access to the low cost of buying feed in great quantities), it probably will not pay for you to buy an older animal.

What you will want to do is make use of your natural pastureland, doing your own shorter "fat feeding" program before sending the animal to your custom slaughterhouse. If this is the case, buy your calf at about 3½ months of age, or right after it's been "weaned" from its mother's milk. You will no doubt pay a prime price for such a calf, but if you can keep it for about 6 months or longer, you should have a return on your initial capital investment and save money in the bargain.

The best kind of calf to buy is generally a good bull calf (which when castrated is called a "steer"). Steers generally grow faster in their first year, and larger, than heifer calves, and it is that rate of weight gain which you're looking for in order to get the most meat for the least amount of money. A "good" calf of any sex will usually be one that is of the many beef breeds or crossbreeds. The standard beef breeds in the United States are Hereford, or white-faced with red hair, Black Angus, Red Angus and Short-

horn, usually bred for their short, thick, stocky bodies and rapid gain of weight in the first year of growth. There are countless crossbreeds, and many ranchers prefer them to purebreds, claiming they grow faster.

Calves of any of the dairy breeds can be raised profitably for beef, but they seem to have longer, thinner bodies and longer legs, and so there is more waste at butchering time. Most ranchers agree that the general characteristics to look for when buying a calf are thickness of body (especially through the shoulders and rump) and short, stocky legs. It is also important to choose calves that have proven their hardiness and weight gain in the first 3 months of growth by reaching between 300 and 400 pounds. Try to make sure that the calf you buy comes from good, strong stock, whether it is of the dairy or beef breeds. As in people, the larger the parents, the larger usually are the offspring.

Try to check with people in your area as to the going price for a good calf. Those who can't tell good beef from bad beef at a distance should try to avoid the auction sale yard, and buy from an individual farmer or rancher. If you buy an animal that is not yet castrated, dehorned and vaccinated, you will have to do this yourself or have it done for you. Unless you're willing to learn a few cowboy tricks and wrestle with an animal that is twice your weight or more, try to get your seller or someone with experience to prepare your animal for you. Most calves raised for beef will never be gentle, and a particularly rambunctious calf can be dangerous if not handled properly. Buying a calf and raising it for beef is really an adventure, and after trying it you will more fully appreciate the kind and character of the work that goes into your top sirloin steak.

## CAUTION

Before you attempt to raise any kind of livestock on your land, check with your local zoning regulations or local ordinances to make sure you can do so within the limits of the law.

# FIVE

## Household Helps

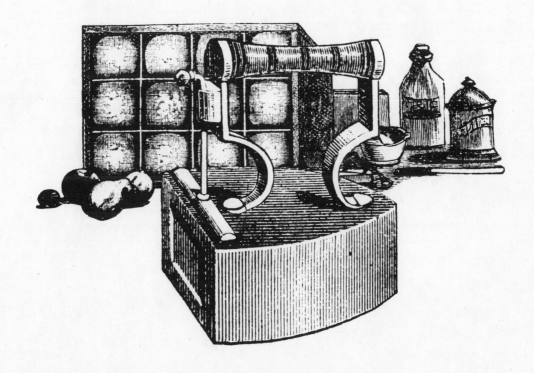

*IF YOU heed the razzle-dazzle of newspaper, magazine
and television ads, you might conclude that before name-brand
household products came along, wash was never white,
floors were never bright and bathtubs had rings as dark as a
country lane on a summer's night. Contrary to what the
commercials would have us believe, there is nothing magical
about getting things clean. There are a few household helps
(Clorox, Calgon and sal soda) that take a good deal of the
"dirty" out of the work involved in keeping a house. These
three are basic ingredients in the bulk of household
"miracle" products sold in supermarkets. If you by-pass the
colorful boxes and the multimillion-dollar advertising pitch,
you can make products that work equally well
for sometimes dollars less.
In addition to these three home helps, there are hundreds
of time-honored, homespun household hints that will help
free you from supermarket buying. Grandmother had
housekeeping problems similar to ours and practical household
formulas for almost any occasion. Vinegar and salt does
clean copper marvelously well, and unscientific hints like
boiling wine stains in milk can work seeming miracles.
If you use your common sense, the advice given in this
book and just an extra bit of elbow grease, you may be on
your way to breaking the name-brand habit.*

# HELPFUL
# HOUSEHOLD FORMULAS

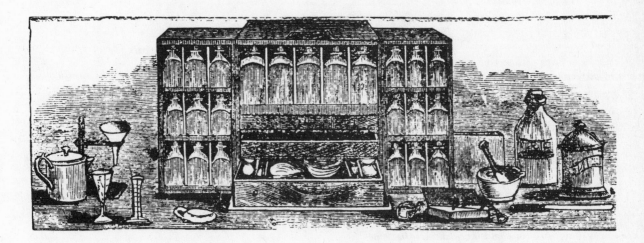

Many of the products frequently used around the house—from library paste to window putty—are actually simple formulations easily made in the kitchen. Following are a number of these you can make easily, quickly and for substantially less than they would cost at your local supermarket or hardware store.

## *Household Paste*

*For pasting paper, mounting photos and for general use around the house and by young craftsmen, this paste can easily be made from ingredients you probably have in your cupboard right now.*

(YIELD: ABOUT 1½ CUPS)

1½ Cups water
½ Cup cornstarch
2 Tablespoons light corn syrup
1 Teaspoon white vinegar
½ Teaspoon oil of wintergreen

Pour ¾ cup of the water into a medium-sized saucepan. Stir ¼ cup of the cornstarch, the syrup and the vinegar into the water and heat over a medium flame, stirring constantly until the mixture thickens. Remove from the heat and set aside.

Pour the remaining ¾ cup of water into a small mixing bowl and stir in the remaining ¼ cup of cornstarch until smooth. Add this to the hot mixture and stir slowly until smooth.

Stir in the ½ teaspoon of oil of wintergreen to act as a preservative.

This paste may be used at once, although it will be thicker and better after standing for 24 hours. Store in a tightly closed jar. It should stay soft and usable for at least 2 months.

### Simple Flour Paste

*Here is a quick, easy paste for children's arts and crafts, and general paper-pasting around the house. You can whip it up in 5 minutes.*

(YIELD: ABOUT 1½ CUPS)

¼ Cup all-purpose flour
7 Tablespoons cold water
1½ Cups boiling water

Stir the flour into the cold water to form a smooth paste. Mix this into the boiling water and continue to boil over a very low heat for 5 minutes, stirring constantly to ensure against lumps. Allow to cool before using.

### Fine Library Paste

*This is a formulation you can use to paste up important pictures, articles and so on. It will not yellow with time and is apparently the same formulation used by many museums and libraries.*

(YIELD: ABOUT 1 QUART)

9 Ounces all-purpose flour
2½ Pints water
1/16 Ounce alum
1/16 Fluid ounces formaldehyde

Mix the flour into enough of the water to form a smooth, thin paste. Bring the rest of the water to a boil and add the alum. Stir until dissolved. Add the flour paste to the boiling water and continue to heat over a very low flame for 5 minutes more, stirring constantly. Remove from the heat, stir in the formaldehyde and allow to cool. Store in a tightly lidded jar.

### Paper-Hanging Paste

*Here's an easy-to-make wallpaper paste that does an effective job.*

2 Cups cold water
3 Cups all-purpose flour
6 Cups boiling water

¾ Ounce Alum
¼ Cup hot water

Pour the cold water into a bowl. Add the flour, a little at a time, stirring well to form a smooth paste. Pour the paste into a pot containing the boiling water and continue to heat and stir gently until the mixture thickens. Dissolve the alum in the hot water and add to the paste mix.

### Finger Paints

*It is easy and far less expensive to make your own finger paints for your children's use or for general craft use—prints, stenciling, silk screens and so on.*

½ Cup cornstarch
3 Cups cold water
¼ Ounce unflavored gelatin
½ Cup soap flakes
Coloring

Mix the cornstarch into ¾ cup of the cold water in a medium-sized pan. Meanwhile, soak the gelatin in ¼ cup of the cold water. Add the remaining 2 cups of cold water to the cornstarch mixture and bring to a slow boil, stirring constantly.

Remove from the heat and stir in the softened gelatin. Add the soap flakes and continue to stir until the soap is thoroughly dissolved. Pour the mixture into 5 or 6 small, lidded jars and mix 1 teaspoonful of a different colored food coloring into each jar. If you would like white paint, use precipitated chalk or whiting for pigment.

If you prefer, one teaspoon of household dye may be substituted for the food coloring. The dye is less expensive and the colors are stronger, but food coloring is safer in case fingers end up in the mouth.

## Homemade Tracing Paper

*This homemade product works just as well as the average grade of commercial tracing paper and is much less expensive besides.*

Simply mix 1 ounce of gum turpentine with 1 ounce of Canadian Balsam and apply the mixture to one side of a sheet of unsized white paper with a brush or cotton wad.

If the paper is not sufficiently transparent for your use, apply another coat.

## Paint Brush Cleaner

Dried out, apparently useless paint brushes can be cleaned with a trisodium phosphate solution. Place 3 to 4 ounces of trisodium phosphate into a quart of very hot water in a wide-mouthed can or jar. Soak the hardened brush in the solution, press against the bottom of the can to soften, and spread bristles. Alternately soak, press and brush the paint out of the bristles with an old comb until all the paint has been removed. Rinse well, dry and store.

CAUTION: Wear rubber gloves and do not splatter the solution about.

## Paint Remover

Trisodium phosphate mixed in a solution of 1 pound per gallon of hot water makes an excellent paint remover. Brush on, allow to stand for approximately half an hour, and then scrape off the softened paint with a paint scraper or putty knife. Rinse the surface with plain water and dry immediately.

CAUTION: Wear rubber gloves and do not splatter the solution.

## Tar Remover

Spots of tar that adhere to your car or other metal surfaces may be easily removed with linseed oil. Put a few drops of oil on each spot, allow to soak until the tar has softened, and then wipe off with a soft, clean cloth.

## Simple Glazier's Putty

*Here is an easily made putty, which is certainly adequate for general use around the house.*

*18 Ounces whiting*
*10 Fluid ounces boiled linseed oil*

Mix the whiting well into the linseed oil until the putty has assumed a workable consistency. Differences in the grades of whiting may require you to add more of one or the other of the ingredients to achieve the desired consistency. Store in a tightly capped glass jar or can and, ideally, allow to stand for several days before using. If your putty becomes too hard, you can always blend more oil into it, and vice versa.

## Substitute Machine Oil

Mix 2 parts mineral oil, 2 parts 20 SAE automobile motor oil and 1 part kerosene together and you have a good lubricating oil for small electric tools and appliances for far less than you pay for small cans of conventional "machine oil."

# POLISHERS & CLEANERS FOR HOUSEHOLD METALS

In any household, there are many metal objects that require constant care to keep them looking bright. Instead of spending money needlessly on overpriced commercial polishes and metal cleaners, you might want to try making them at home. Most metal polishes consist of an abrasive material mixed with a lubricating liquid, which is also an aid in removing dirt and tarnish. The abrasives used in metal polishes should not be so hard that they scratch the surface of the metal you are cleaning, but should be hard enough to remove oxidized surface coatings and dirt. The liquid used in the polish must be fairly neutral so that it does not corrode or damage the metal.

Oxide of iron, or "jewelers' rouge," powdered talc or whiting are good abrasives to use in cleaning your silverware and highly polished articles, since they are rather soft. Abrasives for harder, less polished surfaces include diatomaceous earth, silica dust (a kind of sand) and tripoli. Good liquids to mix with your abrasives are heavy oils, soaps, paste waxes, soap solutions and many other materials to be mentioned in reference to specific metals in this chapter.

Here are some more specific formulas and procedures for cleaning your household metals:

### Aluminum Utensils

Aluminum, which is the one metal probably more widely used in the kitchen than any other, is relatively soft and porous. As a consequence it is easily discolored. If your aluminum pots and pans are tarnished, restoring them is no particular problem. Any of the methods below will produce satisfactory results.

· Use your discolored pot to cook rhubarb, tomatoes or any mildly acidic food.

· Boil a half-water, half-vinegar solution in the pan.

· Boil a solution of water and cream of tartar in the utensil.

To clean and polish aluminum pots, pans, panels or whatever, mix up a batch of the following formula:

½ *Ounce trisodium phosphate*
24 *Fluid ounces water*
2 *Fluid ounces water glass*
4 *Ounces tripoli (fine grade)*

Dissolve the trisodium phosphate in the water. Stir in the water glass. Sift in the tripoli powder, which will not actually dissolve but will remain in suspension.

Shake well before using, apply with a soft cloth and rub in one direction. Final-polish with a clean, soft rag or soft felt.

### Bronze and Brass

Any unlacquered bronze or brass object or utensil requires little more than a warm, acidic material to remove ordinary tarnish.

Rub with hot vinegar, hot buttermilk, tomato or citrus juice or a salt and vinegar mixture. Rinse with clean water and dry with a soft, clean rag.

### Copper Pots

Keep the copper pots and pans you use for cooking particularly clean. Copper oxide in food is dangerous.

The methods mentioned above for brass and bronze work very well on copper. For starters you might try ordinary catsup straight from the bottle. It generally does an amazingly good job!

A good, nontoxic polish you can make at home follows:

10 *Ounces Liquid Soap (see page 261)*
½ *Ounce cream of tartar*
½ *Ounce jewelers' rouge*
½ *Ounce magnesium carbonate*
1 *Ounce precipitated chalk*

Heat the soap in the upper part of a double boiler. Stir gently while you add the cream of tartar, jewelers' rouge, magnesium carbonate and precipitated chalk. As the solution cools it will form a paste, which will be most convenient to use if you pour it into a fairly wide mouthed, shallow container.

### Chrome

Chrome is an extremely hard metal, and chances are that unless it is badly discolored, soap, warm water and a soft cloth will restore it.

Whiting mixed with water to the consistency of paste will do a good job as well, and a particularly good chrome paste may be made by mixing equal parts of whiting and orthodichlorobenzene by weight. Simply spread the paste on the surface to be cleaned with a cloth and polish with a clean, soft cloth or paper towel.

### Iron

Iron, which is a ferrous metal, rusts. The solution to the problem is to keep iron pots and skillets dry. If they are not in frequent use, coat the surface with a salt-free oil or fat, wrap in paper and plastic and store in a warm dry place.

Rust spots may be scoured away with steel wool and cleanser. More extensive rusting may be removed with sandpaper, a vigorously wielded steel-bristled brush, or a steel-wire wheel set in an electric drill.

### Pewter

Pewter, which is basically zinc, is a soft, easily abraded metal. Dull-finished pewter may be cleaned with a fine pumice powder mixed with water and rubbed on with a clean, soft cloth or paper towel.

Polished pewter, which has a much finer surface than the dull-finished variety, should be polished with a soft rag and jewelers' rouge. After polishing, wash with hot, soapy water and dry thoroughly.

### Silver

Silver, lovely metal though it is, has the drawback of tarnishing easily. Silver objects that are not used for food should be waxed. Two coats of a good grade of paste wax (butchers' wax is excellent)—the second applied only after the first has dried thoroughly—will inhibit the formation of tarnish. After applying, buff well with a very soft, clean rag.

If, in several months, the wax has yellowed considerably, remove by washing in hot, soapy or detergent water, and apply fresh wax.

Fine, water-clear varnishes are available in spray cans. They will provide good antitarnish protection for silver, copper, bronze and other ornamental objects. Application is a problem, however. They should only be used at room temperature (65 to 70 degrees F.), preferably on a dry day, and must be used sparingly. Excess spray builds up very rapidly and tends to get very runny and messy-looking. I much prefer the wax method. It is easier, surer and cheaper.

When silver is stored, it is a good idea to wrap it well in polyethylene food storage bags. These keep the air out and the silver relatively tarnish-free.

An alternate storage technique that works well requires the use of clean cotton flannel. Soak your flannel in a solution of 2 ounces zinc acetate per quart of water. After soaking, squeeze out the excess moisture, dry well and use to wrap your clean, freshly washed silver pieces.

### How to Clean Silver

Silver polishes are legion. There are probably dozens of formulas that work well, and most of them can be made at home. One simple and effective scratch-free method involves the use of precipitated chalk or whiting. Either of these substances moistened with a little ammonia and applied with a soft rag will do a fair job. Rinse after using and dry well.

An easy-to-make liquid polish requires the use of . . .

> *16 Ounces water*
> *2 Ounces soap flakes*
> *4 Ounces whiting*
> *½ Ounce ammonia*

Heat the water and dissolve in it the soap flakes and whiting. When the solution has cooled, add the ammonia and store in a well-corked bottle. Shake well before using.

Of course, the easiest way to clean silver is by the dip method. You dunk your silver into the dip solution dirty and it emerges shiny and bright. Drawbacks to the dip method are the facts that it leaves the silver with a slightly dulled surface, which will require occasional buffing to restore the shine, and that it tends to stain stainless steel knife blades. Do not leave your silver in for more than an instant, and rinse in cool water immediately after dipping.

A good silver-dip formula follows. Handle the acid carefully.

> *5 Parts hydrochloric acid (38% concentration)*
> *8 Parts thiourea*
> *½ Part liquid dishwashing detergent*
> *86 Parts water*

### Stainless Steel Pots and Pans

Steel wool and old-fashioned elbow grease probably are still the most effective way to remove burned-on food marks from stainless steel. A good cleanser helps.

### Tinware

Tin is an extremely soft metal. When used on pots or pans it is applied in a very thin coating. Clean it infrequently and gently, or you will wear through to the parent metal underneath. To remove burned-on foods, boil washing soda and water in the utensil for 3 or 4 minutes. If the tin-plated object is small, boil it in the washing soda solution for 3 or 4 minutes.

### Scouring Powder for Kitchen Utensils

> *4 Parts powdered soap*
> *1 Part powdered borax*
> *1 Part soda ash*
> *7 Parts fine pumice*

Mix thoroughly by stirring and running through a fine (100 mesh) sieve. To use, shake the powder onto dampened utensils. Rub with a damp cloth and then rinse. Do not use on highly polished ware.

### Nonscratching Scouring Powder

Measure out 9 parts of whiting or precipitated chalk and 1 part of trisodium phosphate. Mix thoroughly by shaking together in a box or bag for several minutes. This mixture is an inexpensive, nonscratching, effective compound for cleaning porcelain, brass, copper, nickel and stainless steel. To use, moisten and rub the surface with a cloth.

# HOW TO
# CLEAN MARBLE

Down through the years much has been written on the care and cleaning of marble. The fact is that even under the best of circumstances marble is difficult to restore, and in some instances, depending on the particular type of stain, virtually impossible, but if you follow the directions below, you should get more than satisfactory results.

The hardest part of your job may be securing the necessary materials in small quantities. The best place to obtain cleaning and polishing supplies is directly from the people who know marble best. Try "Marble Dealers" listed in the yellow pages. For detailed and interesting information on the subject, write to the Marble Institute of America or the Vermont Marble Company, both of which are listed as sources of supply at the back of this book.

## GENERAL CLEANING

To remove general soil from polished marble, plain water applied with a soft, clean cloth will do, but if the marble shows signs of heavy use and exposure, use a mild household laundry detergent in warm water. Dirt in unpolished marble can generally be removed by scrubbing well with a fiber or other stiff brush. Rinse both polished and unpolished marble with plenty of water immediately after cleaning, and dry quickly with a cloth or chamois to avoid streaks and water spots.

Since marble is a very porous stone and will absorb foreign substances quickly, it is best to attack stains as they appear. Before treating any stain, first determine its nature and the appropriate treatment.

If your unpolished marble is really dirty, try cleaning it by the poultice method rather than scrubbing it. Make a thick paste of household detergent and water and apply it to the entire marble surface with your hand or a towel in a layer at least ¼ inch thick. Cover this layer with a plastic sheet or a cloth kept damp for at least 24 hours. Let the poultice dry another 24 hours, then remove it, flush the entire surface with water and dry with a clean cloth or chamois.

## TREATING STAINS

### Copper and Bronze Stains

Copper and bronze stains usually result from the oxidation of fittings or inlays in the marble, and are most frequently a light green or muddy brown in color. These can usually be removed by using a poultice made from 1 part ammonium chloride (sal ammoniac) mixed with 4 parts whiting and a little household ammonia. Apply the paste over the stain. After it has dried thoroughly, rinse away with clear water and wipe dry with a soft cloth or chamois. Repeat the process if necessary.

### Iron and Rust Stains

If you catch rust stains when they're fresh, they can usually be washed off with household detergent and water. If that doesn't work, try a fine pumice powder or a mild scouring powder and water. There is another method that usually works wonders, but it might also dull the polish on your marble, making it necessary to repolish. Sprinkle sodium hydrosulphite powder (a dye remover that can be purchased where you buy household dyes), mixed with enough water to dampen it, over the stain and leave it for not more than half an hour. Rinse away the powder and immediately wash the stained area with sodium citrate. Wash with water, rinse and dry.

### Tea, Coffee, Soft Drink, Wine and Tobacco Stains

These stains, along with those caused by some inks and dyes, can usually be removed by bleaching the stone. Wash the stained area with warm water and dry it well. If your marble can be laid horizontally, pour on a little household chlorine bleach in liquid form or a 6 percent solution of hydrogen peroxide activated with a few drops of household ammonia. (Do not add ammonia to chlorine bleach, as this will release poisonous chlorine gas.) If your marble is vertical, use a heavy poultice made of whiting or talc mixed with either above-mentioned bleach, let the layer dry, remove it, rinse with clean water and dry the stone.

Any remaining color or stain can usually be bleached away by using a poultice of hydrogen peroxide or liquid chlorine bleach made into a paste by mixing it with whiting or talc. Spread this paste in a layer over the stained area, let it dry, remove the poultice, rinse the stained area with clean water and dry it thoroughly. Repeat the procedure if necessary.

### Superficial Smoke Stains

Superficial smoke stains (such as those that accumulate on marble around fireplaces as opposed to those caused by close contact with fire) can usually be taken out of marble by washing the stained area with an abrasive cleaner.

## POLISHING

For dull spots on marble, which are often mistaken for stains, try using the tin dioxide polishing material generally used by professionals. In the stone trade this substance is known as "putty powder" or "polishing powder." Sprinkle this powder lightly over the dull spot and buff steadily with a felt pad, a piece of short-nap wool carpeting or chamois dampened with water. Keep adding water and powder to the spot, rubbing back and forth in a straight line and stick with it until the surface is uniformly polished and matches the surrounding areas. Rinse and dry thoroughly with a soft cloth.

# REMOVING SPOTS
# & STAINS
# FROM FABRICS

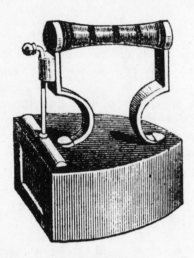
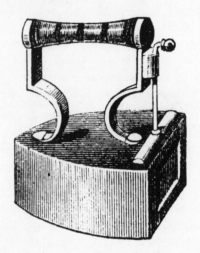

In any household, especially those with children, spots and stains are a daily problem. The usual method of stain removal in this consumer society is to drive the stain to the local cleaner and pay his bill. Some stains do need professional attention, but many simple stains can be removed at home in as much time as it takes to fight the traffic to the cleaner's or wait at the checkout line in a supermarket. And the price is usually much, much less.

Learn the simple methods for removing stains at home. Then act promptly when a fabric is stained. Many stains that can be removed easily when they are fresh are difficult or impossible to remove later, particularly after they are set by heat.

## SELECTING THE METHOD

Successful stain removal starts with the selection of a method that is suited to both stain and fabric.

### Kind of Stain

Identify the stain, if possible. The treatment for one kind of stain may set another. If you cannot determine what caused the stain, it will help if you can tell whether it is a greasy stain, a nongreasy stain or a combination of the two.

### Kind of Fabric

Before using any stain remover, be sure it will not harm the fabric.

Some stain removers that do not damage fibers may change the appearance of the treated area so that it looks as bad as or worse than the original stain. They may, for example, cause fading or bleeding of dyes, loss of luster, shrinkage or stretching of the fabric. They may remove nonpermanent finishes or designs. It is often difficult to use any stain remover on such fabrics as satins, crepes, taffetas, silk and rayon moirés, gabardines and velvets without causing some change in appearance.

To determine whether a stain remover will change the appearance of the fabric to be treated, test it first on a sample of the material, or on a hidden part of the article—a seam allowance, hem, inside of pocket or tail of a blouse or shirt.

If the substance needed to remove the stain seems to damage the fiber or change the appearance of the fabric, then you must send the stained article to a professional dry cleaner. He has the skill, the special equipment and the reagents that enable him to handle many of the more difficult stains and fabrics.

## TREATING THE STAIN

Follow directions accurately. Use solutions only in the strengths recommended and for the length of time given.

Work carefully and patiently. Results often depend as much on the way the job is done as on the remover used.

Observe all precautions given for the use of removers that are flammable, that give off poisonous vapors or that are poisonous if swallowed.

## STAIN REMOVERS AND HOW TO USE THEM

### Absorbent Materials

Useful absorbent materials are absorbent powders, absorbent cotton, sponges, white or fast-color paper towels, facial tissues and soft cloths.

ABSORBENT POWDERS: Cornstarch, cornmeal, talc or powdered chalk will remove some fresh stains, such as grease spatters. They are also used with solvents.

Spread absorbent powder over the stain before it dries. Remove powder as it absorbs the stain by shaking or brushing it off; or use the upholstery attachment of a vacuum cleaner.

After the surface stain has been removed, work fresh powder into the stain, then remove as before. Repeat with fresh powder until as much stain as possible has been absorbed.

It may be difficult to use this method success-fully on some dark-colored articles that cannot be washed. If the white powder cannot be completely removed, it may be more conspicuous on dark materials than the original stain.

OTHER ABSORBENT MATERIALS: Absorbent cloths, absorbent cotton, absorbent paper, blotters and sponges can be used to soak up staining liquids before they soak into a fabric. If much of the liquid can be absorbed quickly, the stain will be smaller and easier to remove than it would be otherwise. This technique will work only on fabrics that absorb the staining liquid slowly. It is often useful on such articles as rugs, upholstered furniture and heavy coats.

Hold the absorbent material so that the staining liquid is absorbed into it rather than forced deeper into the fabric. If the stain is not greasy, you may be able to remove some of the liquid that has soaked into the fabric by adding a little water to the stain and absorbing this immediately with the absorbent material. Repeat as long as any stain is absorbed.

These materials are also used to absorb stains as they are loosened from fabrics by liquid stain removers.

### Soaps and Detergents

Soaps and detergents will remove many non-greasy stains and some greasy stains. They act as lubricants, coating insoluble particles of staining material with a smooth, slippery film. The particles can then be rinsed out of the fabric.

Liquid detergents are especially useful. They are in the concentrated form needed to remove stains, and can easily be worked into the fabric and rinsed out of it.

WASHABLE ARTICLES: For surface stains, rub soap or detergent lightly into the dampened spot or rub in liquid detergent. Rinse the stained area or wash the article as usual.

If a stain is deeply embedded, work the soap or detergent thoroughly into the fabric. One way to do this is to rub soap or detergent lightly into the stained area, then holding the fabric with both hands, work the stained area back and forth between your thumbs. Bend the yarns sharply so that the individual fibers in the yarn rub against one another. It is this bending of yarns, rather than rubbing the surface of the fabric, that is effective in removing the stain. Go over the entire stained area in this way. Then rinse thoroughly.

On articles such as rugs, on heavy fabrics that cannot be bent easily, or on woolen fabrics that might be felted by too much bending of the yarn, work the soap or detergent into the fabric with the edge of a spoon.

NONWASHABLE ARTICLES: Work soap or detergent into the stained area in the same way as for washable articles. Dilute liquid detergents with an equal volume of water. Use as little soap or detergent as possible, because it is difficult to remove excess without wetting a large area of the fabric. Rinse thoroughly by sponging the spot with cool water or by forcing water through the stain with a syringe. If alcohol is safe for the fabric, use it instead of water to rinse the fabric. It is easier to rinse out the soap or detergent with alcohol, and the fabric will dry more quickly.

## Solvents

Many common stains can be removed with the right solvent. Different kinds of solvents are needed for nongreasy and for greasy stains. Water is the most useful solvent for many common nongreasy stains, and it is the only solvent that is neither flammable nor poisonous. When using other solvents, follow carefully the safety precautions listed.

With the exceptions of acetone and trichloroethylene, the solvents recommended here will not dissolve or seriously damage the fibers in the fabric. They may, however, change the appearance of the fabric so much that the article is no longer usable. Solvents may dissolve dyes and finishes or cause other changes, such as dulling of the luster and shrinking or stretching of the treated area. Test to be sure the solvent will not change the appearance of the treated area.

To test, use a solvent on a swatch of similar material or on a hidden part of the article exactly as you would to remove a stain.

SOLVENTS FOR NONGREASY STAINS: Water or water with a detergent will remove many nongreasy stains.

Acetone, alcohol, amyl acetate and turpentine are needed for other nongreasy stains. All are available at drug and hardware stores.

*Acetone* is used for removing such stains as fingernail polish and ballpoint ink. It should not be used on acetate, Arnel, Dynel or Verel. Flammable. Poison.

*Alcohol* (rubbing) is used for a number of stains if it is safe for the dye in the fabric. It should be diluted with 2 parts of water for use on acetate. Flammable. Poison.

*Amyl acetate* (chemically pure) is used for the same stains as acetone; it can be used on fabrics that are damaged by acetone. However, impure (technical grade) amyl acetate may damage the same fabrics as acetone. Flammable. Poison.

*Turpentine* is used on paint stains. Flammable. Poison.

GREASE SOLVENTS: Special solvents, such as those used by dry cleaners, are needed for greasy stains. These are available at drug, grocery and auto-supply stores.

No solvents are available that will effectively remove greasy spots without hazard to the user. Some are flammable; all of those commonly used are poisonous. Serious illness or death can result from swallowing the liquids or from breathing too large an amount of the vapors.

HOW TO USE SOLVENTS: Place the stained areas on a pad of soft cloth or other absorbent material. Place stained side down, if possible, so that the stain can be washed out of the fabric, not through it.

Dampen a pad of cotton or soft cloth with the solvent. Sponge the back of the stain with the pad. Repeated applications of only a small amount of solvent are better than a few applications of larger amounts.

Work from the center of the stain toward its outside edge, using light brushing or tamping motions. Professional dry cleaners have found that a fabric is less likely to ring if worked in this direction rather than from the outside edge toward the center. Avoid hard rubbing that might roughen the surface of the fabric. Sponge the stain irregularly around the edges so that there will be no definite line when the fabric dries.

Change the absorbent pad under the fabric and the pad used for sponging as soon as they are soiled to avoid transferring the stain back to the fabric.

For hardened stains (such as old paint or tar stains), place an absorbent pad or blotter dampened with the solvent on the stain. Allow time for the solvent to soften the stain; replace the pad as needed. Finish by sponging the stain.

For stains on delicate fabrics that cannot be sponged without chafing the surface or displacing the yarns, place an absorbent pad or blotter dampened with the solvent on the stain. Replace pad as needed. Do not sponge.

Dry fabrics as rapidly as possible.

On fabrics that tend to form rings: If a fabric tends to form rings when sponged with a solvent, use either of the following methods:

· Use method previously described, with these variations. Barely dampen the sponging pad with solvent. Apply only enough solvent to dampen the fabric—not so much that the solvent spreads out beyond the point of application. Take extra care, in sponging the stain around the edges, to make sure there will be no definite line when the fabric dries. Dry the fabric as rapidly as possible. On some fabrics the formation of rings can be prevented by placing the treated area on a dry, absorbent pad and rubbing it lightly with the palm of the hand; be sure the fabric is flat and free from wrinkles before you rub it. Or place it on the palm of one hand and rub it with the other. Rub with the crosswise or lengthwise thread of the material.

· Or use a solvent-absorbent powder mixture. Add just enough solvent to cornstarch, talc or other absorbent powder to make a thick, crumbly mixture. To make sure the mixture is dry enough, test it first on a scrap of similar material. The solvent should not spread out on the cloth beyond the edge of the mixture.

Apply the mixture over the stained area and work it into the fabric with gentle tamping or rubbing motions. Allow the mixture to dry on the stain. Brush off and repeat if necessary.

It may be difficult to use this mixture successfully on some dark-colored articles that cannot be washed. If the white powder cannot be completely removed, it may be more conspicuous on dark materials than the original stain.

To remove rings: Once rings have formed on a fabric they may be difficult to remove.

If the article is washable, work a soap or detergent thoroughly into the dampened ring. Then rinse thoroughly.

If the article is not washable, you may be able to remove the ring by rubbing the fabric between your thumbs, or scratching it lightly with a fingernail. A solvent-absorbent powder mixture, used as described above, may also remove rings.

## CHEMICAL STAIN REMOVERS

Chemical stain removers will take out many stains that cannot be removed by absorbents, detergents or solvents. The chemical removers react with such stains to form new compounds that are colorless or soluble, or both.

Because some may react with the fiber as well as with the stain, chemical removers are more likely to damage fabrics than the other types of removers. Test before using and follow carefully all directions for their use.

Chemical stain removers include bleaches, acetic acid, ammonia, iodine, oxalic acid and sodium thiosulfate.

### Bleaches

Bleaches are the most widely used of the chemical stain removers and the ones most likely to damage fibers and fade dyes if directions are not carefully followed. Bleaches should not be used in metal containers because metals may hasten the action of the bleach and thus increase the chance of fabric damage.

Three kinds of bleaches are recommended for home use—chlorine bleaches, peroxygen bleaches and color removers.

The first two kinds of bleaches generally remove the same types of stains and, if safe for the fabric, can be used interchangeably. If one bleach is more effective than the others for a particular stain, it is recommended in the directions for removing the stain.

Color removers are generally used for types of stains for which the first two are not effective.

CHLORINE BLEACHES: These are sold at grocery stores under various brand names. They may be in liquid, granular or tablet form.

PEROXYGEN BLEACHES: These include sodium perborate, potassium monopersulfate, and hydrogen peroxide.

Sodium Perborate is available as pure sodium perborate powder at drug stores. Powdered bleaches containing sodium perborate or potassium monopersulfate as the active ingredient are sold under various brand names at grocery stores.

The 3 percent hydrogen peroxide used for bleaching is sold in drugstores.

COLOR REMOVERS: These are sold under various brand names in drug and grocery stores.

## Other Chemical Stain Removers

ACETIC ACID OR VINEGAR: Used for neutralizing alkalies and for restoring colors changed by the action of alkalies. Use 10 percent acetic acid available from drugstores. Or substitute white vinegar, which contains 5 percent acetic acid.

AMMONIA: Used for neutralizing acids and restoring colors changed by the action of acids. Use 10 percent ammonia solution, or substitute household ammonia. Avoid breathing ammonia fumes. Poison if swallowed.

OXALIC ACID: Used for rust and other metallic stains. Sold in crystalline form at drugstores. Poison if swallowed.

SODIUM THIOSULFATE: Used only for removing iodine and chlorine stains. Sold in crystalline form at drugstores and as "hypo" at photographers' supply stores.

## How to Use Chemical Stain Removers

Try a mild treatment first. Dampen the stain with cool water and stretch the stained area over a bowl or place on an absorbent pad. Apply liquid removers with a medicine dropper. Or

sprinkle dry removers over the dampened spot. Or, if the article is washable, the stained area or the whole article can be soaked in a solution of the remover.

Do not let the remover dry on the fabric. If it is necessary to keep the remover on the stain for more than a few minutes, keep the area wet by placing a pad of cotton dampened with the remover—or with water if a dry remover is used —on the stain. Keep the cotton damp until the stain is removed.

Rinse the remover from washable articles by sponging the area repeatedly with a cloth dampened with water or by rinsing the area or whole garment in clear water.

To rinse the remover from nonwashable articles, sponge repeatedly with a cloth dampened with water. Or while the treated area is still damp, place it on a clean sponge. Use a syringe to force water through the spot. The sponge, by absorbing water, helps to keep moisture from spreading to surrounding dry areas. If you prefer, stretch the treated area over a bowl. Then force water through the spot.

If stains cannot be removed by a mild treatment, try a stronger treatment. For a stronger treatment:

· Lengthen the treatment time.

· Use a more concentrated solution of the remover.

· Or raise the temperature of the water or the solution.

Note, however, that stronger treatments increase the danger of damage to the fabric.

Additional directions for using each of the chemical stain removers are given on the following pages.

## Directions for Chlorine Bleaches

Do not use chlorine bleaches on fabrics that contain silk, wool or spandex fibers, polyurethane foams, or on a fabric with a special finish (such as those used to improve such properties as wrinkle resistance, shrinkage resistance, crispness or sheen, or to produce durable embossed and sculptured designs) unless the manufacturer states on the label that chlorine bleach is safe.

The resin in some of these finishes absorbs and retains chlorine, which weakens, and sometimes yellows, the fabric. Some fabrics are not weakened or yellowed until they are ironed; then damage may be severe. Test all dyed fabrics for colorfastness. Do not use in metal containers.

WASHABLE ARTICLES (mild treatment): Mix 2 tablespoons liquid bleach with 1 quart cool water. Apply to small stains with a medicine dropper; soak large stains in the solution. Leave on the stain for 5 to 15 minutes, then rinse well with water. Repeat if necessary. For bleaches in granular or tablet form, follow directions on the package.

WASHABLE ARTICLES (strong treatment): Mix equal parts liquid bleach and water. Apply the solution to small stains with a medicine dropper. If the stain is large, dip the stained area in the solution and rinse immediately with water. Repeat if necessary. Be sure all bleach is rinsed out of the fabric.

NONWASHABLE ARTICLES (mild treatment): Mix 1 teaspoon liquid bleach with 1 cup cool water. Apply to the stain with a medicine dropper. Leave on the stain for 5 to 15 minutes, then rinse well with water. Repeat if necessary. For bleaches in granular or tablet form, follow directions on the package.

A strong treatment is not recommended, However, if the stain cannot be removed in any other way, the strong treatment given above for washable articles may be used.

## Powdered Peroxygen Bleaches

These include sodium perborate and potassium monopersulfate bleaches. Do not use strong treatments on fabrics that contain wool, silk or Dynel because these treatments call for hot water. Hot water shrinks Dynel; hot solutions are not safe for silk and wool. Test all dyed fabrics for colorfastness. Do not use in metal containers.

WASHABLE ARTICLES (mild treatment): Mix 1 to 2 tablespoons powdered peroxygen bleach with 1 pint lukewarm water (for wool, silk and Dynel)

or 1 pint hot water (for other fabrics). Mix just before using; the solution loses strength on standing.

Cover the stained area with the solution or soak the entire article. Soak until the stain is removed (this may take several hours, or overnight). Rinse well.

If wool or silk is yellowed by the bleach solution, sponge with 10 percent acetic acid or vinegar to remove yellowing, then rinse with water.

WASHABLE ARTICLES (strong treatment): Sprinkle powdered peroxygen bleach on the stain. Dip the stain into very hot or boiling water; the stain should be removed in a few minutes. Rinse well. Repeat if necessary.

NONWASHABLE ARTICLES (mild treatment): Sprinkle powdered peroxygen bleach on the stain. Cover with a pad of cotton dampened with water. Use lukewarm water for wool, silk and Dynel; hot water for other fabrics. Keep damp until the stain is removed (this may take several hours or more). Rinse well.

Or mix 1 to 2 tablespoons powdered peroxygen bleach with 1 pint lukewarm water (for wool, silk and Dynel) or 1 pint hot water (for other fabrics). Mix just before using; the solution loses strength on standing. Apply to the stain with a medicine dropper. Keep damp until the stain is removed. Rinse well.

If wool or silk is yellowed by the bleach solution, sponge with 10 percent acetic acid or vinegar to remove yellowing, then rinse with water.

NONWASHABLE ARTICLES (strong treatment): Dampen the stain with cool water. Sprinkle powdered peroxygen bleach on the stain. With spoon or medicine dropper, pour a small amount of boiling water on the stain. Use a sponge or absorbent pad under the stain to absorb the water. Rinse well. Repeat if necessary.

## Hydrogen Peroxide

A 3 percent solution of hydrogen peroxide is safe for all fibers; it acts slowly on stains. This solution loses strength on storage. Test all dyed fabrics for colorfastness. Do not use in metal containers.

WASHABLE AND NONWASHABLE ARTICLES (mild treatment): Moisten the stain with a few drops of a 3 percent solution of hydrogen peroxide. Expose the stain to direct sunlight. Add hydrogen peroxide as needed to keep the stained area moist until the stain is removed.

If the above treatment does not remove the stain, add a few drops of household ammonia to about 1 tablespoon of hydrogen peroxide. Moisten the stain immediately with this mixture, and cover with a pad of cotton dampened with the same mixture. Keep damp until the stain is removed (it may take several hours or more). Rinse well.

WASHABLE AND NONWASHABLE ARTICLES (strong treatment): Cover the stain with a cloth dampened with a 3 percent solution of the hydrogen peroxide.

Cover with a dry cloth and press with an iron as hot as is safe for the fiber. Rinse well.

### Color Removers

Color removers are safe for all fibers, but fade or remove many dyes. If a test of the color remover on the fabric shows that the remover causes a distinct color change rather than fading, you may be able to restore the original color by rinsing immediately, then drying the article in air. If the color remover fades the color, the original color cannot be restored. Do not use in metal containers.

WASHABLE AND NONWASHABLE ARTICLES (mild treatment): Dissolve ¼ teaspoon color remover in ½ cup cool water. Wet the stain with a few drops of the solution. Cover the stain for 1 to 15 minutes with a pad of cotton dampened with the solution. Rinse well. Repeat if necessary.

WASHABLE AND NONWASHABLE ARTICLES (strong treatment): For large stains on white or colorfast fabrics, follow the directions on the package. For all other stains, dissolve ¼ teaspoon color remover in ½ cup boiling water. Drop the hot solution on the stain with a medicine dropper. Rinse immediately. Repeat if necessary.

### Directions for Other Chemical Stain Removers

Treatments are the same for washable and nonwashable articles. Unless otherwise indicated,

treatment is strengthened by increasing the time the remover is left on the fabric.

ACETIC ACID, VINEGAR: Moisten the stain with 10 percent acetic acid or vinegar. Keep the fabric wet until the stain is removed. Rinse with water. Safe for all fibers, but may change the color of some dyes.

If the dye changes color, rinse the stain with water. Then try to restore the color by moistening the stain with ammonia as directed below.

AMMONIA: For all fabrics except those that contain wool or silk, moisten the stain with 10 percent ammonia or household ammonia. Keep the stain wet until it is removed. Rinse with water. If the color of a dye is changed by ammonia, try to restore the color after rinsing by moistening with acetic acid or vinegar. Rinse with water.

For wool or silk, dilute ammonia with an equal volume of water. Moisten the stain with this solution and keep it moist until the stain is removed. Rinse with water. Add a small amount of vinegar to the last rinse. If the color of a dye is changed by ammonia, try to restore the color after rinsing by moistening with acetic acid or vinegar. Rinse with water.

OXALIC ACID: Safe for all fibers, but may change the color of some dyes. If the dye changes color after treatment, rinse the stain with water. Then try to restore the color by moistening stain with ammonia as directed above. May cause fabric damage if not rinsed out of fabric. Poison.

Mild treatment: Dissolve 1 tablespoon of oxalic acid crystals in 1 cup of warm water. Keep the stain wet with this solution until it is removed. Rinse thoroughly with water.

Strong treatment: Dissolve 1 tablespoon of oxalic acid in one cup of water as hot as is safe for fabric. Use as for mild treatment.

Or, for all fabrics except nylon, sprinkle crystals on the dampened stain and dip in a pan of very hot water. Rinse thoroughly.

## GENERAL METHODS

### Greasy Stains

WASHABLE ARTICLES: Regular washing, either by hand or by machine, removes some greasy stains.

Some can be removed by rubbing soap or detergent into the stain and then rinsing with warm water. On some wash-and-wear or permanent-press fabrics, it may be necessary to rub soap or detergent thoroughly into the stain and allow it to stand for several hours, or overnight, before rinsing.

Often, however, you will need to use a grease solvent (see page 228); this is effective even after an article has been washed.

Sponge the stain thoroughly with the grease solvent. Dry. Repeat if necessary. It often takes extra time and patience to remove greasy stains from a fabric with a special finish.

A yellow stain may remain after solvent treatment if the stain has been set by age or heat. To remove the yellow stain, use a chlorine or peroxygen bleach (see pages 229–31). If safe for the fabric, the strong sodium perborate treatment (see page 230) is usually the most effective for these stains.

NONWASHABLE ARTICLES: Sponge the stain well with a grease solvent (see page 228). Dry. Repeat if necessary. It often takes extra time and patience to remove greasy stains from fabrics with a special finish.

A yellow stain may remain after solvent treatment if the stain has been set by age or heat. To remove the yellow stain, use a chlorine or peroxygen bleach (see pages 229–31). If safe for the fabric, the strong sodium perborate treatment (see page 230) is usually the most effective for these stains.

### Nongreasy Stains

Many fresh stains can be removed by simple treatments. Stains set by heat or age may be difficult or impossible to remove.

WASHABLE ARTICLES: Some nongreasy stains are removed by regular laundry methods; others are set by them.

Sponge the stain with cool water. Or soak the stain in cool water for 30 minutes or longer; some stains require an overnight soak. If the stain remains after sponging or soaking, work a soap or detergent into it, then rinse. If a stain remains after detergent treatment, use a chlorine or peroxygen bleach (see pages 229–31).

NONWASHABLE ARTICLES: Sponge the stain with cool water. Or force cool water through the stain with a small syringe, using a sponge under the stain to absorb the water. If the stain remains, rub soap or detergent on the stain and work it into the fabric. Rinse.

A final sponging with alcohol helps to remove the soap or detergent and to dry the fabric more quickly. Test the alcohol on the fabric first to be sure it does not affect the dye. Dilute alcohol with 2 parts of water before using it on acetate.

If the stain remains after rinsing, use a chlorine or peroxygen bleach (see pages 229–31).

### Combination Stains

Combination stains are caused by materials that contain both greasy and nongreasy substances.

WASHABLE ARTICLES: Sponge the stain with cool water. Or soak in cool water for 30 minutes or longer. If the stain remains, work soap or detergent into the stain, then rinse thoroughly. Allow the article to dry.

If a greasy stain remains, sponge with a grease solvent (see page 228). Allow the article to dry. Repeat if necessary.

If a colored stain remains after the fabric dries, use a chlorine or peroxygen bleach (see pages 229–31).

NONWASHABLE ARTICLES: Sponge the stain with cool water. Or force cool water through the stain with a small syringe, using a sponge under the stain to absorb the water. If a stain remains, rub soap or detergent on the stain and work it into the fabric. Rinse the spot well with water. Allow article to dry.

If a greasy stain remains, sponge with a grease solvent (see page 228). Allow to dry. Repeat if necessary.

If a colored stain remains after the fabric dries, use a chlorine or peroxygen bleach (see pages 229–31).

## PRECAUTIONS

### *When Using Any Solvent Except Water*

Solvents—except water—are poisonous if swallowed or if their vapors are inhaled; some also are flammable. Use solvents carefully.

Work out of doors or in a well-ventilated room (open several doors and windows).

Do not breathe solvent vapors. They are poisonous. Arrange work so that fumes are blown away from you, by a fan or breeze from an open door or window. Do not lean close to your work.

Solvent vapors are heavier than air and tend to settle unless there is forced ventilation. Do not allow small children to play on the floor in a room where solvents are used.

Use only a small quantity of solvent at a time. Unless you are working outdoors, do not pour solvents into an open bowl.

If you spill solvent on your skin, wash it off immediately.

Observe any additional warnings given on labels of solvent containers.

### *In Addition, When Using Flammable Solvents*

Do not use near open flames, including pilot lights on gas equipment.

Do not use where there is a chance that sparks from electrical equipment or from static electricity may ignite the solvent or vapors. Never use flammable solvents in a washing machine. Never put articles that have been dampened with a flammable solvent in a dryer.

### *When Storing Solvents*

When solvents are not in use, keep them tightly stoppered in a place out of the reach of children. In addition to giving off poisonous fumes, solvents are also poisonous if swallowed.

Store flammable solvents where they cannot be ignited by flames or electric sparks.

## SPECIFIC STAINS

### *Acids*

If an acid is spilled on a fabric, rinse the area with water immediately. Then apply ammonia to the stain and rinse again with water.

### *Adhesive Tape*

Scrape gummy matter from the stain carefully with a dull table knife; avoid damaging fabric. Sponge with a grease solvent (see page 228).

### *Alcoholic Beverages*

Refer to Nongreasy Stains (page 233) or sponge the stain with rubbing alcohol (provided alcohol does not affect the color of the garment). If the fabric is acetate, dilute alcohol with 2 parts of water. If the stain remains, use a chlorine or peroxygen bleach (see pages 229–31).

Some dyes bleed when they come into contact with the alcohol in drinks, causing a loss of color or a ring around the edge of the stain. In either instance the fabric cannot be restored.

### *Alkalies*

Immediately rinse the area with water, apply vinegar and rinse again with water.

### *Antiperspirants*

Sponge thoroughly with soap or detergent and warm water. If stain persists, use a chlorine or peroxygen bleach (see pages 229–31).

Some antiperspirants contain acids that may damage fabrics or cause color changes. Try sponging with ammonia. For use on silk or wool, dilute the ammonia with an equal volume of water.

### *Blood*

Refer to Nongreasy Stains (page 233).

If the stain persists after soap or detergent treatment, apply a few drops of ammonia and repeat the detergent treatment. Rinse and follow with bleach treatment if necessary.

### Bluing

Refer to Nongreasy Stains (page 233).

### Butter

Refer to Greasy Stains (page 232).

### Candle Wax

First remove as much wax as possible. Then place the stain between several layers of facial tissue and press with a warm iron. Sponge the stain that remains with a grease solvent (see page 228).

Or, if fabric will not be affected, pour boiling water through the area and remove any remaining stain with grease solvent.

### Car Grease

Refer to Greasy Stains (page 232).

### Candy

For chocolate and syrup stains, refer to Combination Stains (page 233). For other candy stains, refer to Nongreasy Stains (page 233).

### Catsup

Refer to Nongreasy Stains (page 233).

### Chili Sauce

Refer to Nongreasy Stains (page 233).

### Chewing Gum

Scrape off as much gum as possible. (This is easier if you first harden the gum by applying an ice cube.) Sponge the remaining stain with a grease solvent (see page 228).

### Chlorine

Treat the fabric before ironing whenever possible. Rinse the fabric thoroughly with water. Then soak for 30 minutes or longer in a sodium thiosulfate solution (1 teaspoon per quart of warm water). Rinse thoroughly.

### Chocolate

Refer to Combination Stains (page 233).

### Cocoa

Refer to Nongreasy Stains (page 233).

### Coffee

With cream, refer to Combination Stains (page 233). Without cream, refer to Nongreasy Stains (page 233).

### Cosmetics

FOR WASHABLE ARTICLES: apply undiluted liquid detergent to the stain, or dampen the stain and rub in soap or detergent until thick suds are formed; work in until the stain is gone. Rinse well. (If the stain persists, dry the fabric and then repeat the procedure.)

FOR NONWASHABLE ARTICLES: sponge with a grease solvent (see page 228). If the stain is not removed, it may pay to take a chance and treat it as though for a washable article.

### Crayon

Refer to Cosmetics (above).

### Cream

Refer to Combination Stains (page 233).

### Deodorants

Refer to Antiperspirants (page 234).

### Dyes

Refer to Nongreasy Stains (page 233). If bleach is required, use a chlorine bleach or color remover (see pages 229–30).

A long soak in sudsy water is often effective on fresh dye stains.

### Egg

Refer to Nongreasy Stains (page 233).

### Eye Shadow

Refer to Cosmetics (page 235).

### Fingernail Polish

Sponge the stain with acetone or amyl acetate (see page 228). Use amyl acetate on acetate, Arnel, Dynel and Verel. Use acetone on other fabrics.

Nail polish removers may be used; however, before using on acetate, Arnel, Dynel or Verel, test on scrap of fabric.

### Food Coloring

Refer to Nongreasy Stains (page 233).

### Fruit, Fruit Juices

Refer to Nongreasy Stains (page 233).

If safe for the fabric, pour boiling water through the spot from a height of 1 to 3 feet.

When any fruit juice is spilled on a fabric, it is a good idea to sponge the spot immediately with cool water. Some fruit juices, citrus among them, are invisible on the fabric after they dry, but turn yellow on aging or heating. This yellow stain may be difficult to remove.

### Furniture Polish

Refer to Greasy Stains (page 232).

If the polish contains wood stain, follow the directions given for Paint (page 239).

### Glue, Mucilage, Adhesives

For airplane glue or household cement, sponge the stain with acetone or amyl acetate (see page 228). Use amyl acetate on acetate, Arnel, Dynel and Verel; use acetone on other fabrics.

For casein glue, refer to Nongreasy Stains (page 233).

For plastic glue, wash the stain with soap or detergent and water before glue hardens; some types cannot be removed after they have hardened.

The following treatment will remove some dried plastic glue stains. Immerse the stain in hot 10 percent acetic acid or vinegar. Keep the acid or vinegar at or near the boiling point until the stain is removed (this may take 15 minutes or longer). Rinse with water.

For rubber cement, scrape gummy matter from the stain carefully; avoid damaging the fabric. Sponge thoroughly with a grease solvent (see page 228).

For other types of glue or mucilage, follow directions for Nongreasy Stains (page 233), except for soaking the stain in hot water instead of cool.

### Grass, Flowers, Foliage

FOR WASHABLE ARTICLES: work soap or detergent into the stain, then rinse. Or, if safe for dye, sponge the stain with alcohol (see page 228). Dilute alcohol with 2 parts of water for use on acetate.

If the stain persists, use a chlorine or peroxygen bleach (see pages 229–31).

FOR NONWASHABLE ARTICLES: use the same method, but try alcohol first if it is safe for the dye.

### Gravy

Refer to Combination Stains (page 233).

### Ice Cream

Refer to Combination Stains (page 233).

### Ink (Ballpoint)

Sponge the stain repeatedly with acetone or amyl acetate (see page 228). Use amyl acetate on acetate, Arnel, Dynel and Verel; use acetone on other fabrics. This will remove fresh stains. Old stains may also require bleaching (see page 229).

Washing removes some types of ballpoint ink stains but sets others. To see if the stain will wash out, mark a scrap of similar material with the ink and wash it.

### Ink (Drawing)

BLACK (India ink): Treat the stain as soon as possible. These stains are very hard to remove if dry.

For washable articles, force water through the stain until all loose pigment is removed. Wash with soap or detergent as often as necessary. Then soak the stain in warm suds containing 1 to 4 tablespoons of ammonia per quart of water. Dried stains may need to be soaked overnight.

Or force water through the stain until all loose pigment is removed, wet the spot with ammonia and work soap or detergent into the stain. Rinse. Repeat if necessary.

For nonwashable articles, force water through the stain until all loose pigment is removed. Next, sponge the stain with a solution of water and ammonia (1 tablespoon of ammonia per cup of water). Rinse with water. If the stain persists, moisten with ammonia and work soap or detergent into it. Rinse. Repeat if necessary.

If ammonia changes the color of the fabric, sponge first with water, then moisten with vinegar. Rinse well.

COLORS OTHER THAN BLACK: refer to Nongreasy Stains (page 233). If bleach is needed, use a color remover (see page 230) if safe for the dye. If the color remover is not safe for the dye, try other bleaches.

### Ink (Mimeograph and Printing)

For fresh stains, refer to Greasy Stains (page 232) or sponge with turpentine (see page 228).

For stubborn stains, refer to Paint, Varnish (page 239).

### Ink (Writing)

FOR WASHABLE ARTICLES: follow directions for Nongreasy Stains (page 233). Because writing inks vary greatly in composition, it may be necessary to try more than one kind of bleach.

Try a chlorine bleach (see page 229) on all fabrics for which it is safe. For other fabrics, try peroxygen bleach (see page 229). A few types of ink require treatment with color removers.

A strong bleach treatment may be needed. However, a strong bleach may leave a faded spot on some colored fabrics.

If a yellow stain remains after bleaching, treat as a rust stain (see page 240).

FOR NONWASHABLE ARTICLES: if possible, use a blotter (for small stains) or absorbent powder to remove excess ink before it soaks into the fabric. Then follow directions for washable articles.

### Lard

Refer to Greasy Stains (page 232).

### Lipstick

Refer to Cosmetics (page 235).

### Makeup (Liquid)

Refer to Cosmetics (page 235).

### Margarine

Refer to Greasy Stains (page 232).

### Mascara

Refer to Cosmetics (page 235).

### Mayonnaise

Refer to Combination Stains (page 233).

### Meat Juice

Refer to Combination Stains (page 233).

### Medicines

Because so many different substances are used in medicines, it is not possible to give methods for removing all such stains.

For oily, gummy and tarry medicines, refer to Greasy Stains (page 232).

For medicines in sugar syrup or water, wash the stain out with water.

For medicines dissolved in alcohol (tinctures), sponge the stain with alcohol (see page 228). Dilute with 2 parts water for use on acetate.

For medicines that contain iron, refer to Rust (page 240).

For medicines that contain dyes, follow directions for dyes (see page 236).

### Mercurochrome, Merthiolate, Metaphen

For washable articles, soak overnight in a warm soap or detergent solution that contains 4 tablespoons of ammonia to each quart of water.

For nonwashable articles, if alcohol is safe for the dye, sponge with alcohol (see page 228) as long as any of the stain is removed. Dilute alcohol with 2 parts water for use on acetate.

If a stain remains, place a pad of cotton saturated with alcohol on the stain. Keep the pad wet until the stain is removed (this may take an hour or more).

If alcohol is not safe for the dye, wet the stain with liquid detergent. Add a drop of ammonia with a medicine dropper. Rinse with water. Repeat if necessary.

### Metal

To remove stains caused by tarnished brass, copper, tin and other metals, use vinegar, lemon juice, acetic acid (see page 230) or oxalic acid (see page 230). Use lemon juice according to the directions given for vinegar. The two acids, because they are stronger, will remove stains that cannot be removed by vinegar or lemon juice.

As soon as the stain is removed, rinse well with water.

Do not use chlorine or peroxygen bleaches. These bleaches may cause damage because the metal in the stain hastens their action.

### Mildew

For washable articles, treat mildew spots while they are fresh, before the mold growth has a chance to weaken the fabric.

Wash the mildewed article thoroughly. Dry in the sun. If the stain remains, treat with a chlorine or peroxygen bleach (see page 230).

For nonwashable articles, send the article to the dry cleaner promptly.

### Milk

Refer to Nongreasy Stains (page 233).

### Mud

Let the stain dry, then brush well. If the stain remains, refer to Nongreasy Stains (page 233). Stains from iron-rich clays not removed by this method should be treated as rust stains (see page 240).

### Mustard

For washable articles, rub soap or detergent into the dampened stain, then rinse. If the stain is not removed, soak the article in a hot detergent solution for several hours, or overnight if necessary.

If the stain persists, use a bleach (see page 229). Strong sodium perborate treatment (see page 230), if safe for the fabric, is often the most effective bleach.

For nonwashable articles, if safe for the dye,

sponge the stain with alcohol. Dilute alcohol with 2 parts water for use on acetate.

If alcohol cannot be used, or if it does not remove the stain completely, follow the treatment for washable articles (see page 233), but omit the soaking.

### Oil (Fish-Liver Oil, Linseed Oil, Machine Oil, Mineral Oil, Vegetable Oil)

Refer to Greasy Stains (page 232).

### Paint, Varnish

Treat stains promptly. They are always harder—and sometimes impossible—to remove after they have dried on the fabric. Because there are so many different kinds of paints and varnishes, no one method will remove all stains. Read the label on the container; if a certain solvent is recommended as a thinner, it may be more effective in removing stains than the solvents recommended.

FOR WASHABLE ARTICLES: Rub soap or detergent into the stain and wash. If the stain has dried, or is only partially removed by washing, sponge with turpentine (see page 228) until no more paint or varnish is removed; for aluminum paint stains, trichloroethylene may be more effective than turpentine; do not use this solvent on Arnel or Kodel.

While the stain is still wet with the solvent, work soap or detergent into it, put the article in hot water and soak it overnight. Thorough washing will then remove most types of paint stains.

If the stain remains, repeat the treatment.

FOR NONWASHABLE ARTICLES: Sponge fresh stains with turpentine (see page 228) until no more paint is removed; for aluminum paint stains, trichloroethylene may be more effective than turpentine. Do not use trichloroethylene on Arnel or Kodel.

If necessary, loosen the paint by covering the stain for 30 minutes or longer with a pad of cotton dampened with the solvent. Repeat the sponging.

If the stain remains, put a drop of liquid de-

tergent on the stain and work it into the fabric with the edge of a spoon.

Alternatively, sponge the stain with turpentine (see page 228) and treat with detergent as many times as necessary.

If alcohol is safe for the dye, sponge the stain with alcohol to remove the turpentine and detergent. (Dilute with 2 parts water for use on acetate.) If alcohol is not safe for the dye, sponge the stain first with warm soap or detergent solution, then with water.

### Perfume

Refer to Alcoholic Beverages (page 234).

### Perspiration

Wash or sponge thoroughly with soap or detergent and warm water. Work carefully because some fabrics are weakened by perspiration; silk is the fiber most easily damaged.

If perspiration has changed the color of the fabric, try to restore it by treating it with ammonia or vinegar (see page 230). Apply ammonia to fresh stains; rinse with water. Apply vinegar to old stains; rinse with water.

If an oily stain remains, refer to Greasy Stains (page 232).

Remove any yellow discoloration with a chlorine or peroxygen bleach (see page 230). If safe for the fabric, the strong sodium perborate treatment (see page 230) is often the most effective for these stains.

### Plastic

To remove stains caused by plastic hangers or buttons that have softened and adhered to the fabric, use amyl acetate or trichloroethylene. Test colored fabrics to be sure the dye does not bleed. Do not use trichloroethylene on Arnel or Kodel.

Sponge the stain with a pad of absorbent cloth or cotton moistened with the solvent. In using these solvents, observe the precautions listed on page 228.

If the plastic has been absorbed in the fabric, it may be necessary to place a pad wet with the solvent on the spot and let it remain until the plastic has softened. Sponge with a fresh pad moistened with the solvent. Repeat until all the plastic has been removed.

### Rust

Moisten the stain with oxalic acid solution (1 tablespoon of oxalic acid crystals in 1 cup warm water). If the stain is not removed by a single treatment, heat the oxalic acid solution and repeat.

If the stain is stubborn, place the oxalic acid crystals directly on the stain. Moisten with water as hot as is safe for fabric and allow to stand a few minutes, or dip in hot water. Repeat if necessary. (Do not use this method on nylon.)

Rinse the article thoroughly. If allowed to dry in fabric, oxalic acid will cause damage.

PRECAUTION: Oxalic acid is poison if swallowed.

If safe for the fabric, boil the stained article in a solution containing 4 teaspoons of cream of tartar to each pint of water. Boil until the stain is removed. Rinse thoroughly.

Spread the stained portion over a pan of boiling water and squeeze lemon juice on it.

Or sprinkle salt on the stain, squeeze lemon juice on it, and spread in the sun to dry. Rinse thoroughly. Repeat if necessary.

Color removers (see page 230) can be used to remove rust stains from white fabrics.

### Salad Dressing

Refer to Combination Stains (page 233).

### Sauces

Refer to Combination Stains (page 233).

### Scorch

If the article is washable, refer to Nongreasy Stains (page 233).

To remove light scorch from an article that is nonwashable, apply hydrogen peroxide as directed on pages 231–32. The strong treatment may be needed to remove the scorch stain. Repeat if necessary.

Severe scorch cannot be removed because the fabric has been damaged.

### Shellac

Sponge the stain with alcohol, or soak the stain in alcohol (see page 228). Dilute with 2 parts water for use on acetate. If alcohol bleeds the dye, try turpentine (see Paint, page 239).

### Shoe Polish

Because there are many different kinds of shoe polish, no one method will remove all stains. It may be necessary to try more than one of the methods given below.

· Refer to Cosmetics (page 235).

· Sponge the stain with alcohol if safe for the dye in the fabric. Dilute with 2 parts water for use on acetate.

· Sponge the stain with a grease solvent or turpentine (see page 228). If turpentine is used, remove it by sponging with a warm soap or detergent solution or with alcohol.

· If the stain is not removed by any of these methods, use a chlorine or peroxygen bleach (see pages 229–230). The strong sodium perborate treatment, if safe for the fabric, is often the most effective bleach.

### Smoke

Refer to Cosmetics (page 235).

### Soft Drinks

Refer to Nongreasy Stains (page 233).

When any soft drink is spilled on a fabric, sponge the spot immediately with cool water. Some soft drinks are invisible after they dry, but turn yellow on aging or heating. The yellow stain may be difficult to remove.

### Soot

Refer to Cosmetics (page 235).

### Soups

Refer to Combination Stains (see page 233).

### Syrup

Refer to Combination Stains (see page 233).

### Tar

Refer to Greasy Stains (see page 232).

If the stain is not removed by this method, sponge with turpentine (see page 228).

### Tea

Refer to Coffee (see page 235).

### Tobacco

Refer to Grass (see page 236).

### Unknown Stains

If a stain appears greasy, treat it as a Greasy Stain (see page 236). Otherwise, treat it as a Nongreasy Stain (see page 233).

See also Yellowing (below).

### Urine

To remove stains caused by normal urine, refer to Nongreasy Stains (see page 233).

If the color of the fabric has been changed, sponge with ammonia (see page 230). If this treatment does not restore the color, sponging with acetic acid or vinegar may help (see page 230).

If the stain is not removed by the method given above, refer to Medicines (page 238) and Yellowing (below).

### Vegetables

Refer to Nongreasy Stains (see page 233).

### Wax (Floor, Furniture, Car)

Refer to Greasy Stains (see page 232).

### Yellowing, Brown Stains

To remove storage stains from fabrics, or unknown yellow or yellow-brown stains, use as many of the following treatments as necessary (if safe for the fabric) in the following order:

- Wash.
- Use a mild treatment of a chlorine or peroxygen bleach (see pages 229–30).
- Use the oxalic acid method for treating rust stains (see page 240).
- Use a strong treatment of a chlorine or peroxygen bleach.

# HELP IN
# THE KITCHEN

The kitchen is the center of the house, and the person who tends the kitchen is the center of the home and the true protector of the family. It doesn't matter who this central figure may be —woman, man or child—as long as she or he is responsible and has some feeling of the importance of the work at hand.

The best method of kitchen maintenance is a system whereby every member of the family who consumes the food prepared in the kitchen devotes some time to its upkeep. This system prevents any one member of the household from becoming so inundated with kitchen work that whatever satisfactions might normally be derived are negated by the overbearing drudgery of the tasks involved.

The kitchen has traditionally been a warm, secure place where the preparing of food for the common meal, a central family activity, has provided a meeting place where problems and aspirations can be discussed in an atmosphere of mutual trust and concern. Some television commercials and women's magazines give the impression that a kitchen should be kept spotlessly white and antiseptically clean, like a hospital operating room, but in my opinion a good kitchen ought

to be at least as comfortable and pleasant to spend time in as any other room in the house. It seems silly to have food preparation locked away and out of sight in a separate room that has no other function. The chopping, mixing and cooking of food should be openly shared by all members of the family. There's no reason to try to make your kitchen absolutely spotless, a place where no one can feel at home. True, you'll want to keep your dishes properly clean because it's unpleasant to eat from dirty ones. You'll scrub down your table and counter areas because otherwise they'll get encrusted with food and attract pests. Refrigerators must be cleaned occasionally to prevent mold and off-odors. Sinks must be kept unclogged and garbage disposed of. But these things can be accomplished simply and without undue effort or expense if you take the natural route, make cleaning products yourself, try the old ways that were the wise ways before everything was flashily boxed and set in dazzling rows on a supermarket shelf.

We seem to have the notion that the more attractive the box and the higher the price, the more effective the product will be. In truth, many products advertised so persistently and packaged so elegantly are merely incredibly inexpensive common chemicals, easily available and tremendously effective if only you know where to find them and how to use them. If you think the information in this section is too simple to be worthwhile, you have probably fallen victim to the advertising that is pushing up the price of your present household cleaning items. And as far as I know, propaganda never cleaned a single dish, sink or toilet bowl.

## GENERAL CLEANING

Here are some general ideas to help you with your kitchen cleaning jobs:

### Sink Drains

A good way to keep your drains and traps clean without corroding your plumbing is to pour 3 tablespoons of washing soda down the drain at least once a week, following it with 3 or 4 quarts of very hot water.

### Gas Ranges

To clean clogged gas burners and broilers, soak them from 5 to 10 minutes in very hot water to which 3 heaping tablespoons of washing soda have been added. Boiling the burners hastens the cleaning action, but you must never boil them in an aluminum pan!

### Refrigerators and Freezers

Refrigerator and freezer interiors can be cleaned by sprinkling baking soda on a damp cloth and wiping vigorously. Use 3 tablespoons of baking soda in 1 quart of warm water to clean ice trays, food containers and crisper boxes. Rinse with clean, hot water and wipe dry. Baking soda not only cleans without scratching, but it also removes unpleasant odors.

### Garbage Pails

Keep your garbage pails clean—and sanitary—by rinsing down regularly with a washing soda solution (about 4 ounces per pail).

### Grease

Spilled grease should be blotted up with paper towels. Wipe up any remaining residue with a rag dipped in alcohol. Wipe again with clean paper towels.

### Grills (From Oven or Barbecue)

To clean those grease-encrusted grills, liberally sprinkle with washing soda and brush vigorously with a wire or other stiff brush.

### Irons (Steam-Type)

The inside of most steam irons, just like the interior of any boiler, can corrode from accumulations of mineral deposits from "hard" water. These deposits can be removed with relative ease by the use of Calgon, a water-softening agent, once a month. This clears the water reservoir of the iron and opens the steam holes. Use 1 teaspoon of Calgon to 8 ounces of water. Pour the solution into the iron and set the heat control at medium high. As soon as the iron begins to steam, hold it out at arm's length and shake it gently over the sink to circulate the water. Be careful not to scald yourself! Keep the hot solution in the iron for 10 to 15 minutes. Shake frequently. Drain out the solution and rinse with plain water. Refill the iron with plain water and repeat the procedure, heating and shaking until you are sure all the Calgon and sludge have been rinsed out. Drain the iron again and rinse several more times.

### Dishwashing Hints

When washing dishes by hand, it's a good idea to condition the water first in order to prevent dulling film. In conditioned water, grease and dirt remain in suspension and are washed down the drain without leaving a ring on the dishpan or spots on dishes. First, dissolve 2½ teaspoons of Calgon in a dishpan full of hot water (add more if the water is very "hard"). You'll find you only need half the amount of soap or detergent that you usually use.

Start with clear glassware. Then wash silver, dishes and finally pots and pans. Change dishwater when necessary. Rinse glassware, dishes and all utensils with hot water and let dry.

To make dishwashing easier, wash your dishes as soon as you're finished with them while the rest of the meal is cooking. Many iron pots and pans shouldn't be "washed" at all because they might lose their "seasoning." They should merely be wiped and rinsed and dried.

Do not dry dishes unless it is absolutely necessary because of lack of kitchen space. It is best to let dishes drip-dry in an appropriate draining apparatus or on a draining board, because dishtowels, unless scrupulously clean, can spread bacteria.

### Glassware That Sparkles

To make glassware sparkle, add a little laundry bluing to the water.

### Stuck Drinking Glasses

A hint on drying glasses:

To separate nested drinking glasses that have been stuck together, fill the top glass with ice water and lower the bottom glass into a basin of hot water. The upper glass will contract slightly and the bottom one will expand, permitting the glasses to be separated.

### Greasy Dishes

To cut the grease when washing greasy dishes, put a few drops of ammonia into the dishwater.

### Baking Dishes

Soak encrusted baking and casserole dishes in cold water, sprinkle in a little baking soda and let stand several hours. Wash as usual.

### Scorch Marks on Glass, Porcelain or Unchipped Enamelware

Scorch marks may be easily removed with a solution of 1 cup household liquid chlorine bleach to 4 cups water. Fill the utensil above the scorch marks and slowly bring to a boil. Discard the chlorine solution, wash the utensil as usual, then rinse and dry.

### Scorched Pots and Pans

To remove scorch marks, fill the pan with cold water and 2½ tablespoons of liquid chlorine bleach. Allow to soak for 2 to 3 hours. Discard the chlorine solution, rinse well and rub with an abrasive soap pad.

### Coffeepots

A good way to remove the film of coffee oils and residue that regular soap and detergents can't reach is to wash your glass or stainless steel (do not use this procedure for aluminum or it might damage the pot) in a solution of 3 tablespoons of baking soda in 1 quart of warm water. If you prefer, you can put the coffee maker through its regular boiling or percolating using the same solution in place of coffee, after first removing the aluminum basket or strainer. Rinse your coffeepot in hot water and dry it well. Don't immerse electric appliances in water unless the manufacturer specifically indicates that you may.

### Jugs, Jars, Vacuum Bottles, Etc.

Musty food containers can be made odor-free by washing as usual and then soaking in a mild solution of baking soda and warm water (2 tablespoons per quart). Rinse in plain, hot water and allow to air-dry. (Do not use this method on aluminum.)

### Electric Appliances

Unless you know for sure that your appliance is immersible, don't plunge it into water. Wipe clean with an absorbent towel, and fill with a mild detergent solution to which has been added 1½ tablespoons of Calgon. Boil briskly for several minutes, rinse, wash and dry as usual.

### Frying Pans

To cure a new skillet or frying pan (one that is not coated with Teflon), add 1 cup of vinegar and bring it to a boil. Tilt the skillet to make sure the vinegar washes up the sides. Drain the skillet, let cool and wipe dry. Rub in cooking oil, heat the skillet again and wipe clean.

### Grease Remover for Nonmetal Surfaces

A good grease-cutter for porcelain, plastic or glass kitchen surfaces (for example, your sink) is baking soda, because it scours without scratching. Sprinkle it on, scour with a damp cloth, rinse and let dry.

### To Clean Oily Bottles

Fill the bottle up one-third of the way with cool tap water mixed with several tablespoons of ammonia. Stopper the bottle and shake it until suds form, then drain and rinse several times with clean water.

### To Sterilize Glass, China and Porcelain Dishes

If there is sickness in the house, the patient's dishes may be sterilized by washing as usual and then soaking for 10 minutes in a liquid chlorine bleach solution (⅔ cup bleach per gallon of very hot water). Rinse as usual and air-dry.

### To Sterilize Metal Utensils

Wash as usual, scald with boiling water and allow to air-dry.

### A Good Dishwashing Solution

To make a good dishwashing solution, drop soap scraps and slivers into a jar half-filled with water and keep close to the sink.

### Washing Dishcloths

To wash dishcloths clean, first soak in a light ammonia solution.

### Soap Powder

To make your own soap powder, run leftover bits and pieces through your meat grinder. Wash thoroughly before grinding food.

### To Maintain Chopping and Carving Boards

You can keep your chopping boards from staining and getting waterlogged (which, when dry, will cause them to warp and splinter) by applying two or three coats of raw linseed oil. Let the linseed oil soak in a couple of hours, then wipe off any excess and rub the board with a coarse cloth. Repeat the procedure after 2 days or so, let the chopping board dry and it's ready for use. After long use, another application of linseed oil may be necessary. Generally, do not soak chopping boards in water or wash them in an automatic dishwasher; wipe them down to keep them clean.

### To Clean Chopping and Carving Boards

Mix ¼ cup salt with ¼ cup borax and vigorously rub over the board with a rough cloth. Wipe clean with a damp cloth.

## TO DEODORIZE, DISINFECT AND REMOVE STAINS

Kitchen sinks, dishes, tubs, basins and woodwork can be disinfected and deodorized with a solution of ¾ cup of liquid chlorine bleach per gallon of warm water. Wash with soap and water first and then wipe on the bleach solution. Keep stubborn stains wet for 5 or 10 minutes. (Do not use on bare metal surfaces and do not use a natural sponge to apply.)

### Refrigerator Deodorizer I

Remove food from the refrigerator and wash the walls, shelves and drawers with a solution of ⅓ cup chlorine bleach and 2 quarts warm water. Rinse all surfaces with plain warm water. Air for 15 or 20 minutes. Replace the food.

### Refrigerator Deodorizer II

Remove the food from the refrigerator and wash it well with a solution of ¼ cup baking soda mixed with 2 quarts warm water. Rinse with warm water. Replace the food, along with the open box of baking soda. Odors will be effectively absorbed for 2 months.

### Window and Mirror Cleaner

Keep a bottle of cold tea to clean mirrors, windowpanes and varnished surfaces. Use warm tea if there are flyspecks.

### Tarnish Remover I

Mix salt and water to form a paste. Use a soft cloth to remove tarnish from silver.

### Tarnish Remover II

Regular baking soda can be used in place of silver polish for removing tarnish. Rub the silver with baking soda until clean. This method takes a bit more effort but it does work.

### Tarnish Remover III

Rub with ammonia.

### To Make Polished Stainless Steel Shine

Moisten a soft cloth with several drops of baby oil. Wipe all surfaces with even strokes.

### Stainless Steel Cleanser

Remove persistent rust stains from stainless steel with lighter fluid and a soft rag.

### Improvised Copper Cleansers

Save lemon halves after the juice has been squeezed from them. When your copper needs cleaning, dip the cut side of the lemon half in salt and rub well.

If you have no lemons in the house and your copper pots need cleaning, try using toothpaste spread on a soft cloth.

Catsup is also a good substitute for commercial copper cleaners. Apply with a soft cloth.

### Chrome Cleaner

Baking soda and a dry cloth will usually give chrome a brilliant shine.

### To Freshen the Air in a Room

When the air in a room gets musty, set out an open dish of vinegar. For faster results, dip one end of a towel in vinegar and whirl around rapidly.

### Another Room Deodorizer

Get rid of stale tobacco odors by filling a large bowl with 3 quarts hot water and 1 cup of ammonia. Close all doors and windows and let the liquid stand overnight. Be sure the ammonia mixture is placed high enough so that pets and/or children cannot get into it.

### Removing Food Odors

Garlic, onion, cabbage or fish odors can be removed from your chopping board by washing the board thoroughly and then keeping it wet for 10 to 15 minutes with a solution of ¾ cup of liquid chlorine bleach per gallon of warm water. Rinse and dry well.

## MISCELLANEOUS HOUSEHOLD TIPS

### Quick and Easy Grease Solvent

*Use this instead of commercial grease solvent to remove grimy oil or grease from hands.*

½ Cup vegetable shortening
⅓ Cup cornmeal
¼ Cup powdered soap (not soap powder, which may be fortified)

Mix well and store in a jar with a lid.

### Hand Cleaner

To clean your hands easily after doing a greasy job, rub them with vaseline before you start to work.

### Natural Beauty Knee and Elbow Oil

*This is an oil for use as a hand-softening treatment inside rubber dishwashing gloves. This is quite greasy, though, so rub in well and avoid contact with clothing.*

(YIELD: ¼ CUP)

1½ Tablespoons sesame oil
1½ Tablespoons wheat-germ oil
1½ Tablespoons olive oil
Perfumed oil to your liking

Stir all the ingredients until well mixed and place in a clean jar or small bottle with a top.

### To Clean Piano Keys

To clean piano keys, use an alcohol-moistened cloth and wipe with a soft, dry cloth.

### Kitchen Lubricant

To lubricate eggbeaters, meat grinders and food choppers, use glycerin. It keeps oily tastes and smells from your food.

### Cedar Chest

To make a cedar chest out of any wooden box or chest, oil thoroughly once a year with oil of cedar; it will keep moths away as effectively as a real cedar chest.

### Mothproofing Drawers

Red cedar chips sewn into small cloth bags will keep moths out of drawers.

### Hot Water Bottles

To extend the life of a hot water bottle, rub a little glycerin into it occasionally.

### Tight Corks

To remove a tight cork, place a steaming hot dishrag around the neck of the bottle to expand the glass slightly.

### Poor Man's Paint Brush Cleaner

Soak paint-filled brushes in vinegar instead of expensive turpentine and then wash with hot water and liquid soap (see page 261). Blot with paper towels and let dry in a well-ventilated place.

### Gilt Frames

To clean gilt frames, use a soft brush to apply egg white. When dry, rub gently with a soft, clean flannel rag.

### To Waterproof Leather

To waterproof leather, combine 1 cup of tallow with ¼ cup of beeswax and melt over a very low flame. Mix in ½ cup of castor oil and, when cool, apply to any leather item you wish to waterproof.

### Leather Softener

To clean and soften stiff leather, apply 1 part vinegar and 2 parts linseed oil with a soft, clean cloth.

### Candle Cleaner

To clean decorative candles, wipe gently with absorbent cotton dipped in alcohol.

### Cleaner Hands

To keep your hands cleaner when working in the garden, rub soap under your fingernails and around your fingers. They will be much easier to clean afterwards.

### De-Wrinkler

To steam wrinkles out of clothes, hang over a bathtub half-filled with very hot water.

### Wall Cleaner for Painted Walls

Mix ¼ cup turpentine, ½ cup milk, 2 tablespoons liquid soap (see page 261) with 2 quarts hot water. Sponge the walls gently with the mixture. This gives a nice finish to flat or semigloss paint.

### Another Wall Cleaner

To clean painted walls, use a solution of 4 ounces of borax in 1 gallon of water to which 2 tablespoons of ammonia have been added. Do not use soap with this mixture. Wear rubber gloves.

### Hairbrush Cleaner

Comb all hair out of the brush. Mix ⅓ cup of household ammonia in 2 quarts of lukewarm water. Swish the brush across the surface of the water so that only the bristles are moistened. Do not dip the entire brush in the solution. Shake out the excess moisture and place, bristles down, on a towel to dry.

### Swimming Pool Disinfectant

Use 1 pint of liquid chlorine bleach for every 3,000 gallons of water (figure about 7½ gallons of water for every cubic foot of the size of your pool).

### Hi-Fi Record Cleaner

Wash the kitchen sink thoroughly without using any gritty cleansers. Rinse well. Mix 1½ tablespoons liquid soap (see page 261) and 3 gallons tepid water. Dip the record into the soapy water, taking care not to soak the label. Rub with a very soft cloth in the direction of the grooves. Rinse under tepid running tap water. Prop up on edge and allow to air-dry.

### Toilet Bowl Deodorizer

Place ⅓ cup liquid chlorine bleach in the bowl and brush well to eliminate stains. Never use in combination with any other toilet bowl deodorizer or cleanser. Ammonia and lye produce poisonous chlorine gas when mixed with chlorine bleach.

### Picture Hanging Wire

Hang pictures with plastic fishing line. It is very strong and nearly invisible.

### Fire Starters

For campfire, outdoor grill and fireplace starters, dip in melted paraffin wax short pieces of kindling, or sheets of newspaper folded in half and tightly rolled. To be on the safe side, always melt the paraffin in a double boiler, never over an open fire.

### Another Fire Kindler

Here is a fire kindler that will burn hot enough to get a roaring fire going every time. In a double boiler melt 1 pound of resin to which has been added 3 ounces of tallow. When the mixture is melted, stir in enough pine sawdust to make a very thick mixture and spread out on an old board or similar surface on which you have sprinkled sawdust (to keep the mixture from sticking). Score into approximately 1-inch squares with an old knife and break into blocks when cool and hard.

### To Make Your Own Canned Heat

Roll up a 1-inch strip of cardboard, insert in an old tuna or salmon can and pour melted paraffin over the cardboard and into the can to a depth of about ½ inch. Store until needed. When the paraffin is ignited, it burns with a fairly intense heat for a long period of time.

### Washing Pets

Mix some Calgon with the soap in your dog's bath water. For the first and second rinse, use plain Calgon, then rinse with plain water. Your dog's coat will be soft and glossy.

### For Fleas

Scatter pine needles in your dog's bed to drive away fleas.

### To Clean Eyeglasses

A solution of a scant ¼ teaspoon water-softening agent mixed with 1 cup of water will keep your eyeglasses shining clean. Just dip, rinse and dry.

### To Polish Sunglasses

To polish sunglasses, protective eye shields, motorcycle face shields, and so on, that have been lightly scratched, polish gently with ordinary toothpaste and a soft rag or paper towel.

### Super Soap Bubbles

To blow super strong soap bubbles, add a teaspoonful of glycerin to a glass of soapy water for large, strong, super-elastic bubbles.

### For Quick Pouring of Liquids

To pour liquids from narrow-necked bottles quickly, turn the bottle upside down and swirl it rapidly with a circular motion. The liquid is thrown to the sides of the bottle, creating a funnel through which the air enters while the liquid pours freely out the sides. Once the liquid has started to pour you may stop swirling the bottle.

### Soft-Water Bath with No Bathtub Ring

Dissolve several tablespoons of Calgon in your bath water. Soap or bubble bath will produce luxuriant lather and leave no bathtub ring.

### To Clean Fresh Red Wine Stains from Napkins and Tablecloths

Immediately throw wine-stained napkins or tablecloth into a glass, stainless or enamelware pot containing enough mixture of fresh milk and water to amply cover the stained area and bring to a steady boil. Maintain heat (but do not allow to boil over) for 3 to 4 minutes, or until the stain has completely disappeared.

This procedure works wonderfully on fresh red wine stains and probably will do well on older wine stains and on other types of wine stains as well. (See pages 226–33 for more detailed stain-removing information.)

### To Remove Fresh Coffee Stains

The boiled milk procedure outlined above works well on coffee stains, too! If you ever have the problem, try it and see!

### Better Way to Clean Venetian Blinds

Put on a pair of old cotton gloves, dip your hands into a bucket of lukewarm water to which ¼ cup of ammonia has been added and rub your fingers along and beneath the slats of your Venetian blinds, shutters or jalousies. Wash your gloves frequently and dry your blinds as you finish washing them.

### To Keep Putty from Drying Out

Place a piece of linseed-oil-soaked rag on top of the putty in its jar or can and seal tightly.

### To Keep Tobacco Moist

Place some thick, fresh apple parings in with your tobacco.

### Improvised Pincushion

Use a bar of soap as a safe place to keep pins and needles. If you are sewing through tough fabric or leather, keep your needle lubricated with soap for easier stitching.

### To Thaw Pipes Frozen Just Beneath the Surface of the Ground

Scatter quicklime on the ground around the pipe, wet with water and cover the area with old burlap sacks. The heat generated by the chemical action of the lime and water will soon thaw the frozen pipe.

### To Keep Batteries Fresher Longer

Wrap fresh flashlight and radio batteries as tightly as you can in polyethylene sheet or bags, seal well (the object is to make a moisture-proof wrap) and place in your freezer. When ready to use, allow to warm up to room temperature while still wrapped. According to scientific tests, storage at 0 degrees F. or below will cut down the normal rate of energy loss to a remarkable degree.

### Soft Water

To soften water safely and economically, use washing soda.

### Fishy Odors

To rid utensils of fishy odors, place 1 tablespoonful of baking soda in the dishwater.

### More Efficient Radiators

To get greater warmth from radiators, place aluminum foil, shiny side out, behind each one, to reflect heat into the room.

### Oiling Locks

To oil a stiff lock, dip the key in oil and insert into the lock. Repeat several times.

### Rubber Gloves

To slip into rubber gloves more easily, sprinkle in a bit of cornstarch or talcum powder.

### Bathroom Mirrors

To keep bathroom mirrors from clouding up, rub on a light coating of glycerin.

### Cleaning Wallpaper

To remove wallpaper stains, rub with a ball of soft white bread or an artgum eraser.

### Tying Packages

To tie a firm package, first wet your twine thoroughly, and then tie.

### Softening Shoes

To soften water-hardened shoes and boots, pat with a kerosene-soaked rag.

### Bathroom Rings

To remove stubborn rings around the tub, use a rag lightly wetted with kerosene. Then wipe away odors with soapy water.

### Saving Electricity

To save electricity, use 1 bulb of higher wattage in place of several smaller ones. One 100-watt bulb, for example, will throw substantially more light than 2 50s and cost far less.

### Shoe Polish

To save wax shoe polish, combine same-color remnants into one can, hold over low heat and the small bits will melt into a new cake.

### More Light from Bulbs

To get maximum efficiency from light bulbs, keep them, shades and reflectors clean and dust-free.

### To Boil Water Faster

The boiling point of water is raised by the addition of salt to the water. Used in the outer pot of a double boiler, food will cook faster and save fuel.

### Washing Produce

For very soiled fruits, berries and vegetables not very efficiently cleaned in plain water, soak in a solution of water and Calgon (1 tablespoon of Calgon per gallon of water). This will safely remove most soil and insecticide residues. After soaking for 5 minutes, rinse in plain water. For sandy vegetables, mushrooms and salad greens, for example, this method is most effective.

### Nut Meats

Soak unshelled nuts 4 or 5 hours in salted water and you'll have no trouble getting the nut meats out in one piece. Salt keeps the meats from losing flavor, while the water expands the shells.

### Great Percolator Coffee

To make a hearty cup of percolator coffee, bring fresh, clear water to a boil in a clean percolator with the basket removed. Meanwhile measure 2 level tablespoons of coffee per cup of water into the basket. When the water has boiled, set the basket into the pot, cover, and percolate slowly for 7 minutes. Remove the basket and serve. (For still stronger coffee, measure 2 tablespoons per ¾ cup of water.)

### Self-Basting Roasts

To have roasts baste themselves, place the meat in pot, fat side up.

### Salt Shakers

To keep salt flowing, keep one or two dozen grains of uncooked rice in the shaker.

### To Keep Pancakes from Sticking

If you rub your griddle with salt prior to using, pancakes will have less tendency to stick.

### Coating Foods Easily

To coat chicken parts with flour (or doughnuts with sugar, or fish slices with meal, etc.), place small quantity of flour or meal into brown paper bag, add the food, bunch the top closed, and shake.

### Cocoa

To cook smoother cocoa, start in a little bit of water and then add the milk.

### Apple Pies

To perk up apple pies, sprinkle the apple slices with lemon juice before the top crust is placed in position.

### Broiling Foods Faster

To broil foods faster and save fuel, remove from the refrigerator in advance, cover, and allow to reach room temperature before broiling.

### To Save Fuel I

To save gas or electricity and enjoy more tender meat, cook longer over a low flame.

### To Save Fuel II

To save time and fuel, cook vegetables in the bottom half of a double boiler while you cook or heat sauce in the upper pan.

### Mixing Cakes Easily

To mix a cake efficiently, allow all ingredients to reach room temperature before you begin.

### Preserving Freshness

To keep homemade cake fresher longer, keep half an apple in the cake box with it.

### Saving Vitamins

To save vitamins and other nutrients in clean, naturally dried fruits, utilize the water in which they have been soaked. For example, always stew prunes in their soaking water.

### Sweetening Used Fats

To sweeten used cooking oils and fat, boil a cut-up potato in it and then strain.

### Removing Excess Salt

To remove excess salt from your stew, add a quartered potato or two and continue cooking. Taste the potato before serving and discard if it is too salty.

### Juicier Lemons

To get more juice out of a lemon, heat it in a hot water bath before squeezing.

### Tastier Eggs

To get the best results with eggs and egg dishes, always cook at a slow, gentle heat.

### Slicing Pie

To cut a meringue pie, dip the knife in cold water before using.

### Golden-Brown French Fries

To give fried potatoes a lovely golden brown, blot dry and sprinkle very lightly with flour before frying.

### Slicing Angel Cake

To slice angel cake, carefully break apart with the tines of two forks instead of cutting with a knife.

### Avoiding Discoloration

To keep sliced or diced mushrooms, apples and bananas from discoloring, sprinkle with a little lemon juice.

### Tender White Chicken

To tenderize chicken and make the meat white and juicy, dip in lemon juice before cooking.

### Better Rice

To help keep rice grains separated when boiling, add a teaspoon of lemon juice per cup of rice.

### Creaming Butter

To cream butter and sugar more easily when the butter is hard, heat the sugar slightly.

### Freshening Meat

If meat has an off odor but is unspoiled, remove the odor by rubbing on baking soda and then rinsing thoroughly in cold water.

### Measuring Shortening

To measure shortening exactly, try this.

If you require ¼ cup shortening, fill your measuring cup three-quarters full of cold water. Include an ice cube. Now add enough shortening to bring water to the 1 cup level and you have measured precisely ¼ cup shortening! Pour off the water and ice.

### Softening Brown Sugar

To soften brown sugar that has become hard and lumpy, place in a closed container with half an apple for a couple of days. For quicker results, wet a paper towel, wring out thoroughly, place in the box with the sugar, close the cover and refrigerate.

### To Make Sour Milk

To make sour milk for cooking or baking, add 2 tablespoons of vinegar per cup of warm sweet milk. Let stand for several minutes and use wherever recipe calls for sour or buttermilk. (One tablespoon of lemon juice per cup of milk works well, too!)

## HOUSE PLANTS AND GARDEN

### Hanging Basket

To make a novel hanging basket, cut off the top 4 inches of a large carrot, hollow out the center, push a toothpick horizontally through the cut edge and hang it, top down, in a sunny place. Fill the hollow with water and in a short time lovely leaves will cover the carrot.

### Soapsuds Fertilizer

Soapsuds from real soap make a good fertilizer for shrubbery and young plants.

### Potting Cactus

Your cactus will like soil into which 2 heaping tablespoons of charcoal per quart have been mixed.

### House Plant Fertilizer

To make a good house plant fertilizer, let egg shells stand in water for 3 or 4 days and then use the water on plants.

### Watering House Plants

To water house plants properly, do not water daily. Water thoroughly and then let the soil dry out on top before watering again.

### Greener Ferns

To fertilize ferns and make them grow faster and look greener, mix milk into their water every 2 weeks.

### Egg-Shell Flower Pots

To plant seedlings, start in loam-filled egg-shell halves. To make handling easier, keep in egg cartons and transplant each seedling right in the egg shell.

### To Make Cut Flowers Last Longer I

To keep cut flowers fresh longer, drop a lump of sugar into their water.

### To Make Cut Flowers Last Longer II

Mix 2 tablespoons of liquid chlorine bleach per quart of the water into which your flowers are placed. The bleach not only retards the growth of bacteria, enabling your flowers to stay fresh longer, but it intensifies the colors of chrysanthemums and orchids, keeps some flowers from fading and does wonders for roses.

### Rose Rejuvenator

Ordinary soot gathered from fireplaces or chimneys where wood is burned makes a fabulous picker-upper for rose bushes. Place the soot in a bowl or pitcher, dissolve in hot water, cool and use to water your rose bushes every other day or so.

### To Keep Fall Leaves Indoors

Fall foliage will retain its color and vitality longer if you dip the cut ends in melted beeswax.

### To Test Seeds

Seeds will float if placed on the surface of water before they are ripe, and conversely will sink to the bottom if they are sufficiently mature for planting.

### To Change the Color of Red Roses

Work out of doors or in a well-ventilated garage. Place a small mound of sulfur on an old tin plate and hang half a dozen moist red roses with flowers about 4 or 5 inches above the sulfur. Light the sulfur and place an old carton over all. The fumes will turn the roses to variegated pinks and whites.

### To Dye Cut Flowers

Ordinary fabric dyes will produce amusing and sometimes extraordinary color changes in cut flowers. White flowers can become almost any color, yellows become orange or green, pinks and reds become purple, and so on. Simply mix your dye with plain water, cut flower stems at a slant, then immerse your flowers in the usual fashion.

## LAUNDRY AND CLOTHES-CLEANING TIPS

### Soft Blankets

To keep your blankets soft and fluffy, soak in a warm borax and white soap solution for an hour or so. Rinse gently without wringing and hang in the sun to dry. When dry, beat well with a rug beater (or a clean broomstick) on both sides.

### Dingy Curtains

To perk up dingy lace or muslin curtains, boil for half an hour in equal parts of milk and water to which fine laundry soap has been added.

### To Keep Colors from Running

To keep light-colored tie-dyed clothes from running or fading, add one teaspoonful of epsom salts to each gallon of wash water.

### To Keep Clothes from Freezing on Line

To keep clothes from freezing if you hang them out to dry in winter, add approximately half a cup of salt to your rinse water.

Never fold clothing that has been hung out to dry in freezing weather right away. Thaw them first or they may crack.

### Wash Day Tips

Large pieces (sheets, slipcovers, etc.) will dry more quickly if you hang them over parallel clotheslines.

"Drip-drys" should be hung up dripping wet. The water removes the wrinkles.

### Glove Cleaner

To clean a spot on white kid gloves, try a bit of alcohol. It leaves no after-odor and it dries quickly.

### Washing Gloves

Put on your cloth gloves and wash your hands with pure white soap, scrub well, rinse thoroughly and hang up to dry.

### Snow-White Linens

For 1 hour prior to washing, soak your white linens in cold soft water to which cream of tartar has been added (1 teaspoonful per gallon of water).

### Chamois

To wash chamois without having it turn stiff and cardboardlike, follow this procedure. Wash in a mild soap and water solution and do not rinse it or wring it dry; instead let it drip until fairly dry and then rub it well with a bath towel, just the way you would towel-dry your hair. Hang the slightly damp chamois in an airy place that is out of the sun.

# SOAPMAKING
# AT HOME

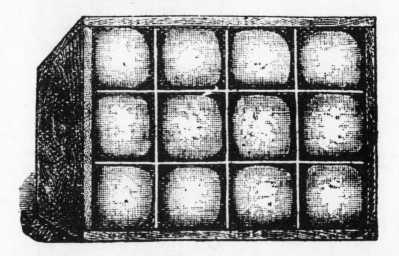

Long before corner drugstores were a part of our American scene, before bulging supermarket shelves became a way of life, even before general stores carried the brown, unwrapped bars, soapmaking was a household task practiced on a regular basis by most homemakers. Today, soaring costs, coupled with the back-to-basics trend, have caused many contemporary householders to return to homey activities practiced by our early American ancestors. Home soapmaking is one such activity.

One of the most gratifying aspects of making your own soap is putting to use those messy leftover fats that clog drains and leak through garbage bags to make slippery puddles on the kitchen floor. You're sure to feel a little pleased with yourself (and rightfully so) when you see your own-made soap stacked up on the shelf, and know it once would have been thrown away with the trash. The money you save by making your own soap is *really* found money!

Soapmaking is not difficult; once you've had a little practice and mastered a few essential techniques, you'll find it easy to turn out a suitable soap for any home purpose.

## INGREDIENTS FOR SOAPMAKING

FATS: These are the most important of the ingredients that go into making soap. The quality of any soap depends on the kind or condition of the fat used. Tallow or lard, or a combination of these two fats, produce best-quality soap. Poultry fats and vegetable oils are also suitable, although they tend to produce a softer, spongy soap unless they are mixed with other fats. Rancid or dirty kitchen fats or those that have been salted or flavored during cooking should be avoided. Fats from very lean cuts of meat should not be used either.

Fresh, clean fat rendered from tallow, pork rinds or uncooked meat trimmings can be made into soap without any further preparation. Waste fat left over from cooking will need to be clarified before soapmaking proceeds. Collect waste fat over a period of time and store it in the refrigerator until ready to use.

To clarify waste fat, melt it slowly in a large kettle, then strain it through several thicknesses of cheesecloth. Measure how many pints of fat are left after straining, place the fat in a clean kettle, and add an equal amount of hot water. Stir the mixture briefly, allow it to come to a boil, and remove it from the heat. Add 4 cups of cold water and allow the kettle to remain undisturbed until the fat cools. The clean fat that rises to the top and firms as the mixture cools is now ready to make into soap.

LYE: The lye, which is combined with water and added to the fat, should be pure flake lye, available from your grocer. Lye in flake form dissolves much faster than does powdered lye. It also comes in convenient 13-ounce containers, just the right amount necessary for the basic soap formula. Never, *ever*, use the lye designed for cleaning drains.

BORAX: Borax is an optional ingredient in soapmaking. Its chief value is to improve the appearance and sudsing action of your soap.

WATER: The water used in soapmaking should be soft. Rainwater is ideal. If the water in your tap is hard, it can be softened if 1 to 2 tablespoons of lye (depending on the hardness of the water) are first mixed into every gallon. This lye-and-water mixture should be prepared at least 48 hours in advance of the soapmaking, so that the hardness has time to settle out.

## SOAPMAKING EQUIPMENT

You will probably find that most of the equipment you will need for making soap is already tucked away somewhere in your kitchen.

KETTLES AND POTS: A kettle of enamel, iron, stainless steel or glass is the only kind of cooking pot suitable to use in soapmaking. The larger the better—minimum size is 8 quarts. Don't use aluminum pots; lye will corrode them. In fact, the use of aluminum should be avoided during all steps of the soapmaking process. A glass or enamel pot with a long handle is excellent for mixing the lye solution.

LONG-HANDLED SPOONS: Either wooden or enamel ones will enable you to stir your soap without danger from burns.

THERMOMETER: This is essential, as correct temperatures are extremely important in making soap. Use the dairy or floating type. One for each pot is helpful to have.

SCALE: Since measurements in soapmaking are precise, a scale comes in very handy.

SOAP MOLDS: To mold the soap you may utilize shallow cardboard or wooden boxes. A shallow enamel pan will also do very nicely. Line the boxes or pans with waxed paper, plastic wrap or a clean cotton cloth first dipped in cold water and then wrung dry. Always prepare your molds with liners in advance of soapmaking, so they'll be ready when needed.

## SAFETY MEASURES

· It is essential that you take adequate care to protect yourself during the soapmaking process. Lye is extremely caustic. Avoid contact of either dry lye or the lye solution with your skin or clothing.

· Wear rubber gloves every step of the way.

· Keep a couple of heavy potholders close by.

· Cover your clothing with an oversized rubber or heavy plastic apron.

· Spread newspapers over your work surfaces and floor.

If, despite your precautions, contact with lye does occur, wash immediately and thoroughly with clear water and then follow by rinsing with diluted vinegar. Call the doctor if you are at all uneasy.

## ADDITIONAL HINTS ON SOAPMAKING

### Fats

Tallow (beef or sheep fat), lard, tallow and lard combinations, olive oil and vegetable oils are the best fats to use (in the order given).

Render your rinds and meat scraps as soon as possible, and store the extracted fat in a tightly covered container in a cool, dry place. When enough is accumulated, plan a day for soap-making.

Fats used in soapmaking should be pure and clean. *Do not use old, rancid or salted fats.*

Always measure your fats accurately. Amounts given in the recipes are by weight. For your convenience you might like to know that 6 pounds of fat equals 6¾ pints, or 13½ cups, of liquid fat.

---

## Lye

In using lye, too, measurements are exceedingly important. Too much lye will make a coarse, crumbly soap.

To repeat, lye reacts upon aluminum, so glass, enamel, cast-iron or stainless steel are the best utensils to use.

---

## Temperatures

Fats and the lye solution must come together (saponify) at the exact temperature called for in the recipe. Therefore, a floating or dairy thermometer is essential. One thermometer for the fat plus one for the lye solution will make your soapmaking much easier.

Different types of fat require different temperatures. Lye solution temperatures also vary according to the type and temperature of the fat used. The following chart may be helpful:

| Types of Fat | Temperature of Fats | Temperature of Lye Solution |
| --- | --- | --- |
| Sweet lard or other soft fats | 80° F.– 85° F. | 70° F.–75° F. |
| Half lard and half tallow | 100° F.–110° F. | 80° F.–85° F. |
| All tallow | 120° F.–130° F. | 90° F.–95° F. |

---

## Aging

Properly prepared soap should be smooth and lustrous when aged, with no bite when touched to the tongue.

Age your soap in a spot free from drafts and cold. Soap that has been exposed to cold during the aging process will turn hard and brittle, and will not lather properly. But do make sure that air has a chance to circulate freely.

Soap made from lard, or soap that has been reclaimed by boiling, needs to age longer than usual before it is ready to use.

Soap that is not neutral (in which the lye is not well incorporated) has a bite when touched to the tongue. Don't handle soap that has separated in this manner. Wear your rubber gloves, cut the soap into small pieces and reboil it as directed on page ooo. Take care—recycled soap boils over easily.

## LAUNDRY SOAP

The following recipe is designed to make 9 pounds of pure, hard, smooth soap, suitable for laundry use. Instructions for making toilet soaps are given later in this chapter.

---

### Basic Laundry Soap

(NOTE: All ounces for this and the recipes that follow are avoirdupois—by weight—not fluid ounces, so get out your household scale.)

> 6 Pounds clean fat (about 13½ cups liquid fat)
> ¼ Cup borax (optional)
> 1 13-ounce can pure flake lye
> 2½ Pints water

Weigh or measure the clean fat, heat slowly over a low flame until completely melted and cool to approximately 110 degrees F. If desired, add the borax at this point. Stir the fat from time to time while it is cooling so that crystals do not form.

Meanwhile, dissolve the lye in the water. A lot of heat will be generated at the outset, so the lye solution will need time to cool down to about 85 degrees F. Keep your face away from the pot as you pour the lye into the water—the solution can get very hot.

When both the fat and the lye solution reach the prescribed temperatures, the time has arrived to mix them together. Some extra finesse is required for this maneuver, since the lye solution cannot be added too fast or too slowly to the fat. Ideally, this solution should be poured in a thin, steady stream as you slowly stir the kettle of fat with a steady, continuous motion. (Get someone to help you if you can.) I keep a large glass coffeepot for just this purpose. The spout, rested on the rim of the soapmaking kettle, helps to regulate the flow of lye solution so that it does not pour in too quickly. A piece of improvised equipment that works as well is a 2-quart glass bottle with a tight, unbent cap in which two holes have been punctured, one opposite the other. Pour the lye solution into the bottle and seal the cap tightly. The stream from the bottle should have just about the correct flow. However, test the bottle method beforehand by pouring plain water into the sink to make sure it works properly.

This adding of lye solution in a thin, steady stream while stirring the fat is really the most important step in soapmaking, so don't rush. Rapid addition of the lye solution or too vigorous stirring may cause separation.

Continue your slow, steady, round-the-pot stirring even after the lye solution has been absorbed. Occasionally run your spoon through the center of the mixture, but do not scrape in any of the dried bits that stick to the top of the sides of the pot. Soon the consistency of the soap will become thick and honeylike. This may take as little as 10, or as long as 20, minutes. If you've been stirring for longer than 20 minutes, and you notice there is a greasy-looking layer on top, the soap mixture may be too warm. Set your kettle in a pan of cool water and continue to stir from the sides and bottom until the mixture thickens to the aforementioned honeylike consistency. On the other hand, should you observe that the soap mixture is lumpy, it may not be warm enough. To remedy this, set the kettle in a pan of very warm water and stir until the lumps disappear and the mixture becomes smooth.

As soon as your soap mixture is the proper color and consistency, it may be poured into your previously readied molds. Set the filled molds in a pan or on a tray, cover with a board or with cardboard, and further insulate with a wool blanket. The heat must be retained so that the soap cools slowly. What was once a soupy, unpleasant-looking mixture will begin to harden into creamy bars of soap. Allow the molds to stand undisturbed for 24 hours, then lift the bars out of the molds by the overlapping edges of the mold liners. Any large bars that emerge from plain molds can be cut into smaller cakes by wrapping them with a fine wire at measured intervals and pulling the wire through the soap.

Once your soap has been cut into the desired size, it *must* be aged for at least two weeks to harden and allow the air to react to any lye not previously incorporated. Place your soap in a spot where the bars will be free from drafts and cold, but arrange them so that air can circulate around them. (For large bars use wire racks salvaged from a discarded oven. Smaller bars fit nicely on racks from old roasting pans.)

You may find that your bars of soap are crumbly or streaked with grease after they are aged, that some of the grease has risen to the top or that there are small blisters of liquid lye solution present. This indicates that separation has taken place at some point in the soapmaking procedure, and that the soap *must* be reprocessed. What went wrong? And when? And why?

Ask yourself these questions: Could the temperature of the fat or the lye solution have been too hot, or too cool? Was I stirring too energetically or too lazily? Did I inadvertently use rancid fat, or fat containing salt?

Whatever the cause, all is not lost—imperfect soap can be reclaimed. Wearing rubber gloves, cut or shave the bars into fine pieces over your soap kettle. Carefully save and add to the kettle any lye solution that has separated out. Add 7 pints of water and melt the soap over low heat, stirring occasionally. As soon as all the lumps have disappeared, increase the heat and gently boil the mixture until it turns thick and forms a syrupy trail when dropped from a spoon. Pour once again into prepared molds and proceed as you did initially.

### Variations

The preceding basic soap recipe is suitable for all home uses. The bars you make can be made to float by simply folding air into your mixture (as you would fold an egg white into a cake) before pouring the soap into the molds. Your soap may be perfumed and colored as you like it. It can be used as is, as laundry soap or shredded into flakes or powder. With a few variations or substitutions of ingredients you can readily produce enough different varieties of soaps to satisfy every need. If you're feeling particularly creative, try cutting the soap into unusual shapes before aging it. Soap that seems soft enough when it's taken from the mold can be rolled into ovals or balls. (Be sure to wear your rubber gloves!)

PERFUMING THE SOAP: Soap easily absorbs odors. Perfume yours by adding any one of the following scents to your basic recipe: 4 teaspoons oil of sassafras, 2 teaspoons oil of wintergreen, 2 teaspoons citronella, 2 teaspoons oil of lavender, 1 teaspoon oil of cloves or 1 teaspoon oil of lemon. Your drugstore can probably supply these. Take care, though, that the scent you use contains no alcohol. Just add your favorite to the soap mixture immediately prior to pouring it into the molds. Stir the scent in evenly and thoroughly.

COLORING THE SOAP: Color adds another dimension to soapmaking. Stir the tints into the soap mixture just before it is poured into the molds. Fluorescein for yellow, Nathol Green for green, and Rhodamine for red are tints generally available in drugstores. Perhaps your druggist can recommend other suitable dyes. And don't overlook colorings from nature. You can extract pinks from tulips or roses and a nice green tint from squeezing beet greens. The trick in coloring soap is to add color *gradually* to the soap mixture. Unless strong colors are your heart's desire, work with small amounts of dye mixed with 2 tablespoons of water until the soap mixture takes on a satisfactory tint. Like the perfumes used in soap, never use any color in soapmaking that contains alcohol. Alcohol fades colors and may cause the soap to separate.

## Soap Flakes or Powdered Soap

The basic recipe makes a fine laundry soap, but you may find flakes or powder useful at times. In this case, pour the soap into bars and allow these to age for only three days, then reduce the soap to flakes with a vegetable shredder. Stir the flakes once in a while as they continue to dry. To produce powdered soap, place the shredded flakes in long glass baking dishes and dry in a warm oven (about 150 degrees F.). When the flakes are thoroughly dry, pulverize them into powder.

Adding borax to the basic recipe will generate sudsing action in laundry soap, flakes or powdered soap.

## Abrasive Hand Soap and Pastes

A good abrasive hand soap effective in removing grease or deeply embedded dirt can be made from the basic soap recipe. Gradually add 5 to 6 pounds of finely ground pumice stone, emery dust or tripoli powder to your thickened soap mixture. Stir until all ingredients are thoroughly blended, then pour into molds and proceed as directed. Don't forget that the volume of soap has been increased, so you'll need to prepare more molds.

To make an abrasive soap paste, take 1½ pounds of Basic Laundry Soap (see page 258) and shred it into pieces. Place the pieces in a kettle, add 3 cups of water and heat only long enough to melt the soap. Blend in 3 ounces of light mineral oil, then remove from the heat and allow to cool. When the mixture thickens nicely, add 2½ pounds of finely ground pumice stone or tripoli powder, mixing it in well until it is thoroughly absorbed. Store the paste in tightly covered jars when not in use, to keep it from drying out.

A small amount of powdered soap can also be combined with other ingredients to produce a paste hand soap designed to eradicate grease and grime. Stir 8 ounces of powdered soap (see above) into 16 ounces of water and allow it to dissolve. Mix 1½ ounces of washing (sal) soda, 2 ounces of borax and ¾ ounce of glycerin with 4½ ounces of water until dissolved. Combine the two mixtures, then thoroughly blend in 10 ounces of powdered pumice.

A variation of the above combination can be achieved by increasing the amounts of washing soda and pumice and using less powdered soap. Pour 30 ounces of water into your soap kettle and place over a low flame. As soon as the water heats, add 4 ounces of powdered soap, 3 ounces of washing soda, and ¾ ounce of borax. Allow these ingredients to dissolve. Stir in ¾ ounce of glycerin, continuing to stir constantly until the mixture thickens, then keep up the stirring while you gradually add 15 ounces of powdered pumice. When the mixture is thick and smooth enough to keep the pumice from settling, pack it into jars and seal it tightly so it won't dry out.

### Soap Powders

At this point it might be useful to mention the basic differences between powdered soap and soap powder. Powdered soap can be made as directed previously from either homemade or purchased bar soap, and consists only of soap. Soap powder, on the other hand, is powdered soap to which varying amounts of alkaline chemicals have been added.

### Dry Hand Powder

A satisfactory dry hand powder that cleans the skin but is not at all harsh can be made by mixing 24 ounces of powdered soap with 12 ounces of fine cornmeal, 18 ounces of powdered borax, and 2¼ ounces of sodium perborate. Put this mixture through an ordinary flour sifter. Repeat this procedure several times. Store the soap until needed in a jar with a shaker top. Wet your hands, sprinkle on an adequate amount of the powdered soap—*et voilà!* Clean hands!

For really rough clean-up jobs, try a slightly different recipe. To 12 ounces of powdered soap, add 15 ounces of fine sawdust, 1½ ounces of borax, and 1½ ounces of trisodium phosphate. Mix thoroughly by shaking through a flour sifter.

### Jellied Soap

Your own jellied soap for washing dishes or clothes can be made in a matter of minutes. Shave 3 pounds of basic soap (see page 258) into your soap kettle. Add 4 quarts of water and bring to a boil. Boil for 10 minutes, then allow to cool until the mixture forms a jelly. Store tightly covered in jars or tins until needed. Be sure to include borax in the basic soap recipe if you want lots of sudsing action.

### Liquid Soap

Soap flakes or powdered soap may be easily converted into a convenient and inexpensive liquid soap suitable for almost any household use, from washing dishes to shampooing your hair. Heat some water in your soap kettle and dissolve in it just enough soap flakes or powdered soap (see page 260) to make a thick paste. Remove the soap paste from the heat, measure it and return it to the kettle. One cup of ethyl rubbing alcohol mixed with 2 cups of warm water should be added to every quart of paste. Mix thoroughly and pour into bottles.

### Rosin Soap

Rosin soap, a good laundry soap with extra lathering power, can be made by slightly varying the basic soap recipe. Begin with only 5 pounds of clean fat and add 1 pound of crushed rosin. Heat the mixture until the rosin is melted or dissolved, then allow it to cool to 100 degrees F. Dissolve 13 ounces (1 can) of lye in 2½ pints of water as directed in the basic formula, but cool the solution to 90 degrees F. Stir the lye solution into the fat-and-rosin mixture and proceed as directed. The result will be a darker and softer soap.

### Saddle Soap

A practical soap for cleaning and preserving leather is the saddle soap you can make by varying the basic soap formula a bit. Use 5 pounds mutton or beef fat, 1 pound coconut oil and 1 13-ounce can of lye. Mix the lye with 2¾ pints of water. The fat and oil should be heated as directed in the basic soap recipe except that the temperatures for both the fat and the lye solution should be a little hotter: 130 degrees F. for the fat and 90 degrees F. for the lye solution when the two are mixed together.

### Linseed Oil Soap

The rapidly accelerating price of linseed oil has made this soap something of a luxury, but the recipe is such a good one I feel I must include it. This linseed oil soap is ideal for washing your car or furniture, since it is soft and particularly easy to apply. Use 1½ pounds of linseed oil and bring it to 100 degrees F. Meanwhile mix 3¼ ounces of lye with 1 pint of water. When the lye solution reaches 90 degrees F., stir it very gradually into the linseed oil. Take care that the amount you have added is well combined with the oil before adding more.

## TOILET SOAPS

While properly made Basic Laundry Soap makes an effective household cleaning agent, improperly made homemade soap will sometimes contain enough free alkali to be undesirable as a toilet soap. For this reason it is important to follow directions *carefully*, age the soap for a sufficient length of time and use one bar from a fresh batch of soap on your hands before you try it on your face. (If you have any doubts that the soap is properly made, do not use it on your face!) If this bar seems to be mild and even in texture your soap is probably correctly made and you may use it as you like. The following toilet soaps are made from high-grade fats to produce superior results.

### Pure Vegetable Soap

Pure vegetable soap is easy to make from the canned shortening available from your grocer's shelf. Weigh out 24 ounces of pure vegetable shortening, 40 ounces of olive oil and 20 ounces of coconut oil and heat in your soap kettle. Meanwhile, dissolve 10½ ounces of pure flake lye in 2 pints of water. Add the lye solution to the melted fats when both are at 96 degrees F. Pour the thickened mixture into molds and age slightly longer than you would with the basic soap recipe—10 days or 2 weeks' further aging is about right.

### Three-Oil Soap

This soap contains vegetable oils combined with lard to produce a high-grade soap. Weigh out

32 ounces of lard, 24 ounces of coconut oil, 20 ounces of olive oil and 9 ounces of castor oil, and heat in your soap kettle. Mix 11½ ounces of pure flake lye with 2 pints of water to make up your lye solution, and add it to the heated fats when both are at 96 degrees F. Pour into molds when the mixture is thick and honeylike. Aging this soap for up to 4 weeks will improve its quality.

### Coconut Oil Soap

Coconut oil soap is serviceable for either bath or shampoo. Heat 4 pounds of coconut oil with 8 ounces of tallow. Mix 1 13-ounce can of pure flake lye with 2½ pints of water. The oil should be 110 degrees F. and the lye solution 70 degrees F. before adding the latter. You'll get copious quantities of rather thin lather from this soap.

### Imitation Castile Soap

Imitation castile soap is a high-grade soap that in many ways is superior to the real article. This recipe calls for 38 ounces of good-grade tallow to be combined with 24 ounces each of olive oil and coconut oil. Weigh the fats out carefully before placing in your soapmaking kettle. Use 2 pints of water to 13 ounces (1 can) of pure flake lye to make up your lye solution. Have both the fats and lye solution at 90 degrees F. before pouring the latter into the fat. Proceed as directed in the basic soap recipe (see page 000).

### Easy and Unusual Toilet Soaps

If you feel like experimenting with soap but haven't the time to start from scratch, try scenting and coloring pure white bar soap to suit your mood.

WINDSOR SOAP: An old-fashioned recipe for making your own Windsor soap directs that new white bar soap be shaved into thin slices, placed in a soap kettle and melted with a bit of water over low heat. Add oil of caraway (or oil of lemon if you like) to scent the soap as it melts. When smooth and syrupy, pour into molds and age for a week, then cut into small squares or roll into small balls and wrap in brightly colored cellophane, twisting each end of the paper to resemble a "candy kiss."

VARIEGATED TOILET SOAP: A soap with brilliantly hued streaks results from the following nineteenth-century recipe:

Bring 3 quarts of "soft" water to a boil. Meanwhile, shred 3 pounds of white toilet soap. Stir the soap into the water, along with 1½ ounces of washing (sal) soda, as it begins to boil. Heat only long enough for the soap to dissolve, then remove the kettle from the flame and stir in ½ ounce of oil of sassafras. Measure 2 cups of the melted soap and divide into separate bowls. To one of the bowls add as much Chinese vermilion "as will lie on a five-cent piece," and stir until thoroughly mixed. Blend a like amount of Chinese blue into the contents of the second bowl. Return the colored cups of soap to the kettle, one at a time, taking care not to stir either color in more than 2 or 3 times after adding it in order to achieve the desired streaks of color. Pour the mixture into molds and proceed as directed. Other colors, usually available in drugstores, may be substituted for the vermilion and blue.

## OTHER USES FOR SOAP

Grandmother used soap to make her life easier in general. Some of her handy hints are still useful today.

• When your needles and pins catch in the material as you sew, lubricate them by sticking them in a bar of soap. They'll slide effortlessly through the stiffest material.

• Store your needles and pins in a soap pincushion—they won't rust.

• Sticking drawers can be easily unstuck with a bar of soap. Simply moisten a corner of a bar of soap and rub it over the drawer runners.

Windows respond equally well if you rub soap up and down the tracks.

Doors that persistently stick will respond to the same treatment.

• Your hands will be easy to clean when dirty jobs beckon if you rub them with wet soap before starting. And don't forget to force your nails into the soap. All you'll need to clean up will be a little water and a nail file.

• Caught with a run in your stockings? A little bit of moistened soap rubbed above and below the run will act as a first-aid measure until you can make more lasting repairs.

• Whip up some artificial snow for your Christmas tree or holiday window designs with soap flakes or powdered soap. Add enough water to make thick suds, twirl with an eggbeater, and use a flat knife to lather your tree branches or windows. Apply some shiny mica or plastic flakes to the still-wet suds to create an authentic sparkle.

• Nails and screws smoothly penetrate even the hardest woods if first rubbed with soap, and the wood is much more likely to withstand splitting, too.

• Use soapsuds to locate a suspected gas leak. Apply to each pipe joint in turn—the leak will blow bubbles to make itself known.

• Wood saws cut more easily when rubbed with soap.

# BEAUTY
# FROM THE EARTH

There is a mystique that surrounds the concoction, the manufacture and the sale of beauty products. An artificial aura of witchcraft, intrigue and scientific sorcery lends enchantment to the mundane stirring and mixing of oils, astringents, and so on that make up even the most commonplace of cosmetics.

Is all of this black magic and hocus-pocus actually necessary? Absolutely! How else · can manufacturers keep you jumping from one product to another? How can they justify all of those four-color, double-spread advertisements, not to mention those five- and ten- and twenty-dollar price tags? The answer is that voodoo and hoodoo are necessary if you are involved in the commercial manufacture or sale of beauty preparations, but they are entirely superfluous if you are merely (merely!) concerned with an effective beauty product.

The fact of the matter is that beauty is really only "earth deep." Throughout history, women have mixed and mashed and stirred, baked and pounded and ground all manner of natural products to enhance or intensify their good looks. Ancient papyrus scrolls recorded beauty formulas used by the queens of the Nile. Du-

Barry and Josephine had their favorite herb blenders. Grandmother and Great-grandmother planted and pulverized seeds and buds and vines and creepers to produce cherished recipes for healthy hair and blooming complexions. Their beauty regimens included no harsh chemicals, no petroleum oils, and yet their fair skin was exquisite, their hair was magnificently thick and glossy.

They knew what we have forgotten—that nature is the greatest miracle worker of all. Natural products contain the richest oils, the purest proteins, the most potent vitamins and minerals, each carefully protected from destruction by nature's own perfect packaging. Beautifiers straight from the soil need no fortifiers, no poisonous preservatives, or tricky outer-space names. They are perfect in a way no manufactured cosmetic can be. Perfectly pure. Perfectly balanced. Perfectly natural.

The woman who faithfully uses natural cosmetics may look forward to beautiful, softer, more youthful-looking skin and hair. She may also save twenty, thirty, even a hundred dollars a year! Such products as honey, eggs, cream, avocado, wheat germ, oatmeal, almond milk, gelatin, sage, cardamom and cucumbers cost a fraction of the price of manufactured cosmetics, and if any of these formulas are left over, you may have them for lunch. No waste, good taste!

Leave the world of synthetic products, harmfully preserved foods and ecologically destructive plastic containers behind you. Walk into the world of Beauty from the Earth and become a natural wonder.

## COSMETICS MADE FROM COMMON HOUSEHOLD ITEMS

A dermatologist, who is also an expert on cosmetics, was quoted in the *New York Times* praising simple skin care routines and inexpensive products:

A light mineral oil, with the excess tissued off, does as much for the skin as the most expensive daytime base, and Vaseline is the equal of the most expensive night cream. They just do not look, smell or feel as good.

Following are a number of simple substitutions using household items. These may be used cosmetically with results as good as or superior to their outrageously priced drug or department store counterparts.

### Milk Compresses for Inflamed Eyes

*My lovely Grandmother Linehan used this remedy for tired eyes. It feels soothing, and the cream in the milk must be marvelous for the tender skin around and under the eyes.*

> 2 Cheesecloth compresses folded into 3- by 3-inch squares about 10 layers thick
> 1/4 Cup each hot milk and hot water

Dip the compresses in a mixture of the hot milk and water. Squeeze out excess so that the cheesecloth is thoroughly saturated but not dripping. Lie with your feet higher than your head and place the hot compresses over your closed eyes

as you slowly count to one hundred. Repeat the process, only this time count slowly to five hundred. (The reason for the counting is so that you are not tempted to look at the clock.) The entire treatment takes about 10 minutes.

### Instant Compresses for Tired Eyes

*Here are ready-made compresses that really hold the heat to rest and brighten tired eyes.*

> 2 Tea bags
> 2 Cups hot water

Steep the tea bags in the hot water for 5 minutes. Remove the bags and squeeze out excess moisture. Lie down with your feet slightly higher than your head, cover your eyelids with the tea bags and rest until the bags are cool.

Be careful not to burn your eyelids. If necessary, cool the bags slightly before you apply them.

### Grandmother's Glycerin and Rosewater Hand Cream

(YIELD: ABOUT 2 CUPS)

> 1 1/2 Cups distilled water
> 3 Teaspoons rose oil (soluble)
> 1/3 Cup glycerin

Blend all the ingredients until smooth and clear. Place in a clean bottle with a top.

### Mouthwash

(YIELD: 1 CUP)

> 1/2 Teaspoon each borax and sodium bicarbonate
> 4 Teaspoons glycerin
> 2/3 Cup distilled water
> 2 Teaspoons alcohol (or vodka), but not *denatured alcohol, which is poison*
> *Flavor and color as desired*

Dissolve the borax, sodium bicarbonate and glycerin in the water. (Warm, if necessary, to help the blending.) Mix with alcohol, add flavoring (such as peppermint oil) and color, if desired, and store in a clean bottle.

## Egg-Rich Face Mask for Removing Blackheads

*Thousands of women actually paid five dollars a package for this product. The manufacturer substituted powdered egg whites for fresh ones (fresh are actually better), and women all over the country used, and loved, this fantastic face mask. The next time you make scrambled eggs, set one uncooked egg white aside for yourself and take the time to give your face a pore-cleaning treatment that actually makes your skin softer than you would believe possible.*

*This mask really tightens and pulls! If you have extremely tender skin or don't like the idea of peeling off the mask, you may rinse instead, but optimum results can only be achieved through the good old pull-and-tug method.*

*This mask is intended only to remove blackheads and should not be used by anyone suffering from acne.*

> 1 Tablespoon plain unflavored gelatin
> 1½ Tablespoons cold milk
> 1 Egg white
> Wheat-germ oil, sesame seed oil, safflower oil, baby oil or a vitamin E capsule

Wash your face to remove all traces of oil and makeup.

In a very small pan, stir the gelatin into the milk. Heat over a *very* low flame for a few seconds until the gelatin melts. Beat the slightly cooled gelatin into the egg white until the mixture is smooth. As soon as it is cool enough to handle, spread the mask evenly over your face (don't wait too long or the mask will harden in the pan). The coating of mask should be thick enough to cover the skin well but not too thick or it will not harden properly. *Do not spread the mask above your upper lip or directly under your eyes.* These areas are particularly sensitive.

Allow the mask to remain on your face until it dries (about 30 minutes). At the expiration of this time, turn up one corner of the edge of the mask along your jaw line and pull lightly upward. The mask should peel off in fairly large pieces. Pull off in short tugs, not in a long stripping motion. This process will really smart, and your skin will be left blushing red and unbelievably smooth. If you look at the underside where the mask made contact with your skin, you will actually see blackheads that have been pulled from your face. The tingle you feel is blood rushing underneath the skin and cleansing from the inside.

It is important, now, to slather your glowing skin with a rich oil. Wheat-germ oil is marvelous, but I generally open a vitamin E capsule and soothe my skin with that. In any case, a non-perfumed oil is best.

## Steaming Rice Pack Facial

*Hot rice holds heat longer than almost anything (be careful not to burn yourself!), and this makes it an ideal pack for stimulating circulation, opening clogged pores and melting smoothing oils into the skin.*

> 1 Cup leftover rice
> ¼ Cup milk
> Cheesecloth, 4 layers thick
> Olive oil, sesame seed oil, wheat-germ oil, etc.

Bring the cooked rice and the milk to a boil and cook until the milk disappears and the rice is quite gummy and thick. Cool slightly, stirring occasionally.

Meanwhile, soak the cheesecloth in the oil. Wrap one towel around your hair and spread another towel on the floor.

When the rice is cool enough not to burn, but still quite warm, use a spoon to spread it between the layers of the cheesecloth. Lie down on the floor with your head on the towel. Arrange the hot rice pack on your face and stay put until the rice is cool. The hot rice keeps the oil on your face warm and working. (The rest will also do you no harm!)

### Rosy-Cheek Face Mask

*Another mask that makes you blush and gets the blood circulating is this cooling, warming favorite.*

1 Egg white
2 Tablespoons cold water
⅛ Teaspoon pure peppermint extract
½ Teaspoon dried mint leaves
1 Drop green food coloring (optional)

Beat all the ingredients together, pat on your face and let dry. Rinse off with cold water.

### Throat Smoother Stick

*A throat cream should melt on contact to smooth those microscopic crinkles. This one does!*

2½ Tablespoons sesame oil
1 Tablespoon each cocoa butter and paraffin wax
1½ Teaspoons beeswax
1 Drop red food coloring

Clean out and have ready an empty make-up base or deodorant stick container.

Measure the sesame oil, cocoa butter, paraffin wax and beeswax into your smallest (unchipped) enamel pan. Place the pan in a slightly larger pan of warm water and heat the mixture until all the ingredients are completely melted. Stir. Remove the pan from the hot water and immediately stir in the food coloring.

Push the base of the deodorant stick all the way to the bottom, and while it is still melted, pour in the wax mixture. Set the stick aside overnight to harden (do not move or disturb it in any way). As soon as the throat smoother stick is firm, it may be used. Refrigerate for longer shelf life.

### Whey Protein Hair Rinse

*Whey, the clear liquid plasma part of the milk left over from cheesemaking, is rich in protein and other nutrients. I've found it to be an excellent body builder and strengthener for the hair. Whey spoils quickly, so you had better freeze small plastic or paper cups of it just as soon as your cheesemaking is out of the "whey." Many expensive commercial hair products now feature milk proteins as one of their main ingredients. This homemade product is just as good and costs you not one cent.*

Work ½ cup of defrosted whey into the wet hair immediately following shampooing. Wrap with a towel, wait for 10 minutes, then rinse well. Towel-dry for a few minutes, then dry as usual.

### Scandinavian Beer-Froth Skin Freshener

*Malt-rich beer is laden with B vitamins, and its combination of natural sugar and alcohol has a tightening effect on the skin. Freshly opened cold beer serves up a tingle along with the bubbles, but stale cold beer is very nearly as refreshing and every bit as efficacious.*

After the beer tightens your pores, splash your face with fresh water and pat dry to remove the telltale odor. One bottle of beer (I like Scandinavian beers best, but the domestic varieties serve just as well and are cheaper) will last twice as long as a commercial skin freshener, and it costs less than half as much.

Keep the beer ice cold. Shake a bit to froth. Pat over face and neck with a ball of cotton. Rinse with very cold water, if you like, and blot dry.

## Mint Tea Bath for Sunburn

*The tannic acid contained in tea is a natural treatment for sunburn. Mint is soothing, and heat helps take the "ouch" out of the burn. All in all, this is the perfect prescription for any sunburn that doesn't require a doctor's care.*

> 5 Tea bags (or 3½ tablespoons loose tea)
> 4¾ Cups boiling water
> 2 Cups fresh mint leaves, packed down (or 3 heaping tablespoons dried mint leaves)
> A tubful of warm water

Steep the tea for 15 minutes in 4 cups of the boiling water. (Break open the tea bags to release the tea.)

In your blender reduce the fresh mint leaves to a slush with the ¾ cup boiling water (or steep the dried leaves in the same amount of boiling water).

Fill a tub to the desired level with warm water. Add the tea (with the tea leaves) and the mint. This will make a fairly unattractive-looking bath, but it will work wonders for your burn.

## Honey Pack for Hair Body

*There are times when your hair needs a bit of additional body and holding power. This hair pack is for those occasions.*

FOR BLONDES ONLY

> ⅓ Cup light honey
> 1 Tablespoon lemon juice

FOR BRUNETTES ONLY

> ⅓ Cup honey (buckwheat is best)
> 1 Tablespoon cider vinegar

Mix the ingredients listed for your hair color. Rub thoroughly into your hair (be it blond or brunette), and wrap in a steaming hot towel. Rinse the towel in water as hot as your hands can stand, then wring out and rewrap your hair. Repeat this process at least 5 times, then rinse your hair well in hot water, allowing the tiniest bit of the honey to remain. Set the hair wet. Dry thoroughly.

Grandmother's only hair-setting preparation was sugar water. This recipe gives better results, along with additional nutrients.

## Easy Nongreasy Egg Shampoo

*An excellent egg shampoo is as close as your kitchen, and each sudsing costs only about 10¢.*

> 1 Small egg
> 1 Tablespoon mild *dishwashing liquid*

Beat the egg until it is frothy and the yolk and the white are well incorporated. Add the dishwashing liquid and continue to beat until the mixture is a beautiful pale yellow and very foamy. This is best when used immediately, but, if necessary, it may be refrigerated and rewhipped lightly.

Remember, when using any *fresh* egg shampoo, use warm, not hot, water.

# COSMETICS UTILIZING FRUITS AND VEGETABLE JUICES

A good many women I know, especially those of European extraction, favor the use of fruit and vegetable juices for softening the skin. Judging by the complexions of these women (and a few are in their sixties) I would tend to believe them. Here are a few recipes gathered from European sources and old manuscripts. I have tried them with excellent results.

CAUTION: These preparations are pure and harmless to most persons. However, if you suffer from an allergy that is aggravated by any of the following ingredients, by all means do not throw caution to the winds and try any of them. The skin very often reacts to external stimuli in the same way it reacts to internal stimuli.

### Melon and Cucumber Cream

*These two natural ingredients add extra freshness and smoothing power to commercial rinse-off cold cream. I find that a jar of the commercial cream will last nearly a year and soften my skin better when a bit is mixed with one or both of these fresh juices.*

⅛ Small melon, peeled
1 Teaspoon lemon juice
¼ Cucumber
  Rinse-off cold cream

Whirl the melon in the blender until it liquefies. Add the lemon juice and strain through wet cheesecloth. Chop the cucumber, skin and all, and blend at high speed for one minute. Strain through cheesecloth. Mix the two juices, cover, label, date and refrigerate.

To use, mix ½ teaspoon juice with ½ teaspoon commercial rinse-off cold cream. Smooth onto face and neck and allow to remain for 10 minutes. Rinse off and pat dry.

### Milk of Lettuce Skin Freshener

*Juice extracted from fresh lettuce leaves (often called "lettuce milk") has long been considered a skin softener. Team it up with a bit of 70 percent ethanol rubbing alcohol and you have an astringent that helps soften the skin as it tingles.*

1 Tablespoon lettuce juice, freshly extracted
1 Tablespoon lemon juice, freshly squeezed
¼ Cup 70 percent ethanol rubbing alcohol

Strain the lettuce milk and lemon juice through one thickness of cheesecloth. Pour the alcohol into a small bottle, add the combined juices and shake well. Label the bottle with the name and date and instructions to shake before using. Refrigerate.

Pat the icy-cold skin freshener on neck, face and wrists for a real wake-up feeling.

### Strawberry Complexion Cream

Crush the strawberries you use to make the juice with a silver fork or a ceramic mortar and pestle and cook the recipe in a glass or unchipped enamel pan. (At any rate, do not use aluminum, copper, brass or iron when mixing this.)

1 Tablespoon oatmeal (or rolled oats)
2 Tablespoons wheat-germ oil
½ Cup strawberry juice

Whirl the oatmeal in a blender or crush it with a mortar and pestle until it is as fine as flour. Mix in the oil and then the strawberry juice. Stir the mixture with a silver spoon and heat it over a low flame, stirring constantly, until thick. Place in a jar, cover with plastic and refrigerate.

## HOME REMEDIES AND PERSONAL HYGIENE

Drugstore products are frequently high-profit items, and while many medications are necessary for your health and well-being, there are many that are much more potent than a mild ailment requires. How foolish to pay two dollars or more for a drug-laden patent cough medicine when you can make old-fashioned honey and lemon, which works wonderfully well for most mild symptoms. If the home remedy does not do the job, there is always time to purchase the higher-priced item.

Following are a few simple products you can make at home and use with good results:

### Before Shave Conditioner

Fill a plastic squeeze bottle with scant ¼ teaspoon water-softening agent and ¼ teaspoon liquid soap (see page 261) mixed with 2 cups water. Splash the face with this solution before shaving.

### After Shave Conditioner

Follow directions given for Before Shave Conditioner (see above) but omit the liquid soap.

### One-Cent Tooth Powder

Dip a wet toothbrush into baking soda and brush as usual. Good for both your own teeth or the store-bought variety. If you seem to need a more gritty substance for getting off stains, dip your toothbrush in a dish of salt and brush as usual.

### Gargle

Mix 2 teaspoons baking soda with 1 quart water. Gargle to sweeten breath.

### No Tangles Rinse for After Shampooing

Add about ½ teaspoon of water-softening agent to 2 quarts of warm water. Use as a rinse after shampooing to keep hair from becoming tangled.

### Good Old-Fashioned Cough Syrup

To make your own cough syrup, juice a lemon, which you have first boiled for 8 to 12 minutes, and mix into 1 cup of honey along with 1 ounce of glycerin; stir well before taking. Take 1 teaspoonful 3 times daily, stirring well before using.

### Sunburn

To relieve sunburn, apply a solution of vinegar and water. Equally effective, mix a very strong solution of ordinary tea, cool and apply to the afflicted area.

### Poison Ivy

To relieve poison ivy, apply used tea leaves (which are rich in tannic acid) to the afflicted areas. Baking soda and water will help to relieve the itch. Most important, do not touch or scratch, because that is what spreads the rash!

### To Remove Ticks

Carefully place a large dab of petroleum jelly over the entire body of the tick. In several hours, after the tick has suffocated, carefully "unscrew" from flesh by gently turning the body of the tick *counter*clockwise. Wash hands and affected area well.

### Internal Mosquito Repellent

If you are attractive to mosquitoes, try taking vitamin B₁ orally. Mosquitoes dislike the taste and may leave you alone to look for fairer game.

### Hot, Tired Feet

To ease aching, tired feet, soak in hot water to which a little vinegar has been added.

### Insect Stings

To relieve stings, apply a paste of baking soda and water, or vinegar, or plain lemon juice.

# SCIENTIFIC NAMES OF COMMON CHEMICALS

A great many of the ingredients listed in formulas presented in this book are called by their popular names. When attempting to purchase them at your local druggist or chemical supply house, it might be helpful to know their scientific names as well. The following list will help in this respect. While it is by no means comprehensive, it will cover anything you will find in this book and a great many more to boot.

| | |
|---|---|
| Alcohol (grain) | Ethyl alcohol |
| Alcohol (wood) | Methyl alcohol |
| Alum (common) | Aluminum potassium sulphate |
| Alumina | Aluminum oxide |
| Antichlor | Sodium thiosulfate |
| Aqua ammonia | Ammonium hydroxide solution |
| Aqua fortis | Nitric acid |
| Aqua regia | Nitric and hydrochloric acids |
| Aromatic spirits of ammonia | Ammonia gas in alcohol |
| Asbestos | Magnesium silicate |
| Aspirin | Acetysalicylic acid |
| Baking soda | Sodium bicarbonate |
| Banana oil | Amyl acetate |
| Benzol | Benzene |
| Bichloride of mercury | Mercuric chloride |
| Black lead | Graphite |
| Black oxide of copper | Cupric oxide |
| Black oxide of mercury | Mercurous oxide |
| Bleaching powder | Calcium hypochlorite |
| Bluestone | Copper sulfate |
| Blue vitriol | Copper sulfate |
| Borax | Sodium borate |
| Brimstone | Sulfur |
| Brine | Strong sodium chloride solution |
| "Butter of" | Chloride or trichloride of |
| Calomel | Mercurous chloride |
| Carbolic acid | Phenol |
| Carbonic acid gas | Carbon dioxide |
| Caustic potash | Potassium hydroxide |
| Caustic soda | Sodium hydroxide |
| Chalk | Calcium carbonate |
| Chile saltpeter | Sodium nitrate |
| Chrome alum | Chromium potassium sulfate |
| Chrome yellow | Lead chromate |
| Copperas | Ferrous sulfate |

| | | | |
|---|---|---|---|
| Cream of tartar | Potassium bitartrate | Potash | Potassium carbonate |
| Crocus powder | Ferric oxide | Prussic acid | Hydrocyanic acid |
| Emery powder | Impure aluminum oxide | Pyro | Pyrogallic acid |
| | | Quicklime | Calcium oxide |
| Epsom salts | Magnesium sulfate | Quicksilver | Mercury |
| Ethanol | Ethyl alcohol | Red lead | Lead tetroxide |
| Fluorspar | Natural calcium fluoride | Rochelle salt | Potassium sodium tartrate |
| Formalin | Formaldehyde | Rouge | Ferric oxide |
| French chalk | Natural magnesium silicate | Sal ammoniac | Ammonium chloride |
| | | Sal soda | Crystalline sodium carbonate |
| Galena | Natural lead sulfide | | |
| Glauber's salt | Sodium sulfate | Salt | Sodium chloride |
| Gypsum | Natural calcium sulfate | Saltpeter | Potassium nitrate |
| Hypo | Sodium thiosulfate | Salt of lemon | Potassium binoxalate |
| Lime (unslaked) | Calcium oxide | Salts of tartar | Potassium carbonate |
| Limewater | Calcium hydroxide solution | Silica | Silicon dioxide |
| | | Slaked lime | Calcium hydroxide |
| Magnesia | Magnesium oxide | Soda ash | Dry sodium carbonate |
| Methanol | Methyl alcohol | Spirit of hartshorn | Ammonia gas in alcohol |
| Methylated spirits | Methyl alcohol | Spirits of salt | Hydrochloric acid |
| "Muriate of" | Chloride of | Spirits of wine | Ethyl alcohol |
| Muriatic acid | Hydrochloric acid | Talc | Magnesium silicate |
| Oil of vitriol | Sulfuric acid | Vinegar | Dilute and impure acetic acid |
| Oil of wintergreen (artificial) | Methyl salicylate | | |
| | | Washing soda | Crystalline sodium carbonate |
| Paris green | Copper aceto-arsenite | | |
| Pearl ash | Potassium carbonate | Water glass | Sodium silicate |
| Peroxide | Peroxide of hydrogen solution | White lead | Basic lead carbonate |
| | | Whiting | Powdered calcium carbonate |
| Plaster of Paris | Calcium sulfate | | |
| Plumbago | Graphite | Wood alcohol | Methyl alcohol |

# SOURCES OF
# SUPPLY

CITY CHEMICAL (132 West 22nd Street, New York, N.Y., 10011, 212-922-2723): This company carries 45,000 chemicals and related items. They have no catalogue, but they seem to have anything you could possibly want. Some items are sold in 1-pound sizes but most are sold in 5-pound quantities. I didn't find them to be too helpful on the phone (except when I knew *exactly* what I needed), but they *will* send orders.

AMEND DRUG AND CHEMICAL: Once a prime supplier of chemicals to individuals, this company has unfortunately moved from its Christopher Street address in the SoHo artists' section of New York City to Irvington, New Jersey, and has discontinued its service to individuals. This is a great pity. The availability of *any* and all materials is what made the SoHo district particularly desirable to artists. As this area becomes more residential the large and small manufacturers and suppliers move away from the city and its problems and everyone suffers. The city loses interest and texture and the companies lose their contacts with humans.

HARRY ROSS (61 Reade St., New York, N.Y. 10007): Hurrah for Harry Ross, who still carries on his person-to-person, over-the-counter business! He carries a limited supply of chemicals, but he will order anything you need and do it willingly, helpfully and courteously. As in other instances, some chemicals can be ordered only in specified quantities from the manufacturer. Mr. Ross also specializes in new and used chemical equipment—beakers for vases or planters, graduates for accurate measuring, mortars and pestles for crushing your whole spices. Extremely accurate thermometers are among interesting items available.

CHR. HANSEN'S LABORATORY, INC. (9015 West Maple Street, Milwaukee, Wis. 53214): Hansen's carries cheesemaking supplies—rennet, cheese colors, starters, etc. They do fill individual orders and seem quite courteous and efficient.

MARBLE INSTITUTE OF AMERICA (1984 Chain Bridge Road, McLean, Va. 22101), or the VERMONT MARBLE COMPANY (61 Main St., Proctor, Vt. 05765), will send you detailed information on the care and cleaning of marble.

## WINEMAKING SUPPLIES

Unless you're fortunate enough to have a local source for winemaking supplies, you'll probably have to write to one of the following for your yeast, acids, etc., plus most of the specialized equipment necessary in winemaking. But never mind—the following companies are ready and willing to handle individual orders. Send for a catalogue from:

*Enology Shop*, 18 North Central Avenue, Hartsdale, N.Y. 10530

*Milan Laboratories*, 57 Spring Street, New York, N.Y. 10012

*Presque Isle Wine Cellars*, 9440 Buffalo Road, North East, Pa. 16428

*Semplex of U.S.A.*, Box 12276, 4805 Lyndale Avenue North, Minneapolis, Minn. 55412

*Wine Art of America, Inc.*, 4324 Geary Boulevard, San Francisco, Calif. 94118
Wine Art has many outlets throughout the country, and can probably give you the location of the one nearest you.

*Sears Roebuck & Co.* lists many winemaking supplies in their catalogue.

## SAUSAGEMAKING SUPPLIES

Your local fine butcher shop probably carries natural casings, but if it does not the Standard Casing Co. Inc., 121 Spring Street, New York, N.Y. 10012, has natural casings of all sizes and shapes. Or write to the International Natural Sausage Casing Association, 505 West 14th Street, Chicago Heights, Ill. 60411, for the name of a supplier nearer your area.

For advice on many of the more technical aspects of dry cleaning, we consulted an expert source: the U. S. Department of Agriculture Home and Garden Bulletin No. 62, "Removing Stains from Fabrics."

Other Departments of Agriculture publications you may want to send for are:

"Protecting Woolens Against Clothes Moths and Carpet Beetles," Home and Garden Bulletin No. 113.

"How to Prevent and Remove Mildew," Home and Garden Bulletin No. 68.

"Family Food Budgeting," Home and Garden Bulletin No. 94.

"Your Money's Worth in Foods," Home and Garden Bulletin No. 183.

"Keeping Food Safe to Eat," Home and Garden Bulletin No. 162.

"Conserving the Nutritive Values in Foods," Home and Garden Bulletin No. 90.

You may secure these bulletins by writing to:

Superintendent of Documents; U. S. Government Printing Office; Washington, D. C. 20402

# Index

## About the Author

―――――――――

YVONNE YOUNG TARR is the bestselling Tastemaker Award–winning author of some twenty cookbooks, including *That's Entertaining, The New York Times Bread and Soup Cookbook, The Ten Minute Gourmet Cookbook, The New York Times Natural Food Dieting Book, The Complete Outdoor Cookbook, Love Portions, Super–Easy Step–by–Step Winemaking, Super–Easy Step–by– Step Book of Special Breads, Yvonne Young Tarr's Low Cholesterol Gourmet, The Squash Cookbook* and *The Tomato Book.*